Marketing Analytics

A Practitioner's Guide to Marketing Analytics
and Research Methods

Marketing Analytics

A Practitioner's Guide to Marketing Analytics and Research Methods

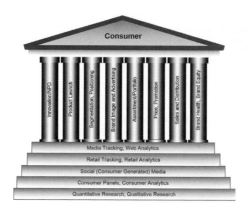

Ashok Charan

World Scientific

NEW JERSEY · LONDON · SINGAPORE · BEIJING · SHANGHAI · HONG KONG · TAIPEI · CHENNAI

Published by

World Scientific Publishing Co. Pte. Ltd.

5 Toh Tuck Link, Singapore 596224

USA office: 27 Warren Street, Suite 401-402, Hackensack, NJ 07601

UK office: 57 Shelton Street, Covent Garden, London WC2H 9HE

Library of Congress Cataloging-in-Publication Data
Charan, Ashok.
    Marketing analytics : a practitioner's guide to marketing analytics and research methods /
Ashok Charan, National University of Singapore.
        pages cm
    ISBN 978-981-4641-36-4 -- ISBN 978-981-4678-57-5 (pbk)
    1. Marketing research--Data processing. 2. Quantitative research. I. Title.
    HF5415.2.C3833 2015
    658.8'3--dc23
                                                                    2014041299

British Library Cataloguing-in-Publication Data
A catalogue record for this book is available from the British Library.

In-house Editor: Li Hongyan

Printed in Singapore

In memory of my father
To my mother
With love and heartfelt gratitude

Preface

The digital age has transformed the very nature of marketing. Armed with smartphones, tablets, PCs and smart TVs, consumers are increasingly hanging out on the internet. Cyberspace has changed the way they communicate, and the way they shop and buy. This fluid, de-centralized and multidirectional medium is changing the way brands engage with consumers.

At the same time, technology and innovation, coupled with the explosion of business data, has fundamentally altered the manner we collect, process, analyse and disseminate market intelligence. The increased volume, variety and velocity of information enables marketers to respond with much greater speed, to changes in the marketplace. Market intelligence is timelier, less expensive, and more accurate and actionable.

Anchored in this age of transformations, *Marketing Analytics* is a practitioner's guide to marketing management in the 21st century. The text devotes considerable attention to the way market analytic techniques and market research processes are being refined and re-engineered.

Given its focus on the methods adopted by practitioners, the book is tailored to the needs of marketing professionals. It is ideal too for business management students who wish to pursue careers in consumer marketing.

Marketing Analytics is structured into six parts — brand, consumer, product, advertising, price and promotion, and retail. Collectively the 22 chapters cover the key aspects of managing brands and categories.

Part I deals with brand, brand image and brand equity. It covers the analytic methods used for developing brand and marketing strategies.

Part II deals with qualitative and quantitative research methods, with emphasis on how these conventional research processes are embracing online platforms. It covers customer segmentation, customer satisfaction and customer value management. It also addresses how consumer panels, consumer analytics and big data enhance our understanding of consumers and their buying behaviour.

Part III is centred on *product*. It deals with the entire new product development process from ideation, concept and product development to product launch. It covers the analytic methods and procedures that are deployed to screen ideas, concepts and products, at each phase of the NPD process.

Part IV is all about *advertising*. It covers the theories of advertising, how new media is transforming the way brands engage with consumers, digital marketing, and research methods for copy testing and advertising tracking.

Part V deals with *price, promotion* and *market mix modelling*. It covers a variety of pricing research methods, and techniques for promotions evaluation. The chapter *Market Mix Modelling* deals with statistical methods of analysis of historical data, to assess the impact of various marketing activities on sales.

The concluding part, *retail*, covers retail tracking, retail analytics, sales and distribution, and category management. It focusses on the use of metrics and analytic techniques to develop sales and distribution plans, and manage categories.

The text also includes seven case studies that have been crafted to facilitate a deeper understanding of the subject.

For more information on the topics covered in the various chapters and appendices, visit the book's website at:

http://bizfaculty.nus.edu/site/bizakc/MarketingAnalytics.

At this site you can access lecture presentations, and soft copies of tables and charts pertaining to the cases in the book. It also serves as the location for introducing fresh content and revisions to the text.

I wrote *Marketing Analytics* with the practitioner in mind. It is intended to impart a thorough understanding of research methods and analytic techniques, to guide you as you craft market strategies, and execute your day to day tasks. I hope that you enjoy reading it, and that it serves you well.

Acknowledgement

My love for marketing grew at what was then a small newly created department at Hindustan Lever. There I had access to a wealth of information in an environment that was conducive to learning. It was in this department, and subsequently at Nielsen, that I acquired the knowledge that made it possible for me to write this book.

I remain indebted to several individuals during my years in the industry, and particularly my team at Nielsen for their support, and to the Nielsen Company for nurturing and rewarding me for 16 years.

Not many years back, academia was unknown territory, and I am immensely grateful to prof. S. Vishwanathan for persuading and encouraging me to teach. A close friend, in some respects, Vish understood me better than I did myself, and he took me down a path that led me to where I am today.

I am greatly indebted to Mr. Chua Hong Koon from World Scientific Publishing, for his guidance and support. I also thank his colleague, Ms. Li Hongyan, for her considerable assistance and patience in editing this text.

For most of my life my mother and father have been my source of strength and stability. It is their unconditional love, sacrifice and faith that gave me an immense advantage in life, and it is to them that I dedicate this book.

Author

Ashok Charan

Associate Professor, NUS Business School, National University of Singapore (ashokcharan.com)

Ashok is the creator of Destiny©, an advanced FMCG business simulator, which he uses for teaching marketing courses to business students and marketing practitioners.

A marketing veteran, he has over 25 years of industry experience in general management, corporate planning, business development, market research and marketing. Prior to joining the NUS Business School, Ashok worked with Nielsen and Unilever. At Nielsen, he assumed a number of roles including Managing Director for Singapore, and Regional Area Client Director – Asia Pacific. His experience spans both business and consumer marketing, and he remains active in consulting in the areas of market research, analytics and data integration.

Ashok is an engineering graduate from the Indian Institute of Technology, Delhi, and a post-graduate in business management (PGDM) from the Indian Institute of Management, Calcutta.

Contents

PART II CONSUMER

PART III PRODUCT

PART IV ADVERTISING

PART V PRICE AND PROMOTION

PART VI RETAIL

APPENDICES

PART I

Brand

CHAPTER 1

Brand and Brand Image

Exhibit 1.1 ArgylePink — "Beyond Rare — The most concentrated form of wealth on earth".

"The word VALUE, it is to be observed, has two different meanings, and sometimes expresses the utility of some particular object, and sometimes the power of purchasing other goods which the possession of that object conveys. The one may be called 'value in use;' the other, 'value in exchange.' The things which have the greatest value in use have frequently little or no value in exchange; on the contrary, those which have the greatest value in exchange have frequently little or no value in use. Nothing is more useful than water: but it will purchase scarce anything; scarce anything can be had in exchange for it. A diamond, on the contrary, has scarce any use-value; but a very great quantity of other goods may frequently be had in exchange for it." — quoted from Adam Smith's An Inquiry into the Nature and Causes of the Wealth of Nations.

Pink Diamonds?

The unknown is synonymous with unease. If a customer is offered diamonds of a peculiar shade, despite how captivating the pitch might be, she is likely to harbour a suspicion that the jewels are not genuine.

If you have not heard of a particular brand, or a product, or a pink diamond, not only do you lack the interest in buying it, you also tend to be dubious of the person or the organization that tries to sell it to you.

And so the discovery of diamonds embedded in an ant hill in the East Kimberley region of Western Australia in October 1979 posed a challenge for Rio Tinto. At the time of the discovery, the notion that diamonds could be intense pink was virtually non-existent. Undoubtedly, associates at the mining company would have pondered how to generate demand for these gems.

Diamonds and water lie at opposite ends of a spectrum. Which you consider more valuable depends on whether you assess them in terms of their "value in use" or their "value in exchange". And while the paradox of value may be explained by the theory of marginal utility and the mechanisms of supply and demand, one might wonder what is it that makes tiny rocks of pure carbon so precious to begin with? Why do so many young men all over the world spend hard earned savings on a glittering diamond ring that, once bought loses over 50% of its monetary value?

The rationale in part lies in their sheer beauty, their famed indestructibility and the strategy adopted by a few dominant players of managing supply. To a greater extent, however, their value is the outcome of *beliefs* and *memorable associations* imparted through marketing. Marketing generates knowledge, awareness, interest, curiosity and status; it makes products *desirable.*

A plethora of memorable media campaigns have contributed to the charm and the allure of diamonds. Great monarchs and famous movie stars have proclaimed their love for these gems. An Archduke in 1477 gave his fiancée a diamond ring when he proposed to her, and men have since followed his example. Over the years a great many images, symbols and beliefs have become associated with diamonds, contributing immensely to their intangible value.

In terms of physical attributes, other than colour, pink diamonds do not lack the qualities of clear diamonds, and they are far rarer. What they lacked at the time of their discovery was awareness, interest and status.

Through branding and marketing, Rio Tinto imbued the pink diamonds with interest and status. Marketing communication powerfully influenced consumers' minds, creating an alluring mystique about their origin and colour. Described in advertisements as "the most revered diamond in the world", the pink gems, through a range of marketing efforts, metamorphosed into the rare, exclusive, and much desired Argyle Pink (Exhibit 1.1). They are now sought after by investors, collectors, celebrities and high net worth individuals, and command a high premium.

The brand, Argyle Pink, captures much of the intangible value that is created through marketing. It makes intangible benefits — such as intrigue, fascination, curiosity, fame — tangible, and associates these attributes with pink diamonds, and more specifically those mined in the Kimberly region. It is the beliefs, symbols, perceptions and associations that consumers hold in their head about the Argyle Pink, that ultimately affects their desire to purchase these diamonds at the premium prices that they command.

Preview

What distinguishes a brand, like the Argyle Pink, from the tangible product are the thoughts and feelings that it evokes. The manner in which these thoughts and feelings are tracked, measured and presented, by means of techniques such as image profiling and perceptual mapping, is the prime focus of this chapter. It introduces the subject of brands and highlights their importance, and reviews the concepts of brand image, positioning, the segmentation and targeting of consumers, and the differentiation of products.

Lesson from the Summer of 1985

"To hear some tell it, April 23, 1985, was a day that will live in marketing infamy ... spawning consumer angst the likes of which no business has ever seen." — The Coca-Cola Company, commenting on the New Coke announcement.

In April 1985, The Coca-Cola Company launched New Coke, and discontinued the production of the original formulation. Taste tests findings clearly indicated consumers' preference for the sweeter New Coke mixture over both regular Coca-Cola and Pepsi. But the consumers' response was not what Coca-Cola had anticipated. At the onset, it was a minority, albeit a vocal one that protested against the transformation of a brand that had become so much a part of their heritage. Their mood was infectious and headquarters in Atlanta started receiving an avalanche of letters expressing anger and dismay.

What transpired was one of the greatest expressions of the will of consumers. Overwhelmed with over 400,000 calls and letters, the company reintroduced Coca-Cola, as Coca-Cola Classic. One can only imagine what the response might have been, if consumers, at that time, were empowered by social media.

The episode gave us a rare glimpse of the enormous depth of emotion that consumers feel for Coca-Cola. A psychiatrist the company hired to listen in on calls told Coca-Cola executives that some callers sounded as if they were discussing the death of a family member.

New Coke was more than a change of formulation. The brand name, logo, and the manner it was presented was altered in one fell swoop. No longer the "the real thing", for many Americans it was the demise of the Coca-Cola that they knew, and had grown to love.

This was a demonstration of the *enormous power that resides in the minds of consumers* for this extraordinary brand. According to Muhtar Kent, the company's chairman & CEO, "Coca-Cola is more than just a drink. It is an idea; it is a vision, a feeling." Great brands like Coca-Cola live beyond generations, becoming part of society's heritage, bonding people together across the globe.

Brand

A brand is defined as a trademark which in the mind of consumers embraces a particular set of values and attributes, both tangible and intangible. Or in the words of David Ogilvy, "a brand is a consumer's idea of a product".

Both descriptions embody two important principles — that brand is different from a product and that the difference resides in the mind of the consumer. *In essence, a brand is the collection of memories, feelings and associations that are linked to it.*

Brand image is the consumers' perception of the brand. Products deliver a set of benefits — functional, rational, emotional, personality, and brand-consumer relationship benefits. The image or profile of a brand relates to how it is perceived on these benefits or attributes.

It is therefore in the interest of marketers to craft a brand's image in a manner that keeps it in tune with the brand's marketing strategy. In a nut shell, this entails choosing which *segments* to target, *differentiating* the brand to appeal to the segments, and *positioning* it distinctly in the minds of target consumers.

What distinguishes a brand from the tangible product is referred to as *brand equity*. The power of the Coca-Cola brand to evoke such an

Interbrand ■●●

01	02	03	04	05	06	07	08
🍎	Google	Coca-Cola	IBM	Microsoft	GE	SAMSUNG	TOYOTA
+21% 118,863 $m	+15% 107,439 $m	+3% 81,563 $m	-8% 72,244 $m	+3% 61,154 $m	-3% 45,480 $m	+15% 45,462 $m	+20% 42,392 $m
09	10	11	12	13	14	15	
M	Mercedes-Benz	BMW	(intel)	Disney	CISCO	amazon	
+1% 42,254 $m	+8% 34,338 $m	+7% 34,214 $m	-8% 34,153 $m	+14% 32,223 $m	+6% 30,936 $m		
16	17	18	19	20	21		
ORACLE	hp	Gillette	LOUIS VUITTON	HONDA	H&M		TOP RISER
+8% 25,980 $m	-8% 23,758 $m	-9% 22,845 $m	-9% 22,552 $m	+17% 21,673 $m	+16% 21,083 $m	+25% 29,478 $m	
22	23	24	25	26	27	28	30
Nike		pepsi	SAP	IKEA	ups	ebay	Pampers
+16% 19,875 $m	+11% 19,510 $m	+7% 19,119 $m	+4% 17,340 $m	+15% 15,885 $m	+5% 14,470 $m	+9% 14,358 $m	+8% 14,078 $m

Exhibit 1.2   Interbrand's 2014 list of top brands *(Source: Interbrand's website).*

intense response from American consumers in 1985 is a reflection of its extraordinary brand equity. Rated by Interbrand (Exhibit 1.2) as one of the most valuable brands in the world, Coca-Cola is beyond doubt an exception. For the vast majority of brands, equity tends to be relatively low.

While branding is popularly associated with consumer marketing, it is of equal importance to business marketing. Interbrand's 2014 list of top brands includes many that are predominantly B2B. Leading global brands, including Google, IBM, Microsoft, GE, Intel, and the big automobile companies, have high proportion of their sales to business markets.

In business marketing, corporate brands position organizations in the minds of their customers. These brands capture intangibles such as integrity, trust, reliability, reputation and professionalism, all of which are of utmost importance in these markets. They are nurtured by delivering value at every customer touch point.

Positioning

Positioning, a concept that relates to product differentiation, was introduced by Jack Trout in 1969 and subsequently, in 1981, popularized by Al Ries and Jack Trout in their bestseller *Positioning: The Battle for Your Mind*. According to the duo, *"positioning is what you do to the mind of the prospect"*. Whereas *differentiation* is the process of distinguishing a *product* or *offering* from others to make it more attractive to a particular target market, positioning is the act of crafting a distinct and valued *image of the brand in the minds of consumers*. In a well-devised strategy, the brand's position drives all elements of the marketing mix.

For example, in the 1970s, the slogan "the real thing", which captured the essence of Coca-Cola's position, resonated strongly with consumers. It was reinforced through memorable campaigns that strengthened the brand's iconic status, and distinguished it from "imitators". (Years later "New Coke" must have come across to Coca-Cola lovers as antithesis of "the real thing".)

In the same era that Coca-Cola was reinforcing its positioning as "the real thing", 7 Up distinguished itself from the big cola brands with its "Uncola" position. The campaign "became part of a counter cultural that symbolized being true to yourself and challenging the status quo" (www.7up.com).

Among the most celebrated examples in positioning is the Volkswagen Beetle's "Think Small" campaign (Exhibit 1.3). In the 1960s when cars were generally big, beautiful and expensive, the Beetle was introduced as a small, awkward looking, inexpensive car. Clearly differentiated and distinctly positioned, the Beetle over the years outsold every car that has ever been made.

Other noteworthy examples of positioning in the automotive sector include BMW's "The ultimate driving machine" and Volvo's "Safety first". To quote from a Volvo advertisement — "Cars are driven by people. The guiding principle behind everything we make at Volvo, therefore, is and must remain — Safety".

Think small.

Our little car isn't so much of a novelty any more.
A couple of dozen college kids don't try to squeeze inside it.
The guy at the gas station doesn't ask where the gas goes.
Nobody even stares at our shape.
In fact, some people who drive our little flivver don't even think 32 miles to the gallon is going any great guns.
Or using five pints of oil instead of five quarts.
Or never needing anti-freeze.
Or racking up 40,000 miles on a set of tires.
That's because once you get used to some of our economies, you don't even think about them any more.
Except when you squeeze into a small parking spot. Or renew your small insurance. Or pay a small repair bill. Or trade in your old VW for a new one.
Think it over.

Exhibit 1.3 Think Small advertisement campaign, crafted in 1959 by Helmut Krone and Julian Koenig at DDB, distinctly positioned and differentiated the VW Beetle from competition. It was ranked the best 20th century campaign by Ad Age, in a survey of North American advertisements.

Dove, a brand that stands for beauty without artifice, has articulated that position via memorable advertising campaigns such as Real Beauty, Evolution, Onslaught and Girls Under Pressure. Positioning the brand as a theme or a social mission (as opposed to a product — moisturizing soap) gave Dove the license to transcend categories. The change in positioning coincided with the brand's extension from soaps and

We are absorbing the GST increase! Because we know every cent counts.

We bring you the first piece of good news on the first day of a new year:
FairPrice is absorbing the 1% GST increase for All items for the month of January 2003.
And we'll continue to absorb the 1% increase for 400 essential items, the whole year through.
You can count on FairPrice to help you save and discover how your savings can really stack up.
Simply because as *Singapore's Very Own* supermarket chain, *We Save, We Care, We Share.*

FairPrice
Singapore's very own

Exhibit 1.4 "Since our birth in 1973, we have changed our name, we have changed our look, and we've changed our logo. One thing that has not changed is our commitment to our social mission." To reinforce its social mission, Singapore's FairPrice supermarket absorbs escalation in the cost of essential goods, for limited periods of time.

cleansers to beauty products in general, including hair-care, deodorants, and skin-care products.

Positioned as a social mission (Exhibit 1.4), the origin of Singapore's FairPrice supermarkets dates back to the 1973 oil crisis, when the country was experiencing hyperinflation fuelled by shortages and hoarding of goods. The National Trades Union Congress set up a supermarket cooperative, NTUC Welcome, to contain prices of essential food products, and the then Prime Minister Lee Kuan Yew officially opened the first outlet. The chain later was renamed FairPrice, and it retains its original social mission to help moderate cost of living for low income households.

Another notable Singaporean example is the Singapore Girl which positions Singapore Airlines as a purveyor of grace and Asian Hospitality. In a crowded market, the Singapore Girl emphatically distinguishes the airline from low-cost carriers as well as other premium airlines.

Brand Image Tracking

Brand image as stated earlier is the consumers' perception of the brand. Products deliver a set of benefits — functional, rational, emotional, personality, and brand-consumer relationship benefits. The image or profile of a brand relates to how it is perceived on these benefits or attributes.

The objective of brand image tracking is to measure consumers' perception of brands through its association with relevant attributes. This is done via quantitative studies where respondents are asked to rate brands on a wide battery of attributes, on a 5 (or 7 or 10) point agree-disagree rating scale. For instance in a shampoo study, a typical question may be as follows:

> *Please rate the following brands of shampoo on each of the statements using a scale of 1 to 5, where*

> 1 *means "Strongly disagree",*
> 2 *means "Disagree",*
> 3 *means "Neither agree nor disagree",*
> 4 *means "Agree" and*
> 5 *means "Strongly agree"*

> a) *Using [brand] makes my hair Shiny and Lustrous*
> b) *[Brand] makes my hair beautiful*
> c) *[Brand] prevents dandruff ...*

Actual	Zhi Zi	Tare	Chitra	Iris	Indigo	Daisy	Okura	Fuji	Inula	AVG
Soft	36	20	18	11	18	13	12	6	6	15.6
Shiny, Lustrous	43	25	18	14	7	13	10	3	4	15.2
Beautiful	35	22	25	9	9	10	10	8	3	14.6
Nourish roots	35	35	14	11	7	8	8	4	4	14.0
Frequent use	30	15	12	8	24	10	10	9	1	13.2
Scalp healthy	33	22	13	8	6	9	8	5	2	11.8
Life, Body and Bounce	30	20	29	13	8	6	9	3	2	13.3
Value for money	20	15	13	5	19	20	12	4	2	12.2
Strengthens hair	23	43	14	10	5	5	8	1	3	12.4
Hair Expert	16	18	43	18	3	3	3	1	3	12.0
Prevents dandruff	11	6	3	3	3	9	13	3	0	5.7
Average	28.4	21.9	18.4	10.0	9.9	9.6	9.4	4.3	2.7	12.7

Exhibit 1.5 Top 2 boxes (Strongly Agree/Agree) ratings for shampoo brands in fictitious research study.

To analyse the data, we usually review boxes 4 and 5 (the top 2 boxes), that is, the percentage of respondent who either "Agree" or "Strongly Agree" with a statement. For instance, with reference to the table in Exhibit 1.5, which summarizes the results for a fictitious shampoo research, 36% of respondents either "Agree" or "Strongly Agree" with the statement "Zhi Zi makes hair soft".

Determining Product Attributes

The product attributes for a brand image tracking study are selected on the basis of their relevance to the study objectives. For instance, if the purpose pertains to advertising and positioning, a broad spectrum of functional and emotional attributes that drive brand choice should be selected. For studies pertaining to product development, focus would shift to product design attributes. Brand owners would typically include the core attributes of their brands as well as those of their direct competitors.

In case of an ongoing research, the attribute list is refined about once a year to reflect change in emphasis in advertising as well as changes in consumers' needs and preferences.

Usage and attitude studies are usually a good source of information on the attributes that consumers deem important. If however no prior information is available or if there is the need to update existing attribute lists, *exploratory attitudinal research* (qualitative in nature)

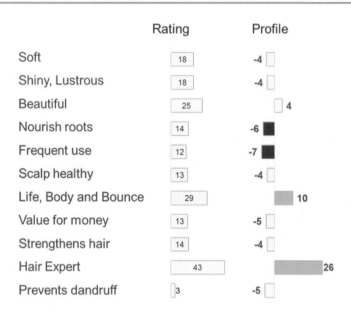

	Rating	Profile
Soft	18	-4
Shiny, Lustrous	18	-4
Beautiful	25	4
Nourish roots	14	-6
Frequent use	12	-7
Scalp healthy	13	-4
Life, Body and Bounce	29	10
Value for money	13	-5
Strengthens hair	14	-4
Hair Expert	43	26
Prevents dandruff	3	-5

Exhibit 1.6 Image rating and profile of a brand.

using focus group discussions, sometimes in combination with physical observation, can help unearth the aspects of a product that consumers find most important.

Image Profiling

The bare numbers depicted in Exhibit 1.5 are not particularly easy to assimilate. Because numbers in general are hard to process, market researchers employ techniques to depict data in a meaningful and visual form that our minds find easier to comprehend.

One method used in the context of drawing a brand's personality, is image profiling, a technique that transforms image rating data to reveal the relative strengths and weaknesses of brands. Observe for instance Exhibit 1.6, which depicts the image profile of a brand. Presentation of data in this form makes it easier to deduce that relative to competing brands, this brand is perceived as the "hair expert" and a brand that

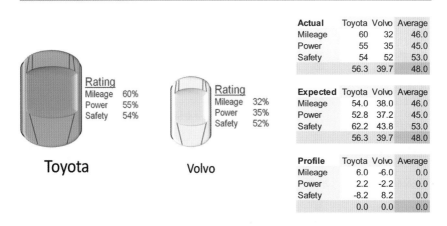

Actual	Toyota	Volvo	Average
Mileage	60	32	46.0
Power	55	35	45.0
Safety	54	52	53.0
	56.3	39.7	48.0

Expected	Toyota	Volvo	Average
Mileage	54.0	38.0	46.0
Power	52.8	37.2	45.0
Safety	62.2	43.8	53.0
	56.3	39.7	48.0

Profile	Toyota	Volvo	Average
Mileage	6.0	-6.0	0.0
Power	2.2	-2.2	0.0
Safety	-8.2	8.2	0.0
	0.0	0.0	0.0

Exhibit 1.7 Fictitious example of image ratings for Toyota and Volvo.

"adds life, body and bounce". It is not perceived as "suitable for frequent use".

The objective in image profiling is to determine what features distinguish one brand from another. While a big brand like Zhi Zi is rated high on all attributes, our aim is to know which of these attributes distinguish it from other brands.

We are aware that people comment more on familiar brands — brand size influences image endorsement. Similarly brands in general are associated more strongly with some attributes (the generic attributes) than others. Image profiling mathematically eliminates influence of brand and attribute "size" to determine each brand's strengths and weaknesses in relation to each other, expressed as variation from what one would expect if the brand were average.

For instance, in Exhibit 1.7, because Toyota is a bigger selling brand, its ratings are generally higher than those for Volvo. With regard to safety, both brands have similar absolute ratings, but *relative to brand size*, Volvo's rating on safety is higher — it is the feature that distinguishes Volvo from Toyota. In terms of image profile it would rate substantially higher than Toyota on this attribute.

Deriving image profile ratings is a two-step process:

Actual	Zhi Zi	Tare	Chitra	Iris	Indigo	Daisy	Okura	Fuji	Inula	AVG
Soft	36	20	18	11	18	13	12	6	6	15.6
Shiny, Lustrous	43	25	18	14	7	13	10	3	4	15.2
Beautiful	35	22	25	9	9	10	10	8	3	14.6
Nourish roots	35	35	14	11	7	8	8	4	4	14.0
Frequent use	30	15	12	8	24	10	10	9	1	13.2
Scalp healthy	33	22	13	8	6	9	8	5	2	11.8
Life, Body and Bounce	30	20	29							13.3
Value for money	20	15	13	$Expected\ Score = \dfrac{21.9 \times 14.0}{12.7} = 24.1$						12.2
Strengthens hair	23	43	14							12.4
Hair Expert	16	18	43	18	3	3	3	1	3	12.0
Prevents dandruff	11	6	3	3	3	9	13	3	0	5.7
Average	28.4	21.9	18.4	10.0	9.9	9.6	9.4	4.3	2.7	12.7

Expected Scores	Zhi Zi	Tare	Chitra	Iris	Indigo	Daisy	Okura	Fuji	Inula	AVG
Soft	35	27	22	12	12	12	11	5	3	15.6
Shiny, Lustrous	34	26	22	12	12	12	11	5	3	15.2
Beautiful	32	25	21	11	11	11	11	5	3	14.6
Nourish roots	31	(24)	20	11	11	11	10	5	3	14.0
Frequent use	29	23	19	10	10	10	10	4	3	13.2
Scalp healthy	26	20	17	9	9	9	9	4	3	11.8
Life, Body and Bounce	30	23	19	10	10	10	10	4	3	13.3
Value for money										12.2
Strengthens hair	$Expected\ Score =$		$\dfrac{AVG(Brand\ Score) \times AVG(Attribute\ Score)}{AVG(ALL\ Scores)}$							12.4
Hair Expert										12.0
Prevents dandruff	13	10	8	4	4	4	4	2	1	5.7
Average	28.4	21.9	18.4	10.0	9.9	9.6	9.4	4.3	2.7	12.7

Exhibit 1.8 Computation of expected score (Example — shampoo).

1. Compute the "expected" score. This reflects the attribute rating that brand would attain, if it was totally undifferentiated. It is computed as follows:

$$Expected\ Score = \frac{AVG(Brand\ Score) \times AVG(Attribute\ Score)}{AVG(All\ Scores)}$$

In the Volvo example the average brand score is 39.7, the average score for the attribute safety is 53, and the overall average is 48. So, Volvo's expected rating on Safety is:

$$Exp\ Score = 39.7 \times 53/48 = 43.8$$

2. Profile rating is the difference between the expected rating and the actual rating. In the case of Volvo, because the actual rating (52) is substantially higher than the expected rating (43.8), the brand's profile on safety is a high positive (+8.2 = 52 − 43.8). Take note that the profile scores eliminate the influence of

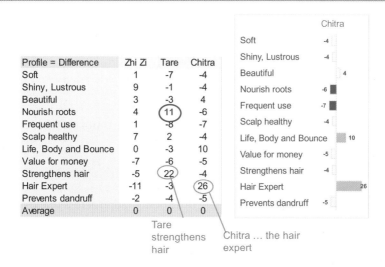

Profile = Difference	Zhi Zi	Tare	Chitra
Soft	1	-7	-4
Shiny, Lustrous	9	-1	-4
Beautiful	3	-3	4
Nourish roots	4	(11)	-6
Frequent use	1	-8	-7
Scalp healthy	7	2	-4
Life, Body and Bounce	0	-3	10
Value for money	-7	-6	-5
Strengthens hair	-5	(22)	-4
Hair Expert	-11	-3	(26)
Prevents dandruff	-2	-4	-5
Average	0	0	0

Tare strengthens hair

Chitra … the hair expert

Exhibit 1.9   Computation of profile rating (image profile = actual − expected scores).

brand and attribute size. This can be seen from total scores, which equal zero, across columns (brands) as well as across rows (attributes).

Reverting to our shampoo example, Exhibits 1.8 and 1.9 illustrate how *Expected Score* and *Profile* rating are computed for Tare shampoo on the attribute "nourish roots". This data tells us that Tare is perceived strong on attributes such as "strengthens hair" and "nourishes roots" and relatively weak on "frequency of use" and "value for money".

Profile rating provides useful understanding of the relative strengths and weaknesses of a brand's image across attributes. This is particularly useful in the context of brand positioning and advertising.

Comparisons Across Time

There is usually some volatility in data due to sampling and non-sampling errors. This becomes pronounced when we compare ratings across time periods. For instance, the average score for all brands may fluctuate from one period to another. Such cross-period fluctuations can be significantly reduced if the data is presented in terms of share of

Attribute = 100

Actual	Zhi Zi	Tare	Chitra	Iris	Indigo	Daisy	Okura	Fuji	Inula	Sum
Soft	26	14	13	8	13	9	9	4	4	100
Shiny, Lustrous	31	18	13	10	5	9	7	2	3	100
Beautiful	27	17	19	7	7	8	8	6	2	100
Nourish roots	28	28	11	9	6	6	6	3	3	100
Frequent use	25	13	10	7	20	8	8	8	1	100
Scalp healthy	31	21	12	8	6	8	8	5	2	100
Life, Body and Bounce	25	17	24	11	7	5	8	3	2	100
Value for money	18	14	12	5	17	18	11	4	2	100
Strengthens hair	21	38	13	9	4	4	7	1	3	100
Hair Expert	15	17	40	17	3	3	3	1	3	100
Prevents dandruff	22	12	6	6	6	18	25	6	0	100
Average	24	19	16	9	8	9	9	4	2	

Exhibit 1.10 (Attribute = 100) Share of attribute rating across brands for a particular time period.

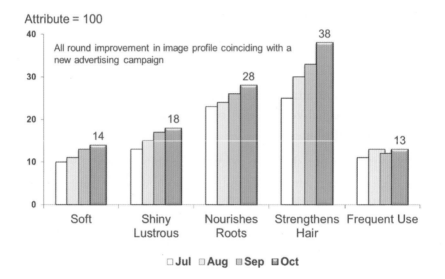

Exhibit 1.11 (Attribute = 100) Share of attribute rating across time for Tare.

attribute rating (also referred to as 'Attribute = 100'), as shown in Exhibits 1.10 and 1.11.

In terms of interpretation, Exhibit 1.10 reveals that Tare's share of ratings (on top 2 boxes) varies from a high of 38% for "strengthens hair" to a low of 12% on "prevents dandruff". Comparisons across time (Exhibit 1.11) reveal that with the exception of "frequent use", the brand is strengthening considerably across the selected set of attributes.

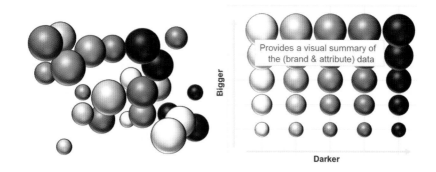

Exhibit 1.12   A set of bubbles that differ in terms of size and shade, depicted along those two dimensions.

The accuracy of the image ratings vary depending on the sample size. The usual standard is to maintain tolerance levels of 3% to 5% at a confidence level of 90% or 95%. Apart from sampling, the research is subject to a variety of other errors including the interviewer's style or his or her demeanour, recording errors, incorrect response by respondents, coding errors and so on. Details about these sampling and non-sampling errors are provided in Appendix A.

Perceptual Mapping

In layman terms, a perceptual map is a two or more dimensional depiction of some entities in a manner that reflects the similarities and differences between the entities. Consider for instance the set of bubbles shown on the left of Exhibit 1.12. These bubbles, which differ in size and shade, are represented on a two-dimensional map so that bubbles that are similar are placed next to one another, and those that differ are further apart.

Similarly by employing statistical techniques like *correspondence analysis*, the brands and their image ratings can also be vividly depicted on a multidimensional perceptual map. Statistical packages like SPSS or SAS are used to craft perceptual maps of brands based on their image profile. The approach is summed up in the following steps:

	Actual		1 Expected Scores		2 Profile = Difference		3 Chi Square		4 Similarity	
	Zhi Zi	Tare	Zhi Zi	Tare	Zhi Zi	Tare	Zhi Zi	Tare	Zhi Zi	Tare
Soft	36	20	34.7	26.8	1.3	-6.8	0.1	1.7	0.1	-1.7
Shiny, Lustrous	43	25	33.9	26.2	9.1	-1.2	2.4	0.1	2.4	-0.1
Beautiful	35	22	32.4	25.1	2.6	-3.1	0.2	0.4	0.2	-0.4
Nourish roots	35	**35**	31.2	**24.1**	3.8	**10.9**	0.5	**4.9**	0.5	**4.9**
Frequent use	30	15	29.5	22.8	0.5	-7.8	0.0	2.6	0.0	-2.6
Scalp healthy	33	22	26.2	20.3	6.8	1.7	1.7	0.1	1.7	0.1
Life, Body and Bounce	30	20	29.7	23.0	0.3	-3.0	0.0	0.4	0.0	-0.4
Value for money	20	15	27.2	21.0	-7.2	-6.0	1.9	1.7	-1.9	-1.7
Strengthens hair	23	43	27.7	21.4	-4.7	21.6	0.8	21.7	-0.8	21.7
Hair Expert	16	18	26.7	20.7	-10.7	-2.7	4.3	0.3	-4.3	-0.3
Prevents dandruff	11	6	12.6	9.8	-1.6	-3.8	0.2	1.4	-0.2	-1.4

Exhibit 1.13   Stepwise approach to producing perceptual map (Example for Zhi Zi and Tare).

1. Compute Expected Score. (Same method as for image profiling)
2. Image Profile = Actual Score – Expected Scores
3. *Standardize* the difference across cells. (Chi-square values)

$$Chi\text{-}square\ value\ =\ \frac{(Profile)^2}{Expected\ Score}$$

4. Compute *Similarity* by applying the sign of the *Profile* to the chi-square values. These values provide a standardized measure of association.
5. Use *correspondence analysis* (CA) to create the perceptual map. CA reduces the numerous attributes that measure different attitudes and perceptions, to a few independent factors that sum up the attributes. These factors become the dimensions for the perceptual map. The attributes and brands are then represented on the multidimensional space in a manner that visually depicts their similarities and differences.

These steps are outlined in Exhibit 1.13 for Tare and Zhi Zi, and the resulting perceptual map is shown in Exhibit 1.14.

The following are some guidelines on how to interpret perceptual maps:

- The closer the products are on the map, the more similar they are perceived to be.

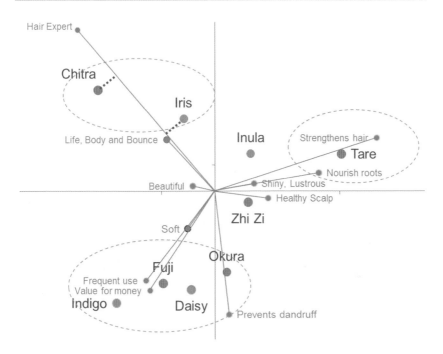

Exhibit 1.14 Perceptual map based on the shampoo data.

- The lines on a perceptual map indicate the different attributes. The longer a line, the greater is the importance of that attribute in differentiating offerings in the market.
- To assess the strength of a brand's position on any attribute, draw an imaginary perpendicular line from the product to the line representing the attribute. The farther an offering is from the origin along the direction of that attribute, the higher is the rating of the offering on that attribute.

  Refer, for instance, to the dotted lines in Exhibit 1.14, drawn from Chitra to form a perpendicular with the vector *Hair Expert*. Since the line from Chitra intersects the attribute vector at a further distance, we can tell that Chitra is positioned more strongly on this attribute than Iris. Notice too that all brands other than Chitra and Iris, would intersect on the negative side of the vector. Compared to other attributes, on an average the association of these brands with the attribute *Hair Expert* is relatively weak.

With regard to the shampoo data, the following are some conclusions one can draw from the perceptual map:

- Attributes such as *Shiny, Lustrous, Soft, Beautiful, Healthy Scalp*, all of which are close to the origin, are generic in nature.
- Attributes like *Hair Expert, Strengthens Hair, Prevents Dandruff, Frequent Use* and *VFM* are more important in distinguishing one brand from another, in people's minds.
- Zhi Zi is centrally located. Usually, this is not a desirable position for most brands. However considering that Zhi Zi is the market leader, and that it comes with a number of variants, it has the capacity to appeal to consumers from different segments.
- On the other hand, a central position is undesirable for a relatively small brand like Inula. To survive, a small or medium size brand should be well differentiated, so that it occupies a profitable niche or segment.
- Indigo, Fuji, Okura and Daisy compete in the same space.
- Tare is uniquely positioned as a brand that strengthens hair and nourishes roots.

Note that the attributes used in this shampoo example pertain primarily to functional, rational aspects such as *makes hair shiny, prevents dandruff, strengthens roots*; and that there is less use in the example of emotive, personality, or brand-consumer relationship benefits. The choice of attributes, as mentioned, is primarily dependent on the purpose and objectives of the study. In this case, the goal might have been to assess the relevance and position of a new brand along functional aspects.

If, on the other hand, a marketer is seeking to understand more clearly the personality of her brand from the perspective of advertising execution, the attributes she might consider using would pertain more to emotive, personality and brand-consumer relationship benefits.

CHAPTER 2

Brand Equity

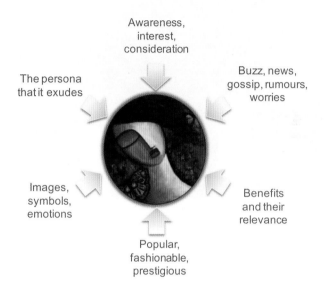

Awareness, interest, consideration

Buzz, news, gossip, rumours, worries

The persona that it exudes

Images, symbols, emotions

Benefits and their relevance

Popular, fashionable, prestigious

Exhibit 2.1 As people get to know a brand they develop thoughts and feelings about the brand.

Brand equity is the incremental value that a brand derives from the thoughts and feelings that it evokes.

Preview

Prior to its launch in 1985, 190,000 taste tests undisputedly confirmed that consumers preferred the New Coke formulation. What mattered, however, was the extraordinary affinity for Coca-Cola, the brand. This state of mind that aroused the outpouring of affection for the brand is its source of equity.

Exhibit 2.2 iPod advertisement *(Courtesy of Apple Inc.).*

This chapter dwells on what constitutes brand equity, how it is measured, and what drives it. The topics covered include loyalty pyramid, net promoter index, net advocacy index, brand equity models and the drivers of brand equity.

The *Shopper Trends* case study that follows this chapter facilitates the development of a deeper understanding of the application of brand equity research.

ZEN versus iPod

Mr. Sim Wong Hoo is one of Singapore's most celebrated entrepreneurs. Rising from the humble beginnings of a computer repair shop, he developed expertise in hardware design, created devices for a variety of computer applications, and set up Creative Technology to mass produce these devices for corporations like Apple. He is best known for his Sound Blaster line of sound card products that dominated the global PC audio market.

Among its many award winning gadgets, Creative's ZEN range of portable media players was a product that the company believed outperformed competition. In 2005, competing with the formidable iPod, Creative invested heavily in a $100 million advertising campaign that stressed ZEN's functional superiority.

That ZEN may not have lived up to Creative's expectations had much to do with the extraordinary strength of the iPod. Yet one also wonders whether ZEN's initial campaign presenting a feature by feature comparison with iPod resonated with the majority of teenagers and young adults. It appeared that at the onset, Creative was marketing a B2C product in a B2B style. A buyer in a business setting would examine closely the product features and price of competing products to decipher which one of them offered superior value. Ordinary consumers however usually do not give as much importance to feature by feature comparisons. For products that reflect their lifestyle, they are swayed more by intangible associations such as symbols, emotions, imagery and relationships with the brand.

The teens and young adults, who were the target market for portable media players, are not the tech-savvy users they are popularly thought to be. Their market has historically been Apple's stronghold. With experience spanning the decades that the company devoted to marketing the Mac and a host of other devices to schools and universities, Apple knew their tastes, preferences and needs. The iPod was advertised to appeal to their senses, and leave them intoxicated with the music.

Interestingly when Apple in 1983 launched the Lisa PC, which at a price tag of $10,000 was intended for business users, the company struggled to cater to the requirements and expectations, such as total solutions and technical support, of the business market. The elements of the marketing mix undergo considerable change when a company moves from one sphere to the other. Apple has traditionally excelled in consumer marketing, whereas Creative's roots lie in business marketing.

ZEN has since carved out its niche within the high tech, great value for money, portable media players, and its campaigns are well targeted for this segment.

It is worth remembering that during its glory days the iPod was Apple's leading brand; that in 2005 it accounted for 39% of Apple's sales. Brand sales peaked in 2008–2009, and roughly 400 million units have sold since its launch in October 2001 till date (2014).

Benefits of Brand Equity

The ZEN versus iPod saga illustrates the power and complexion of brand equity. In *consumer marketing*, the softer aspects pertaining to the brand's affinity with consumers, are often the most potent.

By the time ZEN was launched, iPod had garnered enormous brand equity on a global scale, the benefits of which gave the brand formidable competitive advantage. Some of these benefits are listed below:

- A brand possessing high equity nurtures strong loyalty.
- It can command a price premium.
- Trade cooperation improves as retail partners are more receptive to it.
- Consumers are receptive to the extensions of the brand.
- There is greater interest in acquiring license for a brand with high equity.
- Brand communications become more effective. The brand finds it easier to register messages in the minds of their target consumers.

These benefits reduce friction as products flow from factories to retailers and from retailers to consumers. *They raise profitability*.

At a time when the stakeholders are demanding greater accountability of marketing, the pursuit and measurement of brand equity should gain significance. No other asset compares with a high

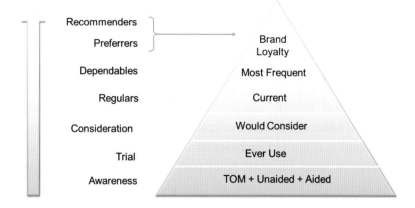

Exhibit 2.3 Loyalty Pyramid.

equity brand, in its potential to generate future cash flow and sustain long term profitability.

The Loyalty Pyramid

The strength of the relationship consumers have with a brand may be gauged via the hierarchy of levels of engagement shown in Exhibit 2.3. Consumers at the base of this loyalty ladder or loyalty pyramid are aware of the brand; it achieves a *presence* in their minds. Moving up, the brand is of *relevance* to consumers who have tried it, or who consider buying it.

Consumers who regularly buy the brand are referred to as *regulars*, and those who buy it most often are called *dependables*. These are behaviourally loyal consumers who drive brand performance.

The pyramid gets thinner from the base to *dependables*. *Trial* is a sub-set of *awareness*, *consideration* is a sub-set of *trial*, *regulars* is a sub-set of *consideration*, and *dependables* is a sub-set of *regulars*.

Brand loyalty represents the highest level of engagement with a brand. Loyal consumers have high level of affinity with the brand; they consider it as their favourite, and are willing to recommend it to others.

Brand loyalty is a state of mind, not a behavioural outcome. A consumer is brand loyal if she has a positive, preferential attitude towards the product or service. *Attitudinal loyalty, emotional loyalty and brand loyalty* are interchangeable terms that allude to this state of mind.

Behavioural loyalty, unlike emotional loyalty, is specifically a behavioural outcome. Defined as brand share amongst brand buyers, it is the quantity of brand purchases by the individual or household as a percentage of total category purchases. For instance, if a consumer drinks 40 cups of Nescafe and 10 cups of other brands of coffee, her behavioural loyalty to Nescafe is 80% over that period of time.

The proportion of consumers that are brand loyal is usually less than those that are dependables, but this is not always the case. Brand loyalty does not always translate to high behavioural loyalty. Availability, affordability and convenience may be constraining factors. For instance, consumers may not be able to buy a preferred brand because is it not available at their regular store.

Similarly, high behavioural loyalty need not be the outcome of brand loyalty. In the case of services like retail banking, due to the inconvenience that it causes, there is reluctance to switch from one service provider to another. Because of reasons such as these, and inertia in general, a customer may continue using a service even after there is erosion in her affinity for the service provider.

Interpreting Loyalty Pyramid Data

In the context of loyalty pyramids, fatter is better. The shifts up and down the adjoining levels of the loyalty pyramid reveal the strengthening and weakening of the brand's interaction with consumers. Comparisons across brands reveal peculiarities that highlight their strengths and weaknesses.

Take for instance the information presented in Exhibit 2.4, which depicts four supermarket banners — Fujimart, SuperFresh, ZerMart and Inulas. The numbers on the right of the bars, with positive and negative signs, reflect the change over previous period. Fujimart for instance has increased its base of *regular shoppers* from 57% in the

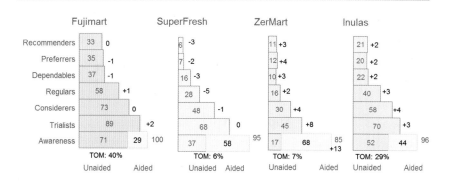

Exhibit 2.4 Loyalty pyramid and brand engagement.

previous time period to 58% (+1). For this retailer there appears to have been a 1% point shift upwards from *considerers* to *regulars*.

Brand awareness is the percentage of consumers who claim they are aware of the brand. It is gauged on three planes — top-of-mind (TOM), spontaneous (unaided) and aided. Top-of-mind awareness is the first brand that comes to mind. Spontaneous or unaided awareness is brand recall without prompting, and aided awareness is brand recall with prompting.

The structural differences between the loyalty pyramids of the banners in Exhibit 2.4 reveal some of the opportunities and challenges they confront. For instance, compared to SuperFresh, ZerMart has much lower base of *regular shoppers* and a significantly higher base of *recommenders* and *preferrers*, reflecting relatively weak behavioural loyalty and strong emotional or attitudinal loyalty. This suggests that while shoppers are attracted, there appears to be some hindrances to shopping at ZerMart.

With only 17% unaided awareness, ZerMart is weak on salience. The data suggests that it is a small, growing banner that offers some distinct advantages over competing stores. This is reflected in the high flow from *regular shoppers* to *dependables* and *recommenders*. However, as yet it is not a well-known banner.

Though the pyramid does not reveal the factors driving its growth, ZerMart clearly appears to be on a high trajectory. Considering its small

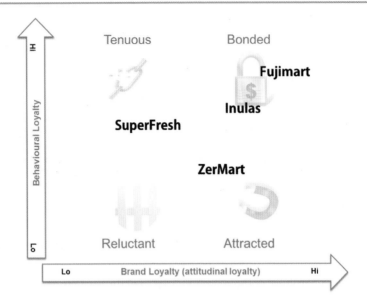

Exhibit 2.5 Loyalty Matrix.

base, the increases at all levels of the loyalty pyramid are quite large. For instance *preferrers* shot up from 8% to 12%, reflecting a large 50% increase.

Fujimart is exceptionally strong commanding 40% top-of-mind awareness, and very high behavioural and emotional loyalty. Inulas is the second largest banner and is experiencing high growth. SuperFresh, on the other and is experiencing considerable erosion, particularly in *regular shoppers.*

By examining their attitudinal and behaviour loyalty for a brand, each of the respondents may be placed into one of four quadrants of the loyalty matrix (Exhibit 2.6):

- Bonded: Customers who are both attitudinally loyal (*recommenders* or *preferrers*) as well as behaviourally loyal (*regulars*).
- Attracted: Customers who are attitudinally loyal, but not behaviourally loyal.
- Tenuous: Customers who are behaviourally loyal, but not attitudinally loyal.

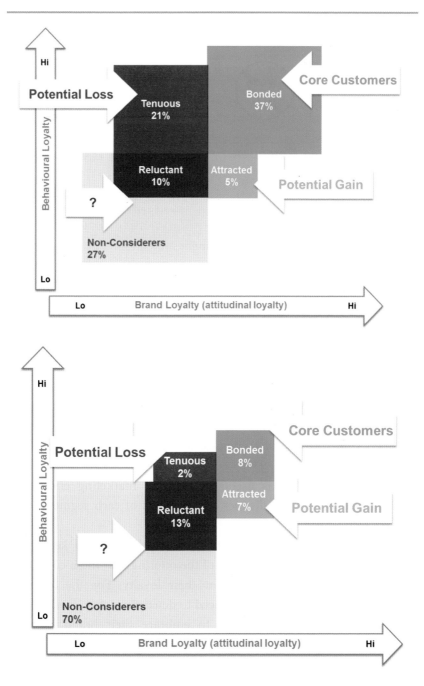

Exhibit 2.6 Loyalty segments for Fujimart (above), ZerMart (below).

Reluctant	Tenuous	Attracted	Bonded
Monitor	**Retention**	**Acquisition**	**Maintenance**
What is undermining attraction?	What is undermining Equity? How to preclude defection?	What "hot buttons" need to be pressed to attain them?	Reinforce, reward and retain.

Exhibit 2.7   Segment strategies.

- Reluctant: Customers who are neither attitudinally nor behaviourally loyal.

The loyalty matrix depicted in Exhibit 2.5 serves as a conceptual summary of how the banners compare with one another. Exhibit 2.6 provides a breakup of Fujimart and ZerMart shoppers across loyalty segments. Fujimart has relatively high *bonded* shoppers who exhibit both behavioural loyalty and attitudinal loyalty. ZerMart on the other hand, relative to its base of *considerers*, has a fairly large base of shoppers who are *attracted* — they exhibit attitudinal loyalty but are not behaviourally loyal.

This categorization is useful in tailoring marketing efforts and strategies to cater to the distinct requirements of each segment (refer Exhibit 2.7).

With *bonded* shoppers, the marketing priority is to keep them bonded by reinforcing the aspects of the offering that these consumers value, and by rewarding them for their loyalty. For the *attracted*, acquisition is the goal. Marketers need to determine what "hot buttons" to press to get these customers to embrace their brand. *Tenuous* shoppers need to be retained. One needs to understand what undermines their brand loyalty, and identify ways of precluding defection. The *reluctant* and the *non-considerers* need to be monitored. In order to target them, marketers need to find ways of attracting them.

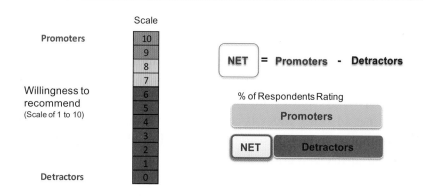

Exhibit 2.8 Net Promoters Index, based on a survey, is the percentage willing to recommend your brand minus those who are not willing to do so.

While the loyalty pyramid and the loyalty matrix analysis reveal some of the strengths and weaknesses of brands, and some of the issues confronting them, additional information is required to chalk out strategies that address these issues. In particular, to identify what undermines brand equity, we need to measure it, and understand what drives it.

A practical approach to measuring brand equity is through its outcomes. If a brand has a large base of loyal consumers, or if it can command a price premium, one may conclude that it possesses high equity.

Net Promoter Index and Net Advocacy Index

Propounded by Fred Reichheld, the *Net Promoter Index* is a straightforward approach, to measuring brand equity. Based on a single metric — "willingness to recommend" — the net promoter index, is the percentage of respondents in a survey who are willing to recommend a brand, minus those who are not willing to do so (Exhibit 2.8).

Nowadays, for brands that exhibit high levels of online engagement, a *Net Advocacy Index* may serve as an indicator of sentiments on the internet. This approach relies on natural language processing (NLP) algorithms to assess the positivity/negativity/neutrality (sentiment analysis) of the multitude of online conversations. NLP is a field of computer science, artificial intelligence and linguistics concerned with the interactions between computers and natural languages.

The net advocacy index is constructed in a manner similar to the net promoter index. Researchers tap into unsolicited consumer generated media, and create the index based on the sentiment of these conversations.

Consumers who are engaged and vocal on the net tend to have strong opinions that may not reflect the viewpoint of other consumers. Because of this, the net advocacy index is heavily biased. One would not recommend it as a measure of brand equity, though it is a useful indicator of how sentiments on the internet are changing.

One limitation of the Net Promoter Index is that it does not reveal the factors influencing or driving brand equity. To be able to act on the data, it is vital for marketers to know how to influence the equity of their brands.

Brand Equity Models

Leading market research agencies have developed proprietary brand equity models that measure brand equity, and tell us what is driving it. Though their terminology differs — "affinity", "bonding", "resonance" or plain "brand loyalty" — the well-known brand equity models are essentially based on measuring surrogates for brand loyalty.

Research firm Millward Brown's equity index, called *Voltage*, is derived from a brand pyramid that is similar to the loyalty pyramid. Voltage is referred to as a brand's "stored energy", or "usable brand equity". It is a reflection of the brand's potential — a high voltage brand has greater potential to gain from its own marketing initiatives and greater capacity to endure the actions of competitors.

A brand signature is crafted based on the strengths and weaknesses of the brand at each of the levels of the brand pyramid, and Voltage is computed from the brand signature.

Research International's model, the *Equity Engine* was developed in 1997 in consultation with David Aaker who is renowned for his theories on brand equity. An equity index is constructed from the perceptions of the brand on a combination of affinity and performance elements. The Equity Engine also computes brand value which is the interaction between brand equity and perceived price relative to other brands in the market (The research firm Research International is now merged with TNS).

Ipsos' model called the *Equity Builder*, places emphasis on brand health which is dependent on brand equity, brand involvement and value. Brand involvement relates to the substitutability of brands; substitutability vitiates the benefits of brand equity. Value, on the other hand, relates to the price differential. Increases in price-gap erode behavioural loyalty.

Brand equity, according to the Ipsos model, is a function of the five factors — differentiation, relevance, popularity, familiarity and quality — described below:

- Differentiation: "Unique or different features, or a distinct image other brands do not have".
- Relevance: "Appropriate, fits my lifestyle and needs".
- Popularity: "A popular brand".
- Familiarity: "Familiar with and understand what this brand is about".
- Quality: "Has consistently high quality".

The Equity Builder model calculates scores for brand equity, brand involvement and value, which are then combined to create an overall brand health score.

Nielsen's *Winning Brands* model was based on Kevin Keller's (1998) consumer based brand equity framework. This model is described in some detail in the following sections.

Computing the Brand Equity Index

The net promoter index is a useful, uncomplicated indicator of brand equity. One may argue that because brand equity is multi-faceted, a series of questions are more appropriate than the single "willingness to recommend" statement used for deriving the net promoter index. In practice, however, it is unlikely to make a substantive difference because the statements used to generate the index are highly correlated.

That said, most brand equity models tend to use a series of three or four statements that reflect the outcomes of brand equity — brand loyalty, willingness to pay a price premium, and the willingness to endure some inconvenience (e.g. travel a distance) to secure the brand. The following statements are used to create Nielsen's Winning Brands' Brand Equity Index:

- If you have to recommend a brand of [category] to somebody which brand would it be?
- Which brand of [category] would you say is your favourite brand? It may or may not be the brand you use/buy most often.
- Can you please indicate which of these statements best describe how much you would be willing to pay for [brand name]?
  - Whatever it costs
  - Even if it costs more than any other brand
  - I would buy even if it costs a lot more than the cheapest brand
  - Even if it costs a bit more than the cheapest brand
  - Only if it costs same as the cheapest brand
  - I would not buy it at all
  - Do not know

There are a variety of approaches that may be used to craft an index; for instance, as depicted in Exhibit 2.9, the equity index may be based on the size of the intersection of the composite measures. In this example, the intersection — i.e. the percent of respondents who rate the brand within top 2 boxes for all the three statements — is 28%. This

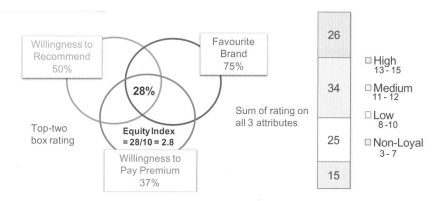

Exhibit 2.9 Equity index based on size of intersection of the composite measures. Consumer segments derived from Likert scale.

intersection value is a reflection of the brand's equity, and on a 10-point scale, the brand's equity index (2.8) is computed by dividing this value by 10.

An alternative approach is to take a weighted average of the ratings on the statements used to determine brand equity, where the weights are obtained through factor analysis.

A Likert scale (i.e. the sum of responses to the statements) may be used to segment consumers based on their affinity to the brand. If a 5-point rating scale is used, the Likert scale for the three statements ranges from 3 (1+1+1) to 15 (5+5+5). In the example, the 26% of the respondents with a composite score of 13 to 15 are classified as loyal, 34% (score 11 or 12) are classified as satisfied, 25% (score 8 to 10) are classified as neutral, and the remaining 15% (score 7 or less) are classified as dissatisfied. While there are no hard rules for the cut-offs, it is preferable that the levels are chosen such that respondents are well distributed across each of the groups. The size of the segments, though, tends to be larger in the middle and smaller at the extremes.

Data Interpretation and Analysis

Of prime interest when analysing brand equity data is the assessment of the impact of marketing initiatives on your brand's equity. To

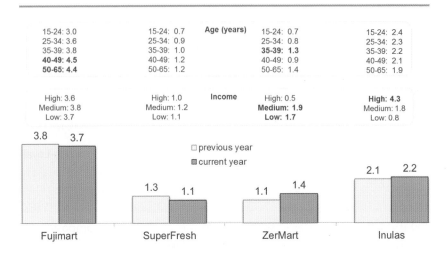

Exhibit 2.10 Store equity indices for some supermarkets.

determine what course of action to take to improve your brand's performance, you will need answers to the following questions:

- What is my brand's equity and how does it compare with competing brands?
- What are my brand's (and my competitor's) strengths and weaknesses?
- Is my brand's equity improving or deteriorating? Which segments are contributing to the improvement/decline?
- What are the factors contributing to the improvement or the decline in equity?

Exhibit 2.10 depicts the store equity indices of some stores based on the Nielsen equity index. The indices, as you will notice, are low for most stores; only Fujimart crosses 3 on this 10-point scale. This reflects the reality in the marketplace. Only a few brands have an equity index that exceeds 3; most brands hover below 1. A ten on this scale would mean that everybody in the market is a loyal customer of the brand and would willingly pay a significant price premium, whereas a zero means that there are no loyal customers and nobody would pay any more than the cheapest price for that brand.

Location	Price and VFM	Variety & Store Experience	Efficiency, Loyalty Program	Quality Products
Convenient location	Value for money	Product availability	Easy to locate items	Quality food products
Near home	Attractive promotions	One stop shop	Good service	Quality fresh food
	Low prices	Spacious	Loyalty program	Quality personal products
	House Brands	Wide range	Ease of parking	
		Comfortable to shop	Efficient checkouts	Quality household products
		Clean Stores		
		Product display		

Exhibit 2.11 Image attributes — Supermarket shopping. Factor analysis summarizes the 22 attributes into 5 factors.

The variations in equity across the demographic groups shown in Exhibit 2.10, reveal the strengths and weaknesses of the brands. Referring back to Exhibit 2.4, observe also how the trends in store equity are reflected in the movements in the loyalty pyramid.

Drivers of Brand Equity

While it yields additional insights, knowledge of how much equity your brand commands does not reveal *the factors contributing to the improvement or the decline in equity*. Only if you know the factors that drive equity, can you recommend a course of action to enhance your brand's equity.

Brand equity, as mentioned earlier, is derived from the thoughts and feelings that the brand evokes. Ultimately it is brand awareness, perceptions, imagery and attitudes that drive equity (Exhibit 2.1). To determine what people think about a brand, we need to track consumers' perception of brands using a multitude of statements that describe different aspects or attributes relating to perceived benefits, imagery, symbols and attitudes.

Exhibit 2.11, which pertains to supermarket shopping, depicts 22 attributes (perceived benefits, imagery, symbolism and attitudes) that portray a banner's image. Taking the same approach as that for brand

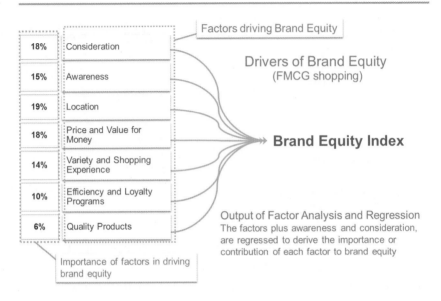

Exhibit 2.12 Deriving the factors' contribution to brand equity.

image tracking, each banner is rated by respondents, on the attribute statements using a 5-point rating scale, where:

> *1 means "Strongly disagree",*
> *2 means "Disagree",*
> *3 means "Neither agree nor disagree",*
> *4 means "Agree" and*
> *5 means "Strongly agree"*

Typically a collection of attributes like those listed in Exhibit 2.11, comprises a number of attributes that are interrelated. Factor analysis reduces these attributes to a smaller set of unobservable independent dimensions called factors. Those attributes that are highly correlated (i.e. fluctuate together) are grouped into the same factor, and those that exhibit low or zero correlation with each other, fall into different factors. Factor loading represents the weight of the attribute on the factor. Attributes with high loading help define the factors.

The factors are named post analysis — usually the researcher chooses an intuitively appealing name based on the attributes that define a factor. For instance in Exhibit 2.11, the factor comprising

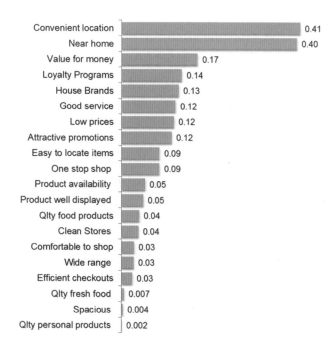

Exhibit 2.13   Relative importance of attributes in driving equity obtained from factor weights and attribute loading on factor.

attributes "product availability", "one stop shop", "comfortable to shop" etc. is labelled "Variety and Store Experience".

The importance of factors in driving brand equity is obtained by regressing the equity index on the factors. And the importance of the attributes is derived from the factor weights and factor loading. The below steps summarize the process as a whole:

- Brands are rated by respondents, on the set of attributes.
- The relatively large number of attributes is reduced to a small number of independent factors, using factor analysis.
- Brand equity index is regressed on the factors, plus awareness (% spontaneous awareness) and consideration (% who consider purchasing), to determine the importance of each of the factors driving brand equity.

Equity Index
$$= f(Awareness, Consideration, Factor_1, Factor_2 \dots Factor_n)$$
$$= \alpha_1 Factor_1 + \alpha_2 Factor_2 + \alpha_3 Factor_3 \dots$$

- The standardized coefficients ($\alpha_1, \alpha_2, \alpha_3 \dots$) obtained from the multiple regression, reflect the importance of the factors. These coefficients have been rebased in Exhibit 2.12 to reflect relative importance.
- The importance of the individual attributes is derived from the factor weights and factor loading. The results for this example are shown in Exhibit 2.13.

Consideration

Whenever habits play a key role in brand choice, consideration becomes an important driver for brand equity. It signals that consumers have made up their minds which brand they want to buy, and their repertoire of brands is limited.

The importance of consideration is also high if the inertia to move from one product offering to another is high. When this is the case, some brands will tend to have relatively high proportion of *tenuous* consumers. These are the customers who remain behaviourally loyal due to the inertia to change, even though their emotional loyalty is low.

Awareness

Salience is likely to be important in low-involvement, habit-driven categories where consumers are less likely to make comparative assessments. In the context of behavioural loyalty, awareness is also important wherever purchases are made over the counter, as is the case with traditional retail channels in many developing countries.

Marketers boost brand awareness or salience with higher frequency advertising, and with the use of brand cues or shortcuts that link to the brand via visuals, sounds or expressions. A brand name and icon, mascot, slogan, music, colour, celebrity etc. can serve as cues. McDonald's, for instance, uses multiple cues including its brand name and icon, golden arches, clown, and its slogan "I'm lovin' it".

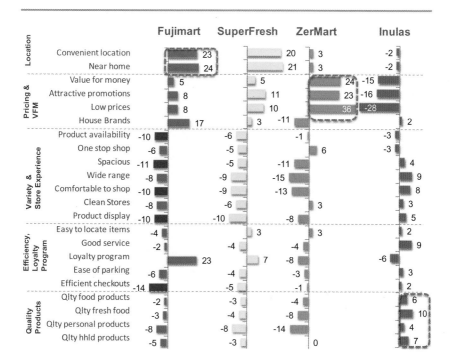

Exhibit 2.14 Image profile of some supermarket banners.

Brand Image

The image profile of supermarket banners in Exhibit 2.14 is constructed using the profiling techniques described in Chapter 1, *Brand and Brand Image*. The attributes are grouped according to factors, with the important factors placed towards the top, and less important ones towards the bottom. This chart reveals the distinct positioning of each of the chains.

The spider charts in Exhibits 2.15–2.18 reveal the strengths and weaknesses of a brand's image from the viewpoint of *regular shoppers*. The approach for constructing these charts is as follows:

- For each supermarket banner the data is filtered so that it includes *only those shoppers who regularly shop at the chain.*

Exhibit 2.15 Image profile analysis of ZerMart and Fujimart.

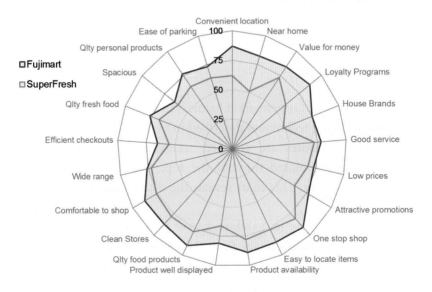

Exhibit 2.16 Image profile analysis of SuperFresh and Fujimart.

- The chart pertains to the top 2 box rating ("strongly agree", "agree") for the chains on each of the attributes. The scale is from 0 at the centre of the web to 100% at the circumference.
- The attributes are arranged in order of importance in a clockwise manner, with the most important attribute at the top.

The analysis reveals how each brand is rated vis-à-vis its competitors. The key points emerging from analysis of the charts in Exhibits 2.14, 2.15–2.17 are as follows:

- ZerMart differentiates on low prices, value for money and attractive promotions. Its "price fighter" strategy appears to be yielding strong gains — the banner's equity index (Exhibit 2.10) surged from 1.1 to 1.4, *dependables* are up from 7% to 10% (Exhibit 2.4), and *preferrers* swelled from 8% to 12% (+50%). Though it is fast increasing, awareness remains low, and shoppers are constrained by the lack of convenient locations.
- SuperFresh is a me-too brand that is competing head-on with a visibly stronger Fujimart. Observe how Fujimart totally envelops it in Exhibit 2.16. This similarity in profile is reflected also in Exhibit 2.14. The chain needs to effectively differentiate.
- The weaker aspects in the Fujimart's image profile (highlighted in Exhibit 2.14) suggest that the chain is experiencing difficulties coping with increased store traffic. The negative skews on efficient check out, spacious, product display and availability, and comfortable shopping experience reflect the growth pains that the chain is probably facing. It seems Fujimart needs to accommodate an ever increasing number of shoppers, and should consider opening more stores, increasing store sizes or entering into larger store formats, hypermarkets for instance.
- Fujimart is stronger on attributes that are of greatest importance to shoppers; its strengths are well aligned to the needs and preferences of shoppers in general.

Case Inulas

The data that we have been referring to over the course of this chapter is apt for studying the application of store equity research. Exhibits 2.4–2.7 depict the loyalty pyramid, loyalty matrix and the loyalty segments for some supermarkets. Exhibit 2.10 depicts their store equity indices. The relevant brand image attributes and factors, factor importance, and attribute importance are covered in Exhibits 2.11–2.13; and the banner image profiles are covered in Exhibits 2.14–2.18. Collectively these exhibits provide thorough insights into customers' shopping behaviour.

Consider the supermarket chain Inulas. At first glance it would appear from Exhibit 2.17 that Inulas is not aligned with shoppers' priorities. It is strong mainly on attributes of low importance, and it is weak on those attributes, namely price and location, that are of greatest importance to shoppers.

It is important to note, however, that whatever strategy Inulas adopts, it must be aligned to the needs and preferences of its target shoppers. It is apparent from Exhibit 2.10 that the banner is targeting upmarket shoppers (Inulas' equity index is 4.3 for high income homes, compared to 0.8 for low income homes). To draw conclusions and recommendations, we should therefore refer to Exhibit 2.18, where the image profile analysis is drawn on the high income segment. As can be seen from this exhibit, the banner's positioning is better aligned with the factors that drive its target shoppers. Moreover, on this base of high income shoppers, Inulas outperforms market leader Fujimart on a number of attributes.

Though "low price" and "value for money" are the prime weak spots, it may not be advisable for Inulas to shifts its focus to these areas as it is hard to alter perceptions 180°, and lowering prices will erode the margins that the chain needs to support superior services. Moreover, by drawing attention to attributes where it is perceived as weak, the chain would inadvertently reinforce their importance in shoppers' minds.

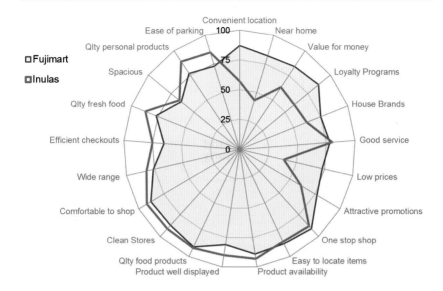

Exhibit 2.17 Image profile of Inulas and Fujimart, *all homes.*

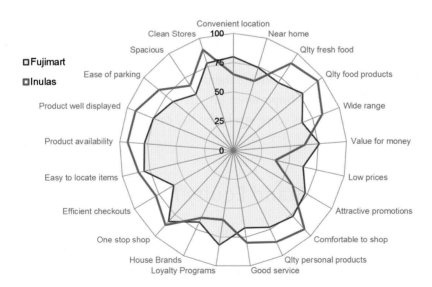

Exhibit 2.18 Image profile of Inulas and Fujimart, *high income homes.*

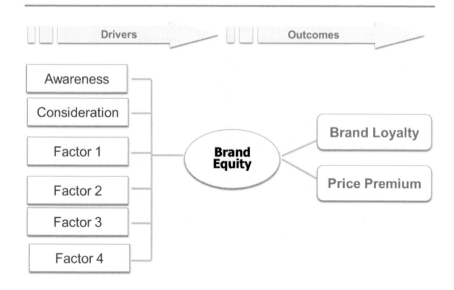

Exhibit 2.19   Overview of Nielsen's Winning Brands Equity Model.

It is advisable instead that Inulas focusses on areas of strength, remaining well differentiated from Fujimart and the other banners. To expand its shopper base, it should evoke through advertising, greater desire amongst shoppers for better quality products, wider variety, and superior shopping experience. Drawing shoppers' attention to these areas of strength would motivate them to shop at Inulas. Markets after all, are dynamic; the importance in driving brand equity, of those attributes where Inulas' core strengths lie, can be reinforced through marketing.

Overview — Brand Equity Model

Exhibit 2.19 summarizes the brand equity model. Brand equity was computed based on measures for the outcomes of brand equity, namely brand loyalty and price premium. The drivers of brand equity were derived based on aspects that relate to what people think and feel about brands in the category, as well as awareness and consideration.

The model delivers an understanding of your brand's relationship with consumers, and its ability to lift consumers up the levels of the loyalty pyramid. You get to know your brand's equity, how it compares with other brands, and how it changes over time. The key driver analysis helps you understand how to strengthen your brand's interaction with consumers thus increasing the brand's loyalty and boosting its equity.

Shopper Trends
Food and Grocery Shopping in Singapore

FMCG Retailing in Singapore — 2006

Singapore's FMCG retail universe, at the broadest level, is split into the upper and the lower trade. The upper trade refers to the organized or modern trade, which includes store formats such as supermarkets like

Note: This case study is prepared for use in class discussions, and it is not intended to illustrate effective or ineffective handling of business situations or processes. Some details presented in the case have been disguised, and the data has been altered.

FairPrice, Sheng Siong and Shop n Save, convenience stores like 7-Eleven, and personal care outlets like Guardian and Watsons. The lower trade comprises a collection of independent stores such as provision shops and sundry kiosks.

Relative to the rest of Asia, FMCG retailing is more concentrated in Singapore. Ever since the opening of NTUC Welcome supermarket in 1973, Singaporean shoppers had been switching from the traditional provision stores and minimarkets to larger modern self-service stores. This change was driven by local and regional retailers, as well as changing shopper needs and expectations. By 2006, the upper trade accounted for as much as 85% of total FMCG sales value in the country, up from about 45% in 1994.

The development of house brands grew with retail concentration. These labels amassed a share of 8% in value terms, making Singapore the lead market for house brands in Asia. For the continent as a whole, house brands represented only 4% share of FMCG sales. That compared poorly with the worldwide average of 16.5%, and the average for Europe where house brands ruled with close to 30% share of market.

House brands can play a pivotal role in the retailer's business strategy. These brands help retailers uniquely position their chain vis-à-vis competition. They offer greater choice to shoppers, generate shopper loyalty and enhance banner equity. Though they are often priced low relative to national brands, they need not compete primarily on price. Many retailers, position one or more of their house brands as premium; for instance First Choice, the premium label at Singapore's Cold Storage supermarkets. Cold Storage also maintains a low end house brand called No Frills.

As regards food and grocery shopping in Singapore, it was largely concentrated within a few supermarket chains, namely FairPrice, Sheng Siong, Shop n Save and Cold Storage. In addition, two small but fast-growing hypermarket chains — Giant and Carrefour — were growing in importance.

Exhibit C1.1 The first NTUC Welcome Supermarket was opened in 1973, followed by the formation of NTUC FairPrice Cooperative Limited in 1983 *(Source: http://www.csr.fairprice.com.sg/oa-journey.html).*

FairPrice

"Since our birth in 1973, we have changed our name, we have changed our look, and we've changed our logo. One thing that has not changed is our commitment to our social mission."

The origin of Singapore's FairPrice supermarkets dates back to the 1973 oil crisis, when the country was experiencing hyperinflation fuelled by shortages and hoarding of goods. The National Trades Union Congress set up a supermarket cooperative, NTUC Welcome, to contain prices of essential food products, and the then Prime Minister Lee Kuan Yew officially opened the first outlet. The chain, which later was renamed

FairPrice, retains its original social mission to help moderate cost of living for low income households.

Over time FairPrice became a well-loved, trusted banner that contributed in numerous ways to the community. Initiatives for the needy included food voucher schemes, used textbooks projects for students, and special discounts for senior citizens. During times of economic recession or periods of high inflation, FairPrice absorbed escalation in the cost of essential goods, through schemes such as the "Stretch Your Dollar" programme in 2007. This programme came with a 5% discount on 500 essential FairPrice house brand products. As much an act of kindness, these initiatives by FairPrice were the means of staying true to their original mission, to help check the cost of living by maintaining low prices.

Launched in 1985, FairPrice's house brands provided another means of moderating the cost of living. The FairPrice label offered a wide range of products at prices that were about 15 to 20% lower than products of comparable quality.

One of the chain's key strengths was its reward programme, which in 2006 extended to about 50% of households in Singapore. These members, essentially FairPrice shareholders, earned patronage rebates and benefit from loyalty programmes when they shopped at FairPrice. While the reward programme was an important driver for store choice, it was felt that the chain could make better use of analytic and customer relationship management techniques to gain deeper insights into the shopping behaviour of their customers.

FairPrice was by far the city's largest retail chain and had been experiencing rapid growth as shoppers migrated from the lower to the upper trade. The chain was experiencing growth pains, grappling with the challenges of rising store traffic, and an increasingly complex supply network.

At that time, FairPrice was also experiencing increased competitive pressures. While in the 1980s and 1990s, almost all supermarket shoppers would shop at the chain, the market was less homogenous by the turn of the century. Shoppers' tastes, needs and values were more

Exhibit C1.2 Sheng Siong, Bedok. *(Source Wikipedia).*

varied, and some of them were increasingly drawn to the diverse formats and experiences offered by competing chains. Even on price, an attribute of importance to its mission, while FairPrice continued to be perceived by the masses as the supermarket offering the lowest prices, a growing minority of shoppers believed that a competitor, Sheng Siong, was offering even better prices.

Sheng Siong

At the time the first NTUC Welcome store was opened, the Lim brothers — Lim Hock Eng, Lim Hock Chee and Lim Hock Leng — were helping out at their father's pig farm in Punggol, a neighbourhood in northeastern Singapore. Their way of life, however, was headed for change. In the 1980s, when the government decided to phase out pig farming, the Lim family was compelled to consider other types of work.

Those days to clear excess stocks, Hock Chee and his wife would sell pork at a rented stall in a supermarket. It turned out that the supermarket chain ran into financial difficulties, and the owner offered his stores for sale to his tenants. With seed capital from their father, Hock Chee and his brothers bought one store, and this outlet was inaugurated in 1985.

Over the initial ten years of operations, Sheng Siong grew slowly from one to three stores. Its scale of operation was relatively small, and the chain found it difficult to command trading terms as favourable as some of its competitors.

The next ten years, however, marked a period of high growth with the opening of 14 new stores. By January 2006, the Lim brothers operated 16 supermarkets and 1 hypermarket, located mainly in neighbourhood suburbs. Yet the chain remained a low-key operator, not indulging in any store advertising or corporate communication efforts.

Mr. Lim Hock Chee has been the key thinker, strategist and showman at the chain. His overarching business strategy was to maintain lowest prices through intense cost controls. Sheng Siong was able to achieve this by maintaining an exceptionally low cost structure. The chain's outlets were located at low rent locations, mainly in neighbourhood suburbs. The company maintained a low wage structure, and indulged in imports to source products from lowest cost suppliers, catering for middle to low income shoppers. The merchandising and shop environment was distinctly no frills, the overheads were low, and there was no advertisement. Procurement was the one key area that Sheng Siong did invest in. The chain set up and maintained robust electronic procurement systems to maintain a smooth, low cost and efficient supply chain.

Shop n Save

Shop n Save was owned by Dairy Farm International (DFI), which also operated a number of other chains in Singapore, including Cold Storage supermarkets, Giant hypermarkets, 7-Eleven convenience stores and Guardian pharmacies.

Exhibit C1.3 Shop n Save store located at the Toa Payoh Hub *(Source: Authority Site Blogs).*

Dairy Farm acquired Shop n Save in 2003, from the Belgian retailer, Delhaize. At the time it was acquired, Shop n Save comprised 35 stores. Two years later, another DFI chain, G-Value, was re-branded Shop n Save, taking the store count of the newly acquired chain from 35 to 46 stores.

Shop n Save stores were located at high traffic locations, which probably was the prime reason why Dairy Farm bought the chain. In terms of performance however, the stores were not as profitable as some of DFI's other chains.

Retail Shopper Trends Research for Food and Grocery Shopping

Nielsen's Retail Shopper Trends is an annual research programme that examines consumer shopping behaviour to determine what drives store choice in FMCG. The study is designed to help FMCG retailers devise strategies to enhance their store equity. Food/grocery shopping and personal care shopping are the two main focus areas of the research.

The study provides an understanding of the image of the major retail banners, assesses their store equity, and determines the factors that drive equity. It also gauges the strength of the engagement of shoppers with the key retail chains, through an analysis tool called the loyalty pyramid.

The methodology and scope of the 2006 edition of the Singapore shopper trend study was as follows:

- City coverage: Singapore.
- Target respondent: Male/female household grocery shoppers aged 15–65 years.
- Interview methodology: Face-to-face interviews.
- Sampling method: Random sampling with quotas for age, gender and race.
- Sample size: 1,300.
- Fieldwork period: 20 January to 3 February 2006.
- Weighting variables: Data weighted proportional to national "main grocery shopper" statistics based on age/gender/location.

Research findings for the study, shown in Exhibits C1.4 to C1.14, provide information on shopper profile across chains, banner profile, banner loyalty, store equity and the factors that drive equity.

Case Exercise

Analyse the research findings for the 2006 Food and Grocery Retail Shopper Trends study for Singapore, and recommend the course of action Sheng Siong, Shop n Save and FairPrice should take, to improve their business performance and store equity. Your recommendations should be supported by the relevant research findings.

Numbers represent difference from profile of all respondents

% All Respondents		FairPrice	Sheng Siong	Shop n Save	Cold Storage	Giant	Carrefour
Race							
Chinese	69%	2	-16	-13	15	3	20
Malay	14%	-4	15	11	-12	10	-10
Others	17%	2	1	2	-3	-12	-10
Occupation:							
PMEBs	25%	2	-15	-1	19	0	17
Other White Collar	19%	-1	4	6	-10	0	-1
Student	4%	0	-2	0	2	4	3
Blue Collar	23%	-3	16	2	-15	3	-10
Housewives	21%	2	-3	-2	-3	-1	-8
Not working	7%	2	1	-4	7	-4	-1
Marital Status:							
Single	16%	3	-7	-5	6	-2	9
Married/Others	84%	-3	7	5	-6	2	-9
No of people in HH:							
1 - 3	33%	-2	2	12	-9	-13	
4 - 5	51%	2	-5	-9	-2	-7	8
6 +	17%	-2	3	-4	10	19	-8

% All Respondents		FairPrice	Sheng Siong	Shop n Save	Cold Storage	Giant	Carrefour
Gender:							
Male	44%	0	7	1	-3	-7	2
Female	56%	0	-7	-1	3	7	-2
Age:							
Age 24 or less	8%	0	-4	1	4	7	5
25-34 years old	22%	-1	0	7	2	-4	5
35-39 years old	13%	-2	4	2	1	7	1
40-49 years old	29%	2	-6	-5	0	-7	-7
50-65 years old	28%	1	6	-5	-8	-2	-3
Household Income							
Low (up to S$2K)	17%	-1	6	-3	-13	3	-12
Middle (S$2~6K)	57%	-1	9	12	-26	1	-1
High (above S$6K)	23%	0	-13	-8	40	-1	14
Not disclosed	3%	1	0	-1	-1	-3	

Base: Those who visit store most often. FairPrice (n=563), Sheng Siong (n=121), Shop n Save (n=98), Cold Storage (n=43), Giant (n=44)

63% of shoppers at Cold Storage are High Income shoppers; i.e., **40% points** above the respondent population proportion (23%)

Exhibit C1.4 Shopper profile of shoppers at Singapore's major supermarkets and hypermarkets.

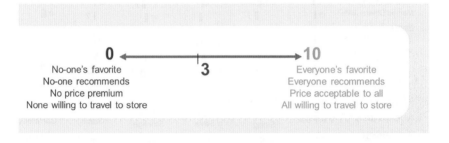

Exhibit C1.5 Supermarket/hypermarket store equity indices — 2005 vs 2006, for food and grocery shopping. The equity indices in the exhibit are based on a 10-point scale where a score of 10 would mean that everybody in the market is a loyal consumer of the brand and would willingly pay a significant price premium, whereas zero means that there are no loyal consumers and nobody would pay any more than the cheapest price for that brand. Most brands on this scale have an equity index of less than 1, and only very strong brands have indices greater than 3.

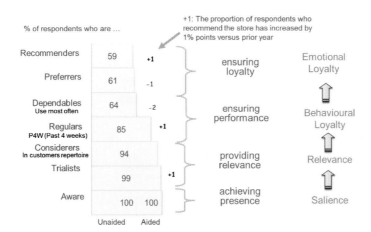

The relationship consumers have with a brand may be gauged via the loyalty pyramid. Consumers at the pyramid's base are aware of the brand; it achieves a *presence* in their minds. Moving up, the brand is of *relevance* to consumers who have tried it, or who consider buying it. Consumers who bought the brand over the past 4 weeks are referred to as *regulars*, and those who buy it most often are called *dependables*. *Regulars* and *dependables* are behaviourally loyal consumers who drive brand performance. Emotionally loyal consumers have high level of affinity with the brand; they consider it as their favourite, and are willing to recommend it to others.

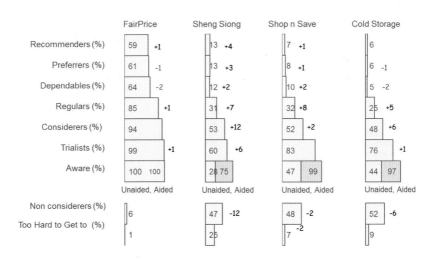

Exhibit C1.6 Loyalty pyramid for major Singaporean supermarkets, for food and grocery shopping.

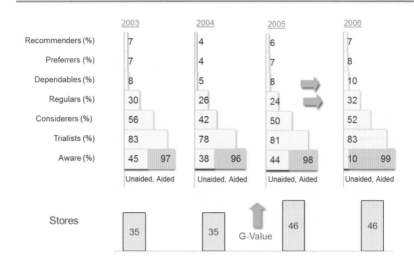

Exhibit C1.7 Loyalty pyramid for Shop n Save, for 2003–2006. The merger with G-Value led to the sharp increase in store count in 2005.

	FairPrice	Sheng Siong	Shop n Save	Cold Storage	Giant	Carrefour
Convenient to get to	83.4	42.3	63.8	43.7	26.1	19.2
Close to home	83.8	42.5	64.1	43.8	26.4	16.8
Value for money	72.3	68.7	53.5	35.8	52.0	28.0
Attractive and Interesting promotion	77.3	69.1	60.8	36.7	55.5	21.2
Low prices for most items	70.7	76.9	55.5	19.4	55.8	10.4
Own brands as a good alternative	75.4	27.6	44.9	46.8	49.3	25.6
Always have what I want in stock	59.7	44.7	44.0	49.3	46.2	76.7
One stop shop	60.9	50.7	43.0	48.5	46.3	60.9
Well presented product display	58.4	34.3	44.9	56.4	45.2	80.8
Modern and comfortable store	59.5	29.8	39.1	60.7	46.6	76.0
Better selection of quality products	53.1	27.6	36.4	54.9	41.9	74.8
Wide product range and variety	56.5	45.6	40.2	52.4	44.7	58.9
Spacious	51.7	32.3	34.6	51.3	52.7	60.9
Easy to find what I need	62.3	46.5	50.4	52.5	44.9	48.9
Staff provide good service	64.5	39.6	44.1	59.2	40.5	58.8
Loyalty program	82.4	31.4	49.9	39.4	46.0	26.6
Ease of parking	54.1	36.2	39.4	48.0	43.7	54.7
Efficient checkout counter	51.8	42.5	42.3	52.4	43.5	72.3
Good range and fresh products	65.9	40.1	46.1	57.3	45.3	58.1
High quality fresh food	63.9	36.0	44.2	61.2	43.2	60.5
Clean and hygienic store	61.5	31.3	42.2	56.2	46.0	82.3
Good quality instant cooked food	54.5	39.4	39.8	52.7	44.1	45.2

Exhibit C1.8 Banner image rating. Top 2 boxes (agree/strongly agree) rating for supermarket banners.

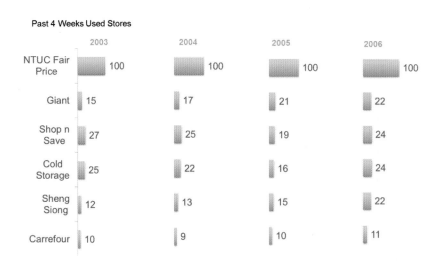

Past 4 Weeks Used Stores

Exhibit C1.9 Proportion of regular FairPrice shoppers who also shopped at other chains over the past 4 weeks.

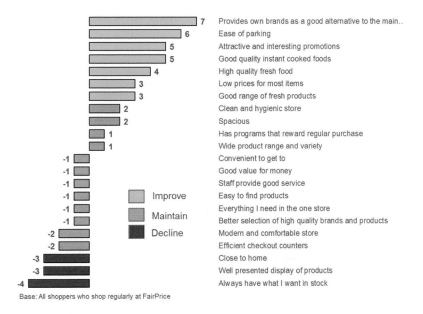

Exhibit C1.10 FairPrice — Image associations score card for 2006 — change versus previous year.

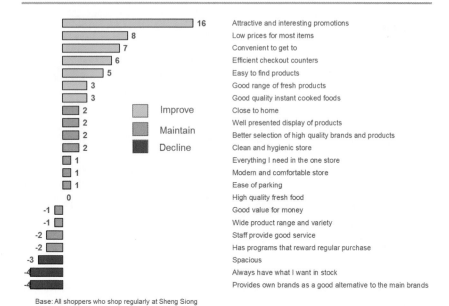

Base: All shoppers who shop regularly at Sheng Siong

Exhibit C1.11   Sheng Siong — Image ratings change over previous year.

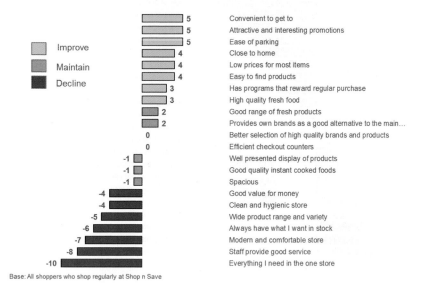

Base: All shoppers who shop regularly at Shop n Save

Exhibit C1.12   Shop n Save — Image ratings change versus previous year.

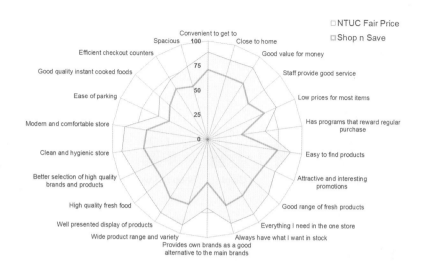

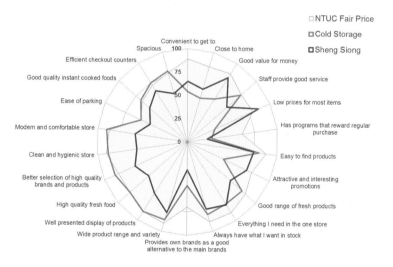

Exhibit C1.13 Image profile analysis for FairPrice and Shop n Save (above), and FairPrice, Sheng Siong and Cold Storage (below). These charts reveal the strengths and weaknesses of a brand's image form the viewpoint of regular shoppers. They are based on only those shoppers who regularly shop at the chain. They depict the top 2 rating box ("strongly agree", "agree") for the chains, and the attributes are arranged in order of importance in a clockwise manner, with the most important attribute ("Convenient to get to"), placed at the top.

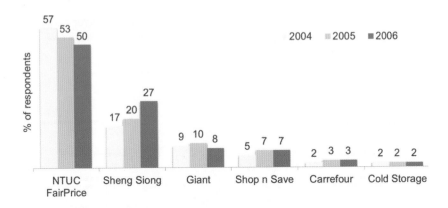

Base: All supermarket/Hypermarket Respondents (N=866)

Exhibit C1.14 Perception on lowest price: Which store offers lowest price for your favourite food and grocery brands?

PART II

Consumer

CHAPTER 3

Segmentation

Exhibit 3.0 Consumers are complicated and unpredictable *(Painting courtesy of Sangeeta Charan, Singaporean artist).*

Schizophrenic Consumers

An ordinary consumer can be extraordinarily unpredictable. She is a daughter, a wife, a mother and a career woman all rolled in one. Not only is she made up of a number of different people, she has different moods; and her needs and preferences are shaped by who she is and what mood she is in at the moment she is considering a purchase.

This unpredictability was highlighted some years back in a Nielsen report. While analysing consumer trends across the globe, the report described consumers as schizophrenic. Often the same consumer, depending on her state of mind, or on what is happening in her life at that moment, is buying products that one would place in diametrically opposite segments:

> *"I usually eat healthy but it has been a hard week and I want to treat myself."*
> *"If I'm just cooking for myself, I go for shortcuts or buy something ready to cook... but when I have friends over, I cook from scratch to make it special."*
> *"I try to eat fresh produce, but I also buy frozen vegetables for when I don't have time for the store."*

Health versus indulgence, value versus premium, fresh versus frozen, large versus small portion, do-it-yourself versus convenience, organic versus local — these conflicting influences reflected in the market trends seen across the globe, highlight the importance of studying consumers in the context in which their needs arise.

Preview

This chapter introduces the concept of need–states, and how they impact on the choices consumers make. It describes the simple decision rules or mental heuristics that consumers rely on for taking low budget purchasing decisions.

The chapter is devoted mainly to the two fundamental approaches to segmentation — a priori and post hoc, and the process of segmentation analysis.

Need-States

Considering the unpredictable nature of consumers, confining them in distinct segments is often not congruent with their behaviour. According to Wendy Gordon (1995), "Brands are bought to reflect the needs of a particular context, be that a mood, an emotion, a habitual circumstance or a practical situation, and thus there are often more differences between the same individual on two different occasions than between two different individuals on the same occasion."

Take for example the soft drinks buying behaviour of a consumer. On a sunny afternoon, in a mood to rejuvenate, he drinks a chilled cola. After exertion, he consumes an isotonic drink. For his daughter's birthday party he buys large PET bottles of orange and cola. During the Chinese New Year season, he purchased large multi-packs of different flavoured drinks. In his office, however he usually sips Jasmine green tea.

A soft drinks marketer may not be able to place this consumer as an individual, within a distinct segment. On the other hand, if she segmented the market in terms of need-states, it would better reflect his buying behaviour as he moves from one need-state to another.

Segmentation

"If you're not thinking segments, you're not thinking." — Theodore Levitt.

The development of your brand's marketing strategy, in a nutshell, entails choosing which segments to target, differentiating the brand to appeal to the segments, and positioning it distinctly in the minds of target consumers.

Market segmentation is typically defined as the process of partitioning a market into groups of consumers with distinct *needs* and *preferences*. For many categories it might be better to describe it as the process of partitioning a market into groups of *consumers' need-states*, reflecting distinct needs, preferences and circumstances. The same consumer often falls into multiple segments, her preferences varying according to her need-states.

Consumer Needs

What exactly constitutes a need? What are the factors that influence consumer buying behaviour? This by itself is big topic, one that is covered in brief, in most marketing management texts. Kotler (2009) describes four underlying influences — cultural, social, personal and psychological. An individual's social class, social network, family, income class, occupation, lifestyle, age, generational cohort, her level on Maslow's needs hierarchy … all these factors and more, shape her beliefs and attitudes. These beliefs and attitudes, coupled with her mood, emotion or circumstance, drive her motivations and buying behaviour, at any moment in time.

The gamut of influences, moods, emotions, and circumstances etc. that drive buying behaviour make segmentation seem a daunting exercise. Yet while the possibilities seem endless all underlying influences do not necessarily shape people's beliefs and attitudes in such a way that it changes their buying behaviour. Depending on the nature of the product category, some influences are more important than others.

Mental Heuristics

Confronted with a whirlwind of information and hundreds of choices in each category, consumers develop simple decision rules or mental heuristics. For low budget purchasing decisions as in FMCG, these rules can be fairly straightforward.

For instance "I always buy Lipton Yellow Label tea". Or for instance the set of rules depicted in Exhibit 3.1, where the consumer prefers Pocari Sweat when it is on promotion, otherwise he buys H-TWO-O. Most brand choice decisions are based on similar, simple decision rules. It saves time and energy.

Rules make shopping behaviour habitual in nature; more often than not a consumer purchases the same set of her usual FMCG brands. Yet there are moments that may trigger a change. Whether it is

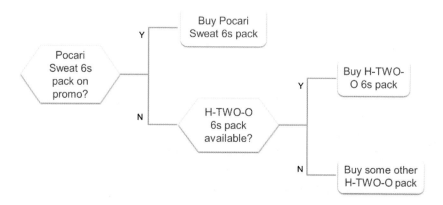

Exhibit 3.1 A consumer's decision rules for buying isotonic drinks.

disappointment with her existing brand, the launch of a new product, the incidence of a stockout, an attractive promotional offer for a competing product or a host of other factors, from time to time she is induced to break out of her habits and try something different. These moments represent the window of opportunity that competing brands seek to exploit.

For segmentation purposes, marketers need to understand the heuristics that dictate consumers' buying habits. What sets of rules apply for each of the different need-states? How do they evolve? What factors influence the formation of the rules? Are the rules backed by an emotional commitment to the brand? What motivations trigger changes to the rules?

The diversity of rules reflects the heterogeneous nature of markets. Marketers can benefit from an understanding of how underlying cultural, social, personal and psychological factors influence the individual's different need-states, and how they in turn lead to the formation of rules.

Forms of Segmentation

Segmentation should be based on consumer needs. The term however is broadly used to describe various ways of classifying consumers or products. For example, take demographic segments. It assumes that the

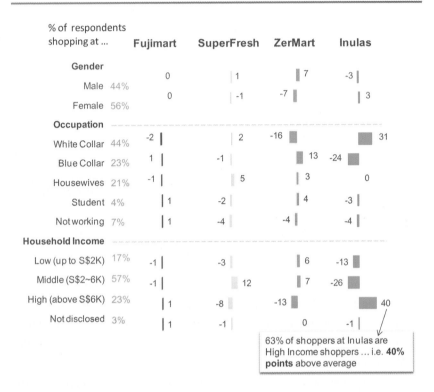

Exhibit 3.2 Skew analysis depicting demographic profile of shoppers at four different supermarket banners.

needs of consumers vary from one demographic group to another, which might be true, though it may not be the ideal or the best way to segment the market.

The objectives of a segmentation exercise also vary. If the exercise pertains to a specific marketing mix decision, the segments are crafted in the context of that element of the mix. For example, a marketer interested in crafting consumer price segments, would use appropriate variables and methods for this purpose.

There are a variety of methods and numerous techniques to segmenting markets. Broadly speaking, these methods may be classified as *a priori*, where the segments are determined in advance; or *post hoc* where analytic techniques are employed to carve segments out from the data.

A Priori Segmentation Methods

Examples of *a priori* methods, where the type and number of segments are determined in advance, include the following:

- Segments where customers are segregated according to observable or pre-existing characteristics such as demographics, geodemographics, psychographics, socialgraphics or personas. Demographic segmentation bases include gender, age, income, race, occupation, marital status, household size, life stage, etc.
- Usage segments that classify customers based on heavy/medium /light use in terms of either quantity or frequency of buying.
- Segments based on behavioural loyalty — solus (100% loyal), core and non-core.
- Segments based on customers' attitudinal loyalty.

A priori segments are easy to define, and easy to reach through advertising in targeted media. Exhibit 3.2, which depicts the demographic profile of some retail banners, reveals that the chain Inulas is targeting high income homes and white collar workers, whereas ZerMart is targeting middle/low income homes and blue collar workers.

Segmentation based on usage and behavioural loyalty is useful in directing marketing efforts to segments on the basis of value to the business. Customer transaction databases in business markets can be used for usage segmentation. In consumer markets usage segments may be crafted from retailers' loyalty panel data, or from consumer panels, or even from data obtained from usage and attitude studies.

Exhibit 3.3 provides an example of usage based segmentation for the "hot beverage" market comprising tea and coffee. The heavy and light hot beverage segments tend to consume more tea, whereas the medium segment comprises mainly coffee drinkers. A manufacturer that dominates the tea category in this market may consider targeting light consumers to induce them to consume more "hot beverage". Targeting the medium segment would be more challenging because converting coffee drinkers to drink tea is unlikely to be an easy task.

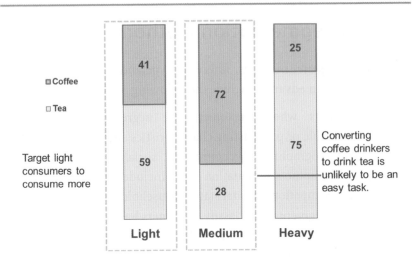

Exhibit 3.3 Usage segmentation of the Tea and Coffee category.

Data from customer satisfaction or brand equity studies (refer to Chapter 6, *Customer Satisfaction and Customer Value* and Chapter 2, *Brand Equity*) may be used for crafting segments based on the customers' loyalty. Another approach to segmentation, the loyalty matrix (described in the *Brand Equity* chapter), combines behavioural loyalty and brand equity. These approaches are useful in tailoring marketing efforts and strategies to cater to the distinct requirements of each loyalty segment.

A limitation with *a priori* methods is that they do not directly reflect the needs of the customers. For some brands and categories, pre-existing characteristics might not yield useful segments.

An important consideration is the feasibility of targeting and tracking consumer segments. For instance, in hot beverage, how does a tea manufacturer engage with light consumers? If light consumers have distinctly different media consumption habits or if they patronize different retail outlets, it becomes feasible to target them. What is likely is that they purchase smaller pack sizes. The tea company may consider directing marketing efforts to motivate small pack consumers to consume more tea.

Post hoc Segmentation Methods

For post hoc segmentation purposes we use characteristics or variables to describe consumers. Characteristics such as demographics, media viewing, web browsing habits and shopping patterns, which may be used to identify and reach consumers are called descriptors or *descriptor variables*. Characteristics that distinguish the segments, typically relating to the needs, preferences, attitudes and usage, are called *basis variables*. Post hoc models use the basis variables for crafting the segments, and the descriptors for targeting them.

The methods may be classified according to whether interdependence or dependence analytic techniques are employed to segment the market.

Interdependence or descriptive methods are suited for strategy development studies where the objective is to understand the market as a whole, and segment it according to the diverse needs, beliefs, attitudes and behaviours of customers, within their distinct need-states. The basis variables for these studies include needs and desired benefits, product usage behaviour, brand loyalty or a combination of these variables.

Dependence or predictive methods are appropriate for taking decisions relating to new products, pricing, advertising or distribution, with the objective of determining which customers to target and how to target them. The basis variables used would depend on the application of the segmentation.

For decisions pertaining to a new product concept, in addition to product related benefits (attributes), the appropriate basis variables may include *product choice,* i.e. the product a respondent chooses or intends to buy.

Store patronage (behavioural store loyalty) and store attributes are the relevant basis variables for studies relating to distribution.

Price sensitivity (price elasticity of demand) forms a good basis variable for studies relating to pricing.

Media habits, customer needs, benefits and attitudes are relevant basis variables for studies pertaining to advertising decisions.

Quality	Cost	Ease of Use	Support

•Durability
•Reliable/trustworthy
  brand
•Range of models
•High technology
•Attractive design
•Speed of printing
•Low noise
•Less paper jams
•Quick drying ink
•Resolution
•Clear/sharp printouts
	•Low-cost ink
	•Low-cost per
	  sheet
	•Low price of
	  printer
	•Low ink
	  consumption
		•Easy to use/install
		•Easy to replace
		  cartridges
		•Compatibility across
		  platforms
		•Supports wide paper
		  sizes
			•Good after-sale
			  service
			•Long warranty
			  period

Exhibit 3.4 Basis variables and factors — inkjet printers example.

Segmentation Analysis

Segmentation analysis is a four-phase process:

- Exploratory attitudinal research (qualitative research): To capture the key basis variables — i.e. the needs, benefits, perceptions and attitudes — that influence brand choice.
- Data collection: From a sample of respondents, obtain responses on basis and descriptor variables.
- Segmentation: Segment the market using the basis variables identified in Phase 1.
- Profiling: Profile the segments using descriptor variables.

Phase 1 — Exploratory attitudinal research

The *exploratory attitudinal research* phase uses focus group discussions, sometimes in combination with physical observation, to capture the basis variables that distinguish one consumer from another. The information from this phase reveals the habits, decision rules and preferences of consumers, and the functional and emotional aspects (product attributes) of the product that drive product or service choice.

Exhibit 3.4 depicts an example from a fictitious inkjet printer market where 21 attributes have been identified as the basis variables.

Phase 2 — Data collection

The remainder of the segmentation analysis is quantitative in nature. In the data collection phase, information is obtained from respondents on the descriptor and basis variables. Questions on needs are framed in the form of agree-disagree or importance rating scales.

Phase 3 — Segmentation

Segmentation involves the following steps:

- Pre-segmentation processing: Factor analysis is conducted to condense the data to a smaller set of independent dimensions called factors.
- Forming Segments: Cluster analysis is used to form segments.

The basis variables usually comprise of groups of variables that are similar or interrelated (correlated). This can cause instability during the formation of clusters. It is therefore important to reduce these correlated variables to a smaller set of unobservable *independent* dimensions called factors. The statistical technique used for this purpose is called *factor analysis*. The data is analysed and represented in a manner such that those variables that are highly correlated (i.e. fluctuate together) are grouped into the same factor and those that exhibit low or zero correlation with each other, fall into different factors. The derived factors represent the original data more concisely, and usually yield more reliable clusters (segments).

For example in Exhibit 3.4, the 21 product attributes are reduced to 4 factors. Variables *low-cost ink, low-cost per sheet, low price of printer* and *low ink consumption* are attributes that are interrelated and have been grouped under a factor that has been named "cost" by the researcher.

Cluster analysis groups together respondents with similar factor scores into clusters (segments). The basis for clustering of respondents for metric data (e.g. rating scales) is the Euclidean distance (or the squared Euclidean distance). In the context of a multidimensional space this is the actual distance between two points and is computed as the square root of the sum of the squares of the differences between the corresponding coordinates. In case of the below data pertaining to respondents A and B, across factors X_1 to X_5, the Euclidean distance is equal to 3:

	X_1	X_2	X_3	X_4	X_5
Respondent A	a_1	a_2	a_3	a_4	a_5
Respondent B	b_1	b_2	b_3	b_4	b_5

	X_1	X_2	X_3	X_4	X_5
Respondent A	5	4	5	4	5
Respondent B	3	4	3	4	4

$$d(A,B) = \sqrt{\sum_{i=1}^{5}(a_i - b_i)^2}$$

$$\sqrt{(5-3)^2 + (4-4)^2 + (5-3)^2 + (4-4)^2 + (5-4)^2} = \sqrt{9} = 3$$

Euclidean distances are computed across each pair of respondents, and the resulting distance matrix is used for forming the segments.

Among the wide range of techniques that are used for clustering data, *K-means* is one that is often recommended. It employs an iterative process to partition the respondents into a pre-specified number of clusters, in such a manner that the Euclidean distance between members within the same clusters is minimized.

An emerging technique, *latent class* clustering is increasingly recommended by a number of market research companies. Present day personal computers have the power to run these resource intensive methods which offer many advantages, including greater flexibility in use of different data formats (nominal, ordinal, continuous) and scaling of variables. They do however require larger samples.

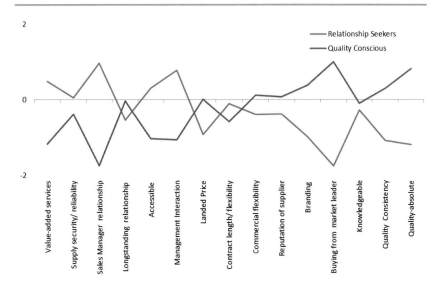

Exhibit 3.5 Segment profile for two segments of a B2B market (Standardized score).

For a detailed description of cluster analysis refer to Hair *et al.* (2009) or any similar text on multivariate data analysis.

Once the segments are formed, they need to be evaluated on the following criteria:

- Heterogeneous: Are there clear differences between the segments? Do they differ in their response to the marketing mix? Do they merit a distinct market strategy, different tactics?
- Substantial: Are the segments large enough in value and profit terms to warrant marketing and product development effort?
- Robust: Can the clusters be generalized to the market as a whole? One approach of assessing the stability of the segments is to split the data at random and cross-validate the solutions.
- Accessible: Is it feasible to reach the segments through appropriate media and product offerings?

Phase 4 — Profiling

In this phase the segmentation is rolled out to the entire customer base. The profile of each segment is created using all relevant variables

Relationship Seekers

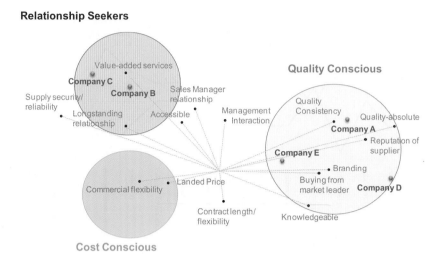

Exhibit 3.6 Perceptual map revealing opportunity areas, and associations between companies, segments and attributes.

including the basis variables used for the clustering as well as the descriptor variables.

There are a few different ways to depict segment profiles. The average standardized scores may be reported as shown in Exhibit 3.5, an example from a B2B market. The plot reveals substantial differences between the two segments — relationship seekers and quality seekers.

The profiles may also be depicted perceptually as shown in Exhibit 3.6 which reveals opportunity areas, and associations between companies, segments and attributes.

To classify customers we rely on a statistical technique called *discriminant analysis*. This technique identifies a set of variables that significantly differentiate each cluster, and is used to place customers into segments.

The segment size can be estimated based on claimed purchases by the respondents.

Targeting

Once the segments are crafted, companies need to identify which ones to target. Their choice depends on a number of factors.

Firstly, it is important that the company has competencies and strengths that are required to compete in the segment. It is easier for a company to succeed in segments, where it possesses competitive advantage.

The size and growth rate of a segment adds to its appeal. The drawback, however, of an attractive segment is that it tends to attract competitors.

The level of competition is an important consideration. It is more difficult to enter a crowded segment than one where customers' needs are not well served.

CHAPTER 4

Qualitative Research

Exhibit 4.0 Focus group discussion *(Photo courtesy of Republic Polytechnic).*

Preview

Qualitative research (qual) reveals what people think and feel, and explores issues by understanding *how* people's attitudes and motivations influence their behaviour. It relies on implicit models of analysis of the participants' verbal and non-verbal communication, their actions and reactions to interpret *why* people feel the way they do.

The distinguishing characteristic of qual is that it is primarily concerned with "how" and "why"; while it serves to explore and investigate, qual does not attempt to measure.

Group discussions and depth interviews, the two commonly used modes of qual are moderated by trained qual researchers. The researchers make use of open-ended interviewing techniques to explore participants' feelings and bring forth emotions into the open in a way that they feel comfortable with.

As shown in Exhibit 4.0, which depicts a focus group in progress, the setting is controlled and the proceedings are recorded. Note also the use of the one way mirror to unobtrusively observe the group discussion.

The topics covered in this chapter include the difference between qual and quant research, consumer generated media and conventional market research, group discussions, interviews, observation, online qual, the design and preparation of a qual study, projective and enabling techniques, body language, and the guidelines for moderating groups.

Difference between Qual and Quant

"The thirty-year war between qualitative and quantitative researchers still flares up in the form of the occasional skirmish with minor injuries on either side, but, on the whole, truce has been declared and happily we are beginning to see signs of co-operation and respect between followers of the two religions. Religions they are, since defenders of either side can still be fanatical and irrational in their denouncements of the other and completely blind to the weaknesses of their own faith." — Wendy Gordon and Roy Langmaid, Qualitative Market Research (1988).

Though the "paradigm wars" between qual and quant is a thing of the past, the above quote alludes to the fundamentally different perspectives that underlie these disciplines. Market researchers often describe themselves as either quantitative (quant) or qualitative. And though the two research forms support one another in addressing business issues, they differ in virtually every aspect of the research process — the type of problem each can solve, the method of sampling, the approach to collecting information, as well as the techniques of analysis. These differences are outlined in Exhibit 4.1.

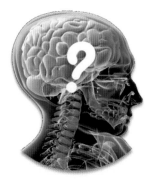 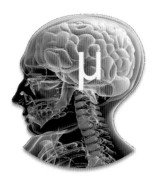

Qual

Objective to examine and explore issues. Expands scope of the investigation.

Subject matter: Covers issues that relate to the conscious and rational as well as the subjective and emotional.

Approach: Qual unearths perceptions and motivations via non-directive interviewing, and draws inferences from observed patterns and themes. It is an adaptive, evolving, unstructured and interactive process.

Sample size is small, purposeful and focused.

Content captured via a wide variety of techniques, is rich, interwoven with verbal responses, non-verbal communication, expressions, actions and reactions.

Quant

Objective to describe, explain, confirm or predict through statistically proven methods of validation and measurement.

Subject matter is relatively simple, conscious and rational.

Approach: Quant methods are explicit and fixed. They rely on directed interviewing of relatively large, statistically valid sample of respondents.

Sample size is large, representative and comprehensive, to meet required accuracy standards and allow for the comparability and generalization of the results.

Content: Verbal responses from a large number of respondents.

Exhibit 4.1 Differences between qual and quant.

The objective in qual is to describe, examine and explore issues, which usually leads to the expansion in the scope of the investigation. Quant on the other hand deals with measurement and validation of hypothesis; it often leads to closure.

A qual focus group constitutes a small sample that is selected for a specific purpose. In comparison, in quant, since measurement is the intent, samples need to be carefully designed and configured. The size of a quant study sample is determined by stipulated accuracy standards, and tends to be relatively large, representative and comprehensive.

The qual advantage arises from quality of content, specifically in terms of its diversity of information. Verbal and non-verbal exchanges, expressions, actions and reactions … all these forms of communication contribute to the wealth of the information that is captured in focus groups, depth interviews and other modes of qual research.

The richness of content allows for the examination of relatively complex issues by tapping the conscious and rational, as well as the subjective and emotional. Qual strives to peel off the outer objectivity that engulfs issues and delve deep into the subjective core; to comprehend not only what people say, but what they actually mean.

The qual framework and process is relatively fluid and relies on implicit models of evaluation and interpretation. On the other hand, the theories, concepts and processes in quant tend to be explicit and fixed.

Consumer Generated Media and Conventional Market Research

Consumer generated media (CGM) — any kind of text, audio, image or video content created by consumers and uploaded on a variety of online media platforms — has emerged as another source of valuable information about consumers. Currently social media is the big wave. Facebook fan pages, such as the Coca-Cola page, which was created by a couple of Coke fans, generate huge volume of on-page engagement.

Conversations of this nature on the net provide a rich source of content about consumers' perceptions, feelings and thoughts.

CGM has many applications in marketing. It aids ideation during new product development and provides an understanding of brand imagery. Consumers' advocacy of a brand reveals their feelings about it, giving us an inkling of the equity of the brand. There are undoubtedly many ways that we may use CGM for research purposes; and as the applications continue to grow, some clarity on the extent to which we may rely on this new media for accurate insights on our brands is desirable. We need to understand the ways it can support, complement or displace conventional quantitative and qualitative research.

Benefits and Limitations of CGM

CGM supports large number of conversations; conversations that emanate from a non-representative albeit influential group of consumers. Information gleaned from these conversations tells us how these highly engaged consumers, who publish content or comment on the web, perceive the brand. However because the sample is so heavily skewed by individuals with fairly strong opinions, their perception or views may not accurately reflect how consumers in general think about the brand.

Marketers too influence opinions as they interact with consumers online. It serves their interest to engage with these consumers, feed them with relevant information and in so doing favourably influence their opinions. While this helps to protect and strengthen their brand, it introduces a further bias on CGM.

Owing to the lack of rigour and discipline, CGM conversations are not representative of the universe, and may contain a strong bias considering that:

    i.   Consumers who are engaged and vocal on the net tend to have strong opinions that do not necessarily reflect the population as a whole;

ii.   their opinions are influenced by other consumers who are active online, as well as marketers who have vested interest in advocating and protecting their brands;

iii.   and consumers who seek information on categories like fast moving consumer goods online are, in numerical terms, minute compared to the universe of consumers.

While representativeness is important where the intent is to measure, as in quant, it is not of critical importance where the intent is to explore, as in qual. In qual we often (though not always) target engaged consumers, people who like to talk about the brand. Consumers who are actively engaged with the brand online would be appropriate, even sought after, for exploring and investigating issues relating to your brand.

One must, however, remain wary of some of the claims that we stumble upon on this subject. Though it has been touted as the "world's largest focus group", CGM is *not a focus group*. It is not a purposeful sample. It lacks moderation, the discipline in approach, and is devoid of projective techniques that researchers use to unlock people's minds in focus groups or depth interviews. It does not therefore substitute qualitative research.

It is, nonetheless, a powerful, revealing medium for *observation*. It allows you to "listen" to *unsolicited* feedback about your brand from hundreds or thousands or millions of consumers, and "see" how they relate to it and how they use it. As natural language processing and text analytics technologies evolve, you increasingly can listen more efficiently to the glut of conversations on the net. The insights that you glean through listening and seeing enable you to:

- Spot market gaps and trends;
- Generate ideas and insights for new products (ideation);
- Learn about existing needs and preferences; uncover new "organic" needs;

- Uncover feelings and emotions arising from marketing initiatives and activities;
- Understand what product categories, product attributes, themes, and which competing brands are associated with your brand (brand image);
- Test advertising;
- Gauge the extent to which these consumers advocate your brand (consumer advocacy).

CGM can trigger new ideas, thoughts and perspectives. You are more likely to encounter the unforeseen via CGM because it yields much more unsolicited information than conventional research which is primarily guided by brand management's existing thoughts and notions about the brand. CGM also reveals consumer vocabulary, i.e. the labels and adjectives used by ordinary people to describe brands and brand-related concepts or themes.

Moreover CGM-based research need not be expensive. Considering the necessity of monitoring online conversations to protect or enhance the reputation of your brand, the incremental cost of drawing further insights from these conversations is not high, and will continue to decline as related technologies improve.

CGM Complements Conventional Market Research

The unsolicited information garnered through CGM feeds conventional research. Consumer vocabulary on the net may help refine the language we use in both qual and quant research. The new ideas and thoughts that emerge from CGM may be explored in greater depth through qual. Quant on the other hand helps to measure and validate, draw conclusions, and assess the extent to which the ideas relate to the masses.

In conclusion, CGM-based research works best in conjunction with conventional market research. While it lacks the rigour and discipline that is necessary to form conclusions about the market as a whole, it is a very valuable medium that allows marketers to listen and engage with a large number of consumers, uncover new product ideas, and spot market gaps and trends. The insights that it generates need to be further explored, measured and validated via conventional research.

Applications of Qualitative Research

Qual is used mainly for exploratory, explanatory or diagnostic, and evaluative or tactical purposes. From a marketing standpoint, it encompasses a wide range of applications, of which the most common include:

- Product development
- Creative development
- Packaging development
- Motivational research
- Semiotics
- Usage and attitudinal research

Exploratory

Qual is the appropriate method to employ when confronted with the unexplored or the unknown. It is used for exploring opportunities and ideas for products, advertising or brand positioning. The need for qual arises when developing new products, entering new markets or when a market undergoes change. In these scenarios qual can provide insights pertaining to wide range of unknowns, including:

- Understanding of usage, attitudes and behaviours;
- Knowledge of product benefits and attributes, and an understanding of what differentiates brands;
- Understanding of how consumers relate to brands;
- Understanding of their purchase decision making process.

Exhibit 4.2 Qualitative research complements quantitative research.

Explanatory or Diagnostic

Qual helps to examine and investigate issues. For instance, if the sales of a new product are not meeting expectations, qual will answer *why* consumers are unwilling to try the product. Similarly if a new product is experiencing low repeat purchase, or if an established product is experiencing a decline, qual will diagnose the reasons, including emotive ones, as to *why* lapsed users stopped buying.

Qual is also extensively used to explore social issues. One example that comes to mind is its use to explain the underlying reasons for declining birth rate. The subjective and emotive responses that qual is able to unearth, help diagnose and explain the real reasons why some couples do not want to have babies.

Evaluative

Qual is often used to assess whether or not a proposed marketing initiative will satisfy its intended objectives. It may also be used to evaluate a set of alternatives. For example, evaluation of product concepts, communication themes or advertisements and pack designs.

Qual with Quant Research

Qual complements quant by addressing different aspects of a business issue (Exhibit 4.2). It may be conducted pre- or post-quant. It serves to screen products/advertising concepts, identify important dimensions and formulate key hypotheses for quantification. It may be used simply for piloting questionnaires to test comprehension, language and flow. Qual can also explore in more depth some issue or problem emerging from quantitative data.

Product Development

Qual is of primary importance in the development of new products. It is widely deployed to assist marketers in spotting gaps and trends in the market, in the *ideation* process, in the conceptualization and filtering of new product concepts, and in the processes leading to the development and launch of products.

You can use qual to attain an in-depth understanding of consumers' attitudes, usage and behaviours, and their aspirations and motivations. This will provide an understanding of the factors that drive brand choice, help you spot opportunities, and trigger ideas for new products.

Workshops engaging target consumers in group discussions are widely used for *concept development* purposes. These concept development workshops serve to explore, develop and improve concepts via an iterative process where consumers assess a number of concepts in detail, and prioritize those deserving further development. They provide for an improved understanding of the strengths and weaknesses of the concepts and serve to guide further development.

Associates from marketing, market research, R&D, and sales are encouraged to participate in the process. Marketers interact with consumers, introduce them to the product ideas and engage with them to flesh out the new product concepts.

Once the product concept is finalized, quant research methods such as BASES simulated test markets provide for a volumetric estimate of the potential of a new concept or product. BASES is discussed in some detail in Chapter 11, *Product Validation.*

A key step in the new product's development is to optimize the elements of *marketing mix,* often by means of a marketing mix workshop. Depending on the nature of the product, the scope of a marketing mix workshop will include some of the following elements — product naming, product usage, advertising and brand positioning, and packaging. It is possible also to broadly gauge how *receptive* respondents are to the product's price, though as far as price *setting* is concerned quantitative methods are more appropriate.

Research methods relating to new product development including ideation, concept development, and development of marketing mix are discussed in more detail in Chapter 9, *New Product Development.*

Creative Development

Qual can provide an understanding of how brands are positioned, their image, their personality, as well as the extent to which they are "stretched".

Creative development research is used to chalk out new directions in advertising or NPD. It helps advertisers refine adcepts, and verify execution details. It is also used in conjunction with quant for screening new advertising, product or positioning concepts, or for copy testing purposes. (Refer to Chapter 15, *Advertising Research* for details on copy testing).

Motivational Research, Semiotics, Usage & Attitude

Motivational research, semiotics and usage & attitude (U&A) are qualitative research methods that support the development of marketing and brand strategy. They directly feed into key marketing processes including insight generation, product development, positioning, development of brand key, and packaging and creative development.

Motivational research explains the underlying *needs* that drive behaviour. It focusses on identifying the *emotional needs* that are central to relationship between the brand and its consumers. Depth interviewing is the most effective and efficient mode for conducting motivational research. It relies heavily on the skills of the researcher to build empathy, and create an atmosphere where the respondent feels uninhibited to express thoughts and emotions.

Semiotics is the study of signs and symbols, and how they are used in different cultures. It allows us to understand the implicit meaning these codes communicate, in the culture and context within which they are used. For example, depending on the context, the colour red signifies distinctly different connotations. It signifies luck and prosperity in the Chinese culture, love or anger in the West, losses in a financial statement, and danger or caution on the roads.

U&A studies provide information about consumer attitudes and usage behaviours for the category and brands. It is important that the scope of these studies, which may be quite wide, is aligned with business objectives. The considerable amount of information that is contained in these studies can be used to *segment consumers* on the basis of their usage as well as their opinions, and identify growth opportunities for brands within the various segments. The information collected includes details of usage dynamics — frequency of use, quantity bought, reasons and occasions for use, brand awareness and usage, demographic of different types of users, attitudes to category or life in general, functional and emotional needs driving category purchase, shopping behaviour, satisfaction/dissatisfaction with category, and issues/problems and their resolution.

Qual followed by quant research is the typical approach for conducting U&A studies. The qual phase usually involves depth interviews/group discussions to explore and identify the issues that need to be tracked in the quant phase.

Packaging Development

Qualitative research for developing and evaluating packaging helps explore new pack designs in terms of appeal and communication. At the early stages of the packaging development, it is essential to understands how effectively the packaging is communicating what the brand stands for — the proposition, brand personality, the key symbols, identifiers and icons.

The Qualitative Advantage

Qualitative research offers many advantages that make it conducive for studies that are exploratory, explanatory and evaluative in nature.

- It is quick and easy to commission and complete.
- It draws on a wide range of stimulus materials and techniques — drawing, sorting, writing, lateral thinking.
- It assesses both verbal and nonverbal responses from the participants.
- It offers the flexibility to modify the process during the course of a study.
- Decision makers can be involved as unobtrusive observers to hear consumers talk about their product. (see Exhibit 4.3)
- Qual reports are often easy to understand. There are no elaborate models and no inferential statistics.
- A variety of topics can be investigated using a wide range of respondents, including children.

Watchouts

- Qual results are not representative of the general population and cannot be projected. Those marketing decisions that rely on the measurement of one or more variables should not be based purely on qual.

Exhibit 4.3   Observing a focus group *(Photo courtesy of Strategic Research Associates).*

- Qualitative lacks the statistical foundation that guides decision makers in quant, as to the significance of the results. It is therefore susceptible to selective perception and interpretation. Marketers and decision makers should be wary of this and remain open to all responses and comments, not merely those findings that they would like to hear.
- Qual findings are exploratory, not conclusive. Decision makers should neither place greater confidence than warranted in the results, nor should they dismiss the findings as inconsequential.

- Low cost should not be the reason to use focus groups as an alternative to quantitative research.
- The unstructured nature of the responses in qual research complicate coding, analysis, and interpretation. Furthermore since analysis in qual is the product of the researcher's implicit models of evaluation and interpretation, it will vary with

researcher. The capability of the researcher is accordingly a determinant of research quality, which introduces a level of inconsistency in qual.

- The growth of online qual has led to the influx of boutique agencies some of which rely more on technology than the soft skills that distinguish a qual researcher. At the same time some end-users enamoured by technology, and lured by low costs, may fail to fully appreciate the true benefits of qual. The resulting commoditization may lead to deterioration in the overall standards of quality of qual research.

Modes of Data Collection

Group discussions, in-depth interviews and observations are the basic approaches to conducting qual studies. In the past these modes relied entirely on real time, in person interaction with participants. While conventional approaches still constitute the bulk of qual research, internet and mobile technologies are steadily transforming qual. Online qual has gained wide acceptance, and mobile qual is gaining popularity. There is a steady transition from real time group discussions at research facilities, face-to-face interviews and physical observations, to asynchronous online discussion boards, video diaries, online journals and blogs.

Group Discussions

Group discussions or focus groups provide for the interaction among participants. They may be conducted online or face-to-face. The group moderator engages with participants, encourages them to communicate with one another, and exchange ideas and comments on each other's experiences or points of view.

Groups are appropriate for a broad range of topics in marketing and social sciences, including for instance areas relating to brand studies, concept testing and advertising testing that are conducive to interactive discussion. The discussion is led by a moderator who introduces the topic, encourages free flow of ideas and coordinates the discussion.

Conventional focus group discussions, conducted at a research facility or an alternative venue, typically comprise of 6 to 8 respondents, usually last about one and half hours, and are recorded on video/DVD for remote viewing of the proceedings. The research facility is fitted with a large one-way glass window — participants cannot see out, but decision makers and researchers can see in.

For those studies where respondents are hard to recruit, or where the subject matter requires focussed attention, mini group discussions comprising 3–5 respondents per group, lasting about one to two hours are the norm. The smaller group size allows for more in-depth and focussed interaction.

Extended Group Discussions lasting about 2.5 to 3 hours and comprising 6–8 respondents per group are appropriate for more complex or detailed issues that require additional time for evaluation. U&A, exploratory or diagnostic research may require extended groups.

When there is polarization of views on a subject, researchers may adopt *Conflict Groups* comprising respondents with different attitudes, habits or views on the subject. These groups may also be extended for 2.5 to 3 hours and are best suited for studies where the intent is to force out deep seated feelings on the subject.

Unlike conventional focus groups *online groups* tend to vary greatly both in size and duration, and are dependent on the online methodology. The duration of discussion boards for instance varies from 2 to 10 days.

Interviews

Interviews are best suited for in-depth probing of personal opinions, beliefs and values on *intimate or sensitive* subject matters, such as personal finance or contraception. They are appropriate too for understanding *complex* psycho-sociological issues, both in marketing as well as social sciences.

We need to rely on interviews also when there are difficulties in recruiting groups such as in the case of high profile respondents or experts/specialists.

Interviews tend to be individual focussed, often requiring the respondent's relevant background history. *Conventional depth interviews* are conducted one-on-one, in person and last about 45-60 minutes. *Paired Interviews or Dyads* comprise 2 respondents — usually friends or a couple — last about 1 to 1½ hours and work best for subjects that require joint decisions. *Triads* comprise 3 respondents usually friends or colleagues, and last about 1½ hours. Triads are appropriate for subjects pertaining to young children, teenagers or experts.

The empathy between researcher and respondent is the key to the success of depth interviews. The methodology relies heavily on the skills of the researcher in building a rapport with the respondent and creating an atmosphere where the respondent feels uninhibited to express thoughts and emotions. She is skilled in reading body language, and uses projective techniques to allow the respondent to express his feelings about a sensitive subject, in a manner he feels comfortable with.

A wide range of online qual platforms including those covered later, are also conducive for in-depth interviewing.

Observation

Pioneered by anthropologists, observation is a technique for understanding human behaviours, perceptions and emotions as they occur. In marketing applications researchers usually observe consumers during shopping trips or at their homes, with the intent to understand shopping dynamics, in-home product usage and ethnography.

Observation research is still largely conducted in-person, though this is both expensive as well as intrusive. While it is feasible to install and maintain video cameras in-store, securing retailer cooperation is often a challenge, and privacy laws need to be taken into consideration. The in-home environment is less complicated, and it is usually convenient to video record participants as they use products, or undertake tasks of interest to the researcher.

With a view to saving costs, researchers, in future, will increasingly rely on user-generated media for recording observations. This is facilitated by the proliferation of mobile recording devices that make it feasible for participants to produce their own video or audio recording of activities. Alternatively participants are asked to maintain online journals or blogs where they write details about the activities and experiences relevant to the research. Considering that individual preferences do vary, qual platforms should support a wide range of media types including text, image, video and audio content.

Online Qual

As consumers increasingly converse on the net, it benefits researchers to engage with them online. Online methods yield greater efficiencies, making it quicker, easier and less expensive to conduct qual studies.

Moving online however requires considerable adaptation. Besides the appreciation of the new technologies, researchers must learn how to initiate and drive interaction online. There is the need to proactively engage with participants, to keep them motivated, encourage them to participate, and ensure that they remain focussed. This is similar to what transpires in conventional in-person qual, except that the researcher needs to adapt to doing so in an online environment.

Basic principles remain the same. The value derived from the research hinges on the quality of the recruitment methods, and the skills of the researcher in moderating the group, interpreting the data, and drawing actionable insights. It is important that the research is designed to invoke an engaging, evolving experience rather than a Q&A style of interaction, which goes better with quant research.

	Text	Audio	Video	Multimedia
Asynchronous	Discussion board Diary, journal, blog Online community		Video diary, journal, blog (webcam)	Discussion board Online community Mobile
Real Time	Text chat Online community	Telephone (audio conferencing)	Video diary, journal, blog	Video diary, journal, blog Online community Mobile

Exhibit 4.3 Online platforms for qual.

The wide variety of online platforms that currently exist are categorized in Exhibit 4.3, in terms of timing (real time, asynchronous) and media type (text, audio, visual and multimedia).

Diary, journal and blog (whether text or video) are intended for individual observation or interview. Rest of the platforms shown in Exhibit 4.3 could be configured for focus groups or in-depth interviews.

Discussion Boards

Discussion boards or bulletin boards are versatile and can generate rich content. Boards involve pre-recruited participants from diverse geographical locations. Their number can vary greatly depending on the nature of the study, though 15–20 respondents would fit the majority of boards. Where the subject matter has greater depth, it is more productive to engage with fewer participants. The duration is also quite flexible; it can last anywhere from 2 to 10 days, and participants typically commit to log in once a day or a few times per day, over the duration of the exercise.

In addition to typing their thoughts, participants can post videos and audios using webcam, audio, and mobile input tools that can incorporate facial expressions and body language into the discussions.

Discussion boards have evolved since the text-based Q&A type bulletin boards of the past. It is important that these platforms are moderated by experienced researchers, or else they could easily degenerate into glorified open-ended Q&A surveys. The inclusion of image, video and audio enables researchers to read non-verbal communication and tacit signs, such as facial expressions, body language cues, tone of voice, inflexion and pauses. Skilled moderators utilize analogies, projectives and other techniques that can help board participants express their hearts and minds through "digital body language", with a remarkable degree of personality and affect.

Video-based Online

Video-based online, which taps on webcam and streaming technology is the closest reflection of in-person focus groups and interviews. Its use is likely to expand rapidly as high-speed internet penetration increases, and as consumers become familiar with video conferencing via free/low-cost platforms like Skype.

As one technological wave follows another on the net, online qual will keep evolving. In the past developers took a bottom up approach accommodating existing tools and technologies to create a range of diverse online platforms, such as those depicted in Exhibit 4.3. In the future these applications ought to be better integrated, providing for real time as well as asynchronous interaction, across multiple media types, within a single platform.

Online Advantages

- Travelling to a research facility is no longer a requirement; participants, researchers and clients may even be dispersed across countries or continents. This not only saves cost but also allows for the participation of respondents who would otherwise find it inconvenient or too time consuming to travel — for instance, busy specialists/professionals or new mothers with babies. Online/telephone platforms also provide access to participants based in politically sensitive or dangerous locations.

- Participants feel relatively secure, relaxed and comfortable participating from their preferred environment, without the physical presence of the moderator and other participants. This also lowers the pressure to conform to the views of others within the group. Practitioners claim that respondents open up more online; that they are candid, honest and critical. They feel less embarrassed, and are willing to express their views on sensitive subjects.

- Participants may choose to remain anonymous within their group. They may do so by using avatars, or usernames that are not their real names. They may also choose to refrain from posting information via media, such as video, that would reveal their identities.

- Online platforms provide for both individual and group interaction. Typically the interface comprises sections or panes on the device screen that can be configured on one-on-one mode or group mode. This allows participants the flexibility to share thoughts individually with the moderator, or with the group as a whole.

- Asynchronous platforms allow participants the convenience of finding time during their day to reflect on the topics, answer the questions, and complete tasks at their own pace.

- Skilled moderators capable of making the interactions engaging and satisfying can get participants to open up and provide thoughtful responses. Asynchronous platforms, where participants are engaged for a few days (or weeks/months as in the case of online communities), provide researchers the time to harvest, probe, and extract an impressive flow of useful information.

- Participants may use a variety of devices to communicate — PC, laptop, tablet or smart phone.

- Many classic projective techniques smoothly translate to online activities where they can be easier to set up, execute and compile. The device keyboard, mouse, screen and software substitute for the cumbersome easel pad, whiteboard and marker pen. Whereas compiling results in face-to-face qualitative studies can be quite laborious, the automation in online qual allows researchers and clients to instantly view aggregate results.

- Online qual can also be more engaging with impactful multi-dimensional visuals and interactive elements such as the drag-and-drop features to construct brand or perception maps, or smiley scales to indicate preferences. Automation could also make tasks such as configuring an ideal product (or combination), by selecting from a set of options, easier and visually engaging.

- Clients can observe from a virtual backroom that allows them to see exactly what the moderator sees. They may confer with the moderator at any time by posting comments that are visible only to the research team.

- Research firms that conduct regular online research save time and money by setting up ongoing, proprietary, online convenience panels.

- Online qual often can be accomplished with greater speed and at lower cost. Besides savings on travel, a confluence of factors such as the explosive growth of social media, spread of broadband connectivity, penetration of computers and smart phones, and the development of online qual platforms, have driven down costs and cycle times.

Online Limitations

- Platforms that rely solely on text communication lead to loss of social cues, while others that rely on audio will suffer the loss of visual cues. If the interviewee cannot be seen (or heard in case of text), the interviewer is unable to read body language, tone of voice, etc. Some cues can be substituted with the use of emoticons such as "smiley" faces, which ameliorate the audio visual deficit to some extent.

- The researcher has limited ability to create a good interview ambience. Unlike face-to-face interviews, there is no scope for standardization of the ambience.
- In asynchronous communication the respondent can deliberate and is less spontaneous.

Commoditization of Qual

"Qualitative research has become a commodity and is in danger of losing its power to shape business strategy and provide inspiring consumer understanding. We are concerned that the pressure for instant results and the belief that respondents mean what they say and say what they mean will simply undermine true insight. Qualitative research needs to reclaim its interpretative potency, assert its expertise, and keep focused on understanding people and brands in their relevant contexts." — Rebecca Wynberg, CEO Global Qualitative Practice, TNS (Source: TNS website).

The barriers of entry into the qualitative research business have historically been relatively low. These barriers receded further with the onset and growth of online qual. Entrants who rely on online platforms, no longer find it necessary to set up brick and mortar research facilities, and automation further reduced their entry costs. The ensuing influx of boutique service providers and do-it-yourself users, led to what the research industry refers to as the commoditization of qual. Their key concern as reflected in Rebecca Wynberg's comment is the tension between quick and dirty applications versus truly interpretative qual research.

The true benefits of qual depend greatly on the skills of the researcher — her ability to actively engage with participants, her use of projecting and enabling techniques, her understanding of human behaviours, motivations, verbal and non-verbal communication, her interpretation of the data, and her ability to draw meaning that relates the research to business issues. In order to reclaim its interpretative potency and reinstate the strategic role of qualitative research, she must be brought back to her rightful place at the core of the qual research process.

Managed Online Panels

Nowadays major market research firms and panel service providers maintain fully managed online panels, comprising pre-screened individuals who have agreed to participate in research studies. Participants are usually incentivized by means of reward point schemes, sweepstakes or cash.

Managed online panels differ from those intended for quant surveys in terms of the type of individuals recruited, and their expectations. Quant research panels, often labelled access panels, are intended primarily for short surveys that take 20 minutes or less. These panels tend to be large varying from a few thousand to hundreds of thousands, within a country. On the other hand, panels intended for qual research tend to be much smaller, and are often referred to as online convenience panels or online market research communities.

Managed panels reflect a shift towards permission-based research. Since panel members have agreed to be approached for research studies, it is through "permission" that research firms seek their participation. This is a step in the right direction — interruption-based recruitment methods can cause annoyance.

Recruitment is controlled, and the profile and participation history of the members is maintained by the service provider. This allows for selectively inviting panellists on the basis that they qualify to match research criteria. Panel management rules also safeguarded against excessively active "professional respondents".

Managed panels are cost-effective. Benefits include fast turnaround, real-time reporting and good response rates.

Research Design and Preparation

Broadly speaking a market research programme arises from the need to address a business issue or business objective. Based on a briefing from end-users, the researcher prepares a research proposal outlining the business objectives, research objectives, and the recommended research programme inclusive of cost estimates. The dual set of objectives need to be clearly articulated and understood at the onset, and should form the basis for the design, analysis and interpretation of the study. The proposal typically undergoes a number of refinements to align it with the needs of the business, before sign-off. The research commences once the proposal has been signed-off.

A qual research programme comprises the following steps:

- Sample design
- Discussion guide
- Data collection
- Analysis and presentation

Sample Design
The sample design is subject to methodology — in-person or online; interviews, groups or observations. The design essentially stipulates who to interview (target respondent), and how many to interview (sample size).

Discussion Guide
The discussion guide is qual's equivalent of a questionnaire. It serves as a checklist of the topics and issues that are to be covered, and the techniques that the moderator might employ during the course of the

discussion. It provides the framework to ask and probe, and prepares the moderator to think through the most effective procedures and techniques to employ, and the appropriate wording and phrasing of questions. The preparation also enables the moderator to decide how she feels about the subject and sort out any biases. Pre-testing or rehearsing the interview helps to refine the guide and prepare the moderator.

Regarding the structure and sequence of the discussion, the moderator needs to carefully consider how and when to introduce stimulus materials, rotate materials and deploy techniques. Sequence is particularly important since what transpires earlier often has an influence on what comes later in the discussion.

The moderator needs to determine how to introduce topics and stimuli, decide on the mode of questioning, prepare appropriate prompts and probes, and anticipate possible responses. The choice of language, words and phrases must remain impartial; the objective is to research, not to advocate.

For in-person group discussions, the researcher should give attention to the ambience. In addition to comfort and convenience, careful consideration should be given to the profile of the participants, the topics of discussion, and the feelings or the emotions that the set up at the research facility might help to induce.

In quant once the questionnaire is released into field there is little scope for flexibility. Qual on the other hand is fluid; moderators have the flexibility to adapt and improvise during the course of group discussions. This is likely to occur more during the opening sessions, when the moderator gets her first taste of interaction with real participants. Should the discussion delve into unanticipated territory, it is a good practice to go with the flow as long as it remains relevant. Moderators reflect on their experiences during the opening night, and if required, alter/amend the discussion guide for subsequent groups.

We don't always say what we mean or mean what we say

Projective and Enabling Techniques

Minds are Hard to Read

People are complicated. The conflict between our real self and our ideal self creates dissonance in our minds. Our words and actions are often shaped by how we want others to perceive us. We do not always say what we mean, or mean what we say.

The reluctance to say what we really think stems from the fear that our thoughts might not be politically, socially or intellectually correct. To avoid embarrassment, and preserve our self-esteem, we use defence mechanisms, and become experts in making ourselves sound rational.

Driven by the need to preserve our image, our responses are mostly stereotypic; they are shaped by how we want others to perceive us. Only occasionally do we express our heartfelt desires and feelings.

Additionally there prevails a tendency to restrict answers to either a rational or an emotional mental state. For instance if we ask a motorcyclist why he bought an expensive racy motorbike, he might cite rational reasons only, such as speed, style and performance. However emotive reasons such as the desire to project a cool, macho image may be of far greater significance. Similarly, emotive reasons such as status and prestige, as well as rational ones such as performance, have bearing on why people buy expensive cars.

There are also times when participants find it difficult to verbalize their thoughts and feelings, and express them in words. For instance they may find it hard to articulate their feelings for Harley Davidson, and their relationship with the brand.

Projective and Enabling Techniques Unlock People's Minds

Due to the barriers cited earlier, asking direct questions in a qual research might not elicit the complete answer nor reveal the underlying issues. To circumvent these barriers, qual researchers employ a wide range of projective and enabling techniques that reduce the gravity of the subject, by viewing the topic from another perspective. They facilitate a deeper exploration of a person's feelings, and bring forth emotions into the open in a way that she feels comfortable with; enabling researchers to understand in greater detail how consumers relate to a subject.

Enabling techniques facilitate the process by making respondents feel more comfortable in expressing their feelings. Projective techniques on the other hand, are indirect interviewing methods which enable participants to project their thoughts, beliefs and feelings onto a third party or into some task situation.

Enabling exercises have no interpretive value; they purely act as facilitators. Projective exercises, on the other hand, can reveal participants' thoughts, feelings and motives.

The projective techniques involve individual/group exercises, followed by discussion and reflection. The moderator probes to decipher the inner thoughts of the respondents. She links individual responses with the group, to gauge whether the views that are expressed have broader appeal. Her aim is to keep the participants talking, in an effort to expand and further explore the thoughts, beliefs and feelings that are expressed by the participants.

From an analytical standpoint, in addition to the verbal content from these exercises, the participants' body language reveals their states of mind, as well as their attitudes, feelings and intentions.

Some commonly used projective techniques are described in the following sections.

Word Association

Stimulus words or phrases are presented one at a time, to participants who are asked to respond with the first word or phrase that comes to their minds. For example:

What's the first thing that comes to your mind when I say "Harley Davidson"? _____

What's the first thing that come to mind when I say "baby"? _____

The exercise yields spontaneous images and associations of subjects such as products or brands. In the conventional face-to-face setting it may be conducted verbally in which case it serves also as a good warm-up exercise.

Third Party Questioning

What do you think the average woman is most worried about when she is going to have a baby? _____
_____

Why do some young men buy racy motorcycles? ____
_____

As can be seen from the above examples, in third party questioning, respondents are asked to describe what other people are thinking, feeling or doing. By projecting in this manner to a third-party, participants are able to express views that they feel may not be politically, socially or intellectually correct.

Sentence Completion

This technique can be used to understand how respondents feel and relate to a subject. The sentences are prepared in advance and once the respondents complete their sentences the results are shared and discussed.

Some examples of sentence completion are as follows:

The thought of having a baby makes me feel _____

I would describe a perfect mother as one who _____

The biggest challenge that a working mother faces is _

I would describe a perfect marriage as one where ___

Personification

Brands and objects are often inanimate and can be hard to describe. It is far easier to relate to people, so by describing the brand as a person, it becomes easier to articulate what the brand is about. Personification provides valuable information on images and characteristics of products, brands or other subjects. Participants are asked to imagine the subject as a person, and describe the personality, lifestyle and other characteristics. For example:

If Lexus were a person, what kind of person would it be?

If Louis Vuitton were a woman, what kind of woman would it be?

If Citibank were an animal, what animal would it be?

A common variation is to ask respondents to imagine the brand as an animal, or as a car, or as some other object, and again to explore the parallels they are thus drawing.

As with all projective content, it is useful to feed participants' responses back into the discussion.

Brand Mapping

Brand mapping provides an understanding of a brand's positioning especially in crowded marketplaces. As shown in the following questions, respondents are asked to group brands or objects according to a set of prompted dimensions.

> Which of these brands do you consider as "young"?
>
> Which of these brands do you consider as "modern"?
>
> Which of these brands do you consider as "elite"?

Drawing and Collage

Based on a theme assigned by the moderator, drawings or collages are prepared by two or more teams. This is a useful medium for expressing intuitive ideas and associations through pictures, colours and other forms of visual art.

For instance, consider the subject of employee satisfaction. In a recent study, participants from the client firm were grouped into teams. Some teams were asked to make a drawing or collage of what the company was like, and other teams were asked to make a drawing or collage of what they would like the company to become.

Another interesting example pertained to a conflict group where participants were divided into teams based on whether or not they were supporters of a political party. The teams were then asked to develop a collage to describe the political party.

The discussion that ensues at the conclusion of these exercises may be quite intense and revealing. Because of its nature, a drawing/collage exercise is best conducted in-person at a research facility.

Bubble Drawings

Participants are invited to fill speech and thought into "bubbles" on a cartoon showing an imaginary situation relevant to the research. For example:

By projecting their thoughts and emotions in this manner, participants feel comfortable to express views that they feel may not be politically, socially or intellectually correct.

Role-Playing

Participants are asked to assume a role pertaining to a product or a situation and to act it out with other participants who assume different roles. As they perform they project their feelings and behaviours into the role. Considering that this exercise can be time consuming, role plays are usually conducted in extended focus groups.

If the roles are to be enacted, then a venue such as a research facility is required. If the roles are not to be enacted, and the research is conducted online, a description of the role may suffice, for instance:

If you were CEO what would you do to improve customer satisfaction?

If your child failed a school examination, what would you say to her?

Laddering

Laddering is an interviewing technique designed to trace the underlying attitudes, feelings and emotions about a subject. It begins with a simple question, followed repeatedly with questions about that response. For example:

Moderator:	"Why don't you want to have a baby?"
Respondent:	"Because I don't have the time to look after a baby."
Moderator :	"Why don't you have the time to look after a baby?"
Respondent:	"I guess I could take some time off work and hire a maid ... but I really don't want to do that."
Moderator :	"Why not?"
...	
...	
Respondent:	"I am really scared. There is so much pressure on children these days and I am afraid my baby, when she grows up will not be able to cope. I am afraid I too won't be able to help her ... my nephew's primary school arithmetic is so difficult!"

Laddering can take the respondent from the functional to the emotional plane. It can help peel off the outer objective layers and delve deeper into the subjective truth — the emotions and the values that are driving behaviours. The previous example for instance, reveals the respondent's anxiety of raising a child in a highly competitive world.

The technique helps to get to the crux of an issue or problem. It can however be intrusive and stressful for the respondent, and should therefore be sparingly used and administered with care.

Exhibit 4.4 Body language reveals the individual's state of mind.

Body Language

Body language is the language of body posture, gestures, facial expressions and eye movements. It reveals an individual's state of mind, his or her attitudes, feelings and intentions, and personality traits such as extroversion, introversion, aggression, greed and rivalry. Indeed the language is so rich that researchers claim 60 to 70% of all meaning is derived from body language. "... *There is no word as clear as body language, once one has learned to read it.*"

Body language is of immense importance in qual. It greatly enriches its content, and empowers researchers to read their respondents' minds. Qualitative researchers need to acquire expertise in the language, so that they can employ it to unlock and read minds, and grasp the full meaning of the messages conveyed to them. The knowledge of body

Exhibit 4.5   Positive and negative resolution, thinking and boredom.

language also helps the moderator to better manage the group engagement and interaction.

Body language is in part innate and instinctive, partly taught and partly imitative. We are experts in using it; we send and receive non-verbal signals all the time, sometimes consciously and sometimes subconsciously. However even though our brains are "programmed" in the use of the language, we are not as capable of reading or interpreting it. Indeed when we try to understand it, it is almost like learning a foreign language. The examples provided next, many of which relate to the visuals in Exhibit 4.5, should give you a flavour of this extensive language.

Positive resolution is evident when a person leans forward with the head nodding in agreement.

Conversely *negative resolution* is evident when a person leans backwards, and moves his or her head from side to side.

That a person is *thinking* or trying to see things more clearly can be gauged if he is raising the head, and gazing, putting on/polishing spectacles.

In Exhibit 4.4, the child placing her head on top of her head suggests that she is deeply interested in what she is viewing. Depending on other body signals, however, hand(s) clasping the head can also be interpreted as a protective helmet against some perceived adversity or problem.

General expanding and opening of the posture, uncrossing of arms are some of the signs that tell us a person is *opening up*.

When a person folds his arms, this can indicate that a person is *closing up*, particularly if it is accompanied by other signals such as the shrinking or diminishing of the posture. The signals suggest that the person is putting up an unconscious barrier between themselves and others.

Boredom is indicated by yawning and/or by the head tilting to one side. It is usually accompanied by vacant staring at the speaker.

A person indicates *uncertainty* by shrugging his shoulders, and shaking his head.

Disinterest is also reflected by the shrugging of shoulders, but in this case it is accompanied by general lack of attention, or the examining of hands, legs and feet.

A person indicates *irritation* by leaning backward and tutting.

A person signals *evaluation* and *indecision* by placing the hand on or around chin/face, drawing down of eyebrows and/or the scratching of the ear/head.

Anxiety is reflected in a tense posture, such as the clutching of the chair.

The *desire to speak* is signalled by a raised finger, direct eye contact and perking up.

Desire to interrupt the speaker is reflected in multiple head nods or other impatient gestures.

Our *eyes* reveal more about our emotions than any other part of our body. Messages are formed from a combination of the gaze, the widening of the eyes, and the movement of the lids and the brows. For example, wide open eyes, with raised brows and raised lids indicate surprise. In addition to eye expression, the manner we exchange looks, the extent of eye contact, and the movement of our eyes also reflect what is going on inside our minds.

The act of controlling our body, so that it refrains from conveying messages that we want to conceal, is called *masking*. However, not all messages are easily masked; there are some body responses, such as perspiration, that are difficult to control. If for instance you are experiencing stress, your anxiety is likely to be reflected through perspiration, and your hands would tend to become clammy.

Guidelines for Moderating Groups

The Do's and Don'ts:

- Impartiality is the mainstay of credibility in research; the moderator must always bear in mind that our purpose is research, not advocacy. If required, she needs to sort out any biases prior to conducting a qual study. During the discussion she should express interest in all shades of opinion, not appear to give approval to any particular point of view, and should take care not to lead or direct respondents with the line of questioning.
- She should use layman/respondents' terminology rather than corporate lingo or technical jargon.
- She should pay constant attention to respondents' body language, and learn to interpret it.
- She should frequently probe to decipher the inner thoughts and feelings of respondents. She should bounce off an individual's response with rest of the group (e.g. "Who else feels like this?") to gauge whether the views that are expressed have broader appeal, and to expand the focus of inquiry.

Handling Potential Problems

Approaches to handling some of the common problems encountered by moderators are listed here.

- Should a *dominant personality* (one who takes control of the discussion) emerge within a group, the moderator will need to actively encourage and elicit the opinions of others within the group, while at the same time turn a cold shoulder to the dominant person.

- *Passive participants* require encouragement and support by making eye contact, calling them by their names and directly asking them questions.
- *Superfluous storytellers* need to be contained so that the discussion may be brought back on course.
- All points of view, including those expressed in an insensitive manner, should be captured, and the feelings acknowledged. In case of *personal attacks*, the moderator should remind all participants to be respectful and not direct feelings at others.
- The moderator should re-energize the group by introducing a break or an activity whenever *fatigue* sets in.
- *Silence* should be respected if it arises from the participants' need to think through their answers. However if it is an uneasy silence such as when respondents are feeling inhibited or are not clear about what's required from them, in that case the moderator should address the cause.

Analysis and Interpretation

There is no recipe on how to interpret a qual study. It is essentially an analytical and creative thinking process that is well organized, logical and impartial; yet it remains subject to the researcher's view of events.

In terms of approach, a descriptive, journalistic report that provides details of the information gathered from the group discussions or interviews is good way to start. It provides information on the topic of discussion, and the participants' reactions, their attitudes, behaviours, responses and needs.

Qual, as you will recall is primarily concerned with "how" and "why", and a descriptive report falls short on this front. Reporting what was said may not entirely explain *why* respondents think or feel the way they do. It does nonetheless provide for a factual understanding of the subject, and prepares the groundwork for the interpretation.

There are a host of factors that the practitioner must take into consideration when interpreting a qual study. To understand what respondents mean, she must take into account what was said verbally and non-verbally, the tone and intensity, the silent moments, the contradictions, the influence of what was said earlier and so on. She needs to identify the underlying patterns in the detail, and draw insights on consumers' motivations. To arrive at conclusions she must relate the meaning of what was said to the business issues and objectives.

Much like a painting, interpretation is intrinsically subjective; it is the researcher's individual viewpoint. The output is a coherent story that relates back to the business issues, yet depending on the individual and the process, the story will tend to vary. This places great importance on the skills of the moderator. Since interpretation depends greatly on experience, skill and judgement, end users tend to be picky, choosing practitioners whose competencies they value and trust. It is the reason why reputed qual researchers are highly sought after.

CHAPTER 5

Quantitative Research

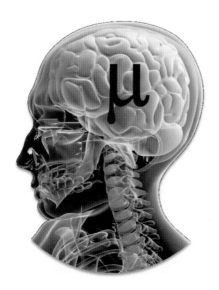

Exhibit 5.0 Quantitative research deals with measurement and validation of hypothesis.

Preview

Quantitative research (quant) is widely used in marketing to methodically investigate markets via theoretical models and statistical techniques. As a marketer, you will find the practical, diverse applications of quant useful for formulating strategies and refining the marketing mix of your brand. Applications such as brand image tracking, market segmentation and measurement of brand equity, discussed in earlier chapters are a few among the multitude of examples of quant in practice.

Some of its key characteristics, in comparison to qualitative research (qual), are described in the previous chapter, *Qualitative Research*, in the section *Comparison between Qual and Quant*.

This chapter covers the basic processes and practices in quant, including topics such as problem definition, research design, questionnaire design, information needs, sampling, data collection, online research, and the analysis process. In essence, it dwells on the following steps involved in implementing a quant study:

- Problem definition
- Research design
- Data collection
- Data processing
- Analysis and recommendations

Problem Definition

A market research programme arises from the need to address a problem or a business need. When the problem is not clearly understood, it is useful to first identify the symptoms, consider the possible causes and the actions that could be taken to resolve the problem. Ultimately some decisions need to be made, and the purpose of the research is to guide decision makers and mitigate their risks.

Once a problem is understood it may be defined by explicitly articulating the business issue, the business objectives that the research needs to address, and the research objectives. A research proposal should start by outlining these objectives.

Descriptive and Inferential Problems

From the previous chapter we know that different forms of research address different types of business needs. Quantitative research can find answers to questions such as: How many people use my brand? What is my brand's brand equity? Is it rising or falling? This type of problem is called *descriptive* — it describes or summarizes observations.

Quant is also well suited for *inferential* problems that interpret the meaning of some descriptive measure or verify a hypothesis. For instance — What are the factors driving brand equity? Do more consumers prefer product formulation 'A' over formulation 'B'? A research question becomes a hypothesis when it is rephrased as a statement that can be proved or disproved. For instance, the prior question may be rephrased as the hypothesis — more consumers prefer product formulation 'A' over formulation 'B'.

Research Design

The problem definition pertains to the research objective — it tells us *what to measure*. The research design pertains to methodology, questionnaire design and sampling — it is concerned with *how to measure*. A good design is essential to ensuring the validity of the results that we eventually report.

The methodology is dependent on the research objective, and the nature of the problem that needs to be solved. This book covers numerous methods for addressing diverse research problems and applications — tracking brand image, measuring brand equity, advertising evaluation, price optimization, product validation and so on.

Questionnaire Design

As the instrument for collecting information from respondents, the questionnaire plays a central role in quant. It must address the research objectives; and while this may sound obvious, it does require considerable thought and preparation, and is clearly crucial to the effectiveness of the research. A good questionnaire design also minimizes non-sampling bias and is an efficient and effective means of acquiring information.

Questionnaire Flow and Question Sequence

Questionnaires typically open with a screener, followed by the main section pertaining to the research topic, and conclude with the section on demographics. The flow should be logical, from the broader, wide-ranging to more specific and focussed questions. Sensitive questions should be placed towards the end.

Order Effects

The question sequence must be carefully considered to avoid *order effects* — biases caused by the sequencing of the questions. Order effects occur when a question earlier in the study has an influence on the response to one or more questions that follow. Take for example, the sequence of questions listed below:

Please rate the colour of this drink.
Please rate the smell of this drink.
Please rate the amount of cocoa in this drink.
Please rate the amount of sugar in this drink.
Please rate the size of chocolate chips in this drink.
What is your overall rating of this drink?

Placing it at the end, a common error, biases the response to the question on "overall rating". If for instance, respondents have a positive (or a negative) feeling for the attributes colour, smell, amount of cocoa, etc. it will influence their response on overall rating. For this reason, questions on overall rating of product, service or experience should precede questions about the various attributes that influence the overall rating.

We also need to be mindful of halo effects. If the respondent has a positive (or a negative) feeling for the first one or two attributes (colour, smell), this might cause a halo affecting her response to some of the subsequent attributes (amount of cocoa, amount of sugar, etc.). The halo effect may be contained by randomizing the sequence of the questions that appear on attribute rating.

Order effects can also occur when the text of a question reveals previously unknown facts to respondents. For example the question "Do you use Timotei shampoo?" makes the respondents aware of the brand Timotei. Accordingly unaided brand awareness questions are placed near the start of the questionnaire, and questions on factual and behavioural information go before questions relating to attitudes and opinions. For instance in advertising tracking, brand awareness questions precede questions on purchase behaviour and brand image, and these are followed by questions pertaining to advertising awareness and diagnostics.

Order bias

Besides the sequencing of questions, the sequencing of choices may also generate bias. This is referred to as *order bias* — it may occur when a respondent is given the opportunity to select answers in multiple choice questions. For instance, given a choice of flavours, colours, ingredients and so on, respondents have the tendency to select items that appear at the top or the bottom of the list. Order bias may be eliminated by randomizing the sequence of the items in the list so that each has the same likelihood of being in any given position in the list.

Open-ended and Close-ended Questions

Questionnaires typically comprise mainly close-ended questions and some open-ended ones. Open-ended questions tend to be of the type — "Do you have any suggestions on how to improve our service?" They solicit additional information from the respondent and allow respondents greater freedom to express themselves. They often yield useful insights that help diagnose issues and interpret responses to close-ended questions e.g. — "Please share the reasons why you stopped using brand A." Open-ended questions may also yield quotable comments (verbatim) that enrich the research findings.

Note however that the exploratory nature of open-ended questions makes them amenable more to qual than quant. Unlike closed-ended questions which offer predetermined lists or categories of possible answers, open-ended questions are not as easy to manage in quant. They are harder to record, code, process, analyse and report, and consequently add to the expense of the study. For these reasons they should be used sparingly in quant studies.

Close-ended questions provide a set of answers from which the respondent must choose. Examples include dichotomous closed questions (For instance Yes/No — Did you drink tea today?), or multiple choice questions. These questions are apt for quant where we aim to close rather than expand the focus of inquiry. Responses are comparable across respondents, and they are quicker, easier and cheaper to administer in field, and process in the office.

Close-ended questions are, however, rigid and may restrict some respondents to a list that does not apply to them. It also prevents them from expressing their complete feelings and experiences; which is why a few open-ended questions provide for good balance.

A good understanding of the subject is required to develop good questions and pre-code lists. Where there is lack of familiarity, exploratory qual study may be carried out prior to quant, to determine the right questions and the anticipated responses. It also helps to pick up the terminology consumers commonly used for terms pertaining to the category.

Information Needs

Research studies typically seek information relating to the respondent's behaviours, her attitudes and her classification. Questionnaires are composed of a mix of these three types of information.

Behaviour Questions

Behaviours ultimately reflect the impact of the marketing mix, and serve as measures for gauging performance. Therefore the aim of behavioural questions is to obtain accurate, fact-based information, and to achieve this, the questions should be framed in a manner that elicits accurate responses.

Of relevance is the choice of these words — "usually" versus "last time". For example, the question "What brand of soft drinks do you *usually* buy?" will elicit a different response from the question "What brand of soft drinks did you buy *last time*?" Responses to "usually buy" exhibit central tendency, i.e., the tendency to gravitate towards the few leading brands that the respondent chooses most of the time. It is appropriate for assessing the individual's purchasing behaviour. On the other hand "buy last time" elicits a wider range of brands that more accurately reflects the behaviour of the population.

Classification Questions

Classification information usually pertains to the respondents' demographics, and is typically used for profile analysis. For instance the profile of consumers (gender, race, age, income, dwelling type, life cycle, etc.) who use Clinic shampoo or the profile of a company (line of business, country of incorporation, sales turnover, number of employees, average age of employee, etc.) that buys Apple computers.

Attitude Questions

Attitudes have a powerful influence on behaviours. These opinions or beliefs have three related yet distinct components — cognitive, affective and intent. Attitudes are measured in terms of both the direction (positive, negative), and the intensity.

Because they are multi-faceted, it usually takes a series of questions to capture people's attitude about a topic. Often a Likert scale is employed to assess their opinion on different aspects of the subject.

Likert Scale

The first step in constructing a Likert scale is to generate statements covering different aspects, both positive and negative, of the subject. For example, a bank interested in assessing customers' attitudes to teller service, may consider the following statements to gauge their level of satisfaction:

> *Efficiently completed transaction/addressed query*
> *Knowledgeable of banks' products and services*
> *Courteous*
> *Provided simple and understandable explanations*

In cases where marketers are dealing with an unfamiliar subject, they may consider qualitative research to determine the statements or aspects that best reflect the respondent's attitude to the subject.

Next we need to determine the direction of the statement — does it reflect a positive or negative attitude towards the teller service? Statements that are positive or negative are retained, and those that are neutral are discarded.

The question to respondents is then framed on a multi-item rating scale, such as the one shown below:

	Strongly disagree	Disagree	Neutral	Agree	Strongly Agree
Efficiently completed transaction/addressed query	1	2	3	4	5
Knowledgeable of banks' products and services	1	2	3	4	5
Courteous	1	2	3	4	5
Provided simple and understandable explanations	1	2	3	4	5

In this example we do not have any negative statements. However if we did, those statements would be reverse scored (i.e. 5 becomes 1, 4 becomes 2 ... and 1 becomes 5) during processing so that there is a uniform scale reflecting the intensity and direction.

A Likert scale is the sum of responses to all the statements or Likert items. In the previous example the scale will range from 4 to 20. It measures what these group of statements represent (i.e. teller satisfaction).

Factor Analysis and Regression

The disadvantage of the Likert scale is that it gives equal weight to all statements. Some statements are more important than others, and some statements are highly correlated to others. Ideally a measure that represents the group of statements, should take these issues into consideration.

In studies where an understanding of the importance of each statement is desirable, researchers may adopt a two-step process — firstly to reduce the statements into a smaller set of uncorrelated factors, and subsequently to determine the importance of each factor.

The statistical technique used to determine the factors is called factor analysis. It reduces the statements to a smaller set of factors — those statements that are highly correlated (i.e. fluctuate together) are grouped into the same factor, and those that exhibit low or zero correlation with each other fall into different factors. A summary measure such as "Overall satisfaction with teller service" may then be regressed on the factors to determine their relative importance. For instance in brand equity research, the equity index is regressed on the factors to derive the importance or contribution of each factor to brand equity.

Rating Scales

Rating scales turn consumer perceptions, attitudes and preferences into something that can be measured and compared. Commonly used scales in quant include numeric (e.g. 0 to 10, 1 to 5, etc.), diagrammatic (e.g. smiley faces), continuous (e.g. slider scales used in online research), and semantic-differential scales (e.g. strongly agree ... strongly disagree, very important ... very unimportant).

Guidelines on Constructing Questions

Here is a list of things you need to watch out for, while framing questions:

- Keep the vocabulary simple. Avoid jargon, technical terms, abbreviations and ambiguous or hard to pronounce words.
- Keep the sentence short and easy to understand. Complex questions or overly detailed wording should be avoided.
- Be specific. Avoid words that lack frame of reference — e.g. often, usually and occasionally.
- Double-barrelled questions should be excluded. Example — "How satisfied are you with your bank and your relationship manager?"
- Refrain from leading or suggestive questions. Example — "Do you agree that Nagara drink has great taste? Yes/No". The purpose of the study is research, not advocacy. This question should accordingly be rephrased as — "Please rate the taste of Nagara drink."
- Avoid emotive questions. Ideologically-loaded expressions or red flags elicit negative responses.
- Do not have questions that are time consuming as these will antagonize respondents.

Sampling

Sampling can easily be misunderstood by marketers. Samples after all are tiny in comparison to the universe, and when research findings contradict marketers' gut feelings, uncertainties may creep in. The basic knowledge of the theory of sampling provided in Appendix A can help marketers' better interpret research results, and bring them to act on the findings with measured level of confidence. The sampling fundamentals covered in this appendix are of relevance to several chapters in this book.

	Hard Copy	Computer-Assisted
Interviewer Administered	Telephone, Face-to-face	CATI (Computer-Assisted Telephone Interviewing) CAPI (Computer-Assisted Personal Interviewing)
Self-Administered	Mail, Diary	Online, MCAPI (Mobile CAPI)

Exhibit 5.1 Methods for collecting quantitative data.

Sampling methodologies in quant vary with the needs of the research as well as the proportion of consumers of the product in the population. For instance, in cases where the proportions are very low, pre-established panels of consumers would be recommended. Or when a sampling frame is not available, as with online research, quota sampling can provide for a balanced respondent profile. Convenience sampling, such as when intercepting respondents at shopping malls, is also used especially for complex studies or when research accompaniments (e.g. product samples) are required. The majority of door-to-door (DTD) and telephone interviews deploy systematic random sampling or a combination of systematic random sampling and some other sampling method.

Standards for sampling error vary depending on the research requirements, however the most commonly used are 95%, 90%, and 99%. If the researcher uses a narrower confidence level (e.g. 99% instead of 95%), the confidence interval becomes wider.

Data Collection

Data collection methods include online, mobile phones, telephone, CATI — computer-assisted telephone interviewing, CLT — controlled location tests (e.g. mall intercepts), CAPI — computer-assisted personal interviewing, DTD, mail and diary. These are categorized in Exhibit 5.1

according to whether administered by interviewer or self, or whether or not computer-assisted. Going forward, the trend is towards online and mobile internet methods assisted by computers.

Each method has its advantages and disadvantages. The choice is dependent on the number of questions and their complexity, the type of stimuli to be used and the sensitivity of the subject. The methodology in turn has an important bearing on the design of the questionnaire.

Online Research

The use of the internet for quantitative research emerged and grew in the 1990s. In the early days there were doubts about its efficacy — Was it representative? Yet, as confidence in its use grew, online research experienced explosive growth.

Online — Advantages

Today, according to the ESOMAR industry reports, online is the most widely used method worldwide for quantitative research. Its benefits, many of which are listed below, give it a distinct advantage over other methods.

- Online research improves respondents' level of interaction and engagement through use of multimedia content — image, video, sound, animation and text. User friendly, engaging features include elements such as sliding scales with smiley faces, 3-dimensional images and interactive exercises. For instance, in some concept clinics or pack tests, respondents are able to see how the choices they make change the visual image of the product or packaging. The richness and depth of participants' responses improves through interactions of this nature that trigger higher levels of involvement.
- The depth and quality of responses also improves as respondents have more time to think and react to open-ended questions. Compared to face-to-face or telephone interviews, in an online setting, respondents feel less pressure to respond

quickly or in a manner that is politically, socially or intellectually correct.

- Online is better suited for obtaining sensitive information since respondents may remain anonymous.
- Being computer-assisted, online research supports better questionnaire controls. It employs software to control the sequencing logic and flow of the questionnaire, check sample quotas, and so on.
- Faster turnaround is achieved as online research is not constrained by the limitation of a physical field force. Respondents can respond concurrently in real time. And as they click their submit buttons, the data is acquired and, in some instances, auto-processed. The resulting improvement in turnaround is a key advantage considering the pace of developments in markets. (The speed-to-market especially for technology products and consumer durables has shrunk from years to months. Marketers of these products, can no longer afford delays in execution due to time consuming market research programmes.)
- Automation and consistency in delivery eliminates interviewing bias in online surveys. (Though this is not likely to be as big an issue since we use more close-ended questions in quant, interviewers can sometimes subtly bias research through their personality, appearance, body language or tone of voice.)
- Respondents' interaction with the specific question pages and stimuli can be tracked in terms of time spent and click-through rates. This may be used for optimization of questionnaire designs. It reveals the more interesting or engaging aspects of the questionnaire. It also helps identify "professional survey takers".
- Online research is not constrained by geographical boundaries or barriers. Whereas certain residential areas may be inaccessible for DTD interviews, this is not an issue with online.

- The participation of respondents such as specialists, professionals or new mothers who would otherwise be hard to get, can be facilitated through specialized access panels.
- Cost savings arise from multiple areas — no fieldwork, savings in data entry and coding. Where applicable there are also savings on the construction of physical stimuli or prototypes, which are substituted by visually appealing graphic images.
- The reduction in costs also affords greater flexibility. It is feasible and affordable to test different variations of questionnaires, stimuli and concepts. It is possible too to change or add questions on the fly.
- In terms of logistics and costs, multi-country studies benefit greatly from the borderless nature of the internet. They are easier to coordinate and execute simultaneously across countries. Online also eliminates the need for the physical presence of teams in each country.

Online — Limitations

For the above reasons, online research is the preferred method that market researchers adopt, when feasible. There are however limitations; and the one that is top of mind is *representativeness*. In quantitative research theory, the notion that samples should be random and representative has prevailed for a long time. Considering that online samples are neither random nor representative, raises a number of questions both from a theoretical as well as a practical standpoint. For instance, it is also debateable also whether conventional methods of data collection are random or representative.

The response rates for conventional offline surveys are low and are getting lower as people's hectic lifestyles undermine their willingness to answer questionnaires on doorsteps or over the telephone. DTD surveys also exclude people who dwell in restricted areas. Moreover surveys often need to be compensated by boosters or quotas. So in reality there are no purely representative samples. Considering that some compromise must be made, decisions ought to be based on a clear understanding of what is required to meet the study objectives.

The vast majority of research studies tend to be broad-based and relative in nature. For instance — Which products do people like more? What attributes are associated with my brand? What are the factors driving customer satisfaction? The biases inherent in online are unlikely to affect the outcome of these studies, provided the research topic has no direct bearing on the internet.

Online samples tend to over-represent high internet usage segments (young, upper/middle class) at the expense of others. Research firms attempt to compensate for this to some extent by recruiting panellists in their access panels that better represent the population as a whole.

Besides representativeness, there are few more limitations of online that need to be taken into consideration:

- Like other self-administered questionnaires, online depends upon respondents being able to comprehend, on their own, what is required. Similarly if the respondent's answer is ambiguous, there is no interviewer present to seek clarification. It is important therefore that questions are clear and to the point. If the topic of discussion is complex, in-person methods may work better.

- The internet has led to the rise of "professional survey takers" — respondents who actively seek online surveys offering paid incentives, and go quickly through the survey without devoting adequate attention to the questions that they answer. Web analytics makes it relatively easy for market research companies to spot these respondents. Most of them have procedures in place to identify the "professionals", and remove their responses from the study.

In summary, online methodology works best for research studies where the target respondents are available online, and representing the entire population (online and offline) is not a necessity from the standpoint of data interpretation. It is important that the questions are clear, concise and easy to answer. The over-representation of internet users will affect the results, particularly for topics that have some bearing on the internet.

Online — Methods

The most common online approach with established research houses is *access panel* based research. These are fully managed online panels comprising pre-screened individuals who have agreed to participate in research studies. Participants are usually incentivized by means of reward point schemes, sweepstakes or cash.

Online research may also be executed via a *banner* or a link that takes respondents to the questionnaire. While this approach is easy and inexpensive to implement, it offers limited controls on the sample, and representativeness is therefore a bigger issue. It should however work well where target respondents are visitors to a particular site.

Whereas banner-based research is open to all, a *client list* based research method is limited by invitation only to a targeted list of respondents. It is appropriate where the research requires purposive sampling.

Interviewer Administered Methods — Advantages

In-person methods are expensive compared to self-completion, yet they do offer a number of advantages, some of which are listed here:

- In-person interviews are recommended for complicated questionnaires because the interviewer can help with clarifications. Interviewers may also probe respondents in order to seek clarifications, or to overcome unwillingness to answer specific questions. Probing also helps enrich responses to open-ended questions.
- Skilled interviewers are capable of building interpersonal rapport thereby sustaining the respondent's interest.
- In-person methods are required in surveying illiterate respondents.
- Interviewer administered questionnaires are also conducive for generating spontaneous "top-of-mind" responses, and would therefore be recommended where this is needed.

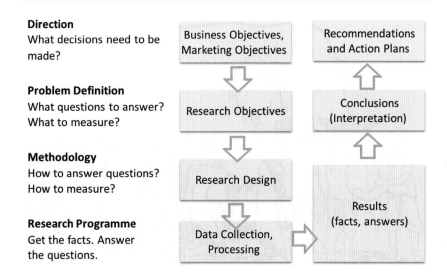

Direction
What decisions need to be made?

Problem Definition
What questions to answer?
What to measure?

Methodology
How to answer questions?
How to measure?

Research Programme
Get the facts. Answer the questions.

Business Objectives, Marketing Objectives

Research Objectives

Research Design

Data Collection, Processing

Recommendations and Action Plans

Conclusions (Interpretation)

Results (facts, answers)

Exhibit 5.2 The research process.

In general face-to-face interviewing has some advantages over telephone interviewing, but it is also more expensive. It is recommended for long and complex questionnaires, and is required for research where the consumer is required to respond to sensorial stimuli. In addition a controlled setting, as in CLTs, allows for a better managed environment, which is beneficial for some studies.

The Analysis Process

The process outlined in Exhibit 5.2 provides a general framework of the market research process.

The business objectives, spelt out in the research proposal, ought to provide a clear *sense of direction*. The objectives are framed to address issues confronting the business, or more specifically the brand. The research process must remain focussed on delivering the recommendations and action plans that address these issues.

The research objectives pose the questions that need to be answered, to illuminate the issues confronting the brand. The research is designed

Exhibit 5.3 Like a jigsaw puzzle, the picture emerges once the facts are pieced together.

to answer these questions and grasp the facts. Conclusions are drawn from the answers, and from the interpretation of the facts. The recommendations ought to spell out *how* to address the business issues.

In order to derive a return on investment, actions need to be taken, based on the research programme. Good recommendations therefore state a course of action, based not only on the knowledge gleaned from the research, but also on other sources of knowledge. A good understanding of the brand's strategy, and the market and business dynamics confronting it, is a prerequisite to crafting meaningful recommendations.

Interpretation and Recommendation

The Elephant and the Blind Men

Once upon a time, there lived six blind men in a village. One day the villagers told them, "Hey, there is an elephant in the village today."

They had no idea what an elephant was like. They decided, "Even though we would not be able to see it, let us go and feel it anyway." All of them went where the elephant was. Every one of them touched the elephant (Exhibit 5.3).

"Hey, the elephant is a pillar," said the first man who touched his leg.

"Oh, no! It is like a rope," said the second man who touched the tail.

"Oh, no! It is like a thick branch of a tree," said the third man who touched the trunk of the elephant.

"It is like a big hand fan" said the fourth man who touched the ear of the elephant.

"It is like a huge wall," said the fifth man who touched the belly of the elephant.

"It is like a solid pipe," Said the sixth man who touched the tusk of the elephant.

*Source: Jain World (*http://www.jainworld.com/literature/story25.htm*).*

Data Linkages

Data is like a jigsaw puzzle; you need to put the pieces together to see the big picture. Individually each piece is factually true — depending on the touchpoint, the elephant has the shape of a pillar, a rope, a branch, a fan, a wall or a pipe. Yet, these conclusions from individual snippets of data are misleading.

Much like the elephant, the business issue must be addressed from different angles. You need to immerse yourself in the data, and put the pieces together to form the complete picture. Most market metrics need to be examined in conjunction with other metrics, not only because each alone presents a restricted view, but also because individual research methodologies have limitations and constraints.

The picture in its entirety is often revealed by looking beyond the confines of a single research study, linking different research studies/sources of knowledge to enhance your understanding of the issues, and improve your confidence in the findings. This use of

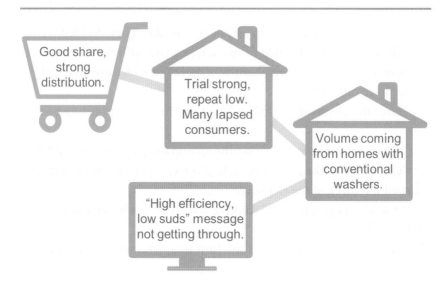

Exhibit 5.4 Piecing together snippets from multiple data sources.

multiple approaches to examine an issue, in order to enhance confidence in the ensuing findings, is referred to as   .

Facts gleaned from any research programme need to be critically examined. Answers often lead to more questions. It is often useful to examine sub-samples and drill deeper for an improved understanding of the marketing issues, provided the data remains statistically significant. Eventually a coherent scenario should emerge.

For example, consider Exhibit 5.4 which pieces together snippets of information about the launch of a new high efficiency detergent.

The findings from retail tracking revealed that the product was well distributed, and market share was above expectations. The conclusions from the quantitative research, however, revealed that though the proportion of consumers who tried this product was quite high, there were many lapsed buyers. This typically is a sign that the brand did not meet the expectations of the consumers who tried it — was there a problem with the product's quality?

Drilling deeper, we realized that the homes trying the detergent powder were primarily having conventional washing machines, whereas the new detergent was intended for high efficiency washers. Lapsed users were reverting back to the conventional detergent brands that they were accustomed to buying.

Consumer panel analysis confirmed that trial rate was high and the repeat buying rate was low. It also predicted that, if corrective actions were not taken, the market share of the new brand will decline to a level that would not meet target expectations.

By filtering the data, we were able to conclude that the repeat buying rate was good among those users who were the intended target. The problem, therefore, was that the brand was not attracting enough of these users.

Qualitative research commissioned at that time, revealed that the key advertising message "high efficiency, low suds", was not registering with target consumers.

Piecing together snippets from diverse data sources equips marketers to make better-informed decisions. In this example, while the low repeat rates and high lapsed usage may have suggested an issue with the product, by drilling deeper into the data and examining multiple sources, it became apparent that the real issue was communication, not product quality.

It is not necessarily desirable that marketers commission multiple research studies to address business issues. That may be too expensive for small or medium-sized brands. What is important is that marketers effectively use their existing sources of information, and that they arrive at conclusions after exhausting plausible, alternative explanations.

CHAPTER 6

Customer Satisfaction and Customer Value

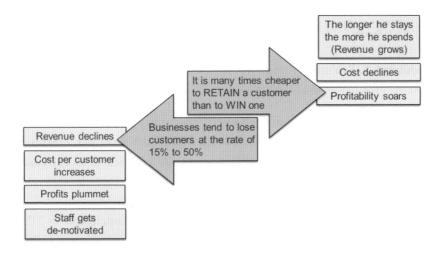

Exhibit 6.0 Impact of Retention and Attrition.

Impact of Retention and Attrition

It is many times cheaper to retain a customer than to win one. As depicted in Exhibit 6.0, the longer customers stay the more they spend. And, as companies get to know them, they become more efficient in serving them. They benefit from economies of scale. Their revenue increases, costs decline and consequently profitability soars. Depending upon the industry, a 5% improvement in customer retention can increase profitability by 25% to 85%, in terms of net present value (Reichheld and Sasser, 1990).

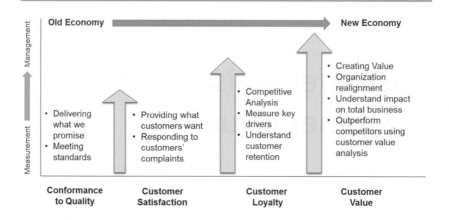

Exhibit: 6.1 Evolution of customer satisfaction. *(Source: Adapted from Bradley Gale,* Managing Customer Value, *2010).*

On the other hand if customers are unhappy, they tend to go elsewhere. With attrition, revenue declines and cost per customer increases. As profits plummet, businesses are compelled to cut costs, often resorting to retrenching employees. That further de-motivates staff, plunging the company into a vicious downward spiral.

These business realities lead to Peter Drucker's conclusion — "The only profit centre is the customer". Retaining customers is not only a marketing prerogative, it is a survival strategy. Poor customer satisfaction eventually leads to bankruptcy and closure of business.

Preview

This chapter imparts an understanding of how to manage customer satisfaction. It covers a wide array of topics on the subject including the evolution of customer satisfaction, the interplay between employee and customer satisfaction, customer loyalty, customer satisfaction measurement, transaction and relationship surveys, drivers of customer loyalty and satisfaction, and the Kano model.

The chapter also provides an overview of customer value management, i.e., the process of creating superior value for target customers and securing an equitable return on the value delivered.

Concepts such as customers' value-in-use and customers' purchasing philosophy are reviewed here.

Evolution of Customer Satisfaction

The better mousetrap once ruled the marketplace. The focus then was "sell what you can make" as opposed to "make what you can sell". During this era customer satisfaction was measured largely in terms of conformance to quality — superior products with zero defects were bound to rule.

Since the days of the better mousetrap, the management of customer satisfaction has evolved considerably (refer to Exhibit 6.1). Now product parity is the norm — it has become increasingly difficult, in many markets, to perceive a substantial difference in performance between competing products that target the same segment. Marketers need to find different ways to differentiate their offering.

At its infancy, customer satisfaction measurement focusses on understanding customer needs, measuring performance and monitoring complaints. Manufacturers respond to complaints, as opposed to quelling them before they surface. The inherent drawback of this reactive approach is that customers often do not take the time to register complaints and allow problems to be addressed. They simply switch, defecting to competitors that better serve their needs and preferences.

In the 1980s and 1990s, a number of companies started measuring customer loyalty, and identifying the factors driving it. Empowered with this understanding, suppliers are able to proactively allocate resources to strengthen those service and product quality areas that raise customer satisfaction and customer loyalty.

Retention, particularly in business markets, is heavily dependent on the value, or the monetary benefit, that the customer is able to derive. Recognizing its importance, in recent years, suppliers are focussing more on creating and delivering customer value. This demands much improved understanding of customers' needs, goals and priorities.

Exhibit 6.2 The service-profit chain. Two voices — voice of the employee, voice of the customer *(Source: Adapted from James L. Heskett, W. Earl Sasser and Leonard A. Schlesinger,* The Service Profit Chain, *1997).*

Suppliers need to realign their organizations, such that they are better geared to creating customer value.

While the evolution of customer satisfaction research has led to superior understanding of customer satisfaction and customer value, organizations still need to meet quality conformance standards, and monitor customer complaints. In the New Economy, conformance to quality remains important, though it no longer differentiates one supplier from another as much as it used to in the Old Economy. Companies cannot win business solely by delivering good quality, though they will certainly lose business if they do not do so.

Customer Satisfaction and Employee Satisfaction

Understanding what drives customer satisfaction, customer loyalty and customer value, empowers leaders to direct their organization's efforts to better serve the needs of their customers. Their strategies however can best be realized through a team that is highly motivated.

The service-profit chain, depicted in (Exhibit 6.2), is a road map for leaders of service organizations that emphasizes the importance of each employee and each customer in driving shareholder value. It is essentially the commonsensical notion that *customer satisfaction strategies begin with employee satisfaction* — by winning their hearts and minds, companies can motivate their employees to improve performance and productivity, for the benefit of customers.

Employee satisfaction is a long debated subject. Numerous theories abound on the nature of human motivation, and many practices prevail within organizations to boost and sustain employee satisfaction. Overwhelming evidence, however, suggests that the challenge of winning the hearts of employees is not an easy one.

The reward and recognition programmes and the "carrot and stick" policies that prevail tend to focus on the individual's need for self-esteem. The negative impact of these policies which drive employees to compete for rewards was emphasized by Kohn in 1993. Earlier in 1989 Stephen Covey described how we are deeply scripted in the win/lose mentality, from the days we compete for grades and medals, to the days we compete for promotions and bonuses. Teams, however, are part of an interdependent reality where success hinges more on cooperation than competition. Perhaps more should be done by way of support to help employees fulfil their need for belonging and self-actualization.

Customer Loyalty

Customer loyalty is akin to the notion of brand loyalty. It is an attitudinal state of mind — customers are "loyal" if they have a positive, preferential attitude towards the service or product, and the organization delivering it.

Attitudinal (or emotional) loyalty differs from behavioural loyalty. The latter reflects the behaviour to buy and to continue to buy a product or service. While attitudinal loyalty may induce behavioural loyalty, the two do not necessarily co-exist. A customer may continue to repurchase for a number of other reasons — force of habit or the inertia to change, convenience, affordability, or the lack of other options.

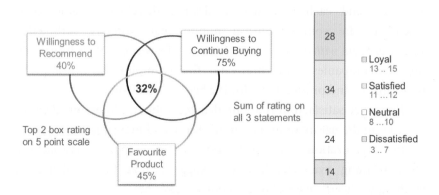

Exhibit 6.3   Defining, measuring and segmenting loyalty. Composite loyalty measure.

Being multi-faceted, customer loyalty is usually measured using a series of statements that reflect different aspect of loyalty. For example:

- Likelihood to recommend the product/service
- Likelihood to continue using it
- Favourite or preferred product/service
- Willingness to pay more for it
- Willingness to overcome inconveniences to secure it

A typical approach to measuring loyalty involves a composite of three (or four) statements such as those shown in the Exhibit 6.3. The scale used in this example is a 5-point scale; the top two boxes are 4 and 5 ("agree" and "strongly agree"), and the composite score, i.e. the sum of the ratings for all three statements, varies from 3 to 15.

There are a variety of ways of crafting a *loyalty index*. One could base it on the intersection — the percentage of respondents who rate the product 4 or 5 (top 2 boxes) for all the three statements. Using this approach, on a 10-point scale, the loyalty index may be derived by dividing intersection score by 10. In the example shown in Exhibit 6.3, this approach yields a loyalty index of 3.2 (32/10).

Alternatively a simple or weighted average of the top two box rating (40, 75, 45) on all three measures, may also serve as a measure for the loyalty index.

The composite score which varies from 3 (1 + 1 + 1) to 15 (5 + 5 + 5) may be used to craft loyalty segments. In the above example, 28% of the respondents with a composite score of 13 to 15 are classified as loyal, 34% (score 11 or 12) are classified as satisfied, 24% (score 8 to 10) are classified as neutral, and the remaining 14% (score 7 or less) are classified as dissatisfied.

Customer Satisfaction Research

Customer satisfaction research focusses on customers' perceptions of their experiences with the products and services of a company, to determine their level of satisfaction. Its primary purpose is to empower management to take measures to improve customer retention.

Applications

Customer satisfaction research *empowers top management* to align their organization to better serve the needs of their customers. It helps them prioritize resources and initiatives in products, services and people development.

Competition benchmarks are of vital importance in interpreting study finding. Dashboards that benchmark performance on key metrics, vis-à-vis major competitors, reveal the areas where the company outperforms as well as those where it lags behind.

Customer retention, as mentioned earlier, is the prime objective. In addition to aligning the organization to better serve customers in general, customer satisfaction research emphasizes the importance of each individual customer. The act of surveying serves as a useful *communications and public relations medium.* Engaging individually with customers through the research, and subsequently following up with them on problem areas, should strengthen customer relationships. It should help *resolve problems* faster and more effectively.

Customer feedback can motivate and guide employees to better serve their customers. It is usually linked with *employee compensation and management incentives,* particularly for organizations with a network of sales offices, branches or stores. These reward schemes work best in conjunction with other performance indicators such as revenue and profit targets.

Derek Allen (2004) aptly describes the relationship between *Customer Relationship Management* (CRM) and Customer Satisfaction Management (CSM) as "symbiotic". CRM systems record internal measures such as transactions, and describe behaviours. It takes customer satisfaction data to "reveal why CRM predictor variables affect CRM outcome variables".

Methodology

Customer satisfaction research services are provided by a number of leading market research companies including Kantar, Market Probe, Ipsos, Nielsen, GfK and JD Power. Consolidation within the industry has helped streamline the offerings. Kantar for instance owns three research houses (TNS, Millward Brown and Research International), each once offering its version of customer satisfaction research solution. Today TRI*M by TNS is the solution promoted by the group. Ipsos' solution is called Loyalty Satisfactor, and Nielsen's brand is eQ (Equity Management System).

The key elements in most of these solutions include measures for loyalty (e.g. eQ Index, TRI*M index), customer segmentation and driver analysis (importance measures).

Traditionally there are two types of customer satisfaction surveys — transaction and relationship. A broad understanding of these surveys should provide for a good appreciation of how customer satisfaction research works.

```
┌────────────────────────────────────────────────┐
│ Introduction, Screener                           │
└────────────────────────────────────────────────┘
```

Transactions relating to the experience of a product, service, channel, process ...

```
┌──────────────────────────────────────────────┐
│ Transaction 1                                  │
│     Overall Experience                         │
│         Overall Satisfaction                   │
│     Satisfaction — product, service, staff     │
│     attributes                                 │
│         Attribute 1                            │
│         Attribute 2                            │
│         Attribute 3 ...                         │
│         Suggestions for improvement            │
│     Competition Benchmarks                     │
│         Attribute 1                            │
│         Attribute 2                            │
│         Attribute 3 ...                         │
│     Problem Resolution                         │
└──────────────────────────────────────────────┘
```

Exhibit 6.4 Structure of a transaction survey.

Transaction Survey

Transaction surveys are designed to measure satisfaction of products and services. They solicit customer feedback on company's employees and are linked to staff and management incentives. They reveal problem areas and alert management to resolve them. They are process driven, decomposing customer interaction on a product or service into specific, discrete touchpoints that characterize the interaction. The structure of a typical transaction survey, depicted in Exhibit 6.4, comprises sections on:

- Overall experience;
- Customer satisfaction on the different aspects or attributes of the transaction;
- Competition benchmarking and;
- Problem resolution.

Based on your experience using ABC bank's ATM, on a scale of 1 to 5, where '1' is not at all satisfied and '5' is highly satisfied, how would you rate your overall satisfaction with the bank?

	Not at all satisfied	Dissatisfied	Neutral	Satisfied	Highly Satisfied
	1	2	3	4	5

Based on your experience using ABC bank's ATM, on a scale of 1 to 5, where '1' is not at all satisfied and '5' is highly satisfied, how would you rate your satisfaction on the following areas?

	Not at all satisfied	Dissatisfied	Neutral	Satisfied	Highly Satisfied
Convenience of location	1	2	3	4	5
Waiting time	1	2	3	4	5
Sense of safety at location	1	2	3	4	5
Ease of use	1	2	3	4	5
Range of facilities	1	2	3	4	5

Exhibit 6.5 Survey questions on rating of bank ABC's ATM service.

For example, consider retail banking. The products and services include teller, relationship manager (RM), credit card, deposits, fixed deposit, unsecured loans, investment, insurance, mortgage and treasury. In addition there exist a number of channels — branches, internet banking, mobile banking, interactive voice response (IVR or hotline), automated teller machine (ATM) and cash dispensing machines. The transaction survey measures customer satisfaction for these products and services, as well as for each of the channels.

Customers' interaction for each service is decomposed into discrete touchpoints. The aim is to generate statements covering different aspects or attributes, of the interaction. Using the example of an ATM service, some statements that capture the different attributes of the transaction are as follows:

- Convenient location
- Waiting time
- Sense of safety at location
- Ease of use
- Range of facilities

The respondents' attitude towards the ATM service may be measured using a Likert scale, similar to the one depicted in Exhibit 6.5.

The importance of the service aspects or attributes is reflected in the correlation of the attribute statements (e.g. "convenience of location") with the rating on "overall satisfaction". If the statement is highly correlated with "overall satisfaction", that suggests that the attribute may have a strong bearing on overall satisfaction.

Note that to pre-empt order effects, the rating on overall satisfaction precedes the rating of the attribute statements.

By decomposing transactions into discrete attribute statements such as those shown in the earlier example, and measuring customers' perceptions on these touchpoints, the survey is able to identify problematic aspects or areas of weakness.

The survey also facilitates performance evaluation — customer satisfaction scores and feedback is directly linked to line staff and management. Performance evaluation is a feature of most bank transaction surveys, especially those where the role of staff is central to the interaction, e.g. "relationship manager" and "teller" surveys.

Competition Benchmarking

Competition benchmarks are very useful in interpreting results in the context of key competitors. They provide best of business comparisons across products and services. The typical approach is to ask customers to rate the competitor that they most frequently transact with on selected metrics including loyalty measures, and key aspects of products and services.

Problem Resolution

The incidence of problems is a crucial KPI — it is often cited by customers as their prime reason for defection. Consequently, customer satisfaction surveys have a section devoted to problem resolution that highlights the problems customers are experiencing, and how effectively they are resolved.

Time Frame

Transaction satisfaction must be measured soon after the interaction — usually within a day or two for low involvement interactions, such as using an ATM. These surveys are often conducted continuously so that management has on-going information on the performance of product, services and staff.

Data Collection

Short transaction satisfaction surveys are best conducted online or via IVR systems. If the target customer base is small or if it is a lengthier survey, in that case, to generate adequate response rates, it is advisable to use computer aided phone interviews. Face-to-face interviews may be considered for most valued customers.

Relationship Survey

Whereas transaction surveys focus on the immediate, and are tactical in nature, relationship surveys are more strategic, measuring in detail the relationship between customers and the company. They encompass perceptions of service and product quality, range and variety, competitiveness of the offering, and service culture and ambience.

The structure of the relationship survey is depicted in Exhibit 6.6. Whereas the transaction survey is centred on individual transactions, the relationship survey cuts across the totality of the relationship with the customer. As such, they should not be linked to the incentive scheme for line management and staff.

Introduction, Screener

Overall Satisfaction

Loyalty Measures

Competition Benchmark on overall experience and loyalty

Product quality, Service Culture, ...

Product I	**Product II ...**
Overall Satisfaction	Overall Satisfaction
Satisfaction - image attributes • Attribute 1 • Attribute 2 • Attribute 3 ... • Suggestions Competition Benchmarks • Attribute 1 • Attribute 2 • Attribute 3 ...	Satisfaction - image attributes • Attribute 1 • Attribute 2 • Attribute 3 ... • Suggestions Competition Benchmarks • Attribute 1 • Attribute 2 • Attribute 3 ...

Problem Resolution

Exhibit 6.6 Structure of a relationship survey.

The first step in analysing the data from a relationship survey would be to summarize information contained in the large number of attributes into a smaller number of factors, through factor analysis.

Taking the hypothetical retail banking example, Exhibit 6.7 depicts the output of a factor analysis. Note that the factors are named post factor analysis by the researcher based on the attributes that define the factor. For instance the attributes "Bank close to home/office", "Convenient ATM locations" and "Superior internet banking facilities" suggest "Accessibility".

Relationship surveys are usually conducted on a periodic basis, annually or quarterly. Since they tend to be relatively long, computer-aided phone interviews are preferred over online surveys.

Hybrid Surveys

While in theory customer satisfaction research adopts two different instruments (transaction and relationship survey), each serving a

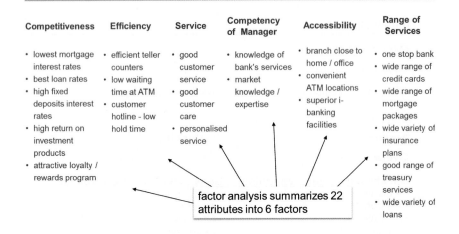

Exhibit 6.7   Large number of attributes summarized through factor analysis.

distinct purpose, in practice it is possible to combine the studies into a single hybrid survey. The hybrid, unlike the transaction survey, is more likely to be administered quarterly than on an ongoing basis. It is nonetheless feasible to link the feedback to specific transactions. And though this approach might not be as elegant as the separate transaction and relationship surveys, it does reduce costs.

Drivers of Customer Loyalty & Satisfaction

Customer satisfaction surveys yield a lot of useful information. For instance:

- How satisfied your customers are on different aspects and attributes of your products and services.
- The type of problems your customers are facing and how they are being resolved.
- How loyal your customers are and whether or not their loyalty is improving.
- How key metrics compare with the competitors that you benchmark against.

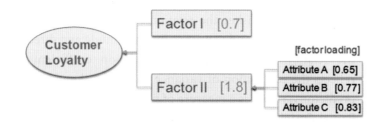

$$Loyalty\ Index\ =\ f\{Factor\ I, Factor\ II\}$$
$$=\ 0.7 \times Factor\ I\ +\ 1.8\ \times\ Factor\ II$$

Exhibit 6.8 Derived importance models determine the importance of attributes in driving business outcomes, for instance customer loyalty as shown above.

In addition to all this valuable information, management needs to know the factors that drive customer loyalty. Only then can they prioritize resources and initiatives in products, services and people development.

Derived importance models employ statistical techniques such as multiple regression to determine the impact of each factor on an outcome such as customer loyalty. The relationship can be represented by equations of the type depicted in Exhibit 6.8. In this hypothetical illustration the model reveals that two factors are important in driving customer loyalty. The coefficients in the equations (0.7 for Factor I and 1.8 for Factor II) determine the importance of each factor, and the factor loading of Attributes A, B and C of (0.65, 0.77 and 0.83 respectively) on Factor II reveal the relative importance of these attributes. This model tells us that Attribute C is more important than Attributes B and A, and Factor II is much more important than Factor I in driving the loyalty index.

There are a number of analytic techniques that may be employed to determine the relationship between each individual attribute (predictor variable) and outcomes such as Loyalty Index or Overall Satisfaction (outcome variable). Some of the commonly used methods are listed below:

- Correlation: establishes the relationship between outcome and predictor variable and expresses the magnitude and direction of the relationship. The squared correlation coefficient which reflects the proportion of variance shared by the outcome and predictor variable, is a measure of relative importance.
- Partial Correlation: The squared partial correlation coefficient reflects the proportion of variance shared by the outcome and predictor variable, after excluding the effects of remaining variables.
- Multivariate Regression: The predictor variables are regressed on the outcome variable to derive the importance or contribution of each predictor to the outcome. The output of a multivariate regression is a model of the type depicted in Exhibit 6.8, where the magnitude of the coefficients of regression reflects the importance of the variables. This is the primary approach used in customer satisfaction research.
- Hierarchical Bayes Regression: subsumes two levels of parameter estimates — the individual (i.e. each respondent) and aggregate. The individual-level coefficients, which reflect the individual's behaviours and attitudes, may be used to segment consumers. The aggregate-level coefficients are parallel to those derived using multiple regression analysis. Hierarchical Bayes is useful for heterogeneous populations. It is a resource-intensive algorithm that is gaining popularity, now that computers are much more powerful than they used to be.

Derived importance framework can be used in various ways with relationship and transaction surveys, to prioritize resources and business initiatives. A common application is to determine the products and services that have greatest impact in driving customer satisfaction. Reverting to the example of retail banking, the coefficients (b_1, b_2, b_3 ... and d_1, d_2, d_3 ...) of the following multivariate regression model, indicate the importance of the banking services in driving overall satisfaction, and the importance of *relationship manager (RM)* attributes in driving "Overall Satisfaction of RM":

$Overall\ satisfaction\ = \mathfrak{f}\{Overall\ satisfaction\ of\ Teller\ (T),$
$Overall\ satisfaction\ of\ Relationship\ Manager\ (RM),$
$Overall\ satisfaction\ of\ Credit\ Card\ (CC),$
$Overall\ satisfaction\ of\ Deposit\ (D),$
$Overall\ satisfaction\ of\ Investment\ (I),$
$Overall\ satisfaction\ of\ Mortgage\ (M),$
$Overall\ satisfaction\ of\ ATM\ (A)\ ...\}$
$$= a + b_1T + b_2RM + b_3CC + b_4D\ ...$$

$Overall\ satisfaction\ of\ RM\ = \mathfrak{f}(Customer\ Service\ (CS),$
$Customer\ Care\ (CC), Personalised\ Service\ (PS),$
$Transaction\ time\ (TT), Knowledge\ of\ market,$
$Knowledge\ of\ bank's\ products\ and\ services\ ...)$
$$= c + d_1CS + d_2CC + d_3PS + d_4TT\ ...$$

To diagnose issues, it is often useful to construct derived importance models for a specific group of respondents (e.g. a loyalty, behavioural, or demographic segment). For instance to determine the factors contributing to dissatisfaction among respondents in the "dissatisfied" segment, a derived importance model would need to crafted for that loyalty segment.

It is also desirable to test for interactions that involve two or more variables. For example, if a customer transacting with a relationship manager experiences good *personalized service (PS)*, and during the same interaction receives useful tips on market developments *Knowledge of market (KM)*, the combined effect may be greater than the sum of the parts. This synergistic impact is captured with the use of an *interaction term (PS × KM)*. Since these interactions do exist, modellers need to test for their presence.

One of the issues with customer satisfaction data is the high incidence of *collinearity*, i.e. the existence of significant relationships among two or more predictor variables. Signs of collinearity include the presence of coefficients with reversed signs, large margins of error on the coefficients and hypersensitivity. The impact of harmful collinearity is mitigated by using analytical approaches such as ridge regression and principal component regression.

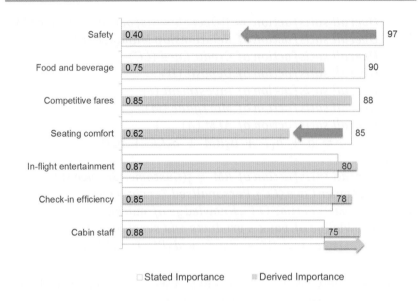

Exhibit 6.9   Air travel: stated importance vs. derived importance.

Interpretation and Recommendation

Stated versus Derived Importance

One might question why we go to the trouble of deriving importance by statistical means. Could we not simply ask respondents to tell us what attributes they consider important? Is there a difference between what respondents claim to be important to them versus what actually drives brand choice?

To appreciate the difference between stated and derived importance, consider the fictitious example in Exhibit 6.9 which pertains to air travel. In this example, almost all respondents (97%) stated that "safety" was important or very important to them. In contrast the derived importance for "safety" is far lower than that for other attributes. In statistics lingo "safety" does not covary with "overall satisfaction".

This suggests that while safety is important to respondents, it is not a key driver for customer satisfaction. Customers do not perceive

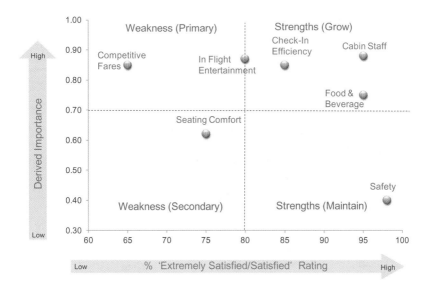

Exhibit 6.10 Joka Airlines: performance and derived importance matrix.

significant differences in the performance of the airlines chosen for this analysis, on the attribute "safety". It does not differentiate one of these airlines from another.

Features that in our example are high on derived importance include "cabin staff", "in-flight entertainment" and "competitive fares". These are the features that differentiate the airlines from one another. Knowing this empowers top management to align their organization to better serve the needs of their customers.

Recommendation

"Firms buy from you for what you are good at (strengths), and despite what you are bad at (weaknesses); for firms that do not buy from you, it is exactly the reverse" — Irwin Gross.

"I will know when our businesses are doing a good job when they can articulate who we should <u>not</u> sell to" — Chuck Lillis, Co-Founder and Managing Partner of LoneTree Capital Partners.

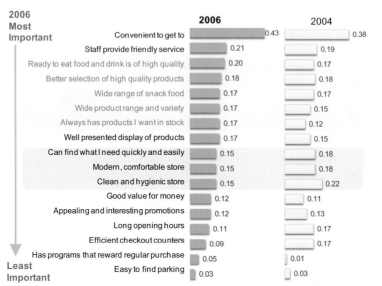

Source: Nielsen's Shopper Trends, Singapore 2004 - 2006

Exhibit 6.11   Changing customer expectations and needs in convenience stores.

The chart in Exhibit 6.10 plots the satisfaction rating of Joka Airlines versus the derived importance of the attributes. This visual summary is useful for drawing conclusions, and for making recommendations: What action should Joka's management take? Which areas should the company prioritize?

It is evident from the exhibit that "competitive fares" is the area of primary weakness for Joka Airlines, and "cabin staff", "food & beverage" and "check-in efficiency" are its primary strengths. Recommendations need to be based not only on the knowledge gleaned from the research programme, but also on the airline's market strategy, and the dynamics of the airline business.

In the context of market strategy we need to know: What segments is Joka Airlines targeting? How does it differentiate from competitors? How is it positioned in the minds of its target customers?

If for instance, Joka's strategy is to offer a premium service with superior in-flight facilities; in that case the results suggest the airline's image is fairly well aligned, though there is scope to improve on in-flight entertainment.

The quotes by Irwin Gross and Chuck Lillis emphasise the importance of knowing your strategy, and staying true to it. If Joka Airlines chose to drop fares in light of its weakness on "competitive fares", its margins will become leaner, and the airline may find it difficult to support superior in-flight facilities with leaner margins. The airline could thus lose its points of differentiation.

Joka Airlines does however need to maintain a *competitive point of parity* on air fares. It may consider adjusting fares if it feels it is unable to negate the competitor's point of difference on "competitive fares".

Changing Customer Expectations

It is observed that parameters such as overall measures of satisfaction and loyalty index are difficult to move. This is because customer expectations are not static. Their expectations tend to grow, and their needs and preferences too are continually changing.

The convenience stores example in Exhibit 6.11 underscores the dynamic nature of key drivers. As their reliance on the channel grows, c-store shoppers in Singapore are driven more by features pertaining to quality, variety and availability of produce as opposed to basic needs such as comfort, cleanliness and hygiene.

From the standpoint of target setting, it is important to appreciate that maintaining a relatively high loyalty index is a fairly good achievement and that despite well-conceived initiatives, overall measures and indices such as loyalty index are hard to move.

The Kano Model

The Kano model is a technique developed by Professor Noriaki Kano that categorizes product and service features in terms of their impact on customer satisfaction. This helps organizations prioritize areas that they need to focus on to enhance customer satisfaction.

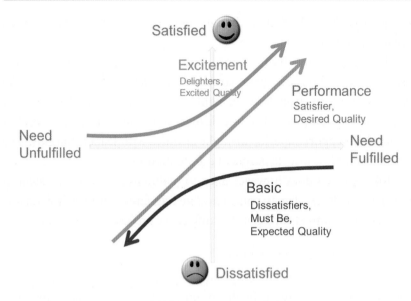

Exhibit 6.12   Kano model.

According to the model, product or service attributes can be grouped into the following categories (see Exhibit 6.12):

- Dissatisfiers are basic attributes that customers expect to be present. These "must be" attributes or hygiene factors are taken for granted and will trigger dissatisfaction if unfulfilled.
- Satisfiers are attributes that generate satisfaction when fulfilled, and dissatisfaction when not fulfilled. Improvement in performance on these attributes produces higher level of satisfaction.
- Delighters are exciting features that customers do not expect, but are delighted when they find them.

Taking the example of air travel, if during check-in you are informed that no seat is available despite a confirmed reservation, you are likely to be highly dissatisfied. It is an attribute that can only trigger unhappiness — if the seat was available, that being an expectation, it would not have generated satisfaction.

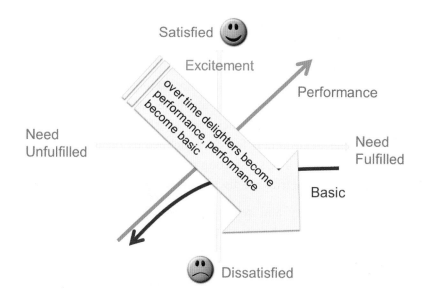

Exhibit 6.13 Product attributes cross categories over time.

On the other hand, if during check-in you are informed that you are upgraded from economy to business class free of charge, you would most likely be delighted. A latent desire, it only evokes satisfaction. If you are not upgraded to business class, you would not be disappointed, because this is not something you were entitled to or expecting in the first place.

Check-in efficiency, cabin service, competitive fares, quality of food and beverage, and in-flight entertainment are performance attributes. The higher the performance on these attributes the greater the satisfaction they generate.

Over time some attributes drift from excitement to performance and from performance to basic, mirroring the rise in customer expectations. Needs and preferences change as customers get accustomed to improvements in market offerings. This is why overall measures of satisfaction and loyalty index tend to remain inert despite improvements in product offerings.

Kano's model speaks of two more categories pertaining to attributes that are less desirable. These are:

- Indifferent quality attributes which offer requirements that customers do not care about or are no longer interested in.
- Reversed quality applies to attributes where the reduction in functionality actually increases satisfaction. For example, a number of customers feel overwhelmed by the extra features in some devices. The satisfaction of these customers may improve as some of the frills are discontinued.

Indifferent quality and reverse quality attributes should be de-emphasised. They may be discontinued or offered on a selective or optional basis.

Customer Feedback

The Kano model is commonly applied in six sigma exercises, where participants brainstorm all aspects about their offerings and categorize them the Kano way. It is recommended however, that any such classification is validated by surveying customers. (In these matters, one should not rely entirely on company's associates because their minds are so heavily influenced by their knowledge and feelings for their offerings, and their specialized skills and knowledge of their market that their perceptions tend to differ greatly from the average consumer).

To ascertain how customers react to a product or service attribute, a pair of questions are formulated in their functional and dysfunctional form. For example, (air travel):

Functional form: How would you feel if your seat is more spacious?

Dysfunctional form: How would you feel if your seat is less spacious?

Functional form: How would you feel if we offered a wider choice of in-flight movies?

Dysfunctional form: How would you feel if we offered a reduced choice of in-flight movies?

Dysfunctional

		like	must be	neutral	live with	dislike
Functional	like		E	E	E	P
	must be	R	I	I	I	B
	neutral	R	I	I	I	B
	live with	R	I	I	I	B
	dislike	R	R	R	R	

E	Excitement	I	Indifferent
P	Performance	R	Reversed
B	Basic		Questionnable

Exhibit 6.14   Functional versus dysfunctional matrix.

The following 5-point scale is used for each form of the question:

I like it that way.
It must be that way.
I am neutral.
I can live with it that way.
I dislike it that why.

The matrix in Exhibit 6.14 depicts the 25 possible combinations of answers to each pair of functional/dysfunctional questions. The answers reveal which category each attribute should be grouped under. For instance if a respondent says she would *like* more "seating space" (functional form) and *dislike* less "seating space" (dysfunctional form), then "seating space" is a performance attribute for this respondent.

The differences in the way they respond to the questions may also be used as a basis for grouping or segmenting customers. For instance, for market research reports, some customers may consider hard copies a basic requirement, others may be indifferent to receiving reports in this form, and still others may not want them at all.

Application and Interpretation

The Kano model is a useful tool for business process improvement. Along with other six sigma techniques it helps companies re-engineer processes so that they are aligned to deliver greater value to their customers. Based on the analysis, listed as follows are actions that should be considered:

- Eliminate features that customers no longer care about. These are "value drains" that cost companies more to provide than their worth to customers. They may have once been of greater interest, but are no longer as relevant to them.
- Focus development efforts on *performance* attributes that customers strongly associate with the company's product offering. Reverting to the air travel example, if Joka Airlines is positioned as a premium service provider, the airline should focus more on attributes like in-flight entertainment, cabin service and quality of food and beverage that enhance customers' in-flight experience.
- Maintain *competitive point of parity* on those performance attributes that are not strongly associated with the company's product offering. A company may choose not to excel in these features, but it cannot afford to fall too far behind competition. For instance, Joka Airlines may charge fares that are higher than some of their competitors, but not so high that they do not negate the competitors' point of difference.
- Maintain *category point of parity* for those attributes that are basic. Category points of parity represent necessary conditions for brand choice.

Decisions relating to business process improvement often cause great anxiety. Associates are accustomed to working in a particular manner, and time and money is invested historically to do things the way they are done. So it can be a little disconcerting to implement

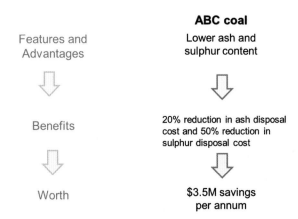

Exhibit 6.15   Value mapping — drilling down from features to worth using example taken from mining coal.

changes to existing processes and offerings. Along with other business improvement techniques, the Kano model helps to guide and facilitate transitions of this nature.

Customer Value

Ultimately, as mentioned at the beginning of this chapter, customer retention is the end goal. Customers in business markets focus predominantly on functionality or performance. They seek to maximize value or the monetary benefit that they may derive. Delivering value to these customers, therefore, is the key to customer acquisition and retention.

Suppliers recognize the importance of value, yet they often lack specific details, estimates or measures to demonstrate the value they deliver. This absence of details creates ambiguity in the minds of customers, leading them to focus more on concrete, unambiguous aspects like cost.

To demonstrate value suppliers need to drill down from the product or service features and advantages to the benefits and from the benefits to value. Take for example, the case of a company that is about to start mining coal at a new mine where the coal has lower ash and sulphur content. The lower ash and sulphur content is the feature or advantage that their coal has to offer (see Exhibit 6.15). This advantage results in the reduction in cost of ash and sulphur disposal — the benefit. For each of its customers, the mining company should also be in a position to translate the benefit, into value terms, based on the cost of disposing sulphur and ash.

Customers' Purchasing Philosophy

With regard to their purchasing philosophy, all customers are not the same. Some think purely in terms of price; their prime objective is to reduce the annual *total spend* of acquisitions. Others think in terms of all associated costs incurred during the lifetime of the product; their priority is to reduce the *total cost of ownership (TCO)*. And there are those who focus on building a supply network that enables them to provide maximum value to their customer. Their objective is to build a *lean enterprise*, where "lean" means creating more value for customers with fewer resources. These three customer purchasing philosophies are called buying orientation, procurement orientation and sales management orientation (Anderson *et al.*, 2009).

Buying orientation focusses narrowly on obtaining the best deal in terms of price, quality, and availability from suppliers. These customers try to maximize power over suppliers and steer clear of risks wherever possible. Negotiations with these customers can degenerate into a distributive win-lose agenda, where parties compete for the margins each can make from the transaction.

Procurement orientation broadens the domain and span of influence of purchasing. In cooperation with suppliers, these customers pursue quality improvements and cost savings, to reduce the TCO. The TCO includes all associated costs incurred during the lifetime of the product, i.e.:

$$Total\ Cost\ of\ Ownership\ (TCO)$$
$$=\ Purchase\ Price$$
$$+\ Product's\ Lifetime\ Expenses$$
$$-\ Salvage\ or\ Resale\ Price$$

The product's lifetime expenses include acquisition costs, conversion costs and disposal costs.

Supply management orientation entails the harmonization of purchasing with the value network, comprising suppliers, suppliers' suppliers, customers and customers' customers, and so on. These companies focus on delivering maximum value to end-users by building a well-synchronized supply network that efficiently completes all processes pertaining to the supply of a product or service, from the development and production, to sales and maintenance.

Only a few organizations have progressed as far as supply management orientation. Some organizations practice procurement orientation, yet the vast majority are still adhering to buying orientation.

Their purchasing philosophy clearly affects the manner in which suppliers are able to deliver value to customers, and how they craft their value proposition. Price drives customers with buying orientation, total lifetime costs are of prime importance to customers that adopt procurement orientation, and value is crucial to customers with a supply management orientation.

Value-in-Use Analysis

Customer value is the worth in monetary terms of the economic, technical, service and social benefits a customer firm receives in exchange for the price it pays for a market offering (Anderson *et al.*, 1993).

It follows that if *Value > Price* there is incentive to purchase. An offering, however, is rarely considered in isolation. Considerations of value take place within the context of one or more competing products. If the incentive to purchase a product A *(Value$_A$ – Price$_A$)* is greater than the incentive to purchase competitor product B *(Value$_B$ – Price$_B$)*, in that case the buyer is likely to prefer A over B. The difference in the incentive to purchase A over its competitor B is termed as *Value in Use (VIU)*.

$$VIU_{A \, versus \, B} = (Value_A - Value_B) - (Price_A - Price_B)$$

VIU analysis determines the monetary benefits of a company's offering, compared to its direct competitors. It allows companies to articulate the true, differentiated value of their offering to their customers.

VIU analysis starts with an in-depth understanding of customers, and the products and services offered by the company and its competitors. A value assessment of costs and benefits in monetary terms is required. Depending on the objective, this exercise may be quite detailed and complex. The relatively simple example that follows serves as an illustration of the approach.

Example — VIU analysis

The ash level of coal at a mine has declined from 10% to 9.5%. Assuming other specifications including price remain the same, customers stand to benefit from savings in ash disposal fees, which are estimated to be US$120 per ton.

	After	Before
Ash %	9.5%	10.0%
Disposal cost per ton of ash (US$)	120	120
Disposal cost per ton of coal (US$)	11.4	12.0

$$VIU_{A \, versus \, B} = (Value_A - Value_B) - (Price_A - Price_B)$$

Since the price has not changed, $VIU_{A \, versus \, B}$ becomes the incremental saving in value, and is equal to 60 cents per ton. On an annual basis a customer consuming a million tons of coal will save US$ 600,000 in ash disposal costs. This improvement in quality, which translates to an increase in value from savings in the ash disposal costs, provides a valid basis for price adjustment. Considering that the savings are fairly significant, the mining company would be interested to know how much increase in price may be justified, on account of the reduced ash content.

VIU Price

VIU Price is the monetary amount at which a customer has no preference between one offering and an alternative offering (VIU = 0). Assuming that the supplier wants to split the benefit of lower ash costs with customers, VIU price will serve as the upper bound for the price adjustment.

$$VIU_{A \; versus \; B} = 0 = (Value_A - Value_B) - (Price_A - Price_B),$$

$$VIU \; Price_A = Price_B + (Value_A - Value_B)$$

If the export price of coal is US$100 per ton, the *VIU Price* for the improved coal is $100 + 60 cents = $100.60 per ton. Based on the improved performance, the mining company can increase the price by as much as 60 cents per ton.

Value Assessment

In order to conduct a VIU analysis companies need to estimate the value in monetary terms of the features and elements of their product or service. Some of the ways to achieve this are listed as follows:

Internal Engineering Tests: This involves laboratory tests conducted to ascertain the difference in the performance of different market offerings. Translating the differences in performance to value estimates often requires some assumptions on the actual in-use conditions at the customers' end.

VIU Research involves the collection of data on costs and benefits from customers. This often entails detailed value stream mapping, and activity-based costing (ABC) concepts and methods, to quantify all expenses related to the use of a product or service. The approach may be used to estimate the TCO of the product. It does however require a high level of cooperation and engagement with customers.

Profiles

Attributes	A	B	C
Oil Change	required	not required	not required
Price	500	500	770
Utility	10	15	10

Exhibit 6.16   Illustration of conjoint analysis — What is the incremental value of eliminating need for oil change?

ABC analysis focusses on the interfaces between customers and suppliers, and on expenditures. It identifies major cost drivers, often revealing opportunities from cost savings.

Research Survey: Customers are interviewed on questions that address how product attributes/value elements affect operations.

Conjoint Analysis: This quantitative research methodology is covered in detail in Chapter 10, *Product Design*. Central to the methodology is the notion of product utility — a latent variable that reflects how desirable or valuable an object is in the mind of the customer. The utility of an offering is assessed from the value (part-worth) of its parts. Conjoint analysis examines customers' responses to offering ratings, rankings or choices, to estimate the part-worth of the various levels of each attribute of a product. Utility is not an absolute unit of measure; only relative values or differences in utilities matter.

The illustration in Exhibit 6.16 provides three profiles of a vacuum pump, which vary on two attributes — the need for oil change and price. Profile *B* offers the benefit that oil change is not required, and its utility is 5 points higher than profile *A*, which requires oil change. Profile *C*, which also does not require oil change and is priced $270 higher, has exactly the same utility as profile *A*. It follows that the benefit of "no oil change" is worth $270 to customers.

Overview — Customer Value Management

Customer Value Management strives to achieve the twin goals of imparting superior value to target customers, and getting an equitable return on the value delivered. To achieve these goals, suppliers must be able to persuasively demonstrate the value of their product offerings relative to competitive alternatives.

Customer value management projects are commissioned to address business issues or opportunities. Teams working on these projects, which may last a number of months, convene over a series of two to three-day workshops, where they brainstorm and chalk out action plans.

Market intelligence is of vital importance. Teams rely on internal experts as well research methods such as the Kano analysis, to determine the value elements or product attributes that they needs to focus on. A value assessment is required to ascertain costs and benefits of these value elements.

Central to the exercise is the construction of an empirical value model based on VIU analysis. The model would generate the VIU and VIU price of the supplier's offering, relative to competing market offerings. It forms the basis for building the business case for change.

Customer buy-in at various stages is crucial to the success of these projects. The cooperation of a few key suppliers helps greatly during value assessment. Particularly in the context of VIU research, the expertise of customers helps greatly in value stream mapping and activity-based costing.

To secure customer buy-in, the business case must be credible, and the opportunities identified must resonate with customers. Estimates and assumptions must be realistic/conservative and all elements of significance must be included in the analysis.

Suppliers should craft customer value propositions that mirror the purchasing orientation of targeted market segments. To resonate with these segments, the customer value propositions should highlight the key points-of-difference that deliver the greatest value to these customers.

CHAPTER 7

Consumer Panels

Exhibit 7.1 Panellist with handheld scanner *(Photo courtesy of Nielsen).*

Preview

A Consumer Panel is a panel of households or individuals whose purchases are monitored on a *continuous* or ongoing basis. In some ways it is similar to a loyalty panel, which comprises loyalty card holders. They both are powerful research platforms that produce streams of continuous customer transaction data, which are ideal for diagnosing the buying behaviour of products and services, where repeat purchasing is the norm.

Though the scope does vary, the research methods described in this chapter apply across the different forms of disaggregate consumers' purchasing data. Unlike consumer panels though, loyalty panels and customer transaction data present only a blinkered view, confined to customers' transactions within the organization. However, because they represent a larger customer base, their data is more tactical/actionable in nature — it allows for the execution of tactics, targeting segments or even individuals, at specific locations, e.g. store, bank, etc.

Consumer panel data is broader in scope as it not confined to an organization's customers. Yet because it is a platform that is specifically created and maintained for research purposes, the data acquisition cost for consumer panels is far greater than that for live sources like customer transaction and loyalty data.

This chapter describes the research methodologies covering a repertoire of analysis metrics and techniques including width and depth of purchase, buyer groups, profile analysis, behavioural brand loyalty, trial and repeat purchase, overlap analysis, basket analysis and gain-loss.

The use of consumer panel data is illustrated in many of the cases featured in this book. In particular the Vizag case, which is centred on consumer panel data, exemplifies the diagnostic capabilities of consumer panels.

Background on Consumer Panels

Exhibit 7.2 depicts the different approaches to tracking sales as goods flow along the path from manufacturer to retailer and from retailer to shopper. The data sourced at retail checkouts offers the most efficient and accurate means of tracking sales. Called the retail index, this is the industry standard for market measurement.

The accuracy of consumer panel data is limited by the panel size, yet it is richer and better suited for diagnosing buying behaviour. In research lingo, data of this nature is called *disaggregate*. Key brand health measures like *brand loyalty*, *%buyers*, *volume per buyer* and so on

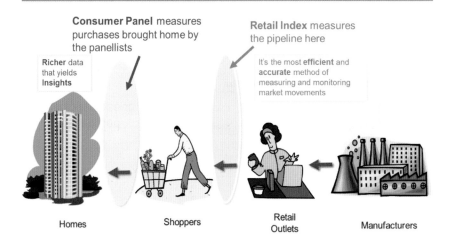

Exhibit 7.2 Different approaches to tracking sales as goods flow along the path from manufacturer to retailer and shopper.

rely on disaggregate data. Other diagnostic analysis like brand switching, repeat buying rate, share forecasting rely on data that must be both continuous and disaggregate.

Typically consumer panels are composed of households/individuals who are representative of the market in terms of relevant characteristics such as household size, life stage, income, dwelling type, ethnic group, geographical location, etc.

The panels in existence today are almost entirely anchored in the fast moving consumer goods (FMCG) sector. There is a considerable, as yet largely unexplored potential for panels in sectors such as finance, telecom and petroleum. Behaviour of usage/consumption of credit cards, mobile phones and petroleum, can provide valuable information that could help shape marketing and business decisions in these sectors.

Nielsen, the largest service provider operates FMCG panels in 28 countries covering about 300,000 households. The first panel was set up by Nielsen in 1932, in the US. The first scan panel, BrandScan was launched in 1986 in Australia by AGB McNair, which subsequently was acquired in 1994 by Nielsen. Today the majority of FMCG consumer panels are scan-based, and the two major service providers are Nielsen and Kantar (TNS).

Exhibit 7.3   Recording of purchases with hand held scanners.

In addition to home panels there are a few out-of-home panels for impulse foods like chocolate, ice cream and soft drink that are consumed out of home.

Research Methodology

Though diary panels are still in existence in a number of developing countries, most panels today are scan panels. Scan technology essentially relies on bar code, scanner, and the telephone network. Panellists record their daily purchases through a menu-driven interface on handheld scanners (see Exhibits 7.1 and 7.3). The scanner is normally perched on a cradle that connects to the telephone line. The data is polled once a week; typically the cradle is programmed to call the service operator's computer and download the data.

In the future, data collection methodology will shift from telephony to wireless and internet. Should ePCs (electronic product codes) replace bar codes, which is unlikely in the near future, ePC readers will replace scanners and the task of recording purchases will become less cumbersome.

The preferred mode of data collection of credit card statements and telecom account statements, in soft copy format, is via email/internet. For motorist panels, even SMS messaging using mobile phones should work well.

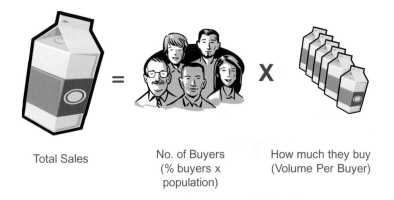

| Total Sales | No. of Buyers (% buyers x population) | How much they buy (Volume Per Buyer) |

Exhibit 7.4 Sales = (Number of buyers) × (Volume per buyer).

In future, with the advent of NFC (near-field communication), it would become much easier to track out of home purchases with smart phones and other mobile devices.

Consumer panels offer a very wide repertoire of analysis; some of the most useful ones are covered in this chapter. The Parfitt–Collins model, a technique that predicts the market share for newly launched products, is covered in Chapter 11, *Product Validation*.

Width and Depth of Purchase

Width and depth of purchase are the two basic components of sales. Width represents the buyer base, and is measured in terms of the percentage of households or individuals that purchase the product in a given time period. Depth represents the amount they purchase, and is measured in terms of *volume or value per buyer.*

> *%Buyers (also referred to as Penetration)*
> *= % of Households (or individuals) that Buy*
>
> *Volume per Buyer*
> *= Volume bought per buying household*
>
> *Value per Buyer = Value bought per buying household*

Exhibit 7.5 Width and depth of purchases for different categories of hot beverages.

Volume, for FMCG products, is usually measured in kg or L (litre). Many products, however, are available in a variety of forms where direct volume comparisons are not valid. For example, tea is available in forms such as leaf tea, dust tea, tea bag and 3-in-1 tea. The appropriate measure would be to translate the volume of each of these forms into an equivalent representing "number of cups". Cups are also the preferred measure for other hot beverages like coffee and malt drinks. For detergents, conversion factors are applied to convert concentrated detergent volume and regular detergent volume, to an equivalent measure referred to as "number of washes".

%Buyers and *volume per buyer* provide a break-up of the components of sales. As illustrated in Exhibit 7.4, *Sales* can be derived by multiplying the number of *Buyers* (*%buyers* × population) with the *volume per buyer* (depth of purchase). A comparison of these measures across categories, brands or items reveals how the basic buying behaviour varies from one product to another. In Exhibit 7.5 for instance, compared to coffee and health food drink (HFD, i.e. malt drink), the market for tea is constrained by its relatively small base of

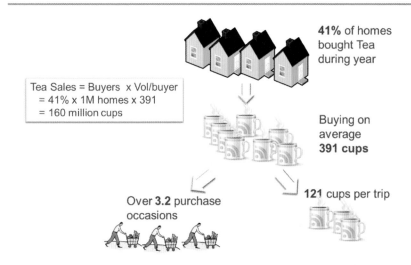

41% of homes bought Tea during year

Tea Sales = Buyers x Vol/buyer
= 41% x 1M homes x 391
= 160 million cups

Buying on average **391 cups**

Over **3.2** purchase occasions

121 cups per trip

Exhibit 7.6 Break down of tea sales in terms of buyers, purchase occasions and cups bought per trip.

buyers. Tea outperforms HFD in terms of *volume per buyer*, but *% buyers* is only 41% for the year as compared to 73% for HFD.

Volume per buyer can be broken down further into number of *purchase trips* and *volume per trip* as depicted in Exhibit 7.6. A review of *% buyers, volume per buyer, purchase trips* and *volume per trip* trends over time reveals whether width or depth of purchases is contributing to the growth or decline of a brand.

Time Period of Analysis

Measures of buying behaviour such as *volume per buyer* and *%buyers* are affected by the length of time period. The percentage of homes that buy a brand (*%buyers*) over a period of one month will usually be significantly smaller than the percentage of homes that buy the brand over a 3-month time period. The same is true for the quantity they purchase, i.e. *volume per buyer*.

The ideal length of period for measurement depends on factors such as the inter-purchase interval (IPI), the type of analysis and the size of panel. The IPI for a product category is the average length of time between purchase trips for that product category. This varies very significantly from one product to another in FMCG. For instance, the IPI for chilled milk is roughly one week whereas for shampoo it is about 3 to 4 months. IPI also varies from country to country. In developing countries where pack sizes are small (shampoos, for instance, are sold in sachets in some countries), the IPI is shorter. Typically for analysis of width and depth of purchase, brand loyalty, profile analysis, purchase basket, etc., the length of the time period should preferably be equal to or greater than the IPI.

The IPI is computed by dividing the total *category volume per buyer* over a relatively large time frame (one or two years) by the *average category volume bought per trip* over the same time frame.

The size of the panel has a bearing on period of analysis, particularly if the panel is relatively small. For measures such as *volume per buyer*, we preferably require a sample of 50 or more to arrive at a fairly reliable estimate. We may not be able to achieve this sample size for a relatively small brand, if the time frame is too short. For example, if the %buyers for a brand is 1% for a month, 2.2% for a quarter and 3% for half a year, and if the continuous panel size is 2,000, then we should preferably set the time frame for the analysis at 6 months so that the resulting sample of buyers (60) exceeds the minimum sample requirement of 50.

Buyer Groups

A buyer group is created by filtering the data, on some criteria, to form a group of households. Grouping households or individuals in this manner allows for drill down analysis of the data.

Demographic groups, segments and user-defined groups are the most common types of buyer groups.

Segmentation

Consumer panel data may be used to segment consumers according to their purchasing behaviour. The statistical techniques deployed to craft segments for panel data are the same as those described in Chapter 3, *Segmentation*. The metrics typically used include spend per month, frequency of shopping, channels/chains visited, brands/segments/categories shopped, etc.

Households may be classified in terms of their store choices (shopper segment) or in terms of their choice of products/brands (consumer segment).

By way of example, in the US, Tesco segments shoppers into the following 5 groups and 10 sub-groups, based on data collected from their Clubcard loyalty panel:

- Convenience. This is further sub-divided into
    o Time-poor, food-rich and
    o Can't cook, won't cook
- Price-sensitive:
    o Stretching the budget
    o Cheapest I can find
- Finer foods:
    o Natural chefs
    o Cooking from scratch
- Mainstream:
    o Kids' stuff
    o Commonplace brands
- Less affluent:
    o Traditional
    o Price sensitive

Consumer segments may also be crafted for a category, based on their category buying behaviour within the category. Since households can exhibit fairly different buying characteristics from one category of goods to another, category-based consumer segments do vary across categories.

Demographic Groups

Important demographic parameters include income, age, ethnic group, household size, presence of children and life stage. The phrase "life stage" refers to the different stages of development of a family. According to a Nielsen definition, life stage groups comprise of categories labelled as *young family, older family, mixed family, adult family* and *young couples*. A young family is one where all the children are below 12 years of age; an older family is one where the children are above 12; mixed families have both "old" (>12 years) and young children; adult families (e.g. empty nest) and young couples do not have any children.

User-defined Buyer Groups

A common approach to crafting buyers groups is in terms of specific behaviour characteristics of the households. There is great flexibility in how these groups may be defined. For example:

- In terms of what they buy: e.g. buy coffee, or buy Nescafe, or buy body wash but not Lux body wash, or buy milk and cheese.
- Where they buy: e.g. shop at Carrefour, or shop at Walmart but not Tesco, or buy Pantene shampoo at Tesco.
- How much they buy or how often they buy: e.g. buy more than 5L of Coca-Cola, or buy Nescafe at least 5 times at Carrefour, or loyalty for Heinz ketchup is greater than 50%, or heavy buyers of Pepsi.

Buyer groups based on heaviness of buying (i.e. *volume per buyer*) are usually segregated into 3 roughly equal groups — Heavy, Medium and Light. Exhibit 7.7 provides a fictitious example for Lipton tea, where heavy buyers who comprise 35% of Lipton's buyer base, contribute 80% of the brand's volume. On the other hand light buyers who also comprise 35% of brand's buyers, contribute merely 5% of the brand's volume.

Once the groups are configured, analysts drill into them in an effort to identify market opportunities. For instance, for the Lipton tea data, while examining the basket of purchases of heavy buyers within hot beverages as a whole, it was found that these were predominantly tea drinkers, with Lipton accounting for 64% of their total hot beverage basket. The medium buyers on the other hand were predominantly coffee drinkers, with coffee accounting for 78% of their total basket.

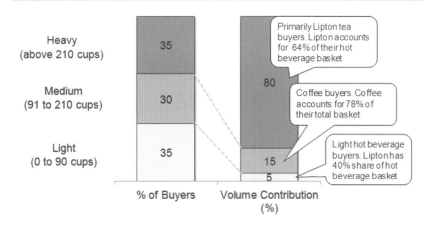

Exhibit 7.7 Buyer groups based on heaviness of buying for Lipton tea.

In contrast the 35% light buyers were quite loyal to Lipton. The reason they contributed only 5% to Lipton's volume was because they were light consumers of hot beverage. The brand's manager might consider different approaches to induce these consumers to consume more Lipton tea.

Before progressing tactics and strategies to exploit the perceived opportunity, the brand manager would need answers to a number of related questions. For instance, what might be the reasons why light consumers consume less hot beverage? Are they small households? Do they consume more out of home? What is the contribution of hot beverage to their share of throat? Most of these questions can be answered by drilling further to obtain relevant details such as demographic profile and beverage consumption habits (beverage basket of purchases).

A tactical plan however, is not always easy to execute with consumer panel data. How for instance do you engage with those consumers that have been identified as your target? In this example it might be via small packs, but often there are practical limitations.

With regard to tactics at a store level, big loyalty panels have an edge over consumer panels. Since they comprise a large proportion of the universe of store shoppers, they are better suited for executing tactical plans.

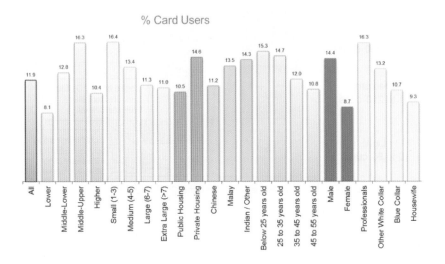

Exhibit 7.8   Demographic profile of users of a specific credit card.

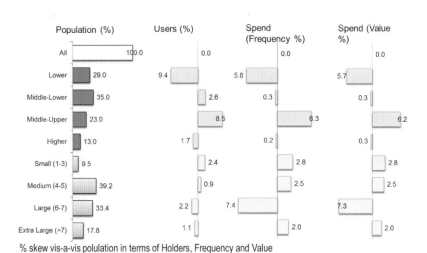

Exhibit 7.9   Skew analysis — users of the credit card.

Profile Analysis

The profile analysis reveals a product's buyer profile in terms of segment or demographic groups. It can be conducted for a brand, category, segment, or a combination of items of interest.

The analysis basically answers the following questions:

- Who buys? — % *buyers* (or % *users*) across groups.
- How much do they buy/spend? — *volume/value per buyer* across groups.
- Who contributes to the brand's volume/value? — distribution of volume/spend.

The demographic profile of holders of a particular credit card is depicted, in terms of % *card users,* in Exhibit 7.8.

The skew analysis for the same data is provided in Exhibit 7.9. This chart gives us the break-up of the credit card users across income levels and across household size. The bar chart on the left tells us the population break-up for this market across income levels: lower income — 29%, middle-lower — 35%, middle-upper — 23% and higher income — 13%. The other charts tell us that the profile of this card's users has a positive skew on middle-upper income and a negative skew on lower income. If there was no skew at all, the break-up of users (%) and spend (%) would be exactly the same as the population break-up. However since there is a -9.4 point skew on lower income, the card's proportion of users in lower income is 29 – 9.4 = 19.6%. Similarly the proportion of users is 37.6% (35 + 2.6) middle-lower income, 31.5% (23 + 8.5) middle-upper and 11.3% (13 – 1.7) higher income.

Profile analysis provides an understanding of which buyer groups (demographic groups, consumer segments) have greater propensity to purchase the brand (or any group of products of interest). The skew analysis best illustrates the areas of strengths and weaknesses. This information can be used for targeting particular buyer groups through product development, advertising, promotions and distribution.

Loyalty	House 1	House 2	House 3	All
Apples	60%	66.7%	100%	75%
Oranges	40%	33.3%	NA	37.5%

Exhibit 7.10   Brand loyalty is brand share among brand buyers.

Brand Loyalty (Behavioural)

Brand Loyalty (in behavioural terms) is defined as the brand's share of total category sales — but only among those households that buy the brand. Or simply brand share among brand buyers.

In the example in Exhibit 7.10, House 1 bought 3 apples and 2 oranges. Its loyalty for apples is 60%, and its loyalty for oranges is 40%. Similarly for House 2, loyalty for apples is 66.7% and for House 3 it is 100%. For all three homes, the combined loyalty for apples is 75%. While computing loyalty for oranges, House 3 is not taken into account — it is not a buying household. The base of buyers for oranges only comprises Houses 1 and 2, and their combined loyalty is 3/8 or 37.5%.

In general there is strong correlation between brand share and brand loyalty. Large, well-established brands experience relatively high brand loyalty. Short term shifts in loyalty however must be viewed in conjunction with other indicators of brand health.

Increases in brand loyalty are not always an indication of improvement in the brand's health. Sometimes when a brand is declining, the buyers who remain with the brand tend to be more loyal than those that exit the brand. This leads to increase in brand loyalty

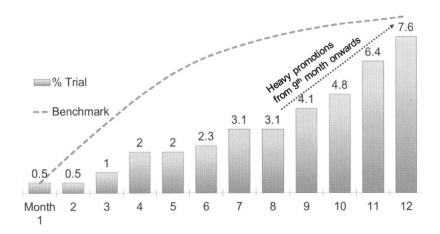

Exhibit 7.11 Trial of a new body wash brand.

even as its volume declines. Conversely, a growing brand attracts new customers who are not as committed or loyal to the brand as its existing customers. In such instances, growth in brand volume results in decrease in brand loyalty.

It is important that the researcher examines loyalty in the context of other measures such as the share, %buyers and brand switching trends. Note also that brand loyalty is dependent on time frame; it will increase as the time frame is reduced. For small time periods, there are fewer purchase trips and consequently less opportunity for the brand buyers to buy other competing brands.

Trial and Repeat Purchase

The success of a new product launch hinges on two factors — its appeal and its adoption.

Appeal: New products generate appeal or desire amongst prospects, to experience the product. This is a function of the *product concept* and the manner in which it is *communicated* through product, packaging,

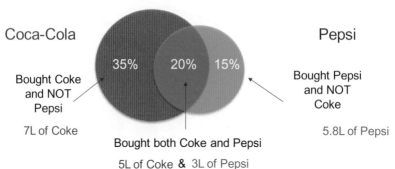

70% of households bought Pepsi and/or Coca-Cola during Jan to March

Coca-Cola

35%   20%   15%

Pepsi

Bought Coke and NOT Pepsi

Bought Pepsi and NOT Coke

7L of Coke

5.8L of Pepsi

Bought both Coke and Pepsi

5L of Coke **&** 3L of Pepsi

Exhibit 7.12   Overlap analysis of Coca-Cola and Pepsi (fictitious example).

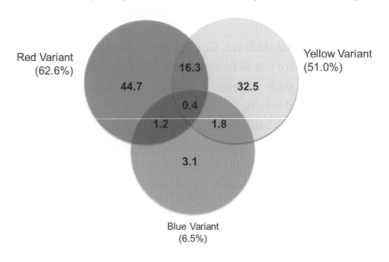

Red Variant (62.6%)

Yellow Variant (51.0%)

16.3

44.7   32.5

0.4

1.2   1.8

3.1

Blue Variant (6.5%)

Exhibit 7.13   Overlap analysis for 3 variants of a brand.

display and advertising. Appeal translates into *trial*; the broader the appeal, the greater the incidence of trial of a new product.

Adoption: This is the willingness to continue buying, *after experiencing* the new brand. It is a function of the extent to which the new product lives up to/exceeds consumer's expectations. Adoption translates into *repeat purchase*; the higher the level of adoption the greater the extent to which the new product gets channelled into the consumer's repertoire of purchases.

Trial and *repeat purchase* are the two metrics we need to closely monitor to assess a new FMCG product's market potential. For the product to succeed, it needs to establish a base of regular consumers who continue to buy it. It must generate appeal so that a substantial number of consumers try it. And once they experience it, an adequate number of them should be willing to continue buying it.

Trial or *cumulative penetration* at a time *t* is the percentage of households or individuals who purchased the product from the time it was launched till time *t*.

The build-up of trial for the new body wash brand shown in Exhibit 7.11 is unusual in that it differs significantly from the benchmark. Usually heavy promotions are scheduled during the early launch phase, but for this brand the promos kicked in more than 6 months post-launch.

%Repeat Purchase is the percentage of buyers who bought more than once. A variation of %Repeat Purchase is the *1 +, 2 +, 3 + %Repeat Buyer,* where the *1 + Repeaters* are those who bought the product at least once, *2 +* at least twice and so on.

Trial and repeat purchase is re-visited in the *Product Validation* chapter which introduces the Parfitt–Collins model for forecasting sales of new products, and provides an understanding of a number of concepts and metrics that relate to the evaluation of new products.

Overlap

Overlap analysis provides a measure of the level of duplication within a group of products. The results of the analysis may be presented in Venn diagrams, such as the ones shown in Exhibits 7.12 and 7.13.

The analysis essentially creates a number of buyer groups, three in the case of the two brand analysis in Exhibit 7.12 — 'Only Coca-Cola', 'Coca-Cola and Pepsi' and 'Only Pepsi'. Drilling into these buyer groups helps marketers address related issues.

For instance, a brand manager might be interested in reducing the number of variants or pack sizes within the brand's range. Besides reviewing other metrics, the brand manager should check whether there are brand buyers who exclusively buy (i.e. *solus buyers*) that variant. In the example in Exhibit 7.13, if variant blue is withdrawn from the market, the buyers that exclusively bought that variant (3.1% of the brand's buyer) are the ones that the brand is most likely to lose.

To take an informed decision the brand manager might want to check what competitor brands fall within the repertoire of these buyers. She can do this by analysing these buyers' basket of purchases.

Basket

The basket is an analysis of transactions by a buyer group. Buyer group, as mentioned earlier, may be a demographic group, a segment, or it may be a user-defined group of consumers, defined on the basis of what they bought, where they bought or how much they bought. It is often defined as buyers of a particular brand, in which case the basket constitutes the repertoire of brands bought by the buyers of that brand.

Exhibit 7.14 depicts the analysis of the petrol basket for Shell 98 for a particular month. The basket reveals that loyalty for Shell 98 is 69.6% in volume (frequency) terms and 70.0% in value terms. These buyers pumped Shell 98 on an average 1.5 times that month, spending $126. It also reveals that 19.4% of Shell 98 motorists pumped Synergy 8000 and that Synergy 8000 constitutes 12.3% of the total spend on average. In total the average Shell 98 motorists spend $180 (pumping 2.1 times) for that month.

The basket analysis is frequently used in internet marketing or e-commerce. For example, the use of recommendations ("Customers who bought this also bought ...") by NetFlix and Amazon, to drive sales and improve customers' on-site experience.

Cross basket, an interesting variation of the basket analysis, analyses the purchases of some other category by a buyer group. For example, the cross basket of shampoo purchases by Dove body wash buyers,

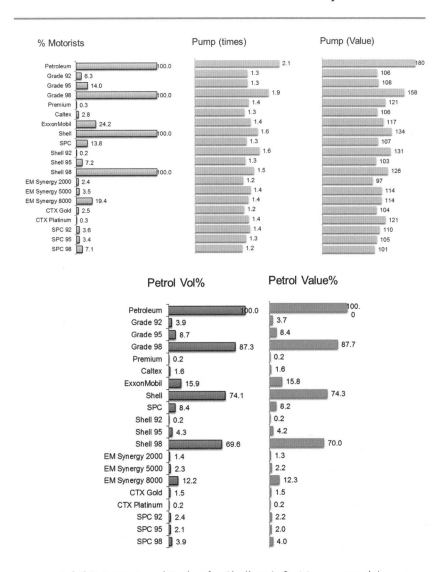

Exhibit 7.14 Petrol Basket for Shell 98 (a fictitious example).

would reveal the repertoire of shampoos bought by Dove body wash buyers.

The basket and cross basket provide a comprehensive understanding of the transactions by the buyer group, and as we will see from the case *Johnson's Body Care*, at the end of this chapter, this is very useful for addressing a variety of business issues.

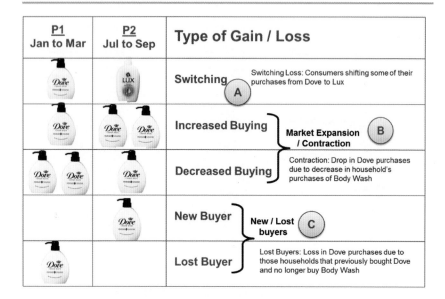

Exhibit 7.15 Types of gains and losses.

Yet another variation of the basket analysis, of great relevance to the retailer, is the *shopping basket*. For instance, it would interest a retailer to know the total spend, and the break-up of that spend across categories, for the shoppers of those brands that they promote most frequently. If a brand buyer's shopping basket is large in terms of quantity and value of purchases, that brand is a potential transaction builder. Retailers want to attract these shoppers to their stores because they spend much more than the average shopper. For example, in most Asian markets, products like cooking oil and rice are transaction builders.

Gain–loss

Also known as brand switching or brand shifting analysis, the objective of gain–loss is to measure competitive shifts in consumer buying in terms of the amount of business each product gains from other products. Much-loved by consumer analysts, it analyses disaggregate

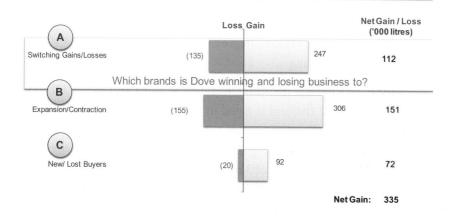

Exhibit 7.16 Analysis summary of gains and losses for Dove (Year 2 versus Year 1) (Fictitious data for illustration only).

	Net Gain/Loss	Interaction Index
Lux	6	76
Shokobutsu	38	65
Kodomo	1	15
Johnsons	96	**344**
PH5.5	1	20
Dettol	-4	34
Follow Me	-18	**128**
Ginvera	-15	**124**
CP Palmolive	-2	43
	112	

Lux (8) 14; Shokobutsu (17) 55; Kodomo (0) 1; Johnsons (28) 124; PH5.5 1; Dettol (15) 11; Follow Me (31) 13; Ginvera (28) 13; CP Palmolive (7) 5

-135 247

◼ Loss (litres) ◻ Gain (litres)

Exhibit 7.17 Analysis for Dove of gains and losses across brands (Year 2 versus Year 1).

data to answer questions relating to switching behaviours — What is my brand's source of growth or decline? Which brands are being cannibalized?

Types of Gains and Losses

Gain–loss reveals the source of growth and decline in a product's sales over two time periods of equal length, in terms of the following:

- New/Lost category buyers
- Increased/Decreased category buying
- Brand Switching

Exhibit 7.15 depicts the different types of gains and losses. Observe that time period *P1* (before) is equal in length to time period *P2* (after), but the periods in this case are not adjoining one another. The analyst might be interested in assessing the impact of an initiative that occurred in Jan-Mar, after an interval of 3 months, when the fluctuations induced by the initiative settle down. External factors such as *seasonality* need to be considered when analysing gain–loss results. In most instances it is preferable that the pre and post periods (*P1* and *P2*) fall within the same season.

Exhibit 7.16 provides an output of the gain–loss analysis for Dove body wash. It tells us that:

- Dove gains a total of 335,000 L in Year 2 over the previous year.
- 112,000 L is the net volume Dove gained from other brands. Households that gained volume from competing brands contributed +247,000 L, and those that lost volume contributed −135,000 L.
- Dove gained 306,000 L from homes that increased purchases of body wash, and lost 155,000 L to those homes that decreased purchase of body wash.
- Homes that bought body wash in Year 2 but not in Year 1, added 92,000 L to Dove's sales. Lapsed body wash buyers accounted for a decline of 20,000 L for Dove.

Exhibit 7.17 zooms into the brand switching behaviour, providing a break-up across brands of the 247,000 litres gained and the 135,000 litres lost due to switching. For instance if we consider Johnson's, Dove gained 124,000 litres in those homes where consumers shifted purchases from Johnson's to Dove, and Dove lost 28,000 litres in those homes where consumers shifted purchases from Dove to Johnson's.

	L	G	Step 1	Step 2 Share ABS	V Volume	Step 3 Adusted	Step 4 Interaction Index
	Loss (litres)	Gain (litres)	ABS(G+L)	(G+L) (%)	Share (%)	Share	(Step2/Step3)
Dove	-	-			10.3	-	
Lux	-8.4	14.4	22.8	6.2	7.3	8.1	76
Shokobutsu	-16.9	55.1	72.0	19.4	26.8	29.9	65
Kodomo	0.0	1.2	1.2	0.3	2.0	2.2	15
Johnsons	-27.7	123.7	151.4	40.8	10.6	11.9	344
PH5.5	0.0	1.2	1.2	0.3	1.4	1.6	20
Dettol	-15.2	10.8	26.0	7.0	18.8	20.9	34
Follow Me	-30.5	12.9	43.4	11.7	8.2	9.1	128
Ginvera	-28.0	12.6	40.6	11.0	7.9	8.8	124
CP Palmolive	-7.2	4.8	12.0	3.2	6.8	7.5	43
	-133.9	236.7	370.6	100.0	100.0	100.0	100

Exhibit 7.18   Computation of Interaction Index.

Interaction Index

Interaction index provides a measure for the extent to which brand buyers interact with other brands. The norm is 100. If the index is above 115, the interaction is significantly above expectation, and if the index is below 85, the interaction is significantly below expectation. The interaction index of 344 between Dove and Johnson's indicates that the propensity of Dove to interact with Johnson's is 3.44 times higher than expected.

The index is computed as follows (refer to Exhibit 7.18):

- Step 1: Compute the total volume transacted (Absolute Gain + Loss).
- Step 2: Compute share of volume transacted.
- Step 3: Compute adjusted volume share after deducting Dove.
  $Adjusted\ Share = V/(100 - 10.3)\%$
  (Where 10.3% is Dove's volume share. The volume share in column V is obtained from the panel data).
- Step 4:

$$Interaction\ Index = \frac{Share\ of\ volume\ transacted}{Adjusted\ Volume\ Share}$$

$$= Step\ 2/Step\ 3$$

The standard gain–loss algorithm assumes proportionate allocation of losses to gains — i.e. losses incurred by brands that lost volume are proportionately allocated to those brands that gained volume. This underestimates interaction between brands that compete strongly, and overestimates the interaction between brands that do not compete strongly. Alternative methods called nested gain–loss and hierarchical gain–loss are described in Appendix B, *The Assumptions and Limitations of Gain–loss Algorithms*. It is important, when interpreting gain–loss results, to remain aware of the method's strengths and limitations that are outlined in this appendix.

Case Example — Johnson's Body Care

Johnson's, a brand that cuts across multiple categories, is a leading brand in hand & body (H&B) lotion and body wash — two categories where market dynamics differs greatly. H&B lotion is a small relatively quiet market where Johnson's often maintains a dominant leadership position. Body wash on the other hand is a cutthroat business with thin margins, as big global brands jostle for market share.

Some years back Johnson's regional leadership was exploring ways to exploit the synergy of the brand across the two categories. They had a few questions on their minds — Could Johnson's equity transcend categories? Could they leverage the brand's equity from one category to another? If so, that would open opportunities to strengthen the brand as well as optimize costs in brand building.

At Nielsen, we picked the Singapore market for in-depth study of the Johnson's brand. One of the analysis, depicted in Exhibit 7.20, provides a break-up of the 21% Johnson's buyers into three buyers groups — those who bought Johnson's H&B only (*H&B only* — 24% of buyers), those who bought Johnson's Body Wash only (*BW only* — 56% of buyers) and those who bought both Johnson's H&B and Johnson's Body Wash (*H&B + BW* — 20% of buyers). For each of the three buyer groups, we examined their behavioural loyalty to the Johnson's brand within H&B and body wash.

Exhibit 7.19 An advertisement of Johnson's Body Wash and Johnson's H&B lotion.

Considering Johnson's dominant position in H&B, it did not come as a surprise that loyalty for Johnson's H&B was high (65-66%) for both *H&B only* and *H&B + BW* buyer groups. What caught our attention, however, was the much higher loyalty of 46% for Johnson's Body Wash, among *H&B + BW* buyers, compared to the 28% loyalty, among *BW only* buyers.

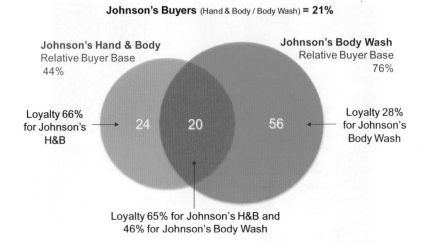

Johnson's Buyers (Hand & Body / Body Wash) **= 21%**

Johnson's Hand & Body
Relative Buyer Base
44%

Johnson's Body Wash
Relative Buyer Base
76%

Loyalty 66%
for Johnson's
H&B   →   24   20   56   ←   Loyalty 28%
                                                            for Johnson's
                                                            Body Wash

Loyalty 65% for Johnson's H&B and
46% for Johnson's Body Wash

Exhibit 7.20 Cross category overlap analysis: Johnson's Hand & Body and Body Wash.

Also revealing was the cross basket analysis of Johnson's H&B buyers. Exhibit 7.21 depicts the body wash basket of purchases by the Johnson's H&B buyers' buyer group. Within this group, Johnson's Body Wash had a commanding share of 27.5% — which is exceptionally high when compared with the 9.5% market share of Johnson's Body Wash, within the panel population as a whole.

In the context of buyer groups, the share of Johnson's Body Wash in total market (9.5%) is called the "fair share" — i.e. the share we would expect if there was nothing extraordinary about a buyer group. The index 27.5/9.5 (= 290 re-based to 100), called the *fair share index*, is extraordinarily high. It tells us that the propensity of a Johnson's H&B buyer to buy Johnson's Body Wash, is 2.9 times higher than that for the average brand buyer.

The cross category overlap analysis, and the cross basket analysis suggested that Johnson's brand equity transcended the categories; that there existed a strong synergistic relationship. Consumers buying both Johnson's product were much more loyal to Johnson's Body Wash. This synergy was leveraged via subsequent marketing efforts such as the joint

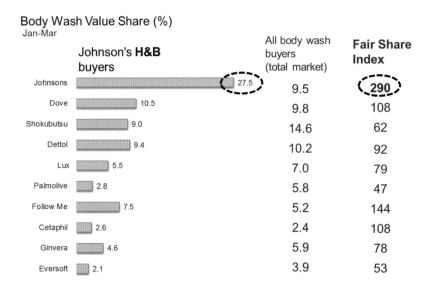

Exhibit 7.21 Cross basket analysis — Johnson's H&B buyers' share of purchases in body wash.

Johnson's body care advertisement, in Exhibit 7.19, of Johnson's Body Wash and Johnson's H&B lotion.

CHAPTER 8

Consumer Analytics and Big Data

"What scares me about this is that you know more about my customers after three months than I know after 30 years." — Lord MacLaurin, Tesco's Chairman (1994).

The "deadly silence", as Clive Humby described it, which followed his presentation felt endless to the nervous 39 year old. It was broken by Lord MacLaurin who uttered the memorable line quoted above.

The analysis of the Clubcard trials presented by Humby, Tim Mason and Grant Harrison, to the Tesco board of directors on 22 November 1994 shattered some long held assumptions. Yet what compelled most was the realization that *Tesco could become UK's market leader by replicating the sales growth Clubcard had achieved during trial.*

Clubcard was launched a few months after the presentation. Tesco subsequently grew at a faster pace than competitors, to become UK's largest retailer. Today one in three UK households has a Clubcard, and Tesco is recognized within the industry as the most successful exponent of loyalty marketing.

Tesco, recognizing the competitive advantage they acquired through their partnership with Dunnhumby, strengthened and protected it over the years. In 2001 they bought a 53% stake in Dunnhumby, and increased this holding to 84% in 2006. By 2010, Clive Humby and his wife Edwina Dunn had sold their entire stake for a total value of approximately £93million, and in October 2010 they resigned from the company, remaining non-executive directors till early 2013.

Preview

Consumer Analytics is the analysis of continuous individual/household level (customer level) behavioural data to address business issues.

The terms *aggregate* and *disaggregate* data provide for a broad categorization of the nature of data. The data that Tesco was accustomed to seeing before the launch of Clubcard was aggregate in nature. They knew how much of each item they sold each week or each day. This is the data that is captured every time a bar code is scanned at the checkout; what it does not reveal is who bought the item.

Disaggregate consumer data on the other hand is consumer or household level data. It is captured for instance when the consumer's loyalty card (e.g. Clubcard) is also scanned at the checkout. The data is *continuous* in nature — we have data for the *same* households/individuals continuously over time.

The term *Consumer Analytics* has been defined in a number of different ways. I would like to use it specifically in the context of consumer level disaggregate data. Consumer panels, loyalty panels, consumer/customer transaction, e-commerce sites, social networking sites, search engines, websites in general — all these sources yield disaggregate, continuous data on the behaviour of individuals, customers or households. It is the analysis of this type of consumer level disaggregate data that I am classifying as consumer analytics.

In the past, the data pertained mainly to consumers' buying and consumption habits, and their tastes and preferences. Now it increasingly also includes their browsing or interaction behaviour on the net.

Interactions include the clicks, navigation paths and browsing activities on websites. The field of web analytics, or the analysis of behaviour of web users, falls largely within the scope of consumer analytics. In addition to refining the elements of the marketing mix, the focus of web analytics lies in improving the effectiveness of the website, in terms of conversion rates and other performance parameters. This subject is covered in brief in Chapter 14, *Digital Marketing*.

While behaviour is the key characteristic of consumer analytics data, it often is enriched by demographic, geographic, psychographic and socialgraphic information.

The methods and techniques covered in Chapter 7, *Consumer Panels*, fall within the field of consumer analytics. The focus in this chapter lies mainly on data management tools and technologies, machine learning techniques, data mining, crowd sourcing and co-creation, optimization techniques and visualization techniques. Big data and cognitive systems are also covered, and so too some of the application areas.

Consumer analytics is not as recent a phenomenon as it is popularly thought to be. Some companies at the forefront of consumer analytics were founded in the 1980s and 1990s. The biggest change over the years is not the science, but rather the technology, and the advent of big data.

Back in the 1990s, to run a resource intense consumer panel analysis over about 35,000 homes in urban India, I would leave one of my PCs on overnight, and it may still be running the next morning. Today a similar analysis would take a second or two to run on my laptop.

Big Data

Big data is the new frontier in consumer analytics. As organizations transact and interact with customers, they are generating a tremendous amount of digital exhaust data — a by-product of business activities. Over the years, this has resulted, in the explosion of business data and its management, along three dimensions — volume, variety and velocity (Laney, 2001).

According to the folks at IBM (Zikopoulos *et al.*, 2012), some enterprises are generating "terabytes of data every hour of every day of the year"; the volume of information stored in the world would grow from hundreds of exabytes (EB 1000^6) of data today to an estimated 35 zetabytes (ZB 1000^7) by 2020.

As more and more data is generated every hour, data velocity has grown tremendously. Much of the data is kept for short duration, and must be analysed as it flows.

Furthermore, with proliferation of smart devices, cameras, microphones, sensors, RFIDs, data has grown in terms of variety and complexity.

Today much of the world's information comprises of huge, fast moving, unstructured data sets that cannot be processed or analysed by means of the conventional methods that apply to structured data. These data sets are collectively referred to today as *big data*. Dealing effectively with them requires new ways of data handling and analysis.

Data Management Tools and Technologies

A wide range of tools and technologies, most of which have existed since several decades, support the application of consumer analytics. More recently, the need to cope with big data led to the emergence of new technologies. Prominent among these are Hadoop and Hadoop-related projects, cloud computing, and cognitive systems.

This section details some of the better known tools and technologies that are currently used for managing structured, unstructured and semi-structured data.

Database

A database is made up of a collection of tables, where data is stored in rows and columns. Relational database management systems (RDBMS) store structured data that may be managed with the use of SQL (structured query language). Non-relational databases, on the other hand, do not store data in tables.

Structured and Unstructured Data

Data that resides in fixed fields (e.g. relational databases, spreadsheet tables) is called structured data and data that does not reside in fixed fields is called unstructured data.

The growth of unstructured data has exploded with the propagation of social media. Examples include free-form text (e.g. social media and other web pages, books, articles, emails), untagged audio, image and video data.

Semi-structured data does not conform to fixed fields but contains tags and other markers to separate data elements. Examples of semi-structured data include XML or HTML-tagged text.

Business Intelligence

The term business intelligence (BI) is used in two different contexts as defined by Forrester Research:

- In the broader context: "Business Intelligence is a set of methodologies, processes, architectures, and technologies that transform raw data into meaningful and useful information used to enable more effective strategic, tactical, and operational insights and decision-making." This definition encompasses a very wide range of theories, methodologies, architectures, and technologies that transform raw data into meaningful and actionable information for business analysis and decision-making.

- In a narrower context, business intelligence refers to "reporting, analytics and dashboards".

A wide range of software applications including IBM Cognos, Oracle Hyperion and SAP NetWeaver provide facilities for retrieving, analysing and reporting data for business intelligence.

Data Marts and Warehouses

A data warehouse is a repository of structured data from diverse data sources, which is optimally designed for reporting and analysis purposes. Data from the different sources is uploaded using ETL (extract, transform and load) tools.

A data mart is a subset of a data warehouse, used to provide data to users usually through business intelligence tools.

Data Integration

Data integration is the process of combining data residing in different sources to present a unified view of the data. In business applications it is often referred to as "Enterprise Information Integration".

There is no universal approach to data integration. Many techniques in this field are still evolving. One approach is the common data storage method, also known as data warehousing. This method extracts data from outside sources, transforms it to fit operational needs, and loads it into a repository, the *data warehouse*. Specialized ETL (*extracts, transforms, and loads*) software tools are used for this purpose.

Because the data has already been extracted, converted and combined, queries to a data warehouse take little time to resolve. From a user or front-end standpoint, data warehousing is therefore an efficient way to work with integrated data. The development of the backend on the other hand, requires considerable thought and effort, and the warehouse needs to be large enough to accommodate the data from the multiple sources, a challenge considering the pace at which some databases are growing.

The key disadvantage with data warehouses is that the information in them is not always current. A data warehouse might not extract and load data very frequently, which means information may not be reliable for time-sensitive applications.

An alternative approach, which is suited for time sensitive data, is for the system to pull data directly from individual networked data sources. The way this is done is by means of mapping the schema for the data sources to a mediated schema. This requires the development of "wrappers" or adapters that transform queries to the mediated schema into appropriate queries over the respective data sources.

Data Fusion

Data fusion is the process of matching two or more data sources at the consumer level to create a unified database. The matching uses information common to both sources, called "linking variables" or "fusion hooks," to pair up consumers from the respective databases. The unified database contains information from the original data sources, simulating single-source data.

For example, data from social media, analysed by natural language processing, can be fused with real-time sales data, to determine what effect a marketing campaign is having on customer sentiment and purchasing behaviour.

Similarly consumer panel data which tells us what consumers buy may be fused with audience measurement data which tells us what programmes they watch. By cross referencing results in this manner, data fusion links purchasing behaviour with media habits to deliver insights that were otherwise not available.

Since it fits into existing analysis systems and requires no additional primary research, data fusion is a cost-effective means of enhancing existing data.

Distributed System

A distributed system comprises a collection of computers, connected via a network. The system uses middleware (software that serves to "glue together" the multiple computers) to enable the connected computers to coordinate their activities and to share the resources of the system, as a single, integrated computing facility.

A distributed system lowers costs because a cluster of lower-end computers can be less expensive than a single higher-end computer. It also improves reliability and scalability — system resources and capabilities can be increased by simply adding more nodes rather than replacing a central computer.

Google File System and Colossus

Google File System (GFS) is a proprietary, scalable distributed file system developed by Google to provide efficient, reliable access to data on large clusters of inexpensive commodity hardware. The successor to GFS is called Colossus.

BigTable

BigTable is a compressed, high performance, and proprietary distributed data storage system built on GFS and other Google technologies. It provides better scalability and control of performance characteristics for Google's applications. The company offers access to BigTable through Google App Engine.

BigTable is used by a number of applications including web indexing, MapReduce, Google Maps, Google Book Search, "My Search History", Google Earth, Blogger.com, Google Code hosting, Orkut, YouTube, and Gmail.

Dynamo

Dynamo is an Amazon proprietary distributed data storage system.

Cassandra

Cassandra is an open source (i.e. free) database management system originally developed at Facebook, designed to handle large data volumes on a distributed system. The system is now managed by Apache Software Foundation.

Cloud Computing

Cloud computing is the delivery of computing as a service rather than a product. Configured as a distributed system, scalable computing resources are provided on users' computers as a utility over the internet.

Hadoop

Hadoop is an open source computing environment that is widely used for large data operations, on distributed clustered systems. Inspired by Google File System and MapReduce, Hadoop was originally developed at Yahoo! and is now managed as a project of the Apache Software Foundation. It is implemented in Java.

Hadoop essentially comprises of the *Hadoop distributed file system* (HDFS), the *Hadoop MapReduce* model, and *Hadoop Common*, which contains libraries and utilities needed by other Hadoop modules.

The HDFS breaks down data into blocks that are distributed across the Hadoop cluster. The MapReduce programme performs two distinct functions — map and reduce. Tasks to be performed on a dataset are broken down into smaller sub-tasks, and distributed to the DataNodes (i.e. worker nodes). The DataNodes process the sub-tasks in parallel, generating a set of intermediate results. The reduce function merges the intermediate values producing the final result.

The Apache Hadoop platform consists of a number of related projects such as Apache Pig, Apache Hive, Apache HBase, Apache Spark, and others.

HBase

HBase, one of a number of projects related to Hadoop, is a column-oriented database management system that runs on top of HDFS. Unlike relational database systems, it does not support a structured query language like SQL. HBase works well with sparse data sets, which are common in many big data use cases. It is managed as a project of the Apache Software Foundation as part of the Hadoop group of services.

Metadata

Metadata is "data about data", i.e. it describes the content and context of data files. A webpage for example, may include metadata specifying what language it is written in, what tools were used to create it, and where to go for more on the subject, allowing web browsers to automatically improve the experience of users.

Consumer Analytic Techniques

Machine Learning Techniques

Machine learning is a branch of artificial intelligence concerned with the development of systems that can learn from empirical data. These systems learn to recognize complex patterns and perform tasks based on these capabilities.

Optical character recognition (OCR) and natural language processing are examples of machine learning. Printed characters are recognized automatically, in OCR systems, based on previous examples. A machine learning system could also be trained to classify different types of transactions (e.g. identify fraudulent transactions) or emails (e.g. distinguish spam).

Pattern Recognition

Pattern recognition is a set of machine learning techniques that classify raw data according to a specific logic or learning procedure. Broadly speaking there are two types of learning procedures — supervised learning and unsupervised learning.

Supervised learning uses training data that consists of a set of pre-labelled instances. Each instance is formally described by a vector of features, which together constitute a description of all known characteristics of the instance. The learning procedure generates a model that attempts to perform as well as possible on the training data, and generalize as well as possible to new data.

Unsupervised learning, on the other hand, works without pre-labelled training data, to find inherent patterns in the data that can then be used to classify data instances. Classification of data based on unsupervised learning is normally known as clustering.

Neural Networks

Neural network (aka artificial neural network) is a nonlinear predictive model that learns through training, and resembles a biological neural network in structure. It can be used for pattern recognition and optimization.

Like other machine learning methods (i.e. systems that learn from data) neural networks have been used to solve a wide variety of tasks including computer vision and speech recognition, classification of customers (e.g. identifying high-risk, high-value customers) or classification of transactions (e.g. fraudulent insurance claims).

Natural Language Processing (NLP)

Natural language processing is a branch of artificial intelligence (more specifically machine learning) and linguistics that deals with the ability of computers to understand natural languages; i.e. enabling computers to derive meaning from human or natural language input. It relates to the area of human-computer interaction. A common application in marketing is use of sentiment analysis on the web to determine how people feel about a particular subject; e.g. a brand, a company or an individual.

Sentiment Analysis

Sentiment analysis uses NLP and other analytic techniques to identify and extract subjective information from textual content such as consumer generated media (social media). It seeks content relating to objects of interest, determines the polarity (favourable, neutral, negative) of the content, and assesses the intensity of the sentiment. The net advocacy index described in Chapter 2, *Brand Equity*, is one example of sentiment analysis to assess how netizens feel about brands.

Ensemble Learning

Ensemble learning is the process by which multiple predictive models, such as classifiers, are combined to improve the predictive performance of the constituent models.

Data Mining

Data mining is the process of scouring and analysing large datasets, and extracting patterns from the data. Data mining techniques combine methods from statistics and machine learning, with database management, to predict behaviours and trends. Data mining allows marketers to take proactive, knowledge-driven decisions. Application areas include:

- Promotions — Identify customers most likely to respond to a promotional offer.
- Direct marketing — Identify prospects most likely to respond to direct marketing campaign.
- Interactive marketing — Predict what web pages an individual accessing a website is most likely to be interested in viewing.
- Market basket analysis — Determine what products or services are commonly purchased together.
- Churn analysis — Identify customers who are likely to drop a product or service, and shift to a competitor.
- Fraud detection — Identify which transactions are most likely to be fraudulent.

Tools used for data mining include neural networks, decision trees, association rule learning, rule induction, genetic algorithms, nearest neighbour, cluster analysis, classification, and regression. Some of these tools are described below.

Rule Induction

Rule induction is an area of machine learning in which formal rules are extracted from a set of observations. The rules extracted may represent a full scientific model of the data, or merely represent local patterns in the data.

The rules are usually stated as expressions of the form:

$$if\ (attribute_1, value_1)\ and\ (attribute_2, value_2)\ and$$
$$... (attribute_n, value_n)\ then\ (decision, value)$$

For example:

$$If\ (urination, frequent)\ and\ (weight\ loss, yes)\ and$$
$$(tiredness, yes)\ and\ (vision, blurred) \rightarrow (diabetes, yes)$$

Association Rule Learning

Association rule learning is a method for discovering interesting relationships (association rules based on the concept of strong rules) among variables in databases. It deploys a range of algorithms to identify strong rules in databases using different measures of "interestingness". For example, shopping basket analysis of loyalty panel data is used to discover interesting relationships between products such as $\{Cheese, Bread\} \rightarrow \{Wine\}$ (i.e. shoppers who buy cheese and bread also tend to buy wine). Information of this nature may be used for merchandising (e.g. special displays) and promotional activities.

Association rule learning is also used in a variety of other applications including web usage mining, intrusion detection, continuous production, and bioinformatics.

Genetic Algorithms

Genetic algorithms optimization techniques are based on the concepts of genetic combination, mutation, and natural selection. Potential solutions are encoded as "chromosomes" that can combine and mutate. Survival within a modelled "environment" depends on fitness or performance of each individual chromosome in the population. These "evolutionary" algorithms are well-suited for solving nonlinear problems. Examples of applications include speech recognition, robotics, planning and scheduling, optimizing portfolio investments and so on.

Classification Techniques

Classification techniques identify the categories where a new observation belongs, based on a set of variables and a training data set containing observations whose category membership is known. The classification rules are derived from the training data set, and the algorithm is referred to as a classifier. Applications include assigning an email into "spam" or "non-spam", or predicting customer behaviour in terms of purchasing, consumption, churn and so on.

Because they use training sets, classification techniques are described as supervised learning. Cluster analysis on the other hand, is unsupervised learning.

Nearest Neighbour

Nearest neighbour is a technique that classifies records in a database based on their similarity.

Cluster Analysis

Cluster analysis is a statistical technique used to form groups of objects with similar characteristics into clusters (segments). In cluster analysis the variables used for clustering are known in advance. Refer to Chapter 3, *Segmentation* for details on the application of cluster analysis for market segmentation.

Sourcing from Social Media

Crowdsourcing

Crowdsourcing is the process of soliciting ideas or content from a large group of people, usually an online community. LEGO IDEAS, an example covered in the chapter *New Product Development*, uses a crowdsourcing programme to source ideas for new Lego projects.

Co-creation

Co-creation is an off-shoot of crowdsourcing, which involves smaller group of individuals with specialized skills. It is used increasingly to generate ideas for the development of advertising and new products.

Examples include consumers building their own shoes (Nike), conceiving their own pizzas (Papa John's), and generating advertising content for companies like Coca-Cola, General Motors and Microsoft.

Optimization/Analysis Techniques

Market Modelling

Many theories abound in marketing on subjects like advertising, brand equity, product optimization, pricing, promotion and so on. Market models "operationalize" these theories into practical solutions using a set of predictive modelling techniques such as regression for instance, to construct models that predict the probability of an outcome.

Market modelling is extensively used in areas such as market segmentation, brand equity analysis, advertising effectiveness, price optimization, promotions evaluation, etc. (For details, refer to Chapter 18, *Market Mix Modelling*).

A/B Testing

A/B testing (aka split testing or bucket testing) is a technique where a control group is compared with one or more test groups, to determine which treatment produces the best results. Examples in marketing include controlled store tests, controlled website tests and copy testing of online advertising. When more than one variable is simultaneously tested (A/B/N testing), multiple test groups need to be formed. In such instances the use of big data helps to ensure that sample sizes are adequate to detect meaningful differences between the groups.

Network Theory and Social Network Analysis

Network theory is a branch of computer science concerned with the relationship between discrete objects. Applications of network theory include logistical networks, gene regulatory networks, metabolic networks, social networks, epistemological networks, etc.

Social network analysis is an application of network theory to analyse social networks. For instance how information travels in a community, or the influence one individual has over others. Applications include identifying opinion leaders to target for marketing.

Spatial Analysis

Spatial analysis or spatial statistics is the study of topological, geometric, or geographic properties of objects. The propagation of *geographic information systems* (GIS) is driving the use and application of spatial analysis in marketing and operations research, for instance, the optimization of the location of stores based on the movement and buying behaviour of target consumers.

R

The R language, an open source programming software environment for statistical computing and graphics, is widely used for developing statistical software and data analysis. It is part of the GNU Project, a collaboration that supports open source projects.

Visualization

Visualization techniques are concerned with depicting data in a form such as images, diagrams, or animations that make it easier for minds to process. Perceptual maps and image profiling are two examples of visualization of data from Chapter 1, *Brand and Brand Image*. Since the advent of big data, the pace of research and innovation in this field has grown substantially. Tag or word clouds, clustergrams, history and spatial information flow are some examples of the techniques used for visualizing big data.

Cognitive Systems — the 3rd Age of Computing

"When Watson defeated Brad Rutter and Ken Jennings in the Jeopardy! Challenge of February 2011, it was clear that a new kind of computing

Exhibit 8.1 Jeopardy! host Alex Trebek with contestants Ken Jennings, Watson, and Brad Rutter *(Courtesy of Jeopardy Productions, Inc.).*

system was emerging — one that could learn, reason, and understand natural language" (Source: IBM Research. Refer also to Exhibit 8.1).

Welcome to the third age of computing. For the first time a computer could answer questions posed in plain English, and beat the very best in a quiz show. That question and answer machine, according to IBM's Manoj Saxena, can now engage a consumer in a dialogue. Systems like Watson can interact with people and assist them in making complex decisions, after interpreting vast amounts of data comprising natural language, images as well as structured information.

As a commercial technology, a cloud enabled Watson may power new consumer and enterprise applications in areas as diverse as cooking recipes, shopping, travel, banking and health care. At the University of Texas MD Anderson Cancer Center, Watson is participating in a "Moon Shots" mission to end cancer. Watson has also been assisting oncologists at the Memorial Sloan Kettering Cancer Center in New York with health data and research around the world.

Whereas computers traditionally were designed for rapid calculations of structured data, cognitive systems process structured and unstructured information akin to how people think. These systems are trained by artificial intelligence and machine learning algorithms to "sense, predict, infer and, in some ways, think".

Benefits

As the Dunnhumby-Tesco saga and the developments surrounding big data suggests, customer behavioural data is the marketer's gold mine. Some key strengths and benefits of disaggregate, continuous behavioural data are listed as follows:

- The potency of the data is largely due to its complexion — continuous, disaggregate. Disaggregate data is far more revealing than aggregate data; therefore better suited for diagnosing consumer behaviour.
- Size. These databases tend to be large enabling the data analyst to drill down into proportionately small customer segments. In particular, transaction data and big data allow for micro segments, or even personalized marketing (e.g. targeted promotions and communications).
- Though not always representative of total market, the data is highly actionable. It allows for the execution of tactics at the customer segment level and at location — i.e. store or bank or website, etc.
- Provides deeper understanding of consumers' buying behaviour. Whereas aggregate data for instance, can compute metrics like market share, disaggregate data goes a step further revealing breadth and depth of consumption, brand loyalty, switching behaviour, purchase baskets and so on.
- Reveals not only current and historical behaviour, it can also predict future behaviour. For example, techniques based on disaggregate data can accurately forecast market share of a new product soon after its launch.

- Estimates growth as well as the sources of growth. (Disaggregate data reveals switching patterns. Refer to gain–loss analysis in Chapter 7, *Consumer Panels*).
- Uncovers the impact of marketing activities in the current time period as well as in the future. Reveals the long term impact of some of these activities.
- Reveals most valuable customers.
- The union of people's physical and the digital world via data integration, yields valuable insights that help better target consumers.
- Accurate and complete information provides for greater transparency and accountability.

People

Consumer analytics is a process of exploration. To address a sticky business issue the analyst starts by examining the upper strata of the data — perhaps market share and standard dashboard metrics. These metrics reveal clues as to where to explore and what to analyse. Each analysis yields further clues taking the analyst along a drill down path to the answers she is looking for.

In addition to the understanding of the technology tools and platforms that support consumer analytics, this requires an understanding of the business, and deep appreciation of the discipline of marketing in that industry. Organizations that use consumer analytics for business decisions are therefore developing in-house capabilities, and augmenting these capabilities by partnering service providers that specialize in the field.

The service providers fall into a two-tier structure. The first tier comprises a host of companies that develop technology tools, platforms and related software. The second tier comprises a slew of companies skilled in the use of these technologies, and specialized in specific sectors. To succeed they need to know the business and market dynamics of their clients' industry.

Needless to add that there is considerable shortage of talent and managerial competencies to exploit the full potential of analytics. Various studies suggest that only a small proportion of companies are using consumer analytics/big data for decision making purposes. Organizations that have made progress are also facing considerable challenges as they strive to derive insight from the variety and volume of the digital consumer data they have access to.

Applications

Nowadays digital data on consumers is ubiquitous, and there are many ways this data is being used to generate valuable insights. Some of the sectors that have progressed most in their use of consumer analytics are listed below:

- Fast moving consumer goods (FMCG) manufacture and retail — brand management, category management, supply chain management, operations. Data sources include — loyalty panels, consumer panels, social graphics, browsing behaviour and geographic information system (GIS) data.
- Digital Media — advertising targeting, website optimization, usage analysis and optimization.
- Conventional Media — advertising targeting, media optimization. (Data sources — media panels, single source data).
- Financial Services — management of brands, products and services; customer relationship management (CRM); credit and risk management.
- Telecommunication service providers — management of brands, products and services; CRM.
- e-Commerce.
- Travel and Leisure.
- Energy and Utilities.

- Gaming/Gambling — segmenting customers and differentiating customer experiences, fraud analysis.
- Government/Public Sector.
- Medicine, Life Sciences — research and discovery based on drug usage analysis.

In general, the applications of consumer analytics serve the objective to enhance customer satisfaction by imparting greater value. They are fairly diverse, though, and vary considerably across industry sectors.

The following examples are intended to illustrate the diversity of applications across two sectors — retailing and credit card services.

Example — Retailer Applications

Loyalty Marketing

Loyalty marketing is the process of utilising customer data to retain and profitably grow existing customers.

It is established on the loyalty paradigm — loyal customers greatly contribute to profits because keeping customers is considerably less expensive than acquiring new ones. The longer they remain loyal, the more they spend and the more profit they generate.

Loyalty marketing is targeted marketing, often through the use of incentives. Statistical analytic techniques are deployed to craft market segments. The typical metrics used include spend per month, frequency of shopping, segments/categories shopped, etc.

When used as a targeted *advertising and promotions medium* for suppliers, the loyalty panel affords the retailer the opportunity to earn revenue as media owner. Using consumer analytics, retailers and their suppliers can finely tune and target marketing messages and promotions to consumers based on their buying behaviour.

Category Management

Consumer analytics is used in category management in numerous ways to optimize the elements of the retailing mix including use of space, promotions and in-store activities and shelf price. It empowers retailers and their suppliers with insights on how to improve category and brand performance in their stores. (The subject is covered in detail in Chapter 22, *Category Management*).

House Brand Management

Consumer analytics may be used to improve the health and performance of house brands. Insights gleaned from the analysis of the data help retailers effectively employ house brands to differentiate their banner, generate shopper loyalty and grow their overall business.

Store Management

Consumer analytics may be used to improve store performance, optimize store count and effectively manage a portfolio of stores. Location of stores may be optimized based on the movement and buying behaviour of target customers tracked via geographical information systems (GIS).

Internet Marketing/e-Commerce

Web analytics, the analysis of the browsing and interaction behaviour of internet users, helps retailers engage customers by bringing personalized offers and relevant products to their attention while on site. For example, NetFlix and Amazon use algorithm-fuelled recommendations ("Customers who bought this also bought ...") to drive sales and improve customers' on-site experience.

Web analytics can help to enhance traffic to website, improve conversion rates and other performance parameters, and evaluate effectiveness of elements of the marketing mix. More information on web analytics is provided in Chapter 14, *Digital Marketing.*

Example — Credit Card Service Applications

Customer Relationship Management

The application areas of customer analytics (including web analytics) in CRM are vast, covering almost every aspect of the CRM process. Broadly speaking, customer analytics empowers issuers with the insights to strengthen their relationship with card holders and increase their card loyalty.

Card Management

Customer analytics can be used very effectively to enhance the performance of cards, and improve the management of a portfolio of cards. A typical *Card Health Barometer* would encompass many analytic-based metrics ranging from usage, spend, demographics and segmentation, loyalty measures, importance measures, financial measures, and a host of special analysis.

Evaluation of Marketing Initiatives

Continuous transaction data helps to effectively track the impact of marketing initiatives over time to provide an assessment of their full impact.

Promotions Evaluation

Market modelling techniques (refer to Chapter 18, *Market Mix Modelling*) are used to evaluate promotions and improve promo plans.

New Launch Evaluation

Customer analytic techniques can forecast usage of a new card, soon after its launch. The launch can also be assessed in terms of sources of growth, extent it cannibalizes other cards, build-up of loyalty and a host of other metrics. In the context of a portfolio of cards, these measures help assess the full costs and benefits of the new card.

Trade Analysis

Customer analytics based trade analysis helps card issuers understand the potential across trade sectors and retail chains. It helps them position cards within their portfolio so that each has unique strengths across sectors and appeals to distinct customer segments. It helps ensure initiatives are better aligned with merchants' strengths and weaknesses, and their customers' preferences.

Reward Programmes

Customer analytics can help evaluate and refine reward programmes so that they are more effective in achieving their goal of increasing card usage and building customer loyalty.

CASE II

Vizag

Exhibit C2.1 Lalitaji, a hard-headed bargain-hunting housewife, was created in reponse to the threat from discount detergent powders, to communicate Surf's value proposition.

The launch into test market of Ariel detergent powder in Vizag, in September 1990 triggered an intense marketing war. The Indian fabric wash market, a major Unilever stronghold, was then worth well over US$1 billion. P&G had entered India in the mid-80s with the acquisition of Richardson Hindustan Limited, and after years of preparation, launched Ariel as its first offensive on Unilever's turf.

Note: Though it is dated, this remains an ideal case on the application of consumer panel data. It is not, however, intended to illustrate effective or ineffective handling of business situations or processes.

The Indian Fabric Wash market in the early 1990s was relatively traditional, almost equally split between detergent powder, detergent bar and the relatively archaic, low cost laundry soap. There was no liquid detergent and prior to the launch of Ariel and Hindustan Lever's Triple Power Rin, there were no concentrates in this vast 900 million people market. Hindustan Lever (HLL) with 3 power brands Rin, Surf and Wheel, had cornered almost 40% of the market. Its nearest rival was a local manufacturer, Nirma, with over 30% market share.

During this period, the penetration of washing machines in India was extremely low. In almost all homes clothes were bucket washed (i.e. soaked overnight in detergent powder and washed by hand). Detergent bars (and in Northern India laundry soaps) were used to remove stains and manually scrub dirt out from shirt collars and other heavily soiled parts of clothing.

The industrial town and sea port of Vishakapatnam, Vizag for short, was once a fishing village. In the early 1990s with a population of about half a million, it was known for its shipyard, steel plant, and other heavy industries. Like most of urban southern India, Vizag was a relatively progressive detergents market where consumers were receptive to new product forms and traditional laundry soaps were no longer in use.

The advent of concentrates coupled with P&G's market entry was of huge significance for HLL. At stake was the large, fast growing Indian fabric wash market. HLL needed to protect its highly lucrative cash cows — Rin, Surf and Wheel. And importantly this was the first time the two global giants were facing one another head-on in India.

Surf dominated the premium segment in detergent powders. The brand's key message centred on performance ("washes whitest"). In advertising, it was the era of Lalitaji (Exhibit C2.1), a hard-headed bargain-hunting housewife who demanded value for money and not just cheap price. Her message — it makes better sense to buy a product that offers good quality and performance, as opposed to something that is cheap ("Sasti cheez or achchi cheez me farak hota hai, bhai saab" ... "there's a difference between cheap and good quality"). In 1990 Surf was perceived as the most powerful and best quality detergent, a position that concentrate powders were about to challenge.

Much like Surf in powder, Rin dominated the premium detergent bar market, and in the 1990s it contributed more to HLL's bottom line than any other brand. In that concentrates possessed greater stain and grime removal properties than conventional powders, there was concern that the use of bars would decline with the growth and development of concentrate powders.

Ariel Microsystem was the first concentrate or compact detergent powder to be launched into India. Like Surf its key message centred on performance ("removes stains as well as tough and stubborn dirt"). The initial ads communicated the wisdom of selecting a superior product that was cost effective on a per-wash basis, despite its high price. When launched into test market, Ariel was technologically superior to any existing product in the Indian detergent market. In addition to being the first among concentrates, it was also the only product to use enzymes as active ingredient for superior detection and removal of stains.

HLL's reaction to the test marketing of Ariel was swift and strong. A fighter brand, Rin Concentrated Powder, later renamed Triple Power Rin (TPR), was launched in Vizag and some other cities. Scientists at HLL's research centre intensified efforts to develop competing concentrate powders using indigenous ingredients. An in-house consumer panel of over a thousand households was set-up in Vizag, within two months of the introduction of Ariel. The launch was extensively studied and research conducted during this period provides a fine example of the use of consumer panels in analysing the advent of a new product form.

Case Analysis

Based on the research findings provided in Exhibits C2.2 to C2.12, address the following questions that were uppermost on the minds of the detergent brand managers at HLL:
- How significant is the demand for concentrates?

- What's the impact of concentrates on the demand for detergent powder and detergent bar?
- To what extent would it change wash habits?
- How cost effective are concentrate powders?
- What's the impact on Unilever, other players?

Recommend what course of action HLL should take to confront the challenges posed by the concentrates.

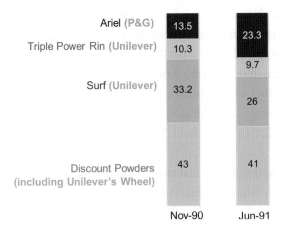

Exhibit C2.2   Value share for detergent powders for Nov-90 and Jun-91.

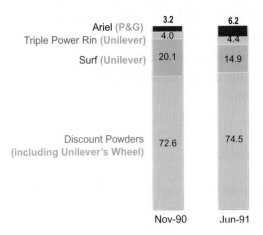

Exhibit C2.3   Volume share for detergent powders for Nov-90 and Jun-91.

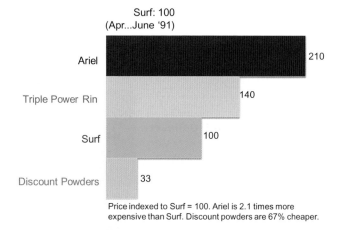

Surf: 100
(Apr...June '91)

Ariel — 210

Triple Power Rin — 140

Surf — 100

Discount Powders — 33

Price indexed to Surf = 100. Ariel is 2.1 times more
expensive than Surf. Discount powders are 67% cheaper.

Exhibit C2.4 Price index (Surf:100).

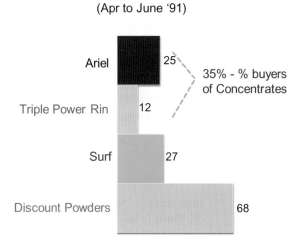

% Buyers
(Apr to June '91)

Ariel — 25

35% - % buyers
of Concentrates

Triple Power Rin — 12

Surf — 27

Discount Powders — 68

Exhibit C2.5 %Buyers – Apr to Jun-91. 25% of Vizag households bought
Ariel during the period Apr to Jun-91, compared to 12% who bought TPR.

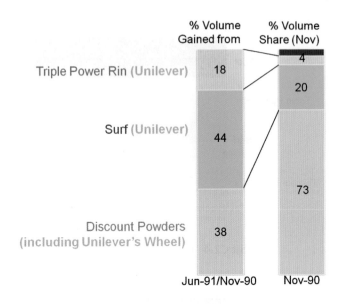

	% Volume Gained from	% Volume Share (Nov)
Triple Power Rin (Unilever)	18	4
		20
Surf (Unilever)	44	
		73
Discount Powders (including Unilever's Wheel)	38	
	Jun-91/Nov-90	Nov-90

Exhibit C2.6   Source of growth of Ariel Jun-91/Nov-90 (in powders). Gain–loss analysis examines household purchases over two time periods to determine the amount of business each brand has gained from each other brand. This analysis reveals the source of growth of Ariel, i.e. which brands are being cannibalised by Ariel and to what extent. The data tells us that 18% of the growth of Ariel over Jun-91/Nov-90 emanates from TPR, and that TPR's share in the market is 4%.

Gains From	(Nov..Jun) % Gain	% Vol Share (Nov 90)	% Vol Share (Jun 91)	Growth Jun/Nov
Ariel		3.2	6.2	78.3%
Triple Power Rin	18	4.0	4.4	1.1%
Surf	44	20.1	14.9	-31.4%
Other Powders	38	72.6	74.5	-4.8%
Total Powders	100	100	100	
Powders	90	52		
Bars	10	48		

Exhibit C2.7   Source of growth of Ariel. Gain–loss Jun-91/Nov-90.

Detergent Powder and Bar: Volume Index

Index (Nov = 100)

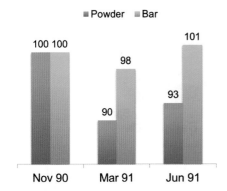

	Nov 90	Mar 91	Jun 91
Volume (tons)	292	273	282
Powder (%)	56	54	54
Bar (%)	44	46	46
Index (Nov=100)	100	93	96
Powder (%)	100	90	93
Bar (%)	100	98	101
Consumption (gm/HHLD)			
Powder + Bar	1,989	1,859	1,917
Powder	1,116	1,007	1,035

Note: Consumption refers to purchases measured as gm / month

Exhibit C2.8   Market structure in terms of volume (tons) and consumption (i.e. purchases in gm/month). In November, soon after concentrates were launched, the average household bought 1,116 gm of detergent powder. Later in March when concentrates achieved relatively high penetration, the average quantity of detergent powder bought per household per month dropped to about 1,000 gm. Note that "detergent power" refers to all detergent powders, including concentrates, and that June is a seasonally high month for detergent sales.

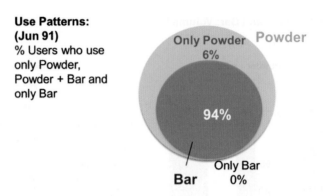

Use Patterns: (Jun 91)
% Users who use only Powder, Powder + Bar and only Bar

Exhibit C2.9   Wash habits for June 1991: All Vizag homes purchased detergent powder and 94% of them also purchased detergent bar. There are no homes that purchased only detergent bar during Jun-91.

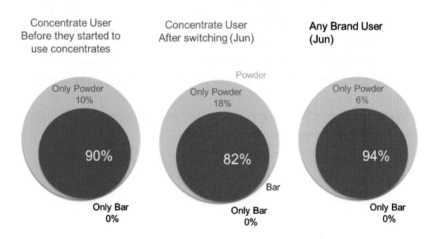

Exhibit C2.10   Wash habits: The usage of detergent powders and bars by concentrate powder buyers, before and after their purchase of concentrates.

	Ariel Buyer	Surf Buyer
Brand	380	700
Powder	740	1,000
Bar	700	750
Wash Basket (gm)	1,440	1,750
Wash Basket (Rs)	49.00	49.50
Loyalty %		
Brand/Powder	51	70
Brand/Basket	26	40

Exhibit C2.11   Wash basket analysis — consumption (purchases) gm/hhld for June-91.

A *wash basket* or *purchase basket* analysis lists out the average purchases of fabric wash products, by a specified buyer group, for a specified period. According to this exhibit, the average Ariel buyer, in the month of June '91, bought 740 gm of detergent power of which 380 gm is Ariel. She also bought 700 gm of detergent bar, and her total wash basket is 1,440 gm, costing Rs 49.

Loyalty is the share of brand purchases to total category purchases by brand buyers. According to this exhibit, 51% of total powder purchased (in weight terms) by Ariel buyers is Ariel powder. While comparing loyalty, one needs to be mindful of the fact that a kg of concentrate has greater throughput than an equivalent weight of normal detergent powder.

% Buyers	Ariel Buyers	TPR Buyers	All Buyers
Solus (use only one powder brand, no bar)	12	14	4
Combine with other powder only	5	4	2
Combine with bar only	55	63	77
Combine bar+other powder	<u>28</u>	<u>19</u>	<u>17</u>
	100	100	100

Exhibit C2.12   Wash habit — product usership (Jun-91). According to this exhibit, for Ariel Buyers, 12% of these buyers bought Ariel and no other product (solus buyers); 5% bought Ariel along with some other powder(s) and did not buy any detergent bars; 55% bought Ariel along with detergent bar(s); 28% bought Ariel with detergent bar(s) and some other detergent powder(s).

Hectomalt

As a product with great heritage experienced decline, its management is confronted with the challenge of resurrecting the brand.

Horlicks

The inspiration for this case comes from a product that traces its origins to 1873 when two brothers from England, William and James Horlicks, founded J & W Horlicks in Chicago to manufacture a patented malted milk drink as an artificial infant food. The product, over a period spanning a hundred and forty years, underwent numerous reincarnations (see Exhibit C3.1), from an infant food to a nutritious drink for adults and children, a provision for explorers and athletes, and an energy booster for soldiers. Milestones include its use as a provision

Note: This case study is prepared for use in class discussions, and it is not intended to illustrate effective or ineffective handling of business situations or processes. The details presented have been disguised, and the data has been altered.

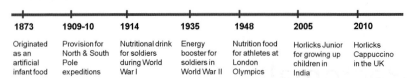

Exhibit C3.1 The Horlicks heritage *(Source: www.horlicks.co.uk/heritage).*

for the North and South Pole expeditions, as nutrition food for athletes at the 1948 London Olympics, and as rations for the British army, navy and air force.

The brand was acquired by the Beecham Group in 1969 and became part of Glaxo's portfolio when the drug giant merged with SmithKline in 2000.

Today Horlicks is popular in India, Malaysia, Singapore and the United Kingdom and is consumed by children as well as adults. In terms of categorization, it is usually placed under a category of malt beverages called health food drinks. The category consists of white drinks such as Horlicks and Complan, and brown cocoa-based drinks such as Milo, Ovaltine and Bournvita. In India where it commands over 50% of the Indian health food drink market, more than two billion cups of Horlicks are consumed annually.

Hectomalt

Owned by Hecto Corporation, a global packaged foods conglomerate, Hectomalt a nutritious malted milk drink grew rapidly during the first half of the 20th century when malnourishment was a global concern. It served the need for affordable nourishment and hunger assuagement during the difficult years of the Great Depression, and the two World Wars.

Over the latter half of the 20th century, the world economy grew strong, global per capita food production increased substantially, and the vast majority of the world's population acquired the means to consume safe and nutritious food in sufficient quantities to meet their dietary needs. In many of the nations where Hectomalt had grown to become a legendary brand, obesity, not hunger, is the concern

nowadays. In these countries people no longer want to put on weight, they want to lose it.

As consumer needs changed Hectomalt was seen to be aging, and it started losing its relevance to consumers in many key markets. The brand's positioning was accordingly refined. In some countries it was positioned as a nourishing bedtime drink that relaxes and makes you sleep and feel better.

While living standards have improved substantially, hunger and poverty still linger in large parts of Africa and Asia, as well as in a number of other countries across the world. According to the Food and Agriculture Organization about 925 million people are chronically hungry, and 2 billion people from time to time lack food security. Particularly for these people, Hectomalt continues to serve as an affordable source of nourishment and hunger assuagement.

Hectomalt's formulation over the years had not changed significantly. It comprised mainly of wheat flour, malted barley and was fortified with a wide range of vitamins and minerals.

Malted barley is obtained through a process called "malting", where barley is germinated allowing enzymes to break down the complex sugars in the grains into simple sugars. Malt extract, a concentrated

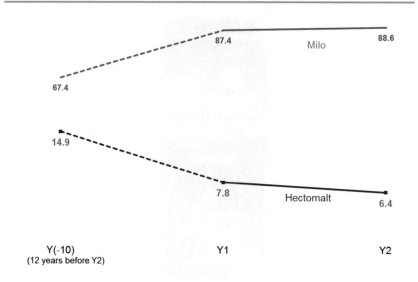

87.4   Milo   88.6

67.4

14.9

7.8   Hectomalt   6.4

Y(-10)   Y1   Y2
(12 years before Y2)

Exhibit C3.2 Volume share of Hectomalt and Milo in Joka's HFD market.

form of malt, is used to make beer, whisky, and beverages like Hectomalt, Milo and Ovaltine that are categorized under health food drinks (HFD).

Even today, the attribute that clearly distinguishes Hectomalt from its competitors, in a number of its key markets, is hunger assuagement. It comes as no surprise that the highest per capita consumption of Hectomalt is known to be in Dharavi, Mumbai. Spread over 535 acres of prime land, Dharavi with an estimated population of anywhere between 500,000 to a million residents, is one of the largest slums in the world.

Hectomalt in Joka

Joka is a small Asian country with a population of 4 million people. A developing economy in the 1950s, Joka has since transformed into a vibrant metropolis. Jokans are affluent and enjoy one of the highest living standards in Asia.

Introduced during the colonial era Hectomalt had century-old heritage in Joka and its neighbouring countries, and it enjoyed immense popularity during most of the 20th century. Towards the end of the century the brand started to experience decline, and the pace of decline accelerated over time. The erosion was reflected not only in Joka, but also in a number of other affluent markets in the region.

Exhibit C3.2 depicts the decline in Hectomalt's market volume share in Joka, from 14.9% to 6.4% over a period of 12 years. During the same period, the dominance of market leader Milo grows substantially as its share increased from 67.4% to 88.6%.

Though prior attempts to reinvigorate Hectomalt in the region helped decelerate the decline, they were unable to arrest it. These attempts included the introduction of new flavours such as Hectomalt Chocolate, as well as new formats such as a ready-to-drink cans and all-in-one sachets.

Market research revealed that the new flavours did not strengthen the brand's equity or its competitive standing. The chocolate variant was pitched against powerful cocoa-based brands like Milo and Ovaltine. Consumers of these brands did not associate Hectomalt with the chocolate segment, and were reluctant to try the chocolate variant. Though the new flavours offered existing Hectomalt consumers greater choice, the true face of the Hectomalt brand remained the "original" variant.

As Hectomalt's regional leadership reflected on the past, they realized the need for clarity in understanding the issues affecting the brand's growth, and in identifying its opportunities and threats. Piecemeal solutions had not worked. As the brand's share plunged to 6.4%, the urgency to reinvigorate the brand was greater than ever before. With the goal to chalk out the strategy to breathe new life into their precious but aging brand, they called for a strategy meet, inviting key company associates and business partners from marketing, market research, advertising and R&D.

Joka, despite its small population, is one of the more significant markets for Hectomalt. It is also a country where the Hectomalt team has access to rich sources of market intelligence through a variety of research services including retail measurement, consumer panel and customized research. In preparation for the strategy meet, Hectomalt's

Exhibit C3.3   Questions confronting the market research team.

research agency, Newton Research has been tasked to seek answers from the market intelligence in Joka, to two fundamental questions:

1.   What are the reasons for the decline of Hectomalt?
2.   What are the opportunities for reviving Hectomalt?

Central to the resurrection strategy is the need to craft the new avatar of Hectomalt, one that is of greater relevance to consumers, well differentiated from competition, and consistent with Hectomalt's core values.

Hectomalt's Marketing Mix

To address the task posed by Hectomalt's management, associates at Newton Research sought answers to the following questions:

1.   What is plaguing Hectomalt? Is it price, place, promotion or product? (Exhibit C3.3).
2.   Is Hectomalt relevant to today's consumers?
3.   Where have the Hectomalt drinkers gone?

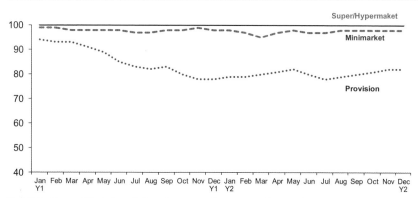

Exhibit C3.4 Weighted distribution of Hectomalt in Joka. Weighted distribution is the proportion of stores handling product weighted by *health food drinks* sales. The weights in this exhibit are computed in value terms.

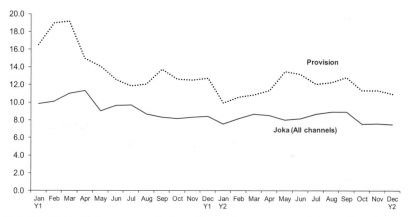

Exhibit C3.5 Volume share in handlers of Hectomalt in Joka and in the provision stores channel. Share in handlers is the share of sales (in *value* terms) within the stores carrying the product.

Place

Health food drinks are essentially sold in three channels in Joka — supermarkets/hypermarkets, minimarkets and provision stores.

There are about a hundred supermarkets, and three hypermarkets in Joka. Collectively they constitute 78% of sales of HFD.

In terms of floor space minimarkets are usually less than half the size of supermarkets, and they have no more than two checkout

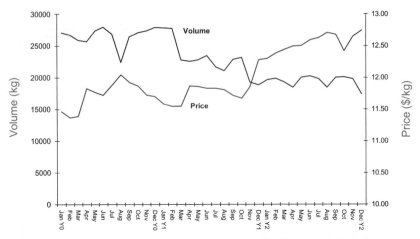

Exhibit C3.6   Trend in price and volume for Hectomalt in Joka.

counters. There are approximately 250 such outlets contributing 15% of HFD sales.

The remaining 7% share of trade emanates from a large base of about 1,500 traditional provision stores. The channel comprises small, family owned stores that lack modern technologies like scanners, and are declining in importance of sales of HFD and other grocery products.

The weighted distribution of Hectomalt is provided in Exhibit C3.4. As can be gauged from this exhibit, in Y2, Hectomalt had 100% distribution in the supermarket/hypermarket channel and close to 100% distribution in the minimarkets. In the provision channel, however, distribution declined from about 94% in Jan Y1 to about 82% in Dec Y2.

The volume share in handlers (Exhibit C3.5) revealed that Hectomalt share within handlers in the provision channel had declined from about 15% at the start of Y1 to 10% at the end of Y2.

Price

Exhibit C3.6 depicts the trend in sales volume and price of Hectomalt in Joka. Based on econometric modelling of weekly scan data, Newton Research came to the conclusion that Hectomalt was price sensitive with estimated price elasticity of demand of -2.3. The model also revealed that given its price elasticity and its price at the end of Y2, a reduction in price would yield an increase in the brand's profitability only if Hectomalt's gross margin was greater than 30%. It was also known that, based on its cost structure in Y2, Hectomalt's gross margin at that time was 25%.

Advertising and Brand Image

Hectomalt's brand management team believe that children are the key influencers of brand choice, but mothers need to be persuaded on the nutritional value and benefits. While it is essential that the brand connects strongly with the aspirations, tastes and preferences of children, it is equally important to target mothers via credible nutritional claims that differentiate the brand from competitor products.

The brand's advertising with its slogan "Taller, Stronger, Sharper" was intended to target children and their mothers and engage them through inspiring children centric messages.

The brand image profile of Hectomalt and Milo depicted in Exhibit C3.7, was obtained from a quantitative research study conducted in Y2. There were indications from this research, that the brand's advertising had low impact. Hectomalt's spend on advertising was low, and its share of spend amounted to about 10% in Y2.

Data sourced from Newton's consumer panel (Exhibit C3.8) provided information on Hectomalt's and Milo's demographic profile.

Product

Jokans consumed a wide range of beverages cutting across categories which delivered a similar set of benefits — energy, nourishment, refreshment, health and so on. As such boundaries between HFD and adjacent categories like growing up milk, tea and coffee were blurred.

Exhibit C3.9, Hectomalt's purchase basket, depicts the Hectomalt buyers' repertoire of brands/categories. Exhibit C3.10 provides the break-up of volume of purchases by Hectomalt consumers, across categories and products.

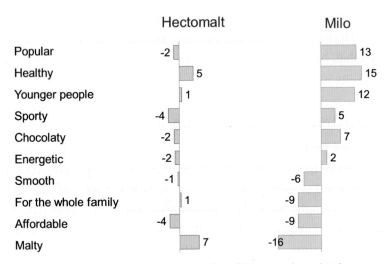

Exhibit C3.7   Brand Image profile of Hectomalt and Milo.

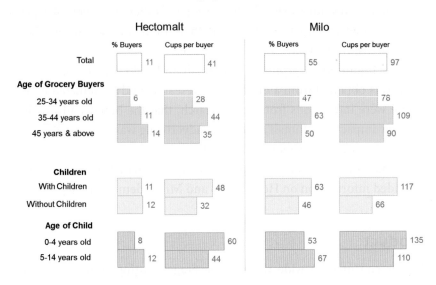

Exhibit C3.8   Demographic profile of Hectomalt and Milo, for Jul–Dec Y2.

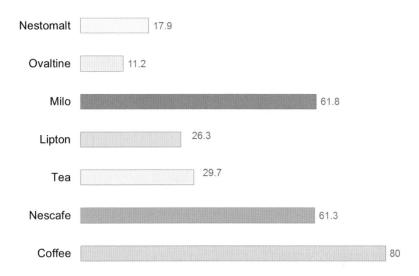

Exhibit C3.9 Purchase basket (%Buyers), Jul–Dec Y2 — products bought by Hectomalt buyers.

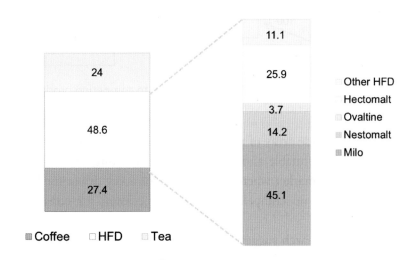

Exhibit C3.10 Purchase basket (Volume %), for Jul–Dec Y2 — break-up of volume of purchases by Hectomalt buyers across categories and HFD brands.

Exhibit C3.11 Gain–loss analysis of Hectomalt in health food drinks, for the full year period Y2 versus Y1.

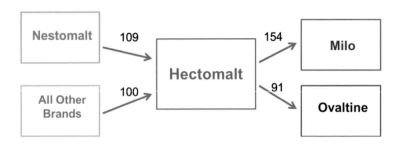

Exhibit C3.12 Net gain–loss ($'000) of Hectomalt to competing products within HFD, for the period Y2 versus Y1.

Amidst this wide array of products Hectomalt appeared vulnerable. It was easily substitutable and did not possess a strong unique selling proposition. In a market where hunger was not a key driver for brand choice, there was no compelling reason or occasion for consuming Hectomalt.

Qualitative research suggested that Hectomalt appeared to be aging and lacked dynamism. The brand was perceived to be boring and not innovative. It was seen to lack visibility, and key brand messages were not registering with consumers.

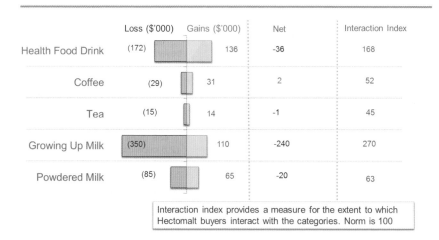

	Loss ($'000)	Gains ($'000)	Net	Interaction Index
Health Food Drink	(172)	136	-36	168
Coffee	(29)	31	2	52
Tea	(15)	14	-1	45
Growing Up Milk	(350)	110	-240	270
Powdered Milk	(85)	65	-20	63

> Interaction index provides a measure for the extent to which Hectomalt buyers interact with the categories. Norm is 100

Exhibit C3.13 Gain–loss analysis of Hectomalt across adjacent categories, for the period Y2 versus Y1.

Hectomalt was also perceived to have distinctive taste — consumers either loved it or hated it. Cocoa-based HFDs like Milo and Ovaltine on the other hand were perceived as uniformly tasty and delivered an enjoyable sensorial experience for the majority of consumers.

Where Have the Hectomalt Drinkers Gone?

The brand management team believed that the erosion of Hectomalt was primarily due to cocoa based HFDs like Milo and Ovaltine. In particular the high negative correlation between Milo's and Hectomalt's market share (Exhibit C3.2) led the team to believe that Milo's aggressive marketing campaigns were impacting Hectomalt sales.

There was also the realization that category boundaries in beverages were porous and there was some concern that the growing up milk category, which emerged in Joka about 20 years ago, might have encroached into the HFD market in general and Hectomalt's business in particular.

To ascertain the true nature of cannibalization of Hectomalt, the team at Newton Research conducted gain–loss analysis of the brand

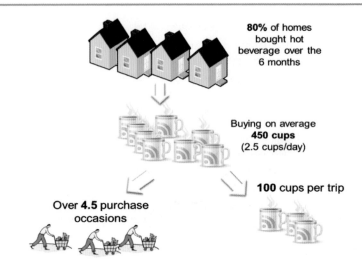

Exhibit C3.14 Hot beverage shopping in Joka, for the period Jul–Dec Y2.

within HFD. The analysis was repeated within a broader spectrum of beverage categories.

Findings from these analyses are provided in Exhibits C3.11, C3.12 and C3.13. Exhibit C3.11 revealed Hectomalt's losses to brands within HFD, and Exhibit C3.13 revealed Hectomalt's losses to adjacent categories, and its interaction with these categories.

It was observed from Exhibit C3.11, which categorizes the gains and losses within HFD, that a large proportion of Hectomalt's loss was due to *market contraction* and *lost category buyers*. Many of the consumers who cut down on Hectomalt consumption, also cut down on HFD consumption. This despite the fact that HFD sales in total were growing by 4.4%.

Hot Beverage

The hot beverage portfolio comprises three categories — coffee, tea and HFD. As can be seen from Exhibit C3.14, 80% of Jokans bought hot beverage over Jul–Dec Y2. On average they purchased 450 cups during the 6 months, over 4.5 purchase occasions, buying 100 cups per purchase occasion.

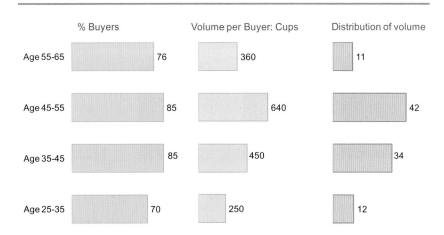

Exhibit C3.15 Hot beverage buying behaviour across age profile of the household grocery shopper, Jul–Dec Y2.

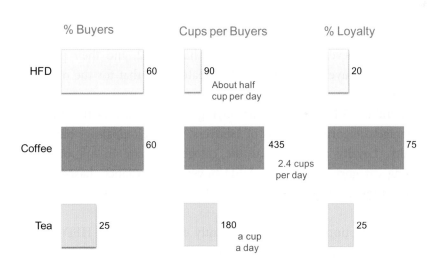

Exhibit C3.16 Hot beverage buying behaviour, Jul–Dec Y2 — width and depth of consumption, loyalty.

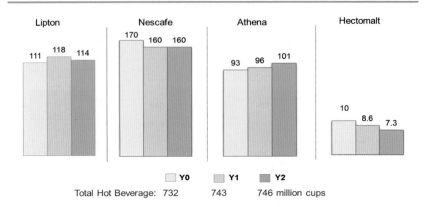

Exhibit C3.17 Sales volume in million cups of major brands in hot beverage market.

The analysis of hot beverage buying behaviour in Exhibit C3.15, across the age profile of shoppers, reveals that households where the grocery buyer is 45 to 55 years old contribute the greatest proportion to hot beverage purchases in Joka. A higher proportion of these homes bought hot beverage over the second half of Y2, and their purchase volume per buyer was substantially greater than that for the other age groups.

Exhibit C3.16 compares the buying behaviour across the three hot beverage categories in terms of %buyers, volume (cups) per buyer and loyalty. Loyalty is defined as the category's share in hot beverages among category buyers. For HFD buyers, for instance, based on the data, HFD purchases account for 20% of their total hot beverage purchases.

Consumption of coffee significantly exceeds that for HFD or Tea. Sixty percent of Jokans bought coffee during Jul–Dec Y2, and they consumed about 2.4 cups per day.

Jokans consumed about 746 million cups of hot beverage during Y2 compared to 743 million cups in Y1 (Exhibit C3.17). The 3 mega brands, Lipton, Nescafe and Milo, account for a little over 50% of the market.

In the context of the total hot beverage market, Hectomalt is a niche brand with a market share that has declined to less than 1% in Y2.

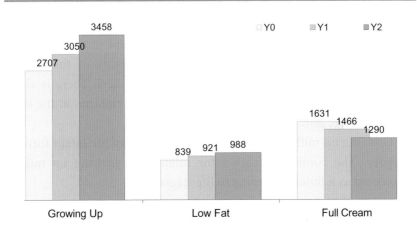

Exhibit C3.18 Powdered milk categories market size (tons) – growing up milk, low fat and full cream milk.

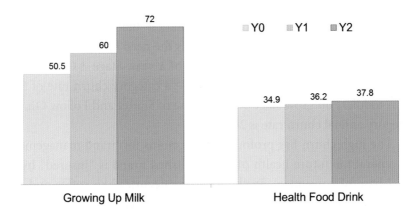

Exhibit C3.19 Health food drink and growing up milk market size ($M).

Growing Up Milk

Growing up milks (GUM) is a relatively young category that came into existence in Joka about 20 years back. It comprises of specially formulated powdered milk products, primarily for toddlers in the age group of one to three years.

The GUM category has grown rapidly since its inception, and, as can be seen from Exhibits C3.18 and C3.19, it is now much larger than other powdered milks and HFDs. The vast majority of this market comprises of drinks for one to three-year-old toddlers. There is also a small segment that comprises products for young children in the three to six-years age group.

Growing up milks are essentially an extension of the infant formula category. The combined market for infant and growing up milk is segmented as follows, according to life stages:

- Stage 1 – Starter: 0 to 6 months
- Stage 2 – Follow On: 6 to 12 months
- Stage 3 – Growing Up: 1 to 3 year old
- Stage 4 – Growing Up: 3 to 6 years old

A defining characteristic of this market that emerges from the segmentation based on the age of child, is the need for constant renewal of the consumer base. Over the course of a year, Stage 3 Growing Up milks lose half of their consumer base — a category churn rate of 50% — as toddlers outgrow stage 3. In the case of Starter and Follow On, the category annual churn rate is 200%.

The high churn has profound implications for brand management. In general the future health of an established brand is "insured" by its loyal base of consumers. In the case of categories like coffee and tea, provided market dynamics do not impact their brand loyalty, big brands can rely on consumption by their loyal consumers for decades, if not a lifetime. That growing up milk and infant formula brands are deprived of their loyal consumers as they grow from one life stage to another, makes them vulnerable to competition.

Manufacturers contain the downside of the churn rate by developing strong umbrella branding that cuts across the life stages. For instance Mead Johnson's range of milks includes Enfalac starter formula, Enfamil follow on formula, and Enfagrow growing up milk that comes in two versions — stage 3 and stage 4.

Mead Johnson also has a mother's supplement called EnfaMama which is positioned as "a nutritional milk supplement formulated to support nutritional needs of a mother and developing baby during pregnancy and later, throughout lactation". EnfaMama allows the Enfa brand to achieve some salience in the minds of mothers, even before her baby is born. This is of relevance in markets like Joka where advertising of starter formulas is not permitted by governments as they strive to promote breastfeeding.

Growing Up Milk Benefits

GUMs are fortified with vitamins and minerals that manufacturers claim aid their mental and physical development. Products may contain ingredients such as AA (arachidonic acid), DHA (docosahexaenoic acid), lutein, choline, taurine and nucleotides. Some quasi medical facts that GUM manufacturers claim about these substances are listed below:

- AA and DHA are polyunsaturated fatty acids which occur naturally in breast milk. They are found throughout the body, particularly in the brain and retina. AA is a precursor to substances called eicosanoids that play a role in immunity and blood clotting. DHA is associated with better visual development.
- Lutein is a carotenoid with antioxidant properties that can be obtained from breast milk, leafy vegetables and egg yolks. It collects in the eyes and protects them from oxidative damage. It may also protect the eye by absorbing blue light, which is high in energy and can harm the retina.
- Choline is required in the production of neurotransmitters (chemical messengers) which relay information between nerve cells.
- Taurine may have a role in supporting normal vision and hearing development.
- Nucleotides are biological molecules that are the building blocks of DNA (nuclei acids) and RNA (ribonucleic acid).

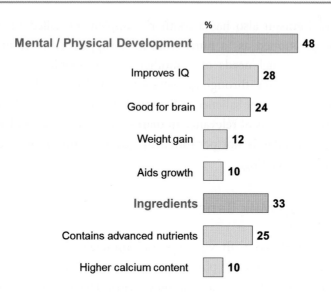

Exhibit C3.20 Reasons for switching to growing up milk (quantitative research) — "What were your reasons for switching to growing up milk?"

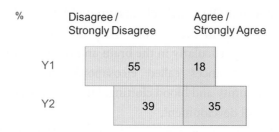

Exhibit C3.21 Price perception (quantitative research) — "Higher price means better quality".

> They are required for the proper functioning of the immune system and aid recovery from diarrhoea, liver-related illness and stress.

Research findings suggest that mothers tend to be influenced by benefit claims about the ingredients (Exhibit C3.20), particularly if the products are endorsed by paediatricians. They are well informed about

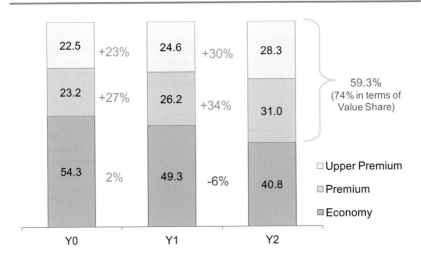

Exhibit C3.22 Growing up milk market volume break-up across price segments.

nutritional aspects of growing up milks and, based on a market research study, associate higher price with better quality (Exhibit C3.21).

Mothers are not prepared to compromise on what many of them believe forms the foundation for their toddler's future. Improved, more expensive GUM products launched into the Joka market in Y1 and Y2 performed well leading to high growth of the *premium* and *upper premium* price segments (Exhibit C3.22). The share of these two segments in value terms reached 74% in Y2, and the average price of GUM products increased by 5.5% and 5.8% over Y1 and Y2. The average price per kg of growing up milk in Y2 was $20.80 compared with $10.47 for health food drink and $12.54 for Hectomalt.

Hectomalt and Growing Up Milks

Consumer panel based analysis provided in Exhibit C3.23, depicts the overlap between Hectomalt and the GUM category, within families with children aged below 10 years. Seventy percent of Hectomalt buyers in this demographic group purchased one or more GUM products during Y2.

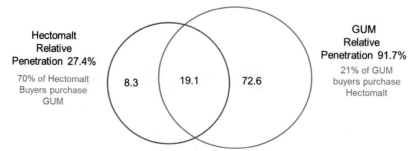

Y2
Base: young/mixed family
(Families with one or more
child aged below 10 years)

Note:
16.5% of young/mixed families buy Hectomalt
and/or GUM :
Penetration = 16.5% (rebased to 100)
Relative penetration =100%

Hectomalt
Relative
Penetration 27.4%

70% of Hectomalt
Buyers purchase
GUM

8.3   19.1   72.6

GUM
Relative
Penetration 91.7%

21% of GUM
buyers purchase
Hectomalt

Exhibit C3.23   Overlap analysis for young families, for Y2, in terms of %buyers.

The level of interaction with the GUM category is also reflected in the gain–loss analysis of Hectomalt in Exhibit C3.13.

Re-inventing Hectomalt

In preparation for the strategy meeting called by Hectomalt's regional leadership team, associates at Newton Research pored over the research findings to gauge the underlying factors leading to the brand's decline, and considered various opportunities for reviving Hectomalt. Reflecting on the recommendations they needed to make to revitalize this aging brand, they realized that more than any piecemeal solution, Hectomalt needed to evolve into a product that had greater relevance to today's target consumers.

PART III

Product

CHAPTER 9

New Product Development

Preview

"They always say time changes things, but you actually have to change them yourself." —Andy Warhol.

In a fast changing world, companies must innovate or face extinction. Yet while new products are essential for survival, they do demand high investments and pose great risks, with uncertainties lingering at all stages of development and launch of products. Numerous studies highlight the high incidence of failure of new initiatives, particularly in

FMCG where failure rates quoted by various sources vary from 75% to as high as 95%. In business markets too, high risks prevail — it is estimated that roughly one in three business-to-business (B2B) products fail.

As such marketers are confronted by two opposing risks associated with product development: investment risk and opportunity risk. In financial terms, the former is the risk of investment losses should a new product fail, and the latter is the risk of losing the opportunity of revenue and profit that a product might have generated, had it not been shelved. Innovative firms tend to focus on opportunity risk while non-innovative firms tend to focus on investment risk. Irrespective of their orientation, to mitigate these risks, marketers need to be data and research driven.

This chapter imparts an understanding of product development by elaborating on the NPD process. The topics covered include innovation, ideation, knowledge immersion, consumer immersion, generation of insights, generation of ideas, concept development, product development and product launch.

Change

"That's one small step for man ... one giant leap for mankind" — *Neil Armstrong.*

A boy once sat on the floor among fellow students at his teacher's home and watched Neil Armstrong step out of Apollo 11. The 20th of July 1969 would go down in history as the day man first stepped on the surface of the moon. For the boy, it was the day he first watched TV.

On the foothills of the outer Himalayas, playing was essentially an outdoor experience. The environment was not his concern. The boy had fresh air to breathe and the great Himalayan ranges as his backdrop. His thoughts were aroused more by hearsay of the presence of leopards in the vicinity, than the ozone layer, a subject he knew nothing about.

His was a life without little luxuries like shampoo, facial tissue, tea bags or calculators. Multiplication tables were memorized. Electricity could not be taken for granted.

In many of the villages where most Indians lived, learning was paperless. It was the age of the qalam (a pen made from bamboo), the takhti (a flat wooden board similar in size to a laptop screen) and the dawaat (ink). Students would dip their qalam in a bottle of dawaat and write on the takhti. They would wash and clean the takhti after school so that it would be ready for use the next day — and their moms would scrub the smudges of dawaat on their hands and clothes.

For the boy, however, pen and paper was a luxury that he took for granted. It was also his means of communication with his mom and dad. But the weekly letters he wrote in class at his boarding school would not always reach the intended destination. The boy was not particularly good at jotting down the numbers in the address, in the correct sequence. And his mom, who was prone to worrying, got into the habit of checking her neighbours' mail boxes. Rotary dial phones were a rarity then, as they are now, in India's capital.

New Delhi at that time a relatively sleepy city; its empty roads would transform into a sea of bicycles at 5 pm. Being skinny wasn't fashionable, as it is now, yet people were thin. Presumably cycling, food shortages and poverty kept people in shape.

Those mornings, the beautiful lush green parks that Delhi is renowned for, exuded a serene, almost deserted aura. A quarter century later, the same parks teem with portly people, walking furiously to shed triglycerides. Cycles had been displaced by scooters in the mid-1970s and '80s, and nowadays there is the perpetual glut of cars choking roads and depleting ozone.

For better or for worse our world never stops changing. The number of bicycles, takhtis, and lanterns has since declined sharply, and so too has the population of leopards (or, for that matter orang-utans, in other parts of the world). Indeed, in less than four decades, little remains of the way of life that the boy was accustomed to.

Innovation

"Here's to the crazy ones. The misfits. The rebels. The troublemakers. The round pegs in the square holes. The ones who see things differently. They're not fond of rules. And they have no respect for the status quo. You can quote them, disagree with them, glorify or vilify them. But the only thing you can't do is ignore them. Because they change things. They push the human race forward. And while some may see them as the crazy ones, we see genius. Because the people who are crazy enough to think they can change the world, are the ones who do". —Apple Inc.

Innovation is invention in commercial use. Edison, for instance, did not *invent* the light bulb; there were others before him who pioneered incandescent bulbs. Thomas Edison and his team of scientists were the *innovators* who made it practical to use light bulbs.

Looking back, as I have done over the decades, reinforces how our lives have been influenced by innovations. In the midst of today's digital era we observe how every sector, whether agriculture, manufacturing, transportation, retail, education or finance, is being shaped by digital technology. As the human race relentlessly moves forward, business leaders recognize the need to innovate and make a conscious choice to do so.

One way of categorizing innovation is in terms of scale. *Incremental Innovation* results in small improvements to the existing design of a product. *Radical Innovation*, on the other hand, yields major enhancements in the performance and functioning of a product. When an innovation is so radical it creates products that deliver a different type of value, it is called a *Breakthrough Innovation*.

Another approach to categorization is on the basis of the impact that an innovation has on existing technologies. *Disruptive Innovation*, a term coined by Clayton Christensen, describes "a process by which a product or service takes root initially in simple applications at the bottom of a market and then relentlessly moves up market, eventually displacing established competitors". *Sustaining Innovation* on the other

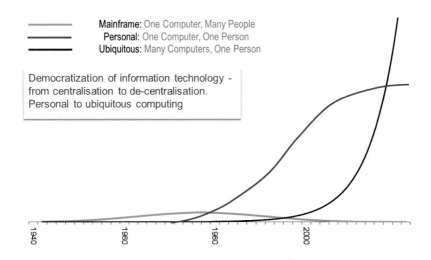

Exhibit 9.1 Illustration of the disruptive changes in the computer industry *(Adapted from a presentation by Mark Weiser/PARC titled "Nomadic Issues in Ubiquitous Computing").*

hand improves on the existing dominant technology to produce offerings that better serve the needs of existing customers. It can be incremental or radical, yet it remains on the same technology vector.

The computer industry is an apt example of a sector that has experienced wave after wave of disruptions, from mainframes to mini-computers, to desktop computers, laptops and smart phones. In half a century, our world moved from virtually no computers, to the "one computer, many people" phase, followed by "one computer, one person", before heading to the age of ubiquitous computing — "many computers, one person" (see Exhibit 9.1).

While popularly perceived in terms of the product dimension, innovation in reality is broad based and cuts across all elements of the mix. Experiences are transformed not only by products or services, but also by the way they are delivered and communicated. These other elements of the mix become important means of differentiation particularly when the product matures.

Take books for instance, while we continue to read them in the form of hard copies, increasingly now, we also read them in soft versions on iPads, Kindles and laptops. We procure them from bookstores as well as from the net. More often we are learning about new titles from friends on Facebook, or authors/publishers who reach us on the net or by email, or from Amazon recommendations. And we may dispose the ones we no longer want to keep by selling them online, or, if it is a soft copy, by clicking the "Delete" button.

For businesses that face disruption, the challenge is how to pursue disruptive technology. As history bears witness technological waves can dislodge existing market leaders. According to Christensen entrenched players find it difficult to pursue disruptive technologies since their infrastructure and operations are geared toward pursuit and support of the established, mature technology. In computers for instance, leadership passed from IBM mainframes, to Digital's minis, to HP, Dell, Lenovo and others in PCs, and Apple and Samsung in smart phones.

New Product Development Process

As depicted in Exhibit 9.2, broadly, there are four phases to new product development (NPD): ideation, concept development, product development and product launch. The activities and information needs listed for each of the phases in this Exhibit are covered in detail in the succeeding sections and chapters.

From a team perspective, a cross-functional approach where some activities can progress concurrently is strongly recommended as it improves the speed-to-market. It also improves communication across departments. Manufacturing for instance needs to translate the soft descriptors they hear from marketing into hard technical specifications, and would be better equipped to do so if involved throughout the NPD process.

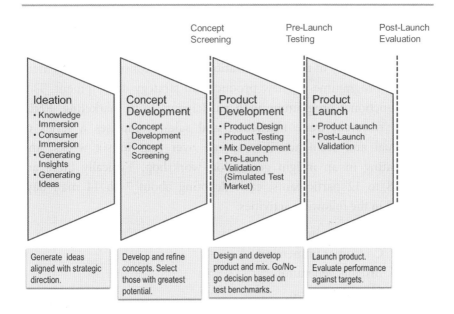

Exhibit 9.2   New product development process.

Ideation

"The real voyage of discovery consists not in seeking new landscapes ... but in having new eyes." —*Marcel Proust.*

Referred to as the fuzzy front-end of innovation, ideation is regarded by many as the most challenging stage in the innovation process.

Ideation begins with insights. Insights yield ideas, and the flow of ideas is the creative force that drives innovation. Gleaned from the tension arising from unmet needs, insights inspire innovation not only in new product development, but in all elements of the marketing mix, and at all stages of the product life cycle.

The Ideation Process

In the context of brand management, an *insight* is a realization that may be channelled to strengthen and grow the brand. It essentially emerges from a penetrating understanding of consumers.

In order, therefore, to succeed in new product development, consumer goods companies need to remain connected with their consumers. Many of these organizations adopt a consumer engagement ideation programme for new product and strategy development. This cross-functional programme with participants from marketing, R&D, market research, trade marketing and sales, comprises a series of individual and team activities spread over four to six weeks, and culminating in an insight generation workshop. Typically there are about 8 to 12 participants, each devoting about 7 to 14 man days engaged in the following activities:

(a) Knowledge immersion
(b) Consumer immersion
(c) Insights generation
(d) Ideas generation

The knowledge immersion and consumer immersion activities are undertaken individually by the participants in preparation for the workshops, where they engage within teams to generate insights and ideas.

(a) Knowledge Immersion

The objective of knowledge immersion is for marketers to understand their consumers' needs and wants, behaviours, values, beliefs and motivations. They need to be aware of the macro trends in consumers' lifestyles, shopping behaviours, and media habits. They need to understand how consumers relate to their markets and product categories, in terms of their usage and habits, and in terms of the functional, rational and emotional product qualities that drive brand choice. And they need to know how consumers relate to their brand in terms of the image that it has formed in their minds, and in terms of how they perceive its performance and benefits, and how they consume it. This understanding is vital for generating insights.

The sources commonly used for gaining the requisite knowledge about consumers are as follows:

- Company's historical knowledge base
- Secondary sources
- Social media
- Primary research

One challenge that corporations often face, is how to leverage the explicit and the tacit *historical knowledge base* that resides within their organization. This dilemma is summed up by the old German saying: "If Siemens only knew what Siemens knows". In big organizations if one seeks information, it is likely that someone else in the organization possesses it. The challenge lies in identifying and reaching that source.

To facilitate the retention and flow of knowledge, companies are developing and maintaining electronic library systems. Unilever for instance developed a knowledge management framework to categorize and pool consumer learning, in a web-based global knowledge bank that the company calls "consumer world". If well implemented, this can greatly empower associates — information that is dispersed around the globe, locked in cupboards and associates' heads, becomes available at their fingertips.

Secondary sources, accessed via the internet or the library, can be a low cost means of obtaining information in areas where gaps continue to exist.

Social media is a powerful, revealing channel for observing and engaging with consumers, particularly for categories that consumers are more involved with. It allows marketers to "listen" to *unsolicited* feedback about their market, their company and their brand from hundreds or even millions of consumers and "see" how they relate to it and how they use it. As natural language processing and text analytics technologies evolve marketers increasingly will be able to listen more efficiently to the glut of conversation on the net, and glean insights and ideas for new products. This source is particularly potent for exploratory research such as new product development, where we seek the unforeseen.

Knowledge immersion empowers associates with an understanding of their consumers that guides and directs them as they progress through the stages in the ideation process. It is an ongoing process; knowledge databanks need to be regularly reviewed and updated, and should any important intelligence gaps emerge, marketers may commission relevant primary research to fill those gaps.

(b) Consumer Immersion

Markets are constantly in a state of flux. All around us we see changes driven by powerful market trends — digitization and personal empowerment through computing and internet, emergence of the net generation and their social media, growth of glamour queens, metrosexuals and ubersexuals, health consciousness, trade modernization, fragmentation of media and so on. The need to immerse in the world of consumers is as acute as ever.

Consumer immersion is all about getting close to consumers so that associates are able to see their brands and their markets through the eyes of their consumers. They get exposed to real consumers and real issues. The main techniques used for immersion into the consumers' world include:

- Day-to-day personal experiences.
- Observing qualitative research sessions such as focus groups or interviews.
- Interviews/probing sessions with consumer.
- Accompanying consumers on their shopping trips.
- Observing consumers in their homes or some other natural setting.
- Video recording or diary maintained by participants. Proliferation of mobile video recording devices makes it feasible for participants to produce their own video recording of activities. Participants are also encouraged to relate any thoughts and emotions that arose during the activities.
- Living with people in their community for a period of time (a week or more). This is known as ethnographic research. It differs in that it involves *participating* in people's lives, whereas

the other techniques mentioned above are confined to *observing* people.

To effectively immerse, associates need to learn to listen emphatically, with the intent to understand. They also need to be cognizant of the effect they may have on participant's behaviour. Observing unobtrusively is important because observation tends to alter behaviour, a phenomenon referred to as the Hawthorne Effect.

In addition to active immersion, marketers rely also on research fields that supplement consumer and knowledge immersion and feed directly into the insight generation and strategy development process. Some of these research fields are listed below:

- *Usage and Attitude* studies provide information about consumer attitudes and usage behaviours for the category and brands. The considerable amount of information that is contained in these studies can be used to segment consumers on the basis of their usage as well as their opinions, and identify growth opportunities for brands within the various segments.
- *Semiotics* is the study of signs and symbols, and how they are used in different cultures. It allows us to understand the implicit meaning these codes communicate, in the culture and context within which they are used. For example, the colour red signifies luck and prosperity in the Chinese culture, love or anger in the West, losses in a financial statement, and danger or caution on the roads.
- *Motivational research* explains the underlying needs that drive behaviour. It focusses on identifying the emotional needs that are central to the relationships between the brand and its consumers.

(c) Generating Insights

Insights provide a penetrating understanding of consumers, their needs and their motivations. They are the substance and the inspiration for breeding ideas and developing concepts. And they are often gleaned from the observations sourced during consumer immersion.

Observation

An observation is a factual, objective record of something read, seen or heard. It is the data that will lead us to identifying the consumer needs. It should be devoid of interpretation or judgement. Observations should not be confined within the category, they should relate to people's day to day lives. Take for example:

- He had a can of Jasmine green tea on his table and took the whole morning to consume it.
- He took off his tie and rolled up his sleeves after the client meeting.
- He walked down the stairs instead of waiting for the elevator.
- He said he likes to eat only at restaurants where the service is prompt.
- He often changed lanes while driving.
- He said powerful, fuel-guzzling cars serve no practical purpose on our busy city roads. People buy them as status symbols to "flaunt" how successful they are.
- He claims that the hybrid car he drives is good for the environment.
- He said he does not buy personal care products. He uses whatever body wash his wife buys.
- He does not use aftershave lotions. He says using scented products makes him feel "artificial".

Observations are captured by associates during consumer immersion, preferably on Post-it notes so they may be grouped and mixed with other observations in the next stage.

Participants share their most interesting observations with the rest of the team. While we tend to focus more on the obvious, insights usually emerge from unexpected sources. Those observations that come as a surprise might be the ones you need to pay attention to.

Clustering Observations

Observations that share common ground are grouped to form clusters. For example the following observations could be grouped together under a cluster named "impatience".

- He walked down the stairs instead of waiting for the elevator.
- He said he likes to eat only at restaurants where the service is prompt.
- He often changed lanes while driving.

Similarly the observations below may be grouped under "my car says what I stand for":

- He said powerful, fuel-guzzling cars serve no practical purpose on our busy city roads. People buy them as status symbols to "flaunt" how successful they are.
- He claims that the hybrid car he drives is good for the environment.

Generating Insights from Observation Clusters

Observation clusters are analysed to determine underlying consumer needs. A technique called laddering can facilitate this process. The team relentlessly keeps asking themselves "why" — why do people say what they say or behave the way they do? Laddering will evoke responses that relate to functional drivers to begin with, but as we persist with questioning, emotional drivers begin to emerge. The process helps to peel off the outer objective layers and delve deeper into the subjective truth — the *emotional needs* that are driving behaviours.

An insight may vary in form; it may reflect generalised human aspect, or it may pertain to a specific situation. Ultimately it uncovers a need that is applicable to a significant proportion of target consumers. It explains their behaviour, and is easy for them to comprehend and relate to.

For instance for the cluster "my car says what I stand for" we may come up with the following needs: individuality and belonging. By relating needs back to brand or category, we create a marketing insight.

In this case it reveals what manufacturers already know: "the car is an expression of the owner's individuality".

(d) Generating Ideas

"If at first the idea is not absurd, then there will be no hope for it." — Albert Einstein.

The next step in the NPD process is to leverage insights in order to generate ideas for new product concepts. A wide variety of approaches may be used to uncover ideas, some of which are described below.

Fulfil Unmet or Poorly Met Needs

An unmet need, or the tension between what is available and what is desirable, opens the door for new product ideas. It is a process of exploration that yields ideas such as the ones listed below:

- The highly successful Old Spice men's body wash campaign of July 2010 ("Anything is possible when your man smells like Old Spice and not a lady"), which targeted women, was based on insights gleaned from the observation that "some men do not buy body wash, they use whatever their woman buys for them".
- The Indian shampoo market surged in the 1990s after sachets packs were launched into the sub-continent. The availability of the low cost sachets made it feasible Indians to use shampoo, at a time when the vast majority of the population could not afford to buy shampoo bottles.
- In 1986 P&G launched the first 2-in-1 shampoo, Pert Plus. Since then a host of 2-in-1 and 3-in-1 products have been launched in categories that range from teas, coffees, and food mixes to thermopads and technology products.
- Diet Coke was launched in 1982 to ease the tension for those who wanted to drink Coca-Cola, but felt it contained too many calories.

- Coca-Cola Zero, launched 22 years later, was the Coca-Cola Company's most successful product after Diet Coke. It initially targeted people who wanted a cola drink that was low in calories and tasted exactly like Coca-Cola. Later it also targeted men who associated "diet" drinks with women.

- Heinz has a tradition for thick, rich ketchup. Indeed it is so thick that it does not flow easily, a point used to impress consumers in their classic "Heinz anticipation" advertisements that first appeared in the late 1970s ("Thick, rich Heinz Ketchup — the taste that's worth the wait"). It was through innovation in packaging that subsequently neutralized this dissatisfier — the first squeezable Heinz bottle was introduced in 1983, and it was in 2001 that the upside-down bottle made its debut.

- In 1978 Sony launched the legendary Walkman for people who wanted to listen to music on the go.

- The need to share information across its computers led the US Department of Defence to development of ARPANET (Advanced Research Projects Agency Network) in 1969. At that time, its broader significance may not have been fully appreciated … it took another 25 years for the advent of the World Wide Web.

- In recent years cloud computing and software as a service are solutions that address the need for greater flexibility and improved efficiencies for businesses as well as individuals.

Make Connections

"All the geniuses here at General Motors kept saying lithium-ion technology is 10 years away, and Toyota agreed with us — and boom, along comes Tesla … How come some tiny little California startup, run by guys who know nothing about the car business, can do this, and we can't?" — General Motors' then Vice Chairman Robert Lutz (2007).

Linking different sources, whether they are observations, consumer needs and emotions, and/or market trends, can create a potent mix that

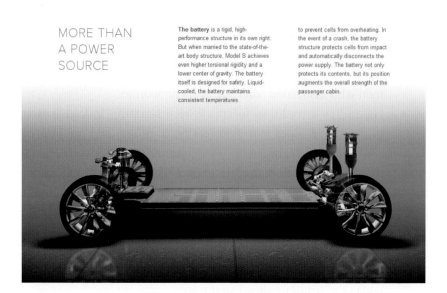

MORE THAN A POWER SOURCE

The **battery** is a rigid, high-performance structure in its own right. But when married to the state-of-the-art body structure, Model S achieves even higher torsional rigidity and a lower center of gravity. The battery itself is designed for safety. Liquid-cooled, the battery maintains consistent temperatures

to prevent cells from overheating. In the event of a crash, the battery structure protects cells from impact and automatically disconnects the power supply. The battery not only protects its contents, but its position augments the overall strength of the passenger cabin.

Exhibit 9.3   Tesla's battery pack stretches across the base of the vehicle.

fuels creative ideas. Take for instance the following examples of products that were conceived by connecting distinct market trends and data patterns:

- The demand for electric vehicles (EVs) stems from the growing desire for cleaner sources of energy as well as advances in lithium-ion batteries. Tesla's plan in February 2014 to build their "giga factory" is reminiscent of IBM's transformation in 1964 from an assembler of computers to also becoming a manufacturing concern that produced the world's largest quantity of integrated circuits. Tesla's giga factory which comes with a similar price tag as IBM's 360, will produce more lithium-ion batteries by 2020 than the total global production in 2013, and reduce battery costs by more than 30%. True to the company's vision the plant will be powered by renewable sources including wind and solar, and it will have facilities to recycle old battery packs. As the company's automobile production capacity soars, and as it achieves economies of scale, it is likely to lead a disruption that will affect almost every aspect of the automobile industry and associated sectors (petroleum, battery, auto components, auto materials etc.). The pace of improvements in performance and technology of EVs suggests that Warren Buffet's prediction that all cars will run on electricity by 2030 might indeed come true.

- Google Maps exploited the opportunity mix created by the proliferation of mobile devices combined with the convenience of reading maps in a soft copy format.
- UP & GO (Australia) nourishing liquid breakfast in a tetra pack targets those who have little or no time to sit for breakfast. Kellogg's All-Bran is also available in liquid format in a number of countries. Both these product leverage the needs for health and on-the-go convenience.
- Yoplait Go-GURT is another product that connects the trend in health with on-the-go convenience. It is a portable, low-fat yogurt that comes in the form of a squeezable tube. Go-GURT may be held in one hand and eaten without a spoon; ideal for children on-the-go.
- Birds Eye Steamfresh, vegetables packed in a unique steamer pack that meets the need for convenience and health.
- Tamagotchi, the electronic pet from Bandai connects the growing interest in electronic gadgets with the trend in keeping smaller pets.

Challenge Conventional Beliefs, Reframe Categories

Creativity is often constrained by strongly held convictions or beliefs, or simply by the way we are accustomed to doing things. Once we are prepared to remove these barriers and cross old boundaries, we often discover new possibilities. For instance:

- Infant milks have been in existence from the early 1900s for babies up to the age of 12 months. When birth rates began to decline even in many developing countries, and manufacturers began to experience the pressures of their shrinking market, they began to question the boundaries they had set. Growing up milk for toddlers aged one to three years was introduced towards the end of the 1980s. The new segment experienced sizzling growth and soon became larger than the traditional infant milk market. Today, growing up milks for toddlers aged above three and children above six are also widely available.

- The discovery of pink diamonds in October 1979 posed a challenge for Rio Tinto. At that time, the notion that diamonds could be intense pink was virtually non-existent. It was through branding and marketing that the company imbued the pink diamonds with an alluring mystique about their origin and colour. Described in advertisements as "the most revered diamond in the world", the Argyle Pink diamonds soon began to command a high premium.

- When Fabuloso, Colgate Palmolive's floor cleaner was launched into some Asian markets, the advertisements conveyed the product's long-lasting fresh scent. The floor cleaner that "smells so good" soon became the market leader in many of these markets.

- Vegemite, an iconic Australian brand ("Real Australians eat Vegemite") was invented by Dr. Cyril P. Callister, a leading Australian food technologist in 1922. For many years the brand's managers viewed Vegemite in the confines of the "yeast-based spreads" category (where it commanded over 90% share). The blinkers were removed at a time when Kraft (who currently own Vegemite) was striving to re-invigorate growth. Reframing categories to spur growth was one of their CEO's top four global endeavours in 2006.

The Vegemite story is still unfolding. Relying far too heavily on social media for research and new ideas, Kraft announced the launch of Vegemite iSnack 2.0 at the revered Melbourne Cricket Ground in September 2009. The response to the launch, which for some days became one of the top three subjects discussed globally on Twitter, can be summed up by the tweet: "So iTried Vegemite's new iSnack today — It is safe to say iHate it." The strategy of growing Vegemite beyond the confines of yeast-based spread is undoubtedly sound. Yet among other factors, what Australians found hard to digest was the dissonance created by the name iSnack 2.0, for a brand that has iconic status. In some ways a repeat of the New Coke saga, it left Vegemite disoriented, still in search of a happy ending.

Discover Benefits

Sometimes an invention or an insight may fail to gain traction because it appears to lack major benefits, or because its intended benefits may not be very relevant or credible. The challenge for such initiatives lies in discovering new benefits that resonate better with consumers. The following are some examples:

- Back in 1968, Dr. Spencer Silver, a scientist at 3M inadvertently created a "low-tack", reusable, adhesive which did not appear to serve a useful purpose. Later in 1974, Art Fry, another 3M associate came up with the idea of using the adhesive to anchor his bookmark in his hymnbook. The idea was subsequently broadened into the concept that we now know as a Post-it note.
- Around 2004, a range of food products known as cosmeceuticals (cosmetics and pharmaceuticals) came into existence. These functional foods for the external appearance, which included products such as Borba water, Essensis yogurt, Fuwarinka candy etc., claimed to improve one's skin, hair or even make you smell better. Though they evoked some interest to begin with, many of these products failed because consumers felt the claims were exaggerated and found them hard to believe.
- In 1992, conducting clinical trial in a small Welsh town called Merthyr Tydfil, researchers from Pfizer realized that their new drug was not very effective for treating angina, its intended purpose. Moreover, it had many side effects in men: back pain, stomach trouble, and long-lasting erections. What seemed like a failure to begin with turned into one of the firm's most

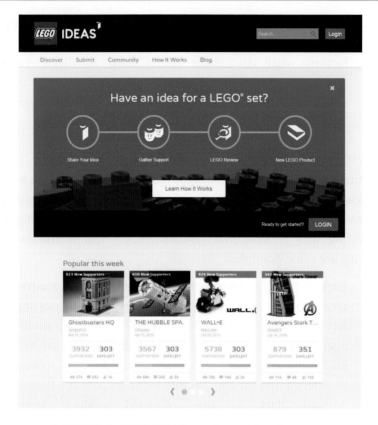

Exhibit 9.4   LEGO IDEAS website — ideas.lego.com

successful drugs. Shifting focus to the side effect, Pfizer eventually developed Viagra.

Co-creation and Crowdsourcing

"The real revolution here is not in the creation of the technology, but the democratization of the technology." —*Chris Anderson.*

Consumers are connected and empowered, and they increasingly express their views and ideas online for brands that they harbour strong feelings for. Their affinity for a brand can be constructively channelled towards co-creation, a process where brand owners collaborate with consumers in creating brand value.

Co-creation is a growing phenomenon; more and more companies encourage consumers to participate in activities for the development of advertising and new products. People are building their own shoes (Nike), rings (Blue Nile), designing their own T-shirts, mugs, cards, calendars etc., conceiving their own pizzas (Papa John's), and developing advertising content for companies as diverse as Coca-Cola, General Motors and Microsoft. These activities, usually contests or games, are helping companies engage with consumers and innovate at low cost.

Take for example LEGO IDEAS, a crowdsourcing programme that invites participants to create a Lego project, share it on the IDEAS website, and seek supporters. Projects that secure 10,000 supporters are reviewed by LEGO for a chance to become an official LEGO product. If the project passes review and is chosen for production, the creator receives 1% of net sales as royalty. As of February 2014 there were 5,563 live projects at LEGO IDEAS and seven co-created products had been launched.

Business Marketing Context

A core distinction between business market customers, vis-à-vis consumers of consumer products, is their focus on functionality and performance. They have systems and processes for evaluating their purchases in a fairly rational manner. To succeed, new offerings need to deliver value and suppliers need to demonstrate exactly how the value is derived. This requires a deep understanding of customers and how they derive value from their products.

The analysis of customer transaction data, via customer satisfaction and relationship management methods, can provide an appreciation of customer needs and preferences, leading to ideas of products or services to better serve the customers.

Value-in-Use analysis covered in Chapter 6, *Customer Satisfaction and Customer Value*, provides for a comprehensive understanding of the value customers derive from a product or service. Value-in-Use (VIU) is the difference in value minus the difference in price that a supplier's new offering provides a customer relative to an alternative offering. And value is the economic, technical, service and social benefit net of all the costs incurred in extracting the benefit. To derive VIU requires a thorough understanding of each individual step in the use of the product or service, i.e. all cost elements need to be accounted for to arrive at the total cost of ownership of the offering by the customer. Moreover this varies from one type of customer to another. Activity-based costing (ABC) methods that quantify all expenses related to the use of a product or service, are often used for this purpose.

Customers as a Source of Ideas

Considering the nature of business markets, it is not surprising that the highest proportion of new product ideas originate with customers. Customers however do differ in a number of ways, and some are more innovative than others.

"Organizations, by their very nature are designed to promote order and routine. They are inhospitable environments for innovation." Levitt's observation applies especially to big companies that tend to be process-centric, focusing on streamlining and minimizing costs. Their heavy investments in existing technologies become a burden when disruptions occur in their markets. Big customers therefore can be relied more on incremental innovations that help improve processes, rather than breakthroughs that disrupt the existing market dynamics.

Lead users on the other hand tend to be innovative companies that identify solutions well before their competitors and suppliers. For example the US Army Signal Corps, needing miniaturized communication equipment, conceived of the use of the PCB (printed circuit board) in their equipment, designed and produced the required PCBs, and sought potential suppliers.

Leap-Frog users are aggressive companies, possibly new entrants pursuing riskier development strategy. Tesla is an apt example of a leap-frog user of lithium batteries, that changed public and industry perception of what an electric car can be.

Salespeople, suppliers, market research agencies and competitors are also important sources that need to be regularly tapped for new product ideas.

Importantly, for ideas to flow, it requires the development of systems to encourage sourcing, and facilitate the submission of ideas. Irrespective of whether it was their original idea or sourced from elsewhere, company's associates need to know how to channel new ideas into the NPD funnel. At the most basic level this requires a destination such as the NPD department, where the ideas may be submitted.

Concept Development

Concept development is the process of developing product concepts, and refining them repeatedly till they convey the envisioned product in a compelling and credible manner.

A product concept is the depiction of an envisioned product. The depiction usually takes the form of a concept board that describe the idea in text, image and/or drawing. A prototype is not recommended at this stage where the concept has yet to undergo substantial refinement.

A cross-functional project team which importantly includes R&D is recommended. To engage consumers in the development effort, the process takes the form of a two or three-stage sequential series of group discussions, sometimes referred to as *concept development clinics*.

In the first stage of group discussions, the concept development team members engage with respondents, introduce them to the product concepts and work with them to explore, prioritise and evolve ideas. After the group discussions, the project team reviews the thoughts that emerged and incorporates them into the refined concept boards.

Subsequent stages of group discussions aim to refine and refine the concepts so that they depict the marketing insight and product benefit in a compelling and credible manner. The improved concept boards are now ready for concept screening.

Concept Screening

Concept screeners help prioritize and select the most promising among a broad range of concepts. In consumer marketing, typically quantitative research methods are used for concept screening, whereas in business marketing qualitative approaches will be used especially where the customer base is limited.

Since no prototype samples are available for respondents to use for evaluation, the sales forecasting capabilities of concept screeners is limited. Unlike simulated test markets, only ballpark volume estimates based on assumed repeat performance can be generated in concept product tests. These screeners, however do serve their intended purpose to prioritize concepts. More details about concept screeners for FMCG products are covered under *Simulated Test Markets* in Chapter 11, *Product Validation*.

Product Development

Design

Once product concepts have been developed and screened, it is time for R&D to design and craft new products from the chosen concepts. Consumer requirements need to be translated into engineering and manufacturing parameters that are measurable and controllable. Engineering needs to make trade-offs so that the product can best satisfy the diverse needs of consumers at a price they are willing to pay.

This process of designing and testing of products is covered in detail in the next chapter, *Product Design*.

Marketing Mix

In addition to the product, other elements of the marketing mix also need to be developed and aligned to form a *holistic, well-coordinated* marketing strategy. These elements include:

- Target definition
- Naming

- Positioning
- Packaging
- Pricing
- Trade emphasis and placement in store

Consumer research can help to explore, develop and refine the marketing mix. This research takes the form of a two or three-stage sequential series of group discussions, sometimes referred to as *marketing mix clinics.*

In the first stage of group discussions, a broad range of options around each element of the marketing mix are explored and prioritized. Consumers participating in the group discussions help to evolve and further develop the stronger ideas. Subsequent stages of group discussions are used to refine and optimize the marketing mix.

Validation

Once the product prototypes are ready and the marketing mix is finalized, a pre-launch validation is called for. This provides for a sales estimate of the new product prior to launch, and is used by management to make the "go/no-go" decision. Besides volume forecasting, validation techniques also provide diagnostic insights on how to improve the marketing mix and optimize performance.

Methods commonly used for validation purposes include simulated test markets (STM) and controlled store tests (CST). STMs are particularly popular with FMCG categories and their use is growing within consumer durables. STM and CST techniques are covered in Chapter 11, *Product Validation.*

Alpha and Beta Testing

In a number of businesses, product prototypes need to be tested by real customers. This is usually a two-stage process. Initial laboratory tests conducted by individuals within the company are referred to as alpha tests. The next stage called beta testing or field testing is at customers' workplace in real usage conditions. Beta testing is the terminology used in the IT sector; manufacturing industries call it field testing.

The feedback after each stage of testing is used to fine tune the new product and iron out any issues.

Test processes need to be thorough to minimize the costs and consequences of in-market failure. The importance of this is highlighted by the numerous well-publicised incidents of product failures. Beta testing should also be well managed to contain the risk of revealing details of the new product to competitors.

Product Launch

"Genius is 1% inspiration and 99% perspiration." — *Thomas Edison.*

Though vital for long term competitiveness, innovation does not guarantee a product's success. Execution is the key. When Vijay Govindarajan and Chris Trimble (authors of *The Other Side of Innovation*) surveyed executives in Fortune 500 companies to rate their organizations' skills on a 10-point scale, participants overwhelmingly believed that their companies were better at generating ideas (average score of six) than at commercializing them (average score of one).

All aspects of brand management, which are covered in this text, come into play in commercialization. The uniqueness of the product influences how it is launched. Novel products require greater investment in all elements of the marketing mix. They also require high level of training, education and adjustment for both internal staff and customers.

An important consideration is whether to launch on a rolling basis from one region to another, or to go global. Global launch provides for faster acceleration in sales and quicker ROI, which in turn can fuel further product development. Yet it is riskier and does require deeper pockets.

A rolling launch allows for savings in investment particularly for technology and consultancy companies, where service and support requirements are quite high. A core launch team can move from region to region, training personnel and supporting launch activities.

Besides delays in the return on investment, a key drawback with rolling launch is that it gives competitors more time to analyse the new launch and respond with a counter strategy.

Launch Evaluation

Once a product is launched, marketers eagerly await sales and market share information to assess how well the product is received by consumers. They need to however remain cognizant that the *early sales and market share readings for a new product do not reveal the product's future performance*, particularly in sectors like FMCG, where goods are repeat purchased. In some cases, the initial sales data may even be misleading. High trials result in encouraging sales growth during launch, prompting companies to expand their supply base. However, if a FMCG product is not generating repeat purchases, irrespective of how good the trial rate might be, it is doomed to fail.

Where repeat purchasing is the norm, a new product can succeed only if it develops a strong base of regular consumers, i.e. a substantial number of consumers must try it, and an adequate number of them must continue to buy it again and again.

To evaluate the launch of a new product, more than sales numbers, companies need to use analytic techniques to forecast and validate the sales potential of the new product. This is important considering also the high proportion of new product failures.

Techniques such as the Parfitt–Collins model, covered in Chapter 11, *Product Validation*, provide reliable sales forecast based on the product's trial and repeat buying rates (RBR). The RBR, which provides an understanding of the rate of adoption, is a critical gauge for the success of the new product, in markets where goods are repeat purchased.

CHAPTER 10

Product Design

Exhibit 10.0 The IBM 360 *(Photo courtesy of IBM).*

IBM 360

"We called this project 'You bet your company'." — Bob Evans, IBM.

One of the greatest feats in the design of computer systems dates back to the mainframe age, at a time when computers were created incompatible. Upgrading to a new computer in the early '60s, meant you needed to redevelop all software, rewrite all programmes. There were, at that time, too many different computers requiring different supporting programmes and different peripheral equipment. IBM's own business divisions produced a "wildly disorganized" array of offerings, as CEO Thomas J. Watson Jr. recalled in his autobiography, *Father, Son & Co.*

It took a "$5,000,000,000 Gamble," as *Fortune* called it, to change the status quo. In addition to the investment risk, gigantic by 1960 standards, the IBM 360 posed major structural risks. It would disrupt every facet of the computer industry. All of IBM's existing computers and peripherals would become obsolete overnight. IBM's head count would grow by 50%. The company, which was essentially an assembler of computer components, and a business service organization, would open five new plants and become the world's largest maker of integrated circuits. Bob Evans, the chairman of the committee that conceived of the IBM 360, said: "We called this project 'You bet your company'."

System 360 was launched on 7 April 1964 as a single compatible line consisting of six computers and 44 peripherals. Besides displacing all existing models, it opened up new fields of computer applications, and served both business and scientific applications. For the first time, all input, output and other peripheral equipment had standard interfaces. For the first time if you bought a new computer you did not need to rewrite your programmes.

The gamble paid off — IBM transformed the world of computing establishing a new global standard. System 360 gave Big Blue a competitive advantage in computer systems that prevailed for decades.

IBM computers that are better known today include *Deep Blue* which beat Garry Kasparov in 1997, and *Watson* which defeated champions in the Jeopardy! quiz show in 2011. Along with the IBM 360, they exemplify the legacy of innovation at a corporation that has topped the US patent list for the past 22 consecutive years.

Preview

Whether it is the compatibility of computers or a light bulb for homes, product ideas are sometimes self-evident. Success in innovation often hinges on the design, development and the execution. In the case of

IBM 360 it was the gargantuan task of re-engineering the architecture of computer systems that led to the establishment of new standards in computing.

In new product development (NPD), once the ideas and concepts have been generated and screened, it is time for R&D to design and craft the new products. They do so by combining art, science, and technology to transform the concepts into new products.

Design Specifications

To begin, consumer requirements need to be translated into engineering and manufacturing parameters that are measurable and controllable. This usually results in some tension between marketing and R&D. Marketers spell out what consumers want, but, to create the new product, what engineers require are technical specifications. A set of methods called quality function deployment (QFD) helps to translate the marketer's description of consumer needs into the engineer's language of technical specifications.

The *house of quality* is a prominent QFD technique that brings together in a "house" configuration the attributes that consumers need and the engineering characteristics that will influence those attributes. Utilizing an inter-relationship matrix to relate the consumer attributes to the engineering characteristics, the technique is able to translate a product concept into the technical specifications for a prototype. It also improves cross-department communication by serving as "a kind of conceptual map that provides the means for inter-functional planning and communication" (Hauser and Clausing, 1988).

Trade-off

A key issue in product design is the trade-off between quality and cost: Are consumers willing to pay for the optimum combination of features that gratify their needs? Are they prepared to pay the additional cost for an improvement in performance?

Designers are also confronted with the challenge of negatively correlated characteristics. For instance, taste versus low calories, taste versus nutrition, power versus safety, ubiquitous versus exclusive, quality versus price and so on. Sometimes a creative solution can satisfy multiple needs. Most of the time, however, a trade-off is called for. To make an informed decision, the designer needs to know the combination of price and features that target consumers finds most desirable.

Conjoint analysis, a technique developed by Paul Green at the Wharton School, answers these questions. It is a predictive technique used to determine customers' preferences for the different features, including price, that make up a product or service.

Conjoint analysis works well for consumer durables and has also been used for FMCG products. Yet sometimes it may become challenging to convey tastes, as in food products, or fragrances, in a conjoint analysis. Sensory research and consumer product testing offer an alternative methodology where preference ratings by consumers are modelled to determine the importance of each attribute.

Sensory Research

Sensory attributes are product properties perceived by one or more of the five senses: visual, tactile (mouth, skin, surface texture, etc.), auditory (crunch, squeak), olfaction (taste, flavour, smell) and kinaesthetic (including feelings such as cooling, burning, and tingling associated with use of a product).

Sensory research is concerned with objectively rating the sensorial attributes of a product using respondents who possess sensory acuity. These respondents can detect sensory properties, and are able to describe them well. They need not be the target market for the product; their role is to provide an objective assessment of the sensorial makeup of the product; something that average consumers are not usually good at. While they are good at telling us what they like and dislike, consumers in general tend to be weak in discerning and describing sensory attributes.

Sensory research is often used in conjunction with consumers' rating of products to provide an explanation of consumers' preferences.

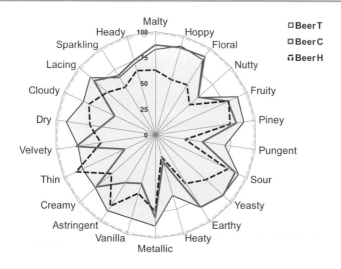

Exhibit 10.1   Sensory profiling of beer brands T, C and H.

For example, if consumers highly rate the smell of a product ("I really like it" or "I like it extremely"), sensory profiling explains what they like about the smell.

Sensory Profiling

Spider charts such as the one shown in Exhibit 10.1, are often used to depict the sensory profile of products. They relate how the product is perceived on the sensory attributes that are associated with the category. The technique commonly used for sensory profiling is called Quantitative Descriptive Analysis (QDA). Listed below are the steps involved in the QDA process:

- Build Attribute list: A sensory panel of about a dozen participants collectively try all products included in the test. Words used by the panellists to describe the sensorial constitution (i.e. visual, tactile, auditory, olfaction and kinaesthetic) of these products are recorded, and a list of descriptors of the sensory attributes is finalized.
- Product Rating: In a blind (unbranded) test, products are rated individually by the panellists on each of the sensory attributes. The assessment is typically repeated at least once to check for

consistency of the ratings. The average rating of each brand is then charted as shown in Exhibit 10.1. Using the principal component analysis (PCA) statistical technique, the brands and their image ratings can also be vividly depicted on a multidimensional perceptual map (Refer to Chapter 1, *Brand and Brand Image* for a description of perceptual maps).

Consumer Product Rating

Sensory profiling in conjunction with consumer rating data can be modelled to yield the relationship between the desirability ("Overall liking") of a product and the sensory attributes. This reveals the importance of each attribute in enhancing the desirability of the product; information that product designers can use to improve products and make trade-off decisions.

In a quantitative research framework, target consumers rate products on a number of different attributes, including overall opinion. A typical question to assess taste for instance, would be worded as follows:

> *How much do you like the taste of this product?*
> > *I like it very much.*
> > *I like it.*
> > *I neither like it nor dislike it.*
> > *I dislike it.*
> > *I dislike it very much.*

Products should be tested *blind* (unbranded). Ideally *monadic in-use* testing is recommended. Monadic, which means only one product is tested by each respondent, is quite an expensive approach, particularly if many products are to be tested.

Comparative testing, where a number of products are tried alongside by respondents, is less expensive. The tendency for respondents in this setting is to compare the products.

An alternative approach, *sequential monadic*, may be adopted where respondents try one product and rate it, move to another product and rate it, and then compare the two. This is recommended when a forced comparison is required. In this case the rating of the product that was tried first is pure monadic, and provides a measure for the initial response to the product.

Triangle Tests

Triangle tests are used where the intent is to verify whether a change in composition can be detected. This is required in case of cost reduction or a change of ingredients exercise. For instance, a soft drink manufacturer may be interested to know whether a reduction in the level of carbonation is noticeable or not.

In triangle tests, participants are asked to identify which two of three products ('item A', 'item A' and 'item B') are the same and which one is different. If the number of participants correctly identifying the different item is statistically significant, it is concluded that difference between item A and item B is perceivable by consumers.

The Kano Model and Conjoint Analysis

As described in Chapter 6, *Customer Satisfaction and Customer Value*, the Kano model is a technique that categorizes product and service features in terms of their impact on customer satisfaction.

The model would, for instance, tell us that brightness, resolution and weight are the features of portable projectors that are explicitly demanded by customers. These features are more effective in differentiating one brand from another.

On the other hand features like a remote control and warranty are requirements that are taken for granted and do not generate an increase in satisfaction. Yet, if unfulfilled, these hygiene factors cause dissatisfaction.

By discriminating product features in this manner, the Kano model filters out those product areas and features that a company should prioritize for research via techniques such as conjoint analysis and the house of quality.

Conjoint analysis takes the focus of inquiry to a deeper level, assessing trade-offs between features, between the ranges of levels of features, and between various price points. It helps in optimize products in terms of their attributes including price, and provides estimates of their market potential.

Conjoint Analysis

Food technologists seek to alter their recipes to achieve what they refer to as the "bliss point", the point at which the composition of ingredients creates the maximum amount of crave. Aeronautical engineers seek to design airplanes that cater to the preferences of the major airlines. Credit card managers seek the combination of features that would incentivize their card holders to spend more on their credit cards. They all are in search of the optimum combination of product features to gratify their target customers.

Conjoint analysis is a method that is commonly used for the above purpose. It is a predictive technique used to determine customers' preferences for the different features that make up a product or service.

Conjoint analysis is based on the notion that consumers evaluate products by assessing the value of its separate yet conjoined parts. Products are made up of a wide range of features or attributes such as brand, ingredients, price etc. each with a range of possibilities or levels. Understanding of attribute importance and their perceived value helps marketers segment markets, refine their marketing mix and develop products with the optimum combination of features to gratify their target customers.

Central to the theory of conjoint analysis is the concept of product utility. *Utility* is a latent variable that reflects how desirable or valuable an object is in the mind of the respondent. The utility of a product is assessed from the value of its parts (part-worth). Conjoint analysis examines consumers' responses to product ratings, rankings or choices, to estimate the part-worth of the various levels of each attribute of a product. Utility is not an absolute unit of measure; only relative values or differences in utilities matter.

The conceptual framework on conjoint analysis originated in mathematical psychology and was applied in marketing in the early 1970s by Professor Paul Green at the Wharton School of the University of Pennsylvania. Over the years new approaches have emerged that make use of computer-aided online research to considerably expand the scope of the technique.

The following sections describe the conjoint methodology in general, and the strengths, weaknesses and the application areas for the different approaches.

Research Design

The design of a conjoint study is tailored to the study objectives. If the objective is to determine the "bliss point", the study's focus will lie on product ingredients. If the objective is to refine the mix to defend against a competitive threat, the focus should be on the key points of differences between products. If the objective is to set price, the emphasis should shift to brand and price.

The selection of the *product attributes* for the research, and their realistic range of values (*levels*) is based on the objectives. Realism in choice of levels ensures that the derived importance of the attribute is not artificially inflated or deflated. For instance, if smaller brands are excluded as is often the case, the importance of the attribute "brand" is underestimated. Or for instance, if the price range is stretched beyond the range prevailing for most products in the market, its importance will be inflated. Both the highest and the lowest prevalent levels ought to be included, and to avoid bias researchers maintain roughly the same number of levels for each attributes. Exhibit 10.2 depicts the attributes and their levels selected for a study on portable projectors.

Given the above set of attributes and levels, there are as many as $4 \times 3 \times 3 \times 2 \times 2 \times 2 = 288$ product possibilities. One such product possibility is the InFocus, 1.2 kg, 2000 lumens, 1280 × 800

Attributes	Levels				Product Profile
Brand	Epson	Dell	InFocus	Optoma	InFocus
Weight (kg)		1.2 kg	1.8 kg	2.4 kg	1.2 kg
Brightness (lumens)		1000	2000	3000	2000
Resolution		1280 x 800		1024 x 768	1280 x 800
Display Technology		DLP		LCD	DLP
Price		$1200		$600	$1200

Exhibit 10.2 Example attributes and levels for portable projectors. Product profile (right).

WXGA, DLP priced at $1,200. These possibilities are referred to as product bundles or product profiles.

The next step in the design of the research is selection of the *analysis methodology*. There are basically three fundamental methods that you need to take into consideration. If the number of attributes in the research is less than 10, *traditional full-profile conjoint analysis* will suffice. Otherwise the use of *Adaptive conjoint,* which accommodates up to 30 attributes, is recommended.

One assumption inherent in both adaptive and tradition conjoint is *pair-wise independence* of attributes. The general notion in conjoint analysis is that consumers evaluate the overall desirability of a product based on the value of its separate (yet conjoined) parts. Pair-wise independence assumes that the overall utility or desirability of the product profile is *additive*, i.e. equal to the sum of its parts. In other words, if the part-worth of the brand InFocus is 3.5, the part-worth for weight 1.2 kg is 2.5, brightness 2000 lumens is 2, resolution 1280 × 800 is 1 and price $1,200 is –2, in that case the utility of the product bundle shown in Exhibit 10.2 is 3.5 + 2.5 + 2 + 1 – 2 = 7.

While the pair-wise independence assumption generally holds true, there are instance when this might not be the case. For example, if the brand Epson is associated strongly with Liquid Crystal Display (LCD) display technology, respondents may desire the brand more when it is bundled with LCD technology. Its part-worth is higher when combined with LCD technology and lower part-worth when it is with Digital Light Processing (DLP). In this case the whole is greater or less than the sum of its parts, and interaction terms must be included in the model.

Interaction effects can be handled by *choice-based conjoint* analysis where consumers undergo a task similar to what they would actually do in the marketplace — choosing a preferred product from a group of products. This approach, along with adaptive conjoint analyses, is described later in the section on developments in conjoint analysis.

Conjoint analysis works by observing how respondents' preferences change as one systematically varies the product features. It examines how they trade-off different aspects of the product, weighing options that have a mix of more desirable and less desirable qualities. The observations allow one to statistically deduce (typically via linear regression) the part-worth of all of the levels across the product attributes.

One approach to deciphering the customers' hierarchy of choices would be to ask respondents to rank or rate all the product profiles (288 in the example of portable projectors). This, however, is neither practical nor necessary, provided one assumes pair-wise independence. The assumption allows for the reduction of the task to a much reduced minimum sample of 12, obtained from the below equation:

> *Minimum sample = Total levels across all attributes − Number of attributes + 1*
>
> $$= (4 + 3 + 3 + 2 + 2 + 3) - 6 + 1 = 17 - 6 + 1 = 12.$$

Normally, however, we include more than the minimum number of profiles, so that all of the discrete attribute levels are well represented in a sample of carefully chosen, well-balanced product concepts.

Data Collection

Online panels are an efficient and cost-effective means of collecting the information for conjoint analysis. They also permit the use of computers to customize the questionnaire, as required for adaptive conjoint.

If an online panel is not available for the research, or if the research requires respondents to sniff or taste product samples, one could conduct live interviews at a booth set up at a controlled location. Controlled location tests (CLT) usually are conducted at high traffic sites such as shopping malls. For instance, for our portable projector study, data could be sourced from a booth located at a mall that is popular for computers and peripherals.

Door-to-door interviewing, though expensive, remains an option for full profile conjoint studies, which do not require the use of computers.

Only respondents interested in buying in the near future should be selected for the survey. Depending on the desired accuracy, sample sizes vary from 200 to 500 respondents.

To facilitate data collection, *product concepts* need to be accurately and vividly depicted. For face-to-face interviews, concept cards are printed out for ease of handling by interviewers and respondents.

The different methodologies essentially require respondents to either rate, rank or select product profiles. Rating scales for conjoint analysis are relatively large varying from 0 to 10 for fewer profiles, and can expand to 0–100 for studies with large number of profiles.

Ranking, which is a more rigorous exercise, requires respondents to sort product samples from most preferred to least preferred. One approach is for respondents to place the profiles into three lots: desirable, neutral and undesirable, and then rank the profiles in each of the three lots. Because it is so time consuming, ranking is infrequently used nowadays.

Data Analysis

Specialized solutions like Sawtooth Software and Bretton-Clark as well as all-purpose statistical packages such as SPSS and SAS, are among the software packages commonly used for conjoint analysis.

Fundamental to conjoint analysis is the derivation of the utility functions. All the study deliverables such as computing attribute

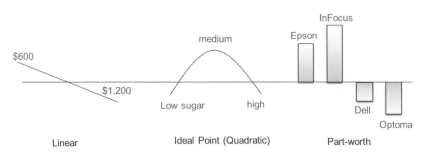

Exhibit 10.3 Basic types of utility functions.

importance, running "what-if" simulations, and examining trade-offs are based on product utility.

Utility functions specify the utility of each level for each attribute, for each individual respondent. Individual-level utilities capture the heterogeneity within the market, allowing for the segmentation of respondents based on their utilities, and permit a wider variety of approaches to market simulations

A common approach to deriving a respondent's utility function is the "part-worth" model that estimates the part-worth utility that survey respondents place on each individual level of a particular attribute. This is particularly appropriate for qualitative features like brand or colour that are unordered. With quantitative features such as price, there is usually a simple relationship between level and its part-worth. Linear models assume a straight-line relationship, as might be appropriate for price. Ideal-point or quadratic models (inverted U-shaped curves) are appropriate when consumers have a preference for a specific level (optimum level), as is the case for level of carbonation or sweetness in soft drinks.

The utilities are usually scaled within a given attribute such that they add up to zero. Referred to as *effects-coded,* the zero point in this approach represents the average. Levels above zero are preferred above average, while those below zero are below average. In an alternative approach called *dummy-coded,* the least preferred value is set to zero, and all other levels are positive values.

Attributes	Levels	Part-Worth	Importance	Relative Importance %
Brand	Epson	1.50	5.15	26.4
	Dell	-1.35		
	InFocus	2.50		
	Optoma	-2.65		
Weight	1.2 kg	1.50	2.50	12.8
	1.8 kg	-0.50		
	2.4 kg	-1.00		
Brightness	1000 lumens	-2.00	3.48	17.8
	2000 lumens	0.52		
	3000 lumens	1.48		
Resolution	1280 x 800	1.89	3.78	19.4
	1024 x 768	-1.89		
Technology	DLP	0.78	1.56	8.0
	LCD	-0.78		
Price	$1,200	-1.53	3.06	15.7
	$600	1.53		
Total			19.53	100.0

Exhibit 10.4 Average part-worths and relative importance of attributes.

Once the utility functions are known, we can compute the utility for any of the possible product profiles by adding the scores for each of the profile's attributes. Going back to the portable projector example we can predict the utility of each of the 288 possible product profiles, for each and every respondent.

Standard Deliverables

Attribute Importance

The average part-worth score across all respondents, as shown in Exhibit 10.4, serves as the analysis summary. It is used to derive the *importance* and the *relative importance of an attribute*. Attribute *importance* is the difference between the highest and lowest utility level of the attribute. *Relative importance* of an attribute is essentially its share of *importance*.

If the distance between the utility levels of an attribute is large, then that attribute will have a larger bearing on the respondents' choice of product than another attribute where the distance is not as large. The distance therefore is a reflection of the importance of the attribute in determining consumer preferences.

It becomes apparent here how the choice of levels has a critical bearing on attribute importance, and why both the highest and the lowest prevalent levels should preferably be included in the design to get unbiased estimates of the importance of attributes. If the levels within an attribute do not cover its entire range its importance is deflated. On the other hand if the range is stretched beyond the prevailing levels in the market, its importance will be inflated.

Since it may not always be desirable or feasible to cover the realistic range of levels within attributes, the correct interpretation of data in Exhibit 10.4 is that for the average consumer, given the attribute properties tested, brand has the highest influence on decision-making, followed by resolution, brightness, price, weight and technology.

Knowledge of the relative importance of various attributes can assist in marketing and advertising decisions. Other factors being equal, one would devote greater attention and resource to improving a product, on attributes that are of greatest importance to target consumers.

Trade-off Analysis

Product developers are constantly faced with trade-offs. For instance, reducing the weight of a portable projector would result in an increase in price as lighter components cost more. Whether this could result in an increase in demand could be gauged by examining the trade-offs that consumers are willing to make.

Exhibit 10.5 provides an illustration of trade-off analysis. In this case the developer of a projector that currently has brightness of 2000 lumens and weighs 1.8 kg, is considering whether to increase the product's brightness to 3000 lumens or reduce the weight to 1.2 kg. Since utility improves by $+2$ (from -0.5 to $+1.5$) if we reduce weight to 1.2 kg compared to $+1$ (from 0.5 to 1.5) if we improve brightness to 3000, the developer can deduce that average consumer will prefer the reduction in weight over the improvement in brightness.

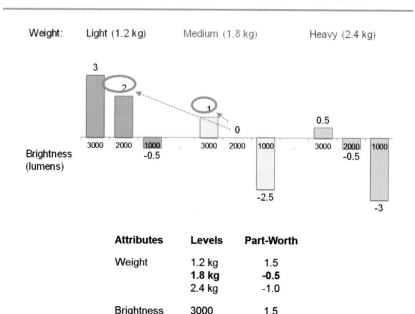

Attributes	Levels	Part-Worth
Weight	1.2 kg	1.5
	1.8 kg	-0.5
	2.4 kg	-1.0
Brightness (lumens)	3000	1.5
	2000	0.5
	1000	-2.0

Exhibit 10.5 Trade-off between brightness and weight for portable projectors.

Market Simulation

For product developers, perhaps the greatest value of conjoint analysis comes from what-if market simulators that are able to predict the changes in consumer preferences across brands should a proposed new product enter the market, or if an existing product is withdrawn.

One approach to market simulation referred to as the *first-choice* model, assumes that a consumer chooses the product that commands the highest utility. As mentioned earlier the utility of each product profile is the sum of the part-worth of its features. Computed for each respondent across all products that exist in the market, the simulation results are aggregated and weighted to yield the consumers' share of preferences within the market.

The first-choice model, where the winner-takes-all is appropriate for markets where consumers tend to buy only one brand or item in the

Product	Utility	e^U	First Choice	Share of Utility	Multinomial Logit
A	1	2.7	0.0	10.0	3.2
B	2	7.4	0.0	20.0	8.7
C	3	20.1	0.0	30.0	23.7
D	4	54.6	100.0	40.0	64.4
	10.0	84.8	100.0	100.0	100.0

Exhibit 10.6 Comparison of first choice, share of utility and multinomial logit methods.

short term, as is the case for consumer durables. It may also apply to categories where brand loyalty is known to be very high.

However, for the majority of FMCG products, consumers tend to maintain a repertoire of brands. The multinomial logit and the share of utility methods are better suited for such products. Exhibit 10.6 provides a comparison of all three methods.

The *share of utility* method allocates volume in proportion to the products' utility. It recognizes that for some categories consumer want variety, and while she may prefer a chicken burger more than other menu options at a fast food restaurant, from time to time she will try some of the other options. In the share of utility method, the utility reflects the proportion of time that the respondent will prefer that option within the specified competitive context. For example if the utility of products A, B, C and D is respectively 1, 2, 3 and 4, then the share of preferences for A is 10% (1/[1 + 2 + 3 + 4]), and share for B, C, and D is 20%, 30% and 40% respectively.

The *multinomial logit* model, takes the following mathematical form:

$$Share_p = \frac{e^{U_p}}{\sum_{i=1}^{n} e^{U_i}}$$

where:

$Share_p$ *is the estimated share of preference for product p.*
U_p *is the estimated utility for product p.*
U_i *is the estimated utility for product i.*
n *is the number of products in the competitive set.*

Share of Preference and Market Share

Conjoint analysis is a highly versatile technique that yields valuable insights for the development of products and their marketing mix. When interpreting the results, however, we need to remain aware that the technique provides estimates of the *share of preference,* which ought not to be confused with share of market.

Besides their preferences for product features, consumers' buying behaviour is dependent on a number of other market factors, including brand and advertising awareness, product knowledge, product perceptions, promotions and distribution.

It takes time for the awareness of a new brand to grow, and for its advertising associations and claims to penetrate minds. Consumers are not fully aware of product details, even for established brands. Their perceptions about a product may be inaccurate, and their choice of brand is usually limited to what is available at the outlets they frequent.

Moreover, market share is not static, it varies over time. Dissemination of information takes time. Trends take time to reach equilibrium. And there is a lag between intent to purchase and date of purchase.

Because many factors that influence market share are not replicated in the conjoint study, the study results are unlikely to accurately reflect buying behaviour. They do however provide an accurate gauge of consumers' preferences for different product features, and this information has many practical applications.

Applications

New Product Development

Conjoint analysis provides knowledge of the relative importance of the various product attributes and the trade-off between attributes. This is of great value to product developers who are constantly striving to enhance the utility of their products.

New product concepts can be simulated to provide an assessment of their market potential, as also an understanding of their source of growth in terms of the amount of business they are likely to gain from other brands (cannibalization).

Market Segmentation

Crafting segments on the basis of the product features that are valued by consumers is an apt approach to segmentation from the standpoint of product development. It aligns well with consumers' needs and preferences, albeit primarily in terms of product related attributes and price.

The segments are identified on the basis of similarities reflected in respondents' utility functions. Cluster analysis is one of a number of methods that can be used for this purpose.

By way of example consider the case of portable projectors. It might be observed that some customers highly value price and display technology, while others value brand, brightness and weight. On examining the profile of the customers, we might find that one segment comprises mainly business customers whereas the other consists primarily of home users. Information of this nature is helpful in product development and targeting customers. At times marketers also discover profitable niches, and develop product offering to serve those niches.

Advertising and Communication

Knowledge of segments and the relative importance of various attributes within each segment helps marketers prioritize their messages in advertising and other forms of brand communication.

Price Elasticity and Cross-Price Elasticity

Where price evaluation is the prime objective of the research, we use two attributes: brand name and price (for the most popular pack size). The brand name, in essence, captures all features associated with the brand.

Because realism is of utmost importance in pricing research, choice-based conjoint is the recommended approach, particularly for FMCG categories.

Developments in Conjoint Analysis

As markets transformed from the mass marketing arena of the 1970s to the personalized marketing era of our digital age, products and services became highly differentiated, offering consumers a multitude of possibilities. The limitations on the number of attributes and their levels inherent in full profile conjoint analysis made it impractical to use this traditional approach.

At the same time, the trend towards online computer aided research facilitated the development and use of adaptive and hybrid conjoint methods, and relatively sophisticated techniques such as adaptive self-explication, which allowed for much larger number of attributes to be accommodated.

Adaptive Conjoint Analysis

Introduced in 1985 by Richard Johnson at Sawtooth Software, adaptive conjoint analysis (ACA) customizes the interview for each respondent, seeking trade-offs only on those attributes and levels, which are of relevance to the respondent.

A good illustration of the ACA process can be found at Sawtooth's website (www.sawtoothsoftware.com) where a sample survey is provided.

It encompasses a four stage interactive computer aided survey, where the responses at each stage serve to customize the questions in subsequent stages.

Stage 1 — Preference rating: Respondent is asked to rate attribute levels from most to least preferred. Sawtooth for example employs a 7-point rating scale from extremely undesirable to extremely desirable.

Stage 2 — Importance rating: Respondent is asked to specify the importance of the difference in levels on a 7-point scale varying from "Extremely important" to "Not at all important".

Example: If the two projectors were the same in all other ways, how important would this difference be to you? InFocus vs. Epson

Stage 3 — Paired comparisons: Depending on the responses to the self-explicated questions (Stages 1 and 2), the survey adapts to present the respondent a set of paired comparisons which are best suited to elicit the respondent's underlying preferences.

Example: If everything else about these two projectors were the same, which would you prefer?

> *Option 1: InFocus, 2000 lumens*
> *Option 2: Epson, 3000 lumens*

Stage 4 — Profile rating: Depending on the responses to the self-explicated questions in Stages 1 and 2, and the trade-offs in Stage 3, the respondent is finally asked to rate a limited set of product profiles on a 0 to 100 scale.

Example: Now we are going to show you four projectors. For each projector, please tell us how likely you are to buy it. Answer using a 100-point scale, where 0 means not likely at all and 100 means definitely would buy it.

Customization based on the response to self-explicated questions, improves the efficiency of the survey. If for instance a respondent has indicated that the InFocus brand is preferable to Epson, and DLP display technology is preferable to LCD, a paired comparison between InFocus-DLP and Epson-LCD becomes redundant. By ensuring that only relevant paired comparisons and profile ratings are shown, ACA substantially trims the task that each respondent is required to perform. The improvement in efficiency allows for the expansion in scale allowing ACA to accommodate designs with as many as 30 attributes.

Choice-based Conjoint Analysis

Choice-based conjoint analysis, an application of *discrete choice modelling*, gained popularity during the 1990s driven by the advantage that it reflects the real world more closely than any of the other approaches to conjoint analysis. Consumers undergo a task similar to what they actually do in the marketplace — choosing a preferred product from a group of products.

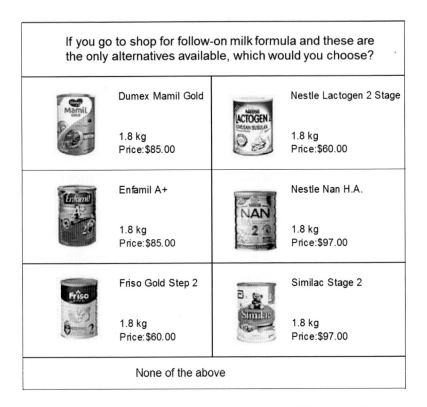

If you go to shop for follow-on milk formula and these are the only alternatives available, which would you choose?

Dumex Mamil Gold 1.8 kg Price:$85.00	**Nestle Lactogen 2 Stage** 1.8 kg Price:$60.00
Enfamil A+ 1.8 kg Price:$85.00	**Nestle Nan H.A.** 1.8 kg Price:$97.00
Friso Gold Step 2 1.8 kg Price:$60.00	**Similac Stage 2** 1.8 kg Price:$97.00
None of the above	

Exhibit 10.7 A choice set used in a research study on follow-on milk formula.

Unlike the other approaches, choice-based conjoint analysis can also estimate higher-order interactions, although we do not need to include these effects for most marketing problems.

Respondents are asked to select a brand from choice sets similar to the one shown in Exhibit 10.7. The choices usually include a "none" choice that can be selected if none of the products appeal to the respondent. The number of choice sets varies from 8 for a small study to 24 for a study with relatively large number of attributes.

Because realism is of utmost importance, choice-based conjoint analysis is the preferred method for pricing research studies.

	IMPORTANCE RATING	Printer Engine	Print Head	Toning System	Paper Feeder	Cartridge System	On-Board Software	New Product (Target)	Current Product	Competitor B	Competitor A
DIRECTION OF IMPROVEMENT		⬆	⬆				⬆	RATING			
CUSTOMER REQUIREMENTS											
Cost under $500	10	●	●	●				3	4	4	3
Quality of print	9		●	●		▲		4	3	3	4
Speed	8					●		4	3	4	3
Noise	6	▲	●	▲	●			3	3	5	4
Printer size	5	●		■	■			4	4	3	4
Number of fonts	4						●	5	5	4	2
Type sizes	4						●	4	4	3	4
Cartridge life	4			■		●		3	3	2	3
New Product (Target)		4	5	5	3	4	4				
Current Product		3	4	5	3	4	3				
Competitor A		3	5	4	2	3	4				
Competitor B		3	4	3	4	5	3				

Relationship
● Strong
■ Moderate
▲ Weak

Rating of products

Exhibit 10.8 Simplified version of the house of quality for laser printers.

House of Quality

The "house of quality" originated at Mitsubishi Kobe shipyard in 1972, as a tool for translating customer requirements into engineering and manufacturing parameters that are measurable and controllable. Over the years its use has spread to a number of sectors including automotive, IT, consumer durables, apparel, and a wide range of B2B products and services.

House of quality is a conceptual framework that provides the means for cross-functional planning and communication, so that marketing, R&D and manufacturing may work together to produce products that reflect the preferences of customers.

Exhibit 10.8 depicts a much simplified version of the house of quality for laser printers. In a typical application there would be about 15 to 50 consumer requirements and 30 to 100 technical requirements.

The building blocks for the house of quality are as follows:

- List of customer requirements (product attributes).
- Importance ratings of these attributes: This may be obtained from product tests where preference ratings by customers are modelled to determine the importance of each attribute. Alternatively conjoint analysis provides the means for determining the importance of attributes and their specific level in terms of part-worth.
- Customer rating of performance on consumer attributes of new product and competing products. This too may be sourced from product tests or conjoint analysis.
- List of engineering characteristics.
- Relationship between customer attributes and engineering characteristics: Whereas the customer requirements spell out customers' preferences, the engineering requirements tell us how the product may be modified. A product's performance on a customer attribute is often affected by multiple design parameters. For instance, the noise level of a laser printer is affected by print head technology, centrifugal fan and paper feeder. The relationship matrix indicates the extent to which each product characteristic affects each customer attribute. These ratings are usually based on the judgement of experienced engineering and marketing associates.
- Relationship within engineering characteristics. The roof matrix specifies whether a change in one characteristic affects another. For instance, improvements in the cartridge system will result in improvements in the toning system.
- Benchmarks: Objective measures of performance on engineering characteristics for the new product and competing products.

- Judgments of technical difficulties, imputed importance and costs of achieving target engineering characteristics (Not shown in Exhibit 10.8).

The house of quality is essentially an elegant approach to depicting comprehensive product design information within a single construct, in a manner that associates from different disciplines can readily comprehend. It improves cross-functional planning and communication, and leads to quicker, superior decisions.

CHAPTER 11

Product Validation

Exhibit 11.0 The first moment of truth: Will she pick the brand up and place it in her cart?

Preview

Consumer goods companies devote considerable time, resource and attention to appeal to the hearts and minds of consumers so that they may powerfully influence them when they seek to find the product, when they initially encounter it, and when they actually experience it. These moments of truth ultimately determine how a new product will perform in the marketplace.

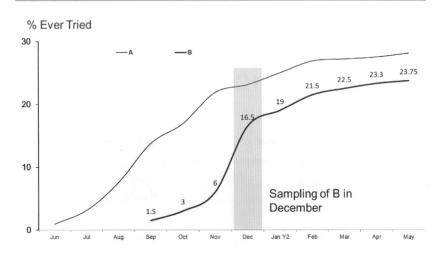

% Ever Tried

Exhibits 11.1 % of consumers who ever bought brands 'A' and 'B'. In the case of 'B' some trials were induced by the sampling exercise in Dec Y1.

For business marketing firms, it is the touchpoints with their customers that represent their moments of truth. Whether it is the customer's interaction with the firm's product or service, or with the employees of the firm, the experiences offer opportunities to build the firm's brand equity.

That the incidence of failure of new products is particularly high in FMCG, stresses the need for pre- and post-launch validation. The validation techniques employed in the industry are based primarily on measures of how well a new product is likely to perform during its moments of truth.

Most of this chapter is devoted to these validation techniques which are categorized as pre-launch and post-launch. The pre-launch methods include simulated test markets such as BASES, MicroTest, Designor and Assessor, and controlled store tests. Post-launch methods include the Parfitt–Collins model which is suited for FMCG, and the Bass Diffusion model which is applicable for consumer durables.

The Hecto Grow case study that follows this chapter, serves to illustrate the application of the Parfitt–Collins model in evaluating the launch of a new product.

Moments of Truth

"We have 50,000 moments of truth every day." — Jan Carlzo, CEO SAS (Scandinavian Airlines System) Group from 1981–1994 referring to every time an SAS employee came into contact with a customer.

In consumer markets, the *First Moment of Truth* (FMOT) is often described as the shopper's first encounter with the brand in-store. There are many moments that lead to this moment — these are the times the consumer initially gets to know the brand. It encompasses the moments she sees the brand on TV, or online, or some other medium; or when she hears about it from a friend. These moments convey the *product concept* to her, and craft her first impression. They generate appeal or the desire to experience the product, and determine whether or not she will try it. The encounter in-store, the moment of truth, is the culmination of these moments; it is where the brand has to close the sale (Exhibit 11.0). Will she pick the brand up and place it in her cart?

A good indicator of a brand's performance at its first moment of truth is the trial rate. Drawn from consumer panel data, the build-up of trial for the two brands labelled 'A' and 'B', in Exhibit 11.1, appears to be fairly strong.

Incidentally, Google coined the term *zero moment of truth* (ZMOT) to refer to the moments before the first, when the consumer searches for products that may or may not exist. By tracking their online behaviour, marketers are able to gauge what consumers are seeking. This is particularly useful information for spotting market trends and gaps, and for generating ideas and insights for new products.

The *second moment of truth* (SMOT) occurs when the consumer uses the product. Product experiences shape her views about the brand, and determine whether she will continue to use it; whether she will adopt it. This collection of moments offer the opportunity to build and strengthen a *relationship* with the consumer; to delight her and to keep her engaged.

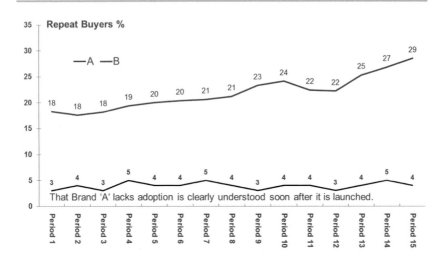

Exhibits 11.2   % of consumers who repeat bought brands 'A' and 'B'.

The repeat buying rate (RBR), which is defined later in the Parfitt–Collins model, captures the essence of SMOT. Derived from consumer panel data, it is an indicator of the propensity of trialists to continue buying the brand, and is measured in the context of their total purchases of the category.

The *repeat buyers %*, depicted in Exhibit 11.2, is also an indicator of the success of a brand at the SMOT. It measures the proportion of trialists who repeat purchase.

Consumer goods companies devote considerable time, resource and attention to appeal to the hearts and minds of consumers so that they may powerfully influence them when they seek to find the product (ZMOT), when they initially encounter it (FMOT), and when they actually experience it (SMOT).

For business marketing firms, it is the touchpoints with their customers that represent their moments of truth. Whether it is the customer's interaction with the firm's product or service, or with the employees of the firm, the experiences offer opportunities to build the firm's brand equity.

% Market Share

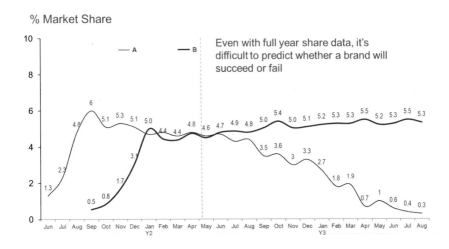

Exhibit 11.3 Market share of brands 'A' and 'B'.

Launch Validation Methods

The moments of truth ultimately determine how a new product will perform. The product can succeed only if it develops a substantial base of regular consumers who, after trying the brand, continue to buy it on an ongoing basis.

Brand 'B', which exhibited strong trial and repeat purchase, gains market share and sustains it over time. On the other hand, Brand 'A', which performed poorly at the SMOT, loses market share, as can be seen from Exhibit 11.3.

The exhibit also highlights that *the early sales and market share readings for a new product do not reveal the product's future performance.* Even by May Y2, one year after Brand 'A' is launched, it is hard to gauge the direction that the brands' share is heading. On the other hand, if the brand's manager was aware of the brand's RBR, she would know its predicament.

That the incidence of failure of new products is particularly high in FMCG, stresses the need for pre- and post-launch validation. The

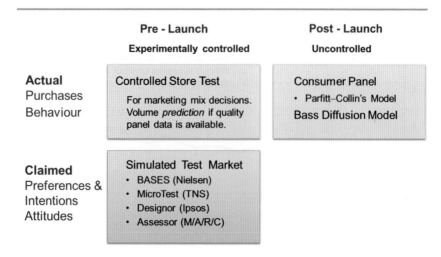

Exhibit 11.4 Pre- and post-launch evaluation methods.

validation techniques are based primarily on measures of how well a new product is likely to perform at its FMOT and SMOT.

Exhibit 11.4 presents some well-known product validation methods. The tools most often used for pre-launch validation are simulated test markets (STM) and controlled test markets, such as controlled store tests. For post-launch validation, the Parfitt–Collin's model, which relies on consumer panel data, works well of FMCG products.

Since STM systems adopt a standardized approach, and their results are accurate and comparable across categories and across markets, they are popular with many FMCG companies. Norms and benchmarks allow these companies to clearly spell out the go/no-go criteria, and many of them have explicit rules and guidelines on the use of STMs for the launch of any major NPD initiative.

Though they are better suited for FMCG products where adoption of products is reflected in consumers' willingness to continue buying, STMs have also successfully been adapted for categories like over-the-counter (OTC) medicines, quick-serve restaurants, durable goods and services.

The Bass diffusion model is used for forecasting sales of goods in categories that are infrequently purchased. The model is versatile and is known to works well for a very wide range of categories and application fields within sectors like consumer durables, computers and technology products, medicine and medical services, agricultural innovations and services, prestige personal care, movies, books and so on. It has limitations, however, from the standpoint of product validation, because accurate estimation of the potential of an innovation usually requires a few years of sales data. By this time, for a newly launched product, key investments in product development, would already have been made. The Bass estimates do however serve as a useful guide for future NPD efforts.

Real world test markets, where a new product is launched into a small representative geographical area, are no longer favoured by marketers. They incur high costs, are time consuming, and are not known to yield superior results over STMs. Moreover a real world test market fully exposes the new initiative to competitors. In the worst case scenario a powerful competitor may be better placed to exploit the benefit of the test market. A case in point is P&G's launch into test market of Ariel concentrate detergent powder in Vizag, India.

Test Market of Ariel in Vizag

The launch of Ariel was of considerable significance as this was P&G's initial assault on to the vast Indian detergent market. Moreover Ariel was the first concentrate powder to be launched in India, and its impact on market dynamics was of great interest to P&G and its competitors.

Hindustan Lever Limited (HLL) responded swiftly to the test market, with a number of competitive manoeuvres. A fighter brand, Rin Concentrate Powder was launched in Vizag. Scientists at HLL's research centre intensified efforts to develop competing concentrate powders using indigenous ingredients. An in-house consumer panel of over a thousand households was also set up by HLL's market research team in Vizag, within a few months of the introduction of Ariel. This panel gave HLL considerable advantage over their arch rivals, in their understanding of the performance of concentrates in the test market.

P&G also lost its first mover advantage. By the time the company was ready to nationally launch Ariel, HLL's Surf Ultra concentrate powder was fully developed, and the two brands were introduced into Indian cities at roughly the same time.

Simulated Test Markets

Simulated test markets (STMs) provide sales estimates of a new product *prior* to their launch. They are used by management to make the "go/no-go" decision prior to the launch of the new product.

Pioneering work in STMs began in the 1960s, and most of the commercially available STM systems were marketed initially in the mid to late '70s. Amongst these the best known are Assessor, BASES, Designor and MicroTest. Mostly similar in nature these tools decompose sales into trial volume and repeat volume, and estimate each of these components to predict the new product's sales volume for the first and second year of launch.

Assessor was developed at the Sloan School in 1973 by Alvin J. Silk and Glen L. Urban, and is currently marketed by M/A/R/C Research.

Julian Bond is credited with developing MicroTest at the MR agency Research International in the 1980s. Research International was acquired by the Kantar Group (WPP) in 1989 and was merged with TNS in 2009.

The research agency Novaction developed Perceptor, a concept testing system that was based on Assessor in 1979, and later in 1986 introduced Designor. The firm was bought over by Ipsos in 2001.

BASES, currently marketed by Nielsen, was developed by Lynn Y.S. Lin at Burke Marketing Research in 1977. Details about BASES, which is currently the leading STM in the market research industry, are provided in the next section.

STMs typically adopt one of two approaches to forecast sales: purchase intent and/or preference. Purchase intent gauges respondents' likelihood of purchase on a 5-point rating scale, and adjusts these claims for overstatement. In the preference approach, participants purchase a product from a competitive set that includes the new product. BASES and MicroTest are designed on purchase intent, whereas Designor and

Assessor were originally based on preference share. Over time, some of the above models have evolved to incorporate elements of both these approaches.

STM interviews are conducted in two stages: concept and after-use. The concept stage yields information on the product's appeal and trial rate. Subsequently, after allowing respondents time to use product samples, the post-usage interview yields information on respondents' likelihood to repurchase the product.

The following information is obtained at both the concept and after-use stages, for forecasting trial and repeat volume:

- Purchase intention: This is gauged through statements that describe how respondents feel about buying the product (See example in Exhibit 11.8).
- Share of preference: Respondents select one or more products from a competitive set displayed on a simulated shelf.
- Claimed units: Respondents are asked how much of the product, if any, they will buy.
- Claimed frequency: Respondents are asked how often, if ever, they would buy the product if it became available.

Besides volume forecasting, STMs provide diagnostic insights on how to improve the marketing mix and optimize performance. They evaluate the strength of the mix on underlying factors that make new products appealing to consumers, such as the following:

- Novelty: Rating product on uniqueness.
- Likeability (and Relevance): Overall liking of the product.
- Credibility: Believability of the statements made about the product.
- Affordability: Price/Value perception.

STM studies also seek to obtain information on product usage, perception on key image and performance attributes, suggested improvement, drivers and inhibiters, and the source of volume (i.e. what product would it replace).

To reliably forecast sales, STMs should test the final mix, or a mix that is close to final. If product development has not reached this stage, a concept product test (CPT) or a concept screener may be the appropriate tool to use.

The insights gleaned from a CPT are a sub-set of those from a STM. Moreover, since there are no product prototypes for respondents to use, there is no after-use survey. Hence only ballpark volume estimates based on assumed repeat performance can be generated in a CPT.

Concept screening systems are useful at an earlier stage in the product development process when marketers are reviewing a broad range of ideas or concepts for further development. Concept screeners help prioritize and select the most promising among these concepts.

Typically STM service providers maintain a suite of products that cater for various stages of development of concept and marketing mix. The BASES suite for instance includes Concept Constructor and BASES SnapShot which are concept screeners, BASES I, a CPT where only concepts, not prototypes, are tested, and BASES II, the full blown STM.

The success of STM systems like BASES is largely because of their intuitive appeal and reputation for accuracy. By and large STM systems claim average deviation within $\pm$ 10% of actual sales. Changes in market dynamics (the internet, faster speed-to-market) have driven numerous incremental improvements in STM systems. They have become more modular in design and take less time to run. The fundamentals, however, of simulated test markets have not changed since their inception over 40 years back.

BASES

BASES (Booz-Allen Sales Estimating System) is a STM which integrates *consumer response* data with manufacturers' *marketing plans* to assess the volumetric potential of concepts and products *prior* to introduction.

The system was developed in 1977 by Lynn Y.S. Lin who at the time was with Burke Marketing Research. Lin was inspired by work on

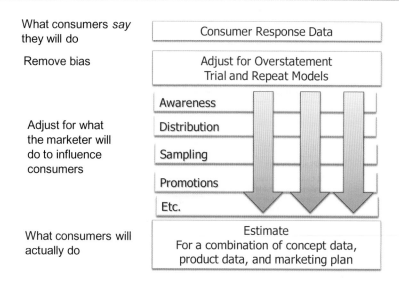

What consumers *say* they will do	Consumer Response Data
Remove bias	Adjust for Overstatement Trial and Repeat Models
Adjust for what the marketer will do to influence consumers	Awareness / Distribution / Sampling / Promotions / Etc.
What consumers will actually do	Estimate For a combination of concept data, product data, and marketing plan

Exhibit 11.5 BASES overview.

market simulators at Pillsbury where he was working prior to joining Burke. BASES was acquired by Nielsen in 1998.

BASES Premise

Consumers do not usually do what they claim to do; and often the difference between claims and behaviours is very significant. This inconvenient truth, which complicates market research in general, must not be overlooked in product validation.

As with other STMs, BASES rides on the premise that there exists a strong correlation between consumers' claimed purchase behaviour and what subsequently transpires in the marketplace. While consumers overstate their intended purchase behaviour, they tend to do so with consistency.

It has been observed that the level of overstatement varies by country, by culture, and by measure. With a database of about 200,000 concept tests (as of 2014), BASES is able to accurately estimate the adjustment factors required to deflate the respondents' claims such that they closely reflect their behaviour.

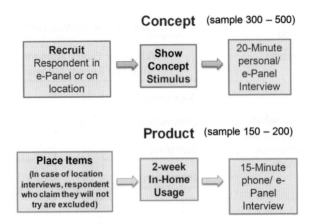

Exhibit 11.6 Data collection at concept and product stage.

Model Structure

An overview of the model is provided in Exhibit 11.5. BASES essentially takes consumer response data (what people say they will do), deflates it to adjust for overstatement, and adjusts for the impact of marketing activities to yield behavioural data (a forecast of what people will actually do).

Data Collection

Online is the preferred and primary mode of data collection as it yields considerable savings in time and cost of study. BASES has e-Panels in a number of markets in North America, Europe and Asia; the largest amongst these is the US e-Panel, comprising 125,000.

Where studies require face-to-face interaction (e.g. sniff or taste tests), mall intercept, controlled location tests and door to door methods are used for interviewing respondents.

The two stage interviewing process is depicted in Exhibit 11.6. The concept stage, where respondents respond to questions on the product concept, yields information on product trial.

In case of face-to-face interviews, those respondents who indicate they will not try the product ("definitely would not try", "probably would not try") are dropped from the product placement stage. For

Introducing new Jasmine ambrosia drink

'Refreshingly Nutritious'

Introducing a new ambrosia drink that is especially made for people seeking a nutritious, appetizing drink that helps release anxiety.

Jasmine is made from nectar and green grape juice. It contains the essence of the Jasmine flower which is known to regulate breathing and reduce tension and anxiety. It contains no preservatives.

Jasmine is a healthy drink that is well suited for the entire family.

Sizes
330 ml: $ 1.20
6 x 330 ml: $ 6.00

Exhibit 11.7 Example of a concept board *(sourced from a student project, where ambrosia is a fictional category).*

e-Panel surveys however, all respondents are moved to the product placement stage, and receive samples. After allowing respondents time to use the product samples, a post-usage interview is conducted to obtain information on respondents' likelihood to repurchase the product.

During the concept stage, either a concept board (like the one shown in Exhibit 11.7) or a commercial is used for conveying the product concept and the brand's positioning. The board contains the information that will be communicated by advertising as well as details on prices, sizes and varieties. Other than that, no additional information about the brand or competitor's products is provided.

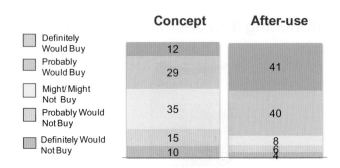

Concept   After-use

Definitely Would Buy

Probably Would Buy

Might/ Might Not Buy

Probably Would Not Buy

Definitely Would Not Buy

Concept: 12, 29, 35, 15, 10

After-use: 41, 40, 8, 6, 4

Exhibit 11.8 Purchase intent — proportion of respondent across a 5-point rating scale.

Analysis and Forecasting

The concept and after-use surveys obtain information for the purpose of volume forecasting. This includes purchase intent, purchase quantity (i.e. the quantity respondents' claim they will buy should they try the product), and the frequency of purchasing should they continue to buy. The new product is rated on the factors that typically evoke consumers' desire to purchase, for instance, novelty, likeability, credibility and affordability. Information is also obtained on product usage, its perception on key image and performance attributes, suggested improvement, drivers and inhibiters, and the source of volume.

Purchase intent is measured on a 5-point rating scale similar to the one shown in the example in Exhibit 11.8. Considering that it pertains to respondents' claimed intent to purchase, we need benchmarks to interpret this information. Whether the top 2 box scores of 41% and 81% for concept and after-use purchase intent are good or bad depends on how they compare with the BASES benchmarks.

BASES database of about 200,000 tests is the primary device used for interpretation. It serves as the source for benchmarks for all key measures, both at the concept and after-use phase. It is noted that while after-use purchase intent strongly correlates with in-market success, purchase intent at the concept phase is not as good a reflection of in-market success. Success targets accordingly are derived from the after-use scores obtained for products that were tested by BASES and that

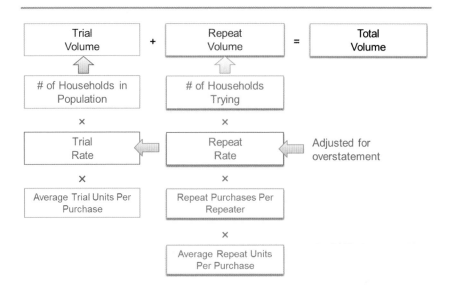

Exhibit 11.9 Volume estimation.

subsequently achieved in-market success. Should a new product score higher than the BASES targets, it will have a high chance for success.

To generate a forecast BASES requires the following inputs on the marketing plan for the new product:

- Introduction dates
- Budget
- Distribution and out-of-stock across retail channels
- Advertising schedule
- Consumer promotion schedule
- Trade promotion schedule
- Retail sales for category and company's internal sales data
- Seasonality

To the extent that execution is not in sync with plan, actual sales volume would differ from the BASES estimates. It is however possible to revise volume estimates based on revisions to the marketing plan.

The volume is forecasted by decomposing total sales into trial and repeat volume, as depicted in Exhibit 11.9. The forecast which pertains to the first two years of launch, yields trial volume, repeat volume, and consumption in terms of average frequency of purchase and the average quantity per occasion.

In terms of key deliverables, BASES provides an estimate of a new product's volume potential. It also estimates the product's source of growth — how much the new product will cannibalize the company's brands, and how much it will gain from competitors. In addition research diagnostics reveal the strengths and weaknesses of the new product initiative, and insights on how to improve the product, its mix and the execution plan.

Controlled Store Test

As the name suggests, Controlled Store Test (CST) is a test conducted in-store to assess the potential of an initiative, usually in relation to a new product. It is appealing because of its real world setting — from the standpoint of a new product launch, the store shelf is the point where the consumers' initial encounters with the product culminate into the act of buying it.

Applications
CST is particularly useful for fine-tuning elements of the mix, for example:

- Special displays and promotions: Determine which type of displays, promotions, in-store sampling and in-store media work best for the brand.
- Merchandizing: Assess the impact on shelf allocation of arrangement such as brands stocked vertically or horizontally.
- Evaluation of different price points, types of packaging, product line mix and extensions.

Note that unless a CST is supported with disaggregate transaction data, such as loyalty panel data, that reveals trial and repeat purchase, it is not a reliable method for *predicting* a product's expected sales or market share.

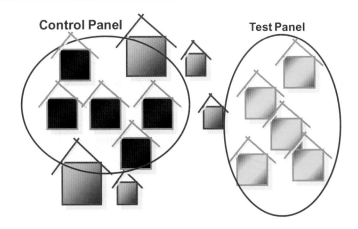

Exhibit 11.10 Matched panel approach: control and test panels.

Methodology

An important prerequisite is the cooperation of one or more retailers. Since their stores are deployed for test purposes, their support is crucial to the success of the research programme.

CST methods require controls in place — stockouts and unintended in-store activities that influence sales are not admissible. For a new product, in-store media such as shelf talkers or floor vision will be required to convey the new product's positioning.

CST is essentially a form of A/B testing. The *matched panel* CST is a commonly used approach that requires two matched panels of stores: Control panel and Test panel. The test panel is where changes to the mix are introduced, whereas the control panel is insulated from these changes. The two panels are matched on a range of criteria including:

- Store size
- Category turnover
- Product range
- Strength of test brand
- Historical trend
- Shopper demographics

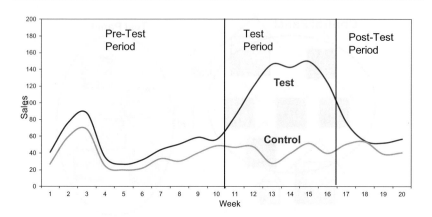

Exhibit 11.11   Analysis of matched panels.

Avg Sales / week	Test Panel	Control Panel
Pre-Test	51.1	37.8
Test phase	128.1	42.5
Post-Test	60.3	46.2
Sales Index		
Pre-Test	100.0	100.0
Test phase	250.6	112.7
Post-Test	117.9	122.3

Exhibit 11.12   Sales summary for CST in Exhibit 11.11.

One advantage of matched panel is that it compensates for seasonality and other environmental factors. Analysis is based on sales trend comparison within the two panels, over a duration that covers the test period and time intervals, before and after the test. Statistical methods such as ANOVA (analysis of variance) may be used to analyse the difference between the two panels, and test their significance.

Consider for example the results of a CST depicted in Exhibits 11.11 and 11.12. The special displays and in-store media activities during the test period resulted in sales volume growth of 122% (250.6 over 112.7).

Latin squares is another approach to CST where an $N \times N$ table (see Exhibit 11.13) is filled with N different scenarios in such a way that each

	Panel 1	Panel 2	Panel 3
Period 1	A	B	C
Period 2	C	A	B
Period 3	B	C	A

Exhibit 11.13 Example of Latin square for 3 different scenarios to be tested, say price: A: $10, B: $12.50, C: $15.

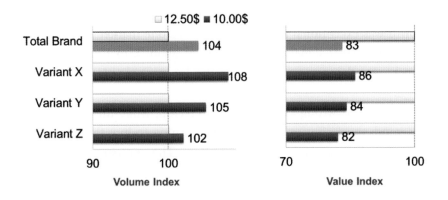

Exhibit 11.14 Case example: impact of a price reduction on sales volume and value.

scenario occurs exactly once in each row (time period) and exactly once in each column (panel of test stores). This approach permits simultaneous evaluation of multiple scenarios. It compensates for seasonality as well as idiosyncrasies across different groups of stores.

Case Example

Objective: To measure impact on sales volume and value of price drop from $12.50 to $10.00 on a shampoo brand with variants *X*, *Y* and *Z*.

Methodology: *Latin Squares*

Analysis in Exhibit 11.14 reveals that this shampoo brand is fairly inelastic. It gains a relatively small 4% in volume, and loses 17% in value, when price is dropped from $12.50 to $10.00, a 20% reduction.

Product Launch Evaluation

Some years back, Treetop, a juice drink in tetra packs was launched into the Indian market. It was a novelty at that time, and sales in the first year were so good that the manufacturer substantially expanded production capacity. But sales plummeted soon after and never recovered.

More recently, in a major offensive, a food conglomerate set up a business division to launch nutritional bars into Asia. Initially the growth was exceptional as the brand entered one market after another. However distress signals began to emerge about 8 to 12 months after launch. Another year or two later the business division was closed down.

What went wrong? In the case of Treetop, while the product trial was good, most consumers were not returning to buy the juice drink after their first, second or third purchase. The company was reading retail sales, which looked very strong in the first year of launch. However, what the sales data did not reveal was the repeat purchase rate, which for Treetop was low. In the second example, while the nutritional bars were filling the distribution pipeline and going on the shelf, not many were going off the shelves. The regional team, for some time, continued to post good aggregate primary sales as they kept entering new territories, expanding their distribution and stretching the pipeline.

Primary sales and retail sales tell us how the product is performing at that time, but as can be gauged from the above examples, they are not a good prediction for the future. On the other hand, consumer panels are particularly good in predicting sales, and should be used for this purpose.

Non-performing products result in financial and opportunity losses; and if corrective actions are not taken promptly, they also impair corporate reputation and dilute brand equity. It is important that such products are identified early after launch, and improved or discontinued before they adversely affect the company's business and its reputation with consumers, retailers and other stake holders.

Considering the high rate of failure, it is important that diagnostic and predictive research continues after the product is launched. Ability to look into the future and gauge the expected share of their new product gives management the confidence they need, to take timely decisions. It gives them the conviction to further invest in performing products, and cut their losses in non-performing products.

The Parfitt–Collins Model

Parfitt–Collins model is a consumer panel based technique for estimating a new product's expected market share soon after it is launched. The basic model was first presented at the 1961 ESOMAR Congress by Baum and Dennis, and subsequently by John Parfitt and Barry Collins at the 1967 MRS Conference.

Market share is a variable, and in an ever changing environment it constantly fluctuates. These fluctuations are more pronounced particularly during the launch of a product when consumers are trying out the product, and manufacturers are strongly promoting it. It usually takes more than a year for the sales baseline to stabilize, fluctuating over a narrower bandwidth. The Parfitt–Collins model's share prediction pertains to new product's expected market share when this relatively stable state occurs.

By decomposing a new product's sales in terms of fundamental growth drivers — trial and repeat purchase — this model is able to estimate the expected share of the new product. These drivers which reveal consumers' desire to try the brand and their willingness to continue buying after experiencing it reflect the brand's ability to succeed at the FMOT and the SMOT.

Purchases on 5th month after trial	New Product	Total Category	The 5th month after trial
Anita	10	20	June
Betty	0	60	August
Claire	5	20	September
Total	15	100	RBR(5) = 15/100 = 15%

Exhibit 11.15 Illustration of RBR: Purchases by three consumers on the fifth month after they first tried the brand.

Trial and Repeat Purchase

To be adopted by consumers, a product must succeed at both the first and the second moments of truth. It can succeed only if it develops a substantial base of regular consumers who are drawn to try the brand, and having tried it, are induced to continue to buy it on an ongoing basis.

Success at the FMOT can be gauged by the trial rate, the proportion of consumers who try the new product. It reflects the attractiveness of the new product concept, how effectively it is communicated, and how well the brand is positioning. The trial rate is also strongly influenced by causal factors such as distribution, promotions and sampling.

Success at the SMOT depends on whether consumers' experiences with the product evoke the desire to continue buying it. It is a function of the extent to which the new product lives up to or exceeds expectations.

Repeat Buying Rate (RBR)

The RBR is a measure of the propensity of consumers to continue buying a product. In terms of definition, RBR(t) is the brand's share among those who repeat purchased the brand t periods (usually the time period is in months) after they first tried it. RBR (5) = 15% means that for the average trialist, the new product constitutes 15% of purchases of the product category, on the 5th interval after trial.

Exhibit 11.15 illustrates how RBR is computed. It depicts three trialists of a new product: Anita, Betty and Claire. Anita bought the new product in January, Betty in March and Claire in April. The fifth interval after trial is June for Anita, August for Betty and September for Claire. On their respective fifth interval, Anita bought 10 units of the new product and 20 units of the category as a whole, Betty bought zero units of the new product and 60 units of the category, and Claire bought 5 units of the new product and 20 units of the category. Their total purchases of the new product (10 + 0 + 5) as a proportion of the total purchases of category (20 + 60 + 20) equals 15%, which by definition is RBR(5).

Note that RBR computation is based on all those who ever tried the new product, which includes current as well as lapsed buyers. It is measured over each purchase occasion after trial — so there exists a whole series of RBRs. RBR(1) is the RBR value at first purchase interval after trial, RBR(2) pertains to the 2nd purchase interval, RBR(3) to the 3rd and so on.

As novelty wears off, the level of interest in a new product is likely to diminish. Promotions and advertising which peak during launch, decline thereafter. With fatigue setting in, RBRs tend to decline before they stabilize. RBR(1) is usually higher than the other RBRs, followed by RBR(2), RBR(3) and so on. Yet the rate of decline rapidly decelerates and RBR values stabilize after the first few intervals, for successful new products. This stable value of the RBR is a measure of consumers' willingness to continue buying a brand. It is the parameter in the Parfitt–Collins model that usually has the greatest bearing on the success of the new product.

Buying Index

Trial Rate × RBR is a fair approximation of a product's expected market share, except that it assumes that the consumers buying the new product tend to buy as much of the category as the average category buyer. To factor the heaviness of buying of the category by consumers of the new product, the Parfitt–Collins model introduces a third parameter, the buying index:

$$Buying\ Index = \frac{[Category\ Volume\ per\ buyer]_{Brand\ Repeaters}}{[Category\ Volume\ per\ buyer]_{ALL\ Category\ Buyers}}$$

The buying index is a measure of the heaviness of buying of the product category by the new brand's repeat buyers, and is computed as the ratio of purchases of category by the brand's repeat buyers over the purchases of category by all category buyers. If, for instance, the buying index is 1.25, it tells us that the average repeat buyer of the brand buys 25% more of the category than the average category buyer.

The Model

$$Market\ Share\ =\ Trial\ Rate \times RBR \times Buying\ Index$$

Provided the sample size is adequate, the above forecast provides a reliable estimate of the brand's baseline market share, till the time market dynamics change. Since dynamics do tend to change, if panel data is readily accessible, marketers should continue to periodically revise estimates of a new product's market share over the first year or two of launch.

The Parfitt–Collins model works best for those categories where the inter-purchase interval is small. Categories like bread and fresh milk for instance, that are purchased at least once a week, can be forecasted within a few weeks of launch. The model also works well for products bought on a monthly or quarterly basis, which included most packaged foods and personal care products. It is not, however, recommended for products that are infrequently re-purchased.

Diagnostics

The underlying patterns for the build-up of trial, RBR and sales are depicted in Exhibit 11.16. The sales trends vary depending on the RBR and the pace of growth of penetration, and there is often a kink or a hump during the first year of launch. The existence of these diverse patterns that may trend up and down explains why early sales data does not provide a good reflection of the share the new product is likely to achieve. Moreover, sales data is also affected by causal factors like promotions and advertising.

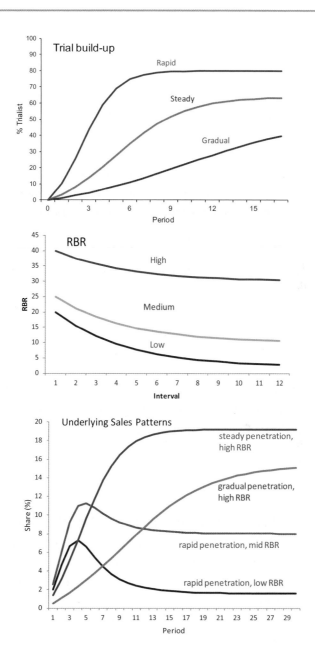

Exhibit 11.16 Trial, RBR and sales patterns.

RBR has a lasting impact and is usually the prime determinant of the long term success of a product. If a product has low RBR, marketers need to investigate, via customized research, the reasons why consumers do not repeat purchase. Raising RBR usually requires refining some of the elements of the marketing mix.

If RBR meets or exceeds expectations but sales are constrained due to low trial rate, marketers may use sampling, price discounts, product displays and other forms of promotions to induce trial. They also need to examine the product proposition and the manner it is communicated, to understand why target consumers do not find the product appealing enough to try it.

Though well-executed promotions yield valuable gains in the trial rate at a time when the new product is striving to gain adoption, their impact in the long run is diluted due to lowering of RBR. The propensity of consumers induced to try the new product through promotions to continue buying the brand is likely to be lower than that for those consumers who were drawn to it, irrespective of the promotion.

Marketers should also use the gain–loss analysis to determine the source of growth of the new product. Of interest is the extent it is cannibalizing the company's other products.

The Bass Diffusion Model

The Parfitt–Collins model is best suited for FMCG products where adoption of products is reflected in consumers' willingness to continue buying. For these products the development of brand loyalty through repeat purchases is the measure of the success of a brand, and this is a function of RBR and trial rate.

In the case of products like consumer durables that are infrequently purchased, trial is a reflection of adoption. For such products, where the consumer's inter-purchase interval extends into years, innovation diffusion models may be used to predict sales.

The Bass diffusion model is one of the most thoroughly researched models in market forecasting. Published in 1969, the model has proven to be versatile in representing the different patterns of adoption of products — from "sleepers", where the sales pick up is gradual, to the "blockbusters". It works well for a very wide range of categories and application fields within sectors like consumer durables, computers and technology products, medicine and medical services, agricultural innovations and services, prestige personal care, movies, books and so on.

The underlying assumption is that adoption by potential customers is triggered by two types of behaviour: innovation and imitation. "Innovation" is driven via influences such as advertising that are **not** dependent on the decisions of others in the social system. Its impact is more pronounced during the early stages of the product life cycle. "Imitation" is the influence of prior adopters through positive word-of-mouth.

The model further assumes:

- Maximum number of potential adopters or buyers is fixed.
- All potential adopters eventually purchase.
- Repeat purchases are not accounted for.

The basic model is represented by the following equations:

$$n(t) = adopters\ via\ 'innovation'$$
$$+ adopters\ via\ 'imitation'$$

$$adopters\ via\ 'innovation' = p \times remaining\ potential$$
$$= p[M - N(t)]$$

$$adopters\ via\ 'imitation'$$
$$= q \times proportion\ of\ adopters$$
$$\times remaining\ potential$$

$$= q\frac{N(t)}{M}[M - N(t)]$$

$$n(t) = p[M - N(t)] + q\frac{N(t)}{M}[M - N(t)] : Equation\ 1$$

where:
$n(t)$ = *number of adopters at time t*
$N(t) = n(0) + n(1) + n(2) + ...\ n(t)$
M = *total number of potential adopters*
p = *coefficient of innovation*
q = *coefficient of imitation*

Exhibit 11.17 provides a comparison of the adoption trajectories for different values of p and q. If $q>p$, as is normally the case for most innovations, then imitation behaviour dominates, and the plot of sales over time will resemble a bell shape. On the other hand, if $q <= p$, as is the case for blockbuster products, then sales peak at introduction and decline in every subsequent time period.

Model Calibration

The model representation (Equation 1) is essentially of the form:

$$X_i = a + bY_i + cY_i^2$$
$$where\ a = pM,\ b = q - p\ and\ c = -q/M.$$

If the innovation has been marketed, estimates of p, q and M from historical sales data may be obtained using a variety of statistical methods applicable for the above functional form. Of these the nonlinear least square method is known to yield better predictions, whereas the ordinary least squares linear regression is the easiest to work with.

If no sales data is available for the innovation, the parameters may be sourced from the diffusion patterns of product categories that exhibited similar characteristics when they were adopted. Estimates of coefficients p and q, for a wide range of product categories are readily available among a host of research publications. Based on a compilation provided in the text *Principles of Marketing Engineering* (Lilien *et al.*, 2013) the average values across a wide range of products is 0.035 for the

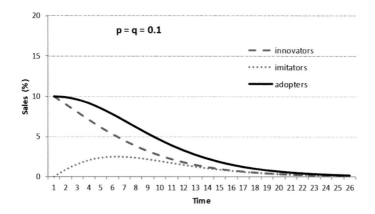

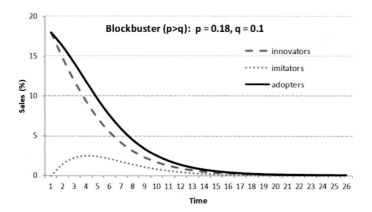

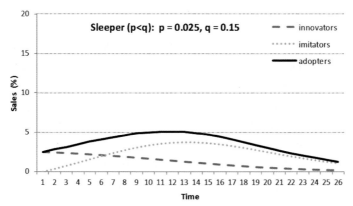

Exhibit 11.17 Adoption patterns for different *p* and *q* values.

coefficient of innovation, and 0.390 for the coefficient of imitation. The book provides industry specific data for agricultural, consumer electronics, appliances, information technology, medical fields and a range of other products and services.

Limitations and Extensions

The assumptions inherent within the model and the inputs that it relies on, give rise to a number of limitations and model extensions including the following:

- The basic Bass model works best for sales patterns that resemble the forms shown in Exhibit 11.17. This may apply for yearly data, but is rarely valid for monthly or quarterly sales data which fluctuates due to causal factors like promotions and advertising.
- Calibration based on sales data may be too late for most firms, and this is particularly true for yearly sales data because big investments in the product would already have been made.
- While the use of analogous category may permit forecasting at earlier stages of product development, the choice of category is crucial. Importantly historical data mostly relates to successful innovations. This bias will result in favourable predictions for new innovations, unless some adjustment is made to factor the probability of failure; which is tricky because data for analogous innovations that failed is often not readily available.
- A prime forecasting objective for marketers is to assess the potential market of a product. Where sales data is not available, the model's reliance on other sources (based on alternative research methods like Delphi or management's intuition), dilutes its utility.
- The basic model assumes that market potential is fixed. This is not true because elements of the marketing mix such as price, advertising, distribution and product keep changing. Extensions to the model allow for the incorporation of the

effects of marketing mix variables, especially price, advertising and sales efforts, on the likelihood of adoption.

- Another extension to the model allows for variation in the coefficient of imitation over time. The impact of word-of-mouth is expected to vary during different stages of the product's life cycle.

- The model is also extended to allow for repeat or replacement purchases.

- Considering that product life cycles have shrunk over the years, and new technologies cannibalize or supersede the old at a faster pace, the validity of the Bass forecast would be limited in duration.

In summary, the Bass diffusion model is a conceptually appealing model that has been extensively researched. Academics have added numerous extensions enhancing the application and accuracy of the model in predicting the diffusion of innovations for categories where repeat purchases occur after many years. A key limitation however is that accurate estimation of the potential of an innovation usually requires a few years of sales data, by which time key investments would already have been made.

CASE IV

Hecto Grow

Hectomalt

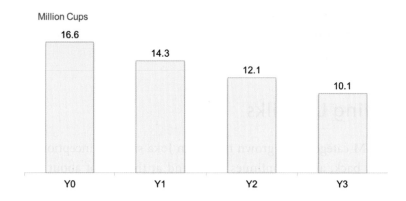

Exhibit C4.1 White malt drinks market experiences decline in Joka.

Hectomalt, a nutritious malted milk drink, experienced a prolonged period of declining sales in Joka, a small, affluent, Asian country with a population of 4 million people. To stem this decline, Hecto Corporation initially tried tweaking Hectomalt in a number of different ways — new flavours, different formats. When this failed to work, a strategy meeting was called about a year back, to seek ways to reinvigorate the brand.

Hectomalt has traditionally been classified in the health food drinks (HFD) category which consists of white drinks such as Hectomalt, and brown cocoa-based drinks such as Milo and Ovaltine. While these drinks are consumed by all age groups, children tend to be the heaviest consumers. The category was growing at a rate of 3% to 5% in recent years, spurred mainly by the cocoa-based drinks. White malt drinks, on the other hand, experienced a steady decline as can be seen from the sales trend in Exhibit C4.1. For the 12 years prior to the strategy meet, Hectomalt's volume share in HFD had plunged from 14.9% to 6.4%.

Note: The data provided in this fictitious case study is disguised.

Hectomalt's formulation comprised mainly of wheat flour, malted barley and a wide range of vitamins and minerals. Its benefits, which include affordable nourishment and hunger assuagement, were of greatest significance across the globe, during the first half of the twentieth century. Even today, Hectomalt continues to serve as an affordable source of nourishment and hunger assuagement in large parts of Asia and Africa where hunger and poverty still linger.

In markets like Joka, however, consumers' preferences and needs had changed over the decades, and sophisticated, specially formulated products like growing up milks (GUM) were better geared to meet the needs of Hectomalt's target consumers.

Growing Up Milks

The GUM category has grown rapidly in Joka since its inception about 20 years back, and it continues to expand at the rate of about 20% in value per annum. It is currently $86 million in size, which makes it more than twice the size of HFDs. Some basic market measures are listed in the following exhibit:

Retail sales estimate	4,150,000	Kg in Y3
Penetration	25	% for year
Volume per household	11,067	gm/year
Purchase vol per trip	1,150	gm
Trips per houshold	9.6	per year
Average purchase cycle	1.2	months

Exhibit C4.2 GUM market (Year 3) – basic measures.

Referred to as *Stage 3*, the majority of the GUM market comprises of specially formulated powdered milk drinks developed for one to three year old toddlers. Brands in this segment need to constantly renew their consumer base. Over the course of a year, growing up milks lose half of their consumer base — a category churn rate of 50% — as toddlers outgrow *Stage 3*. There is also a relatively small segment,

Year 3 Media Spend: $ 17.3M
(All Growing Up Milks)

	Media (%)	TV Spend (%)
Hecto Grow	28	33
Gain	28	30
Dumex	19	17
Neslac	12	5
Nespray	5	4
Grow	3	4
Pediasure	2	3
Promise	2	2
Mead Johnson	1	2

□ TV ■ Press ▨ Magazine ■ Radio ▨ Cinema ■ Bus/Taxi ▨ Hoarding

Exhibit C4.3 GUM market — advertising spend in Year 3.

Stage 4, which comprises products for young children in the 3 to 6 years age group.

Like HFDs, growing up milks also contain vitamins and minerals. In addition, they are fortified with ingredients such as arachidonic acid, docosahexaenoic acid, lutein, choline, taurine and nucleotides that manufacturers claim aid the mental and physical development of toddlers and young children. Research findings in Joka suggest that mothers tend to be influenced by these benefit claims and that they are well informed about nutritional aspects of growing up milks. Moreover they are prepared to pay the premium price of these products as they associate high price with better quality.

Launch of Hecto Grow

At the Y2 strategy meeting, it was concluded that the Hectomalt was losing relevance, and that a substantial proportion of consumers were switching to the GUM category. Bearing this in mind, Hecto Corporation intensified its efforts to develop a GUM product, and Hecto Grow, a malted growing up milk for 1 to 3-year-old toddlers, was launched into the Joka market, in April Y3.

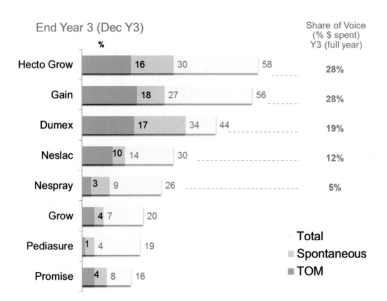

Exhibit C4.4 GUM market – advertising awareness.

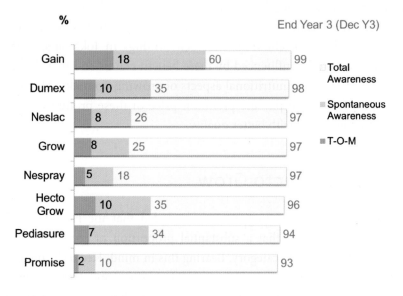

Exhibit C4.5 GUM – brand awareness.

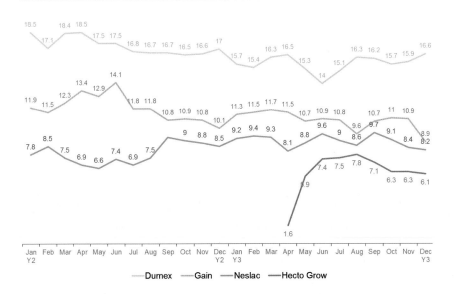

Exhibit C4.6 GUM — market value share.

Hecto Grow's launch was supported by a $4.84 million advertisement campaign of which $4.62 million was on TV, spread over the first 8 months of launch. This translated to a 28% share of voice (spend %) for Year 3 (see Exhibit C4.3) for total media and 33% share of voice on TV.

The heavy advertising resulted in high advertising awareness. As can be seen from Exhibit C4.4, Hecto Grow achieved 16% top-of-mind and 30% spontaneous advertising awareness by December Y3. During the same period, Hecto Grow also achieved 10% top-of-mind and 35% spontaneous brand awareness (Exhibit C4.5).

The brand's market share rose to 7.8% by August Y3, before slipping to 6.1% by year end. The share trend is depicted in Exhibit C4.6, alongside the three brands leading in the GUM category — Dumex, Gain and Neslac.

The supermarket/hypermarket channel is the primary sales channel in Joka, accounting for about 70% of category sales volume. The weekly sales for the three Hecto Grow packs sold in the channel is provided in

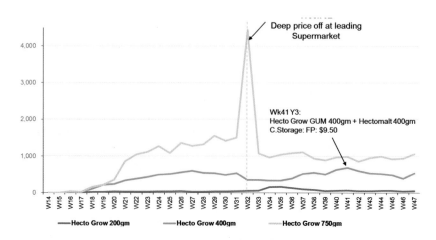

Exhibit C4.7 Sales (kg) of Hecto Grow in supermarkets/hypermarkets.

Exhibit C4.7. It reveals the heavy influence of promotions on the brand's sales within the channel.

The gain–loss analysis findings in Exhibit C4.8 revealed that two-thirds of Hecto Grow's volume was gained from Dumex and Gain. The brand's interaction with these leading brands was also very high, as may be gauged by the gain indices, shown in Exhibit C4.9, which are substantially above 100.

Exhibit C4.10 shows the cumulative proportion of GUM buying households, who tried Hecto Grow. This build-up of trial users or the trial rate of Hecto Grow was significantly above the benchmark average for GUM products.

The conversion from trial to repeat purchase hovered in the range of 35 to 38% (Exhibit C4.11), and repeat buying rate (RBR) stabilized in the range of 32% to 33% (Exhibit C4.12). Whereas trial reflects on the brand's ability to attract new consumers, RBR is a measure of the propensity of the consumers to continue buying a product. By definition, RBR(t) is the brand's share among those who repeat purchased the brand, t periods (usually months) after they first tried it. For instance, RBR(5) = 32.7% means that for the average trialist, Hecto Grow constitutes 32.7% of purchases of the product category, on the 5th interval after trial.

Gain-loss analysis (% volume)
Jan -Jun Y3 vs Jul-Dec Y3

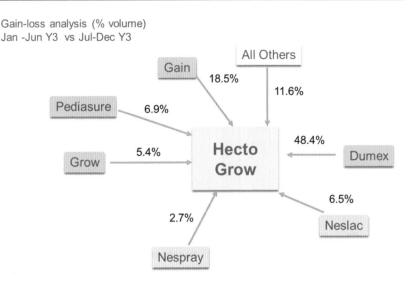

Exhibit C4.8 Hecto Grow gain–loss analysis — source of growth, in volume terms.

Jan -Jun Y3 vs Jul-Dec Y3.

Exhibit C4.9 Gain (interaction) index of Hecto Grow with Neslac, Dumex and Gain.

Trial (%): Cumulative Penetration as % of Category Buyers

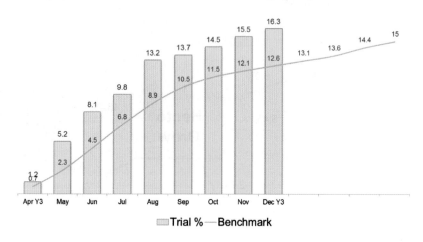

Exhibit C4.10 Hecto Grow trial — %ever tried (base: households buying growing up milks).

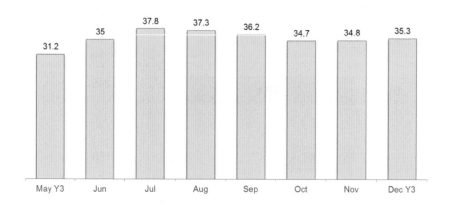

Exhibit C4.11 Hecto Grow % conversion from trial to repeat purchase.

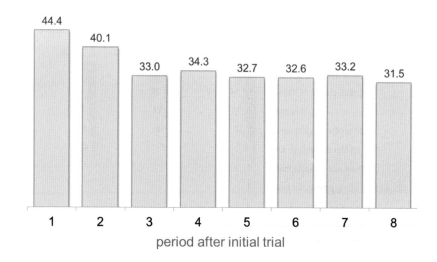

Exhibit C4.12 Repeat buying rate for Hecto Grow (GUM%).

Hecto Grow's buying index was 1.05. This index is a measure of the heaviness of buying of the product category by the new brand's repeat buyers, and is computed as the ratio of purchases of category by the brand's repeat buyers over the purchases of category by all category buyers. That Hecto Grow's buying index is 1.05 tells us that the average repeat buyer of Hecto Grow buys 5% more of the category than the average category buyer.

In a consumer research study conducted in December Y3, Hecto Grow trialists were asked whether there were any aspects about the product that they did not like. Their responses to this open-ended question are summarized in Exhibit C4.13. It reveals that 60% of lapsed consumers said they disliked some aspect about the product, and that one out of four repeat buyers also said they disliked some aspect about the product. The most frequently stated reason for dissatisfaction was that the child did not like the taste.

The same study also confirmed that children are usually the key drivers of brand choice, but, in most cases, their mothers need to be persuaded on nutritional aspects of growing up milks.

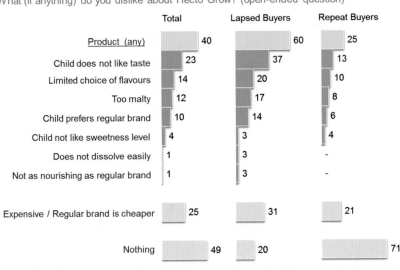

What (if anything) do you dislike about Hecto Grow? (open-ended question)

	Total	Lapsed Buyers	Repeat Buyers
Product (any)	40	60	25
Child does not like taste	23	37	13
Limited choice of flavours	14	20	10
Too malty	12	17	8
Child prefers regular brand	10	14	6
Child not like sweetness level	4	3	4
Does not dissolve easily	1	3	-
Not as nourishing as regular brand	1	3	-
Expensive / Regular brand is cheaper	25	31	21
Nothing	49	20	71

Exhibit C4.13 Aspects about Hecto Grow that consumers claim they dislike.

Hecto Grow and Hectomalt

Hecto Grow was an extension to the Hectomalt brand, and its launch was intended to enhance the equity of the Hecto range of children's drinks as a whole. In the studies that were conducted after the brand's launch, one of the objectives was to ascertain how respondents' perceptions changed after the advent of Hecto Grow. Those respondents who were aware of Hecto Grow were asked to rate the following statements on a 5-point scale varying from "strongly disagree" to "strongly agree":

- I prefer the Hecto range of drinks more now.
- Hecto meets my child's nourishment needs better now.
- I consider Hecto healthier now.

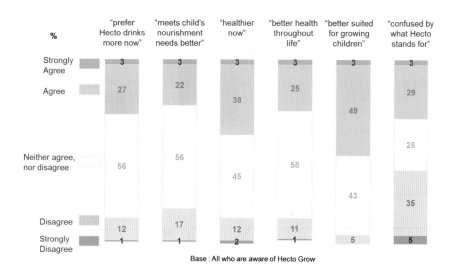

Exhibit C4.14 Perceptions of Hecto's range of drinks, after launch of Hecto Grow.

- Hecto drinks provide better health throughout life.
- Hecto is better suited for growing children.
- I am confused by what the brand Hecto stands for.

The perception ratings charted in Exhibit C4.14 summarize the response to the above question.

Hecto Corporation also had access to studies that assessed the equity of brands in the HFD and GUM markets. The brand equity indices summarized in Exhibit C4.15 were obtained from these studies. These indices are derived based on consumers response to statements that reflect the outcomes of brand equity — i.e. brand loyalty, willingness to pay a price premium, and the willingness to endure some inconvenience (e.g. travel a distance) to secure the brand.

The equity indices in the Exhibit are based on a 10-point scale where a score of 10 would mean that everybody in the market is a loyal consumer of the brand and would willingly pay a significant price premium, whereas zero means that there are no loyal consumers and

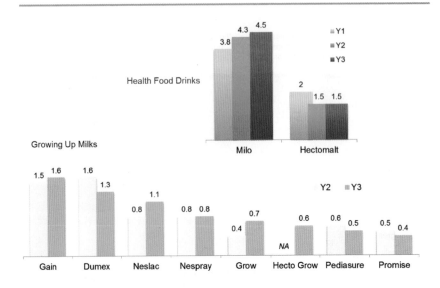

Exhibit C4.15 Brand equity indices – HFD and GUM.

nobody would pay any more than the cheapest price for that brand. Most brands on this scale have an equity index of less than 1, and only very strong brands have indices greater than 3.

It was observed also that the awareness of Hectomalt had improved since the launch of Hecto Grow. As shown in Exhibit C4.16, the brand's top-of-mind awareness in HFD grew from 7% in Y2 to 8.5% in Y3.

The two sister brands were also analysed in detail through Joka's consumer panel. Key observations from this analysis are provided in Exhibits C4.17, C4.18 and C4.19. The duplication or overlap analysis provides an understanding of the proportion of Hecto consuming households who consume both Hectomalt and Hecto Grow. The analysis depicted on Exhibit C4.18 highlights the differences and similarities in their demographic profile. And the cross-purchase basket analysis shown in Exhibit C4.19 reveals the GUM brands bought by Hectomalt buyers who have some children aged below 10 years.

One of the objectives of the analysis was to assess the synergy of the Hecto brand across the two categories. The brand's managers wanted to gain an understanding of the extent to which the brand could transcend categories.

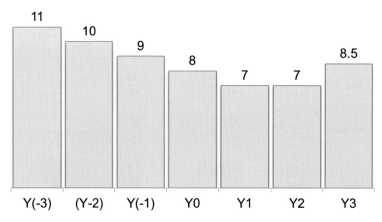

Y(-3): 3 years before Y0

Exhibit C4.16 Hectomalt: top of mind awareness in HFD.

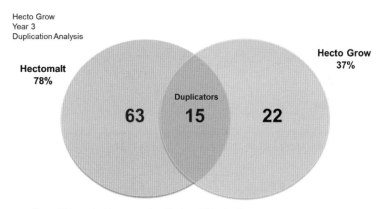

Exhibit C4.17 Hecto Grow/Hectomalt — usage overlap analysis.

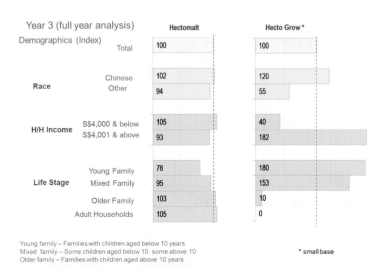

Year 3 (full year analysis)

Young family – Families with children aged below 10 years
Mixed family – Some children aged below 10, some above 10
Older family – Families with children aged above 10 years

* small base

Exhibit C4.18   Demographic profile — Hectomalt and Hecto Grow.

What brands of Growing Up Milks do **Hectomalt** buyers purchase?

Cross-Purchase analysis: Jul-Dec Y3

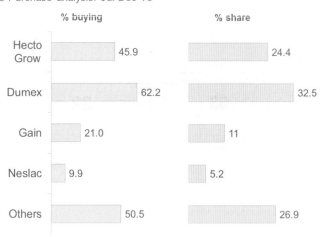

Base: Hectomalt buyers in homes with one or more child aged below 10 years

Exhibit C4.19   GUM brands bought by Hectomalt buyers.

Case Analysis

For this case, assuming the role of brand manager for Hecto Grow, you are required to assess the brand's performance, chalk out plans and initiatives, and set objectives and targets for the brand for the next financial year (Y4). You need to understand how effective was the brand's launch and what is its market potential. You also must determine what needs to be done to further grow the brand and enhance its equity.

Advertising

PART IV
Advertising

CHAPTER 12

How Advertising Works

Come alive with freshness

Totally different LIRIL. Rippled green with the exciting freshness of limes. Tangy, tingling LIRIL... makes a fresh new woman of you.

Liril THE FRESHNESS SOAP with the exciting freshness of limes

A Quality Product by HINDUSTAN LEVER

Exhibit 12.0 Liril "girl in the waterfall" ad featuring Karen Lunel.

Tradition of Great Advertising

"Don't call me a guru. Gurus are not interested in sex." — Shunu Sen.

Several years ago, in the course of being interviewed, I was intrigued by my interviewer, a short, rotund man; his big head perpetually perched a little to one side. Shunu Sen had the knack for engaging and enthralling people. We invariably succumbed to a potent concoction of wisdom, intellect, warmth and, above all else, his wickedly mischievous wit. Talent from within and outside Hindustan Lever revolved around him like planets orbiting a sun, an impression reinforced by the perpetual sight of groups of people flocked outside his room. Shunu's weakness was time management — invariably, he got absorbed with his audience.

Then as the head of marketing at Hindustan Lever (now Hindustan Unilever), and widely regarded as India's marketing guru, Shunu had an eye for great content, and an admiration for talent. Gifted associates from the best advertising agencies rewarded him with unforgettable work, including legendary campaigns for brands such as Surf (Lalitaji), Liril ("girl in the waterfall"), Rin ("zara sa Rin" [just a little Rin]) and Surf Ultra ("daag dhoonte reh jaaoge" [you'll keep searching for the stain]). It was creativity at its very best.

Alyque Padamsee, who is as highly regarded in advertising as Shunu is in marketing, had this to say while speaking of the Liril TV commercial (print version shown above in Exhibit 12.0): "It not only offers you freshness but offers you a sense of freedom. It is not just an ordinary bath. The 'girl in the waterfall' symbolizes that the bathing experience can be *bindaas* ('carefree' in Hindi). For the average Indian woman who is surrounded by chaos, in-laws, husband, children, the ten minutes in the shower are her own, where she can daydream. Now that was so compelling that the Liril ad remained unchanged for 25 years." Liril's sales skyrocketed when the ad was first aired, and the model, Karen Lunel, became an overnight celebrity.

Over an era spanning three decades, Shunu played a defining role in the transformation of consumer marketing in India. He was also the single greatest influencer fuelling the dynamic and highly talented Indian advertising community of the 1980s and 1990s. Indian commercials are often clever, sometimes thought provoking, and almost always entertaining. There is undoubtedly some truth in the claim that at a time when a government channel monopolized the small screen, Indian children were drawn to television by entertaining advertisements.

Shunu's legacy has prevailed, and for those who knew him, I must add that we admired him as much for his capacity to celebrate life in the face of adversity. I write about him to serve as an example of others like him and Padamsee, scattered around the world of marketing and advertising. William Bernbach, David Ogilvy, Leo Burnett, Marion Harper Jr., Maurice and Charles Saatchi, and Rosser Reeves, are some of the best known stars from the industry. There are numerous others across the globe, who remain better known within their spheres of influence. Like Shunu and Padamsee, these legends have contributed immensely to the tradition of great advertising across the globe.

Preview

This chapter is devoted mainly to understanding how advertising works; the mechanisms and the key themes. The following section examines advertising through the ages; the key developments, and their impact on communication and advertising. This is followed by a discussion on advertising mechanisms, and an explanation of the six key themes — salience, persuasion, likeability, symbolism, relationship, emotion — that form the basis for many of the theories on advertising.

Advertising through the Ages

"To communicate is to be human." Word of mouth, the original mode of communication, remains the most persuasive form of advertising. Its impact, though, was curtailed until social media gave people the means to exponentially expand their social network.

Numerous developments have shaped advertising, since the time voice was the primary means of communication, to our age of the internet. Some of these developments are recounted below:

- One of the earliest formal writing systems dates back to Egypt, 3300 BC. At that time ancient Egyptian writing used hieroglyphic characters that combined logographic and alphabetic elements.

- In 2000 BC, the Egyptians started carving public notices in steel, a form of outdoor advertising.
- Johannes Gutenberg, a German goldsmith and printer, invented the printing press in 1439 AD. His major work, the 42-line Gutenberg Bible, marked the start of the printing era.
- The first print advertisement in England was said to have been placed on a church door in 1472.
- Newspaper ads appeared in 1650.
- Fundamental to the success of a business is the need to make customers aware of products and services. It follows that growth in advertising is linked inextricably with developments in industry. Of particular significance is the industrial revolution (1750–1850) which led to explosive growth in the production and supply of goods, and in the advertisement of those goods, in England and Europe.
- The first radio broadcasts were aired in the early 1900s. Years later, in 1919, radio stations began to broadcast continuously. On 2 November 1920, a US radio station (KDKA) aired the first commercial broadcast.
- A number of scientists working on many different technologies spearheaded the invention of the television. The Scottish inventor John Logie Baird gave what is regarded as the first public demonstration of televised silhouette images in motion, at Selfridges Department Store in London, on March 25, 1925. His company (Baird Television Development Company/ Cinema Television) also made the first commercial TV sets in the UK in 1928.
- TV ad revenues surpassed radio and magazine ad sales in 1954.
- The World Wide Web was invented in 1969 with the creation of the Advanced Research Projects Agency (ARPA) Network (ARPANET) by ARPA of the Department of Defense (DOD). ARPANET linked time-sharing computers at four research sites by telephone lines. It took another 25 years for the internet to gain general public awareness.

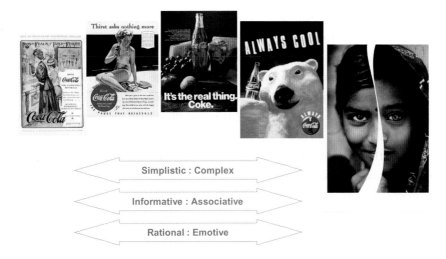

Exhibit 12.1 Coca-Cola advertising over the years (1907, 1940, 1970, 1993, and 2013).

- Banner ads first appeared in 1994.
- Pay-per-click advertising also debuted in 1994.
- Mobile advertising commenced in 1997.
- Google launched AdWords in 2000.
- Video ads appeared on YouTube in 2006.
- Online advertising overtook print and radio in 2011.
- In 2013, for the first time there was a drop in the number of pay-TV subscriptions in the US.

The above developments have had a profound impact on communication, and shaped the manner and the means we use for advertising. The Coca-Cola print advertisements depicted in Exhibit 12.1 reflect the transition over the past 100 years. Some changes relate to technology — sharper images and more vibrant colours. Text was much more prevalent in the past. Advertisements used to be much more informative; nowadays they more associative. Content used to be rational, now we experience a wide spectrum of emotions. Messages were largely simplistic, now they tend to be more complex.

The use of text has declined partly because in an over-communicated environment people have stopped reading commercials. People are also more cynical about advertising; they are less inclined to believe the claims that appear in text. Visuals on the other hand leave behind images and symbols that subtly associate brands with emotions, feelings, values, and an array of diverse attributes.

Consider, for instance, the 2013 "Small World" advert in Exhibit 12.1. One's attention is drawn to the symbols — a bindi on the forehead, the mark of Hinduism, the dupatta covering the head, which is commonly worn by women in Pakistan and India, and the Coca-Cola mnemonic joining the two faces. The message "That what unites us is stronger than that what divides us" is displayed in the "Small World Machines" video commercial on YouTube. The campaign, as a whole inclusive of the Small World vending machines, associates the Coca-Cola brand with values and feelings that people cherish — togetherness, happiness, harmony and peace.

Some of these thoughts and feelings were initially conveyed in previous ads of Coca-Cola. In particular, one is reminded of lines from a 1970s Coca-Cola commercial — "I'd like to teach the world to sing in perfect harmony, I'd like to buy the world a Coke and keep it company".

Media Fragmentation

The expansion of the number of media options and media channels has fragmented audiences. What used to be a mass audience is now dispersed across multiple screens and platforms. While there were barely two or three TV channels in most countries in the 1970s, there are scores if not hundreds of options on cable and TV today. Digital radio and podcasts have split the audience for audio. The internet has further diluted audience concentration. As a result, it is much harder for marketers to reach target consumers.

At an IRI (Information Resources Inc.) summit in 2006, Jesper Wiegandt, then Marketing Director at Procter & Gamble said of the US: "To reach 80% of the population in 1977, you would have needed just three television advertising spots. To reach the same figure today, around 75 spots are required".

It does not help that over time, the cost of TV advertising has grown faster than inflation. Advertising clutter too has grown as a result of an overcrowded marketplace, as also the trend from 30–60 second spots to 10–15 seconds. Further with the help of technology, viewers are able to skip ads by zapping, grazing and channel surfing.

As a result, efficiency and effectiveness has declined sharply, and there is growing disenchantment with mainstream media. Marketers are facing the challenges of lower returns on their advertising spends, greater complexity in reaching their target consumers, and the need to coordinate and integrate their communication programme across multiple media platforms. As they spread their budgets across media, the share of conventional media is in decline.

Advertising Mechanisms

Advertising has a crucial role to play in the development of a brand. It also accounts for bulk of the marketing investment in the brand, and with continued fragmentation of media, the returns are deteriorating. These factors underscore the need to understand how advertising works to strengthen and grow a brand, and how to use it effectively.

There has been considerable progress in advertising theory and research since John Wanamaker lamented the uncertainty of advertising returns. At the same time, however, markets have become more complex, and it has not become any easier to predict the efficacy of a commercial.

Gauging from the advertising elasticity of demand, we do know that the *short term* impact of most advertisements on sales of established brands is far too small to pay for advertising. Only ads that convey a *powerful new* message can *immediately* impact sales. Furthermore, as pointed out by Gordon Brown (Brown 1991), core perceptions and assessments such as "good overall" or "favourite brand" are difficult to immediately improve through advertising. Improvement in such perceptions usually occurs after the consumer has bought the brand.

Why then do brands like Coca-Cola or Pepsi that do not have any powerful new message to convey, persistently advertise?

Reflect for a moment on an advertisement from the past that you remember. I, for instance, can recall an ad that I saw as a 14-year-old in the early 1970s. Referred to as the Hilltop ad ("I'd like to buy the world a Coke and keep it company"), images and lyrics of this ad, which goes as far back as 40 years, remain etched in my memory. Like a number of other remarkable advertisements, the ad highlights two key points.

Firstly, advertising's impact is long-lasting. It goes into the memory and supports sales by sustaining consumers' interest in the brand and enhancing brand perceptions. Secondly, as far as advertising goes, quality matters a great deal more than quantity.

Central to our understanding of advertising therefore, is this question: What is it that makes some advertisements work better than other?

There are literally hundreds of theories on advertising; many hypotheses too, but relatively few facts. The theories attempt to explain how the consumer processes or interprets advertising, and the implications on advertising development and advertising research.

Six frequently repeated themes — salience, persuasion, likeability, symbolism, relationship, emotion — form the basis for many of the theories on advertising. While none of these themes in isolation are able to fully explain how advertising works, collectively they do provide an understanding of the fundamental mechanisms of advertising.

Salience

The unknown, as mentioned at the start, is synonymous with unease. An unheard of brand not only fails to generate interest, it also tends to be regarded as dubious. Curiosity, interest and desire begin with awareness. According to the salience model, the more it resides at top-of-mind, the greater the likelihood that the brand is purchased.

This has implications on both the nature and the quantum of advertising. Brand awareness or salience increases with higher frequency of advertising and the use of brand cues, i.e. shortcuts that

Exhibit 12.2 "Have a Spring Break, Have a Kit Kat".

link to the brand via visuals, sounds or expressions. A brand name, icon, mascot, slogan, music, colour, celebrity etc. can serve as a cue. Coca-Cola, for instance, uses multiple cues including its brand name, logo, mnemonic, red colour, the shape of its bottle, and a slew of slogans over the years, such as "It's the real thing".

Advertising memorabilia is littered with catchy slogans that bring the brand they represent to mind (see Exhibit 12.2). For example: "A diamond is forever", "Just do it", "Have a break", "Because you're worth it", "Eat fresh", "Be stupid", "Think small" and many more.

Salience is likely to be important in low involvement, habit driven categories where consumers are less likely to make comparative assessments. In the context of behavioural loyalty, awareness is also important wherever purchases are made over the counter, as is the case with traditional retail channels in many developing countries.

Persuasion

Persuasive advertisements create a positive shift in disposition towards the brand, usually accompanied amongst non-users by increased intention to use, and increased behavioural loyalty amongst users.

Persuasion is akin to what Brown referred to as "immediate impact". Consumers are persuaded by advertising if it says something new that is relevant and credible. Immediate impact is self-evident — over the years, many remarkable products (e.g. Volkswagen Beetle, Walkman, Pert Plus, iPad, Tesla) that are novel, relevant and credible have experienced immediate sales gains through advertising.

By attracting new users, persuasive advertising has a long term impact on sales. However, these ads become less effective over time, as consumers receptive to the message are persuaded quickly, while those who are not receptive are unlikely to be won over by repeated viewings of the same commercial. To increase their customer base via persuasive advertising, marketers often need to produce a series of advertisements, emphasizing different benefits of the product.

Consider, for example, a government's effort to persuade young couples to have more babies. Officials started by advertising financial support in the form of tax incentives. Some couples were persuaded by these incentives. Those who were not swayed were unlikely to change their minds should the government continue to reiterate the same offer. A new argument was put forward suggesting that it is one's duty (a national service) to country and society to have babies. In their third attempt, the government pursued a programme that tapped people's emotions and feeling, and communicated the enormous joy, fulfilment and unconditional love that children bring to our lives.

Persuasion is the preferred mechanism to appeal to consumers to try new products. It is also the mechanism of choice for impulse products, where it acts as the trigger to tempt people to purchase.

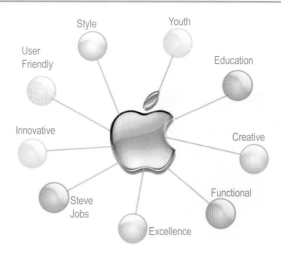

Exhibit 12.3   Attributes associated with Apple products.

Likeability

Liking is essentially classical conditioning — liking for the object (i.e. brand) develops following consistent and long term association with the execution. Likeable advertisements work well for big established brands, imbuing them with interest, appeal and status.

Being a soft measure that can easily be influenced through creative treatment, likeability is particularly popular with advertising agencies. It is also one of the hallmarks of online advertising. Popular and effective commercials on the internet are good at linking the ad's message with the brand, through an entertaining storyline.

Symbolism

In today's markets where product parity is often the norm, what differentiates brands are the symbols, values, images, lifestyles, personalities, relationships and emotions that get associated with them through advertising.

For instance Apple products are favourably associated with aspects like style, youth, innovation, creativity, functionality, excellence etc. (see Exhibit 12.3). Singapore Airlines, through the symbolism of the

☐ wrinkled?
☐ wonderful?

Will society ever accept 'old' can be beautiful? Join the beauty debate.

campaignforrealbeauty.co.uk   *Dove*

Exhibit 12.4   The Real Beauty campaign imbues Dove with social values, concerns and thoughts pertaining to the notion of beauty.

Singapore Girl, is associated with hospitality, grace and beauty. Volvo through a variety of symbols is associated with safety.

Relationship and Involvement

Advertising builds and strengthens the relationship between the consumer and the brand, thus increasing her involvement with the brand. It imbues the brand with the interests, concerns, feelings and values that viewers cherish.

Dove is an example of brand with a history of relationships with women (see Exhibit 12.4). Its testimonials of "real women" in the 1970s focussed on concerns and interest. When it was launched as a shampoo from 2000 onwards, a series of commercials depicted testimonials from different women (e.g., arts undergraduate, business student, buyer, professional dancer) and touched upon their individual hair concerns. Subsequently campaigns like Real Beauty (2003 onwards), Evolution (2006), Onslaught (2007), Pro-age (2007), Girls under Pressure (2008) and Self-Esteem (2011 onwards) imbued Dove with social values, concerns and thoughts dwelling on the notion of beauty. By drawing attention to some deep-rooted concerns on beauty, these campaigns are

Exhibit 12.5 "Embrace Life — Always wear your seat belt" campaign by The Sussex Safer Roads Partnership.

able to attract high viewership on the net, and increase consumers' interest and involvement with Dove.

Emotion

A few years back, a video depicting an ordinary family enacting a driving accident in their sitting room became an internet sensation. No words were uttered in this slow motion 88-second clip that left close to 20 million viewers with a moving reminder to wear their seat belts.

The campaign by The Sussex Safer Roads Partnership taps into our emotions to stimulate and arouse attention (see Exhibit 12.5). The intensity of the emotional charge leaves images and feelings that penetrate our long term memory. Metaphors and symbols exalt the seat belt. The depiction of ordinary folk in an ordinary home, combined with the simplicity of the plot, make viewers relate with ease.

As humans we experience a wide range of emotions that affect our mood, disposition and motivation. According to David Meyers, emotions fundamentally involve "physiological arousal, expressive behaviours, and conscious experience". They could be basic, such as happiness, security and love; or social, such as success, pride, guilt or envy.

Advertising taps these diverse emotions to penetrate our memory associating brands with positive or negative emotional states. The embrace life ad for instance, taps into feelings of love, tenderness, caring, fear, anxiety, shock and relief. The Liril girl advertisement (Exhibit 12.0) evokes the sense of freedom, hedonism and pleasure. Some advertisements reflect ecstasy and euphoria. Others dwell on fear or sorrow. Historical advertisements of Bajaj ("Hamara Bajaj"), the Indian scooter brand, and the Australian icon, Vegemite ("He's doing his bit for his Dad …" [wartime ad]), tap into viewers' sense of national pride.

By infusing deep feelings, these advertisements build emotional bonds that greatly increase consumers' affinity towards the brand. It is a form of classical conditioning; the brand starts to represent those moods, feeling or emotions that it is associated with through advertising.

Measurement Issues

The use of symbols, relationships and emotions in advertising has grown over the years, and so has the level of sophistication. There is less text and more association. From a research perspective, the complexity of evaluating advertising and measuring its impact has increased considerably. Emotions and symbols are harder to gauge than persuasion or salience.

Salience is measured by metrics such as top-of-mind, spontaneous and aided brand awareness. Persuasion is usually measured in terms of pre/post shift in disposition to purchase brand. Note, however, that claimed disposition to purchase normally turns out to be higher than actual behaviour might suggest. What consumer claim they will do is usually not the same as what they actually do.

The likeability of an ad is usually measured in terms of rating on a set of attributes that relate to affinity. Imagery can be measured using the methods described in Chapter 1, *Brand and Brand Image.* Symbolism however is relatively hard to gauge because it is often non-verbal and difficult to describe. As such, it is not always feasible to assess the full significance of symbols.

Consumers' relationships with brands are complex in nature, and consequently difficult to describe or measure. And with regard to emotions, verbal responses do not usually elicit their true nature. Moreover, consumers often find it hard to verbalize emotions, and they may not even be conscious of their existence. In light of this, indirect interviewing methods and non-verbal, physiological approaches are gaining acceptance. Details about these measurement methods and the prevailing techniques in advertising evaluation are covered in Chapter 15, *Advertising Research.*

CHAPTER 13

New Media

Exhibit 13.0 Hundreds of thousands protesters choke the EDSA-Ortigas Avenue intersection calling for the resignation of President Joseph Estrada *(Photo courtesy of Wikipedia).*

Preview

Ordinary people empowered with the social media are interacting and collaborating with increased speed, reach and effectiveness. This has had a profound impact on society, changing the political, economic and cultural landscapes across the globe.

This chapter explores the impact of the new media on marketing and advertising. It embraces a wide range of topics touching on the changing rules and perspectives in marketing, and concepts such as co-creation, permission marketing, the long tail, and inbound and outbound marketing. It also covers trends in media consumption, interactive television, and the basics of the internet.

The Old Order Changeth

The impact of the new media on society is evident from the unprecedented rise in social movements sparked by ordinary people with the means to instantly communicate and collaborate with each other. Lessons from these momentous events bear considerable relevance as marketers struggle to cope with the realities of a social media-empowered marketplace.

Uprisings

"Go 2 EDSA. Wear blk"

Our world is in turmoil. The EDSA revolution in the Philippines in 2001, Moldova's Twitter revolution in 2009, the Arab Spring of 2011, London's BlackBerry riots in 2011, candlelight vigils across India in 2012–13, the Ukraine crisis in 2013–14, and Hong Kong's pro-democracy movement in 2014 — fuelled by the new media, demonstrations of such overwhelming scale have become increasingly common across the globe.

Starting with protests in Tunisia in December 2010, and engulfing 19 countries by 2011–12, the Arab Spring transformed the political landscape across the Arab world. According to the Arab Social Media Report by the Dubai School of Government, nearly 9 in 10 Egyptians and Tunisians surveyed in March 2011 said that Facebook played a role in their involvement in protests and demonstrations. The same report claims that all but one of the protests called for on Facebook ended up coming to life on the streets.

The EDSA revolution of 2001 was perhaps the earliest instance of the use of the new media to force out a national leader. On 17 January, within two hours, over a million Filipinos, many responding to SMS messages, assembled at EDSA (Epifanio de los Santos Avenue) (see Exhibit 13.0) to protest against the vote by the Philippine Congress to set aside key evidence against President Joseph Estrada during his impeachment trial. Three days later on 20 January, Estrada was ousted.

While in recent years we have witnessed upheavals and political change across the globe, a less volatile equilibrium should emerge in the long term. Politicians, recognizing the shift in the balance of power, are changing their methods and their style of leadership. Taking greater pains to stay in touch, they are better at sensing the sentiments of the masses, and are learning how to engage and collaborate with citizens.

Lessons for Marketers

Similarities exist. Citizens are consumers. Their share of purchases, not unlike the count of votes, is a reflection of a brand's power. Conventional brand advertising, like government propaganda, has been one-way communication.

The shift in the balance of power from marketers to consumers mirrors the shifts in the political landscape. Much like politicians, marketers have lost the monopoly on their brand's communication. We are seeing consumers taking the lead in the discussion of products and brands on the net. Just as the governments strive to retain votes, the corporations need to adapt to the social age to maintain and grow their market share. Resembling the political landscape, the new equilibrium in markets is resulting in significant shifts in market dynamics.

Brand missions are not as potent as political ideologies; the business of making soap, soda or soup does not draw as much attention as that of governing a country. It might seem that corporations are less vulnerable; they are unlikely to face a million protestors at their doorstep. Yet marketers do not have the luxury of time to inculcate lessons. Consumers may effortlessly switch allegiance from one brand of soap to another on their next purchase occasion.

Exhibit 13.1   Social media has rapidly grown to become the most pervasive activity on the net.

New Media

At a time when Manila was considered the texting capital of the world, Estrada blamed "the text-messaging generation" for his downfall. During that fateful week, text messaging in the Philippines more than doubled to 70 million messages per day.

New media, however, is not the cause; it is the tool that mobilizes support for the cause. Social media exponentially magnifies the power of word-of-mouth, rapidly generating the critical mass of popular support that is required to instigate an uprising. While it is relatively easy for marketers and governments to exercise control over conventional media, it is neither practical nor feasible to quell the hundreds of thousands of voices on the net.

The unidirectional nature of conventional media allows for tight controls. On TV or radio, while people may choose to switch from one channel or station to another, the content remains centrally controlled.

In contrast, the internet is fluid and decentralized. People go there to watch videos, listen to music, or read about something of interest to them. They may do so whenever and wherever they choose to, and it usually does not cost them anything other than their time.

It is multidirectional. A wide range of web platforms and technologies enable ordinary people to source information from one another. They create their own content and share it with others, a phenomenon popularly known as consumer generated media (CGM) or social media.

Social media (Exhibit 13.1) — any kind of text, audio, image or video content created by consumers and uploaded on a variety of online media platforms — has rapidly grown to become the most pervasive activity on the net. All over the world consumers are communicating online on Facebook, Twitter, Pinterest, Google+ and several other social networks and blogs. As of October 2014, Facebook alone has over 1.35 billion active users.

Social media thrives on engagement between participants. Take Coca-Cola for instance; based on company estimates in 2011, over 80% of Coca-Cola content viewed on YouTube was generated by consumers. The Coca-Cola fan page was started not by the corporation, but by two Coca-Cola enthusiasts from Los Angeles. It is the place where Coca-Cola fans come together and engage; and though The Coca-Cola Company collaborates with the two enthusiasts to maintain the site, the page thrives on the engagement of fans.

The implications for marketing and advertising are profound. The new media marks a shift in power from the corporate to the consumer. While companies stand to lose control, they gain a movement, one that is both an opportunity and a threat. The persuasive power of word-of-mouth outweighs that of advertising, and social media amplifies it. (According to various surveys, 80–90% of consumers claim they trust peer recommendations). An appealing message, pertaining to a product, can become contagious and spread like a virus — possibly yielding extraordinary gains or possibly causing irreparable damage.

New Rules, New Perspectives

"The old order changeth, yielding place to new" — Alfred, Lord Tennyson
(The Passing of Arthur).

The rules of engagement have changed with the empowerment of people. Leaders need to emphatically listen to the masses and keep in tune with their sentiments. There is need for change in style of management and government from dictating to collaborating, from propaganda to engagement, from one-way communication to a dialogue.

Levelling the Marketing Playing Field

The internet is a great leveller. An ordinary person can be heard on the net, and can command influence if he or she is in touch with masses. An unheard of brand, led by a team that embraces new market realities, could gain awareness and build closer relationships with consumers without having to spend the kind of money that is required in conventional advertising. A small political party or a small firm, in tune with the pulse of the people, has the means to connect, and gain influence and power.

Reflect, for instance, on how a relatively unknown, junior senator from Illinois, on 4 November 2008, became the first African American President of the United States of America.

The Advent of Co-creation

"... government of the people, by the people, for the people ..." — Abraham *Lincoln.*

Barack Obama's spectacular victory was the outcome of a *collaborative movement*; a campaign that was built around a strategy of *engaging* with the voters and *listening* to their views and their stories; a campaign that helped build relationships with the masses. Reaching out to five million supporters on 15 different social networks and 50 million viewers on YouTube, his was the first political campaign that truly harnessed the power of social media. It exemplifies co-creation, a concept introduced by Prahalad and Ramaswamy (Prahalad, 2000) that represents the dramatic and challenging transformation towards a two-way communication mode with consumers.

The advent of social media marked the beginning of the *age of listening*. This is not to say that marketers have not been "listening" in the past. They have been doing so through market research, but in a controlled question–answer or stimulus–response environment. What's changed is the ability to "listen" to *unsolicited* feedback about their brand from hundreds or thousands or millions of consumers and "see" how they relate to it and how they use it.

As consumers increasingly express their views and ideas online for brands that they harbour feelings for, companies need to keep abreast of the dialogue, and anticipate opportunities and threats. Today one can ill afford to underestimate the power of a small minority to influence the masses. While companies lose control, they gain a movement, one that's both an opportunity and a threat. And whether this shift in power evolves into something constructive or destructive, is dependent largely on how they respond.

Co-creation is one of the most constructive avenues of channelling consumers' affinity for a brand and their desire to engage with it. It is a process where brand owners collaborate with consumers in creating brand value. To effectively co-create marketers need to listen emphatically to what their consumers are saying with the intent to understand. Once they understand their consumers, brand owners should join the conversations, learn from consumers and share their brand knowledge and expertise; empower consumers to advocate their brands, and become empowered by consumers to shape the future of their brands in a manner that is meaningful to the people who matter.

A related concept, *crowdsourcing* is the process of soliciting ideas or content from a large group of people, usually an online community. LEGO IDEAS, an example covered in Chapter 9, *New Product Development*, uses a crowdsourcing programme to source ideas for new Lego projects.

Permission Marketing

As they face the reality of the new media, marketers are embracing a number of new marketing perspectives. Permission marketing, a term popularized by Seth Godin is "the privilege (not the right) of delivering anticipated, personal and relevant messages to people who actually want to get them" (Godin, 1999). Opting into newsfeeds, signing up for alerts and following friends on social media are examples of permission marketing. It works by inducing consumers to grant permission via relevant and interesting content, or by means of attractive incentives such as discounts or free samples.

Riding the Long Tail

Chris Anderson in 2004 introduced us to the concept of the long tail. The physical world, he points out, is a world of scarcity. In the context of the entertainment industry, stores have a limited amount of shelf space, coaxial cables can transmit no more than a fixed number of TV channels, radio spectrums can carry only a fixed number of stations, and there are, of course, only 24 hours a day of programming.

To justify their existence in brick-and-mortar establishments like movie theatres, book stores, record stores, DVD rental shops, videogame stores etc., products must deliver returns that cover the costs of manufacture, distribution, rent, and inventory holding. "In the tyranny of physical space, an audience too thinly spread is the same as no audience at all" (Anderson, 2008).

The internet transported us to the world of abundance, of unlimited shelf space, and low manufacturing and distribution costs. With hits and misses on equal economic footing, "popularity no longer has a monopoly on profitability" (Anderson, 2008). Amazon, iTunes, Netflix and a host of other online distributors can viably carry hundreds of thousands of books, songs and movies — and they have discovered that the market for these products does exist.

This is the Long Tail. The combined volume of these non-hits often represents the bulk of the market. For instance, based on the limited data made available, the share of books ranked 10,000+ in sales at

Amazon, is roughly 60%. Not surprisingly, companies like Amazon and Netflix that tap into the opportunity that the long tail represents, are growing rapidly.

In the context of media consumption habits, today's online consumers have unlimited choice. And as they explore and discover their unique personal tastes, media consumption on the web is getting shattered into numerous miniscule fragments. Advertisers for mass market brands will find it increasingly challenging to reach target consumers, in substantial numbers, on the internet.

Inbound and Outbound Marketing

Inbound marketing, a term coined by Brian Halligan (2010), relies on a pull strategy based on being discovered by customers on the net through content and social media marketing, rather than pushing messages out to them. With inbound marketing, according to Scott (2011), marketers "earn their way in" by publishing helpful information. It contrasts with outbound marketing which involves interrupt advertising, cold-calling, brochures, direct mail, email and other forms of buying (or bugging for) attention.

Inbound marketing works well for small companies with limited resources who would rather have customers find them on the net than spend advertising dollars to attract their attention. It works by earning the attention of customers by publishing content that is relevant and interesting to their target.

Though it attracts criticism, conventional or "interrupt" advertising, as it is disparagingly called, is not in decline. On the contrary it is rapidly spreading across the new media. Even as marketers embrace internet platforms and inbound marketing, on the advertising front, conventional outbound approaches reign supreme and will continue to do so for the foreseeable future.

Inbound and permission marketing rests partly on the assumption that consumers know where to seek what they want. The role of marketing, however, encompasses the task of reaching out to target consumers, including those who may not have heard of your offering, or may not have a conscious desire to acquire it.

The reality is that the big advertisers need big audiences, and it is not feasible to reach the masses purely through inbound marketing. While the notion of viral marketing is very appealing, even iconic brands find it difficult to successfully create viral campaigns. To spread their message to the masses, large consumer brands need to develop a well-rounded relationship with their consumers, by integrating offline with online, outbound with inbound marketing. And though much of their online advertising continues to interrupt, viewers often have the option to skip video ads after watching a few mandatory seconds.

From the marketers' standpoint, the use of web analytics to target and tailor marketing campaigns, and to measure their success, is a major boon. It permits them to fine-tune their marketing initiatives thereby improving their returns on marketing investments.

Undoubtedly there are great opportunities and challenges confronting marketing and advertising. The rules have changed. Listening and engaging takes priority even as brands continue to talk to consumers. In addition to "consumer impressions" (number of people who get to see or hear an advertisement), marketers are increasingly tracking "consumer expressions" (people who engage with the brand). The media environment is in a state of flux, and as new technologies come into play, it is not clear where exactly it might be heading.

Turning Point for Television

Over the years we became accustomed to the ways of mainstream media. To watch a TV programme for instance, we had to be home in front of the small screen at the time the programme was broadcast, and hope that our spouse or daughter was not tuned to some other TV show at that time. There was no fast-forward or rewind, we were unable to pause if we needed a break, and should we have missed some portion or episode of a show, we may not have got another opportunity to see it. Advertisements interrupted our viewing experience, and irrespective of whether we lived in Sidhbari, Singapore or San Francisco, the fees we paid for the service were high and had been increasing.

For those who were born after 1980, the way we were accustomed to viewing TV must seem peculiar. These Generation Y (the millennials) and Generation Z youths spend a lot more time on their personal digital devices connected to the net, and a lot less time in front of the TV or radio. Most of the media they consume is free of charge.

Thankfully for them, the web has transformed the way media is delivered and consumed. Like a black hole, it has the capacity to attract and absorb almost every type of media in unlimited quantities, and it is doing so at a phenomenal rate. Contemporary devices allow us to tap the net at any time, from any location, access the vast repository of content on personal devices, and stream it to our smartphone, tablet, computer or TV. Not surprisingly, media delivery and consumption is undergoing change. And TVs are becoming smart.

Consumer Trends — Media Consumption

Taking the US as the lead market, here are some signs that reveal the transformation within the media industry:

- Pay-TV hit a turning point in 2012. The growth rate which was in decline for a few years, hit negative territory for the first time in 2013. That year the number of subscribers across the entire pay-TV industry in the US dropped by 251,000, the first full-year decline, according to research firm SNL Kagan.

- Of considerable significance are the shifts within the pay-TV industry, where wireless services are experiencing high growth. Telco TV providers added 1.6 million subscriptions during 2013, an 18% growth rate, largely at the expense of cable providers, who collectively lost 2 million video subscriptions. Wireless TV is better aligned with changing lifestyles. Take for instance AT&T's U-verse proposition: "Enjoy live TV in the palm of your hand! With Uverse.com and the U-verse app, you can enjoy live TV channels or access thousands of hit TV shows On Demand from your computer, smartphone, or tablet at no extra cost."

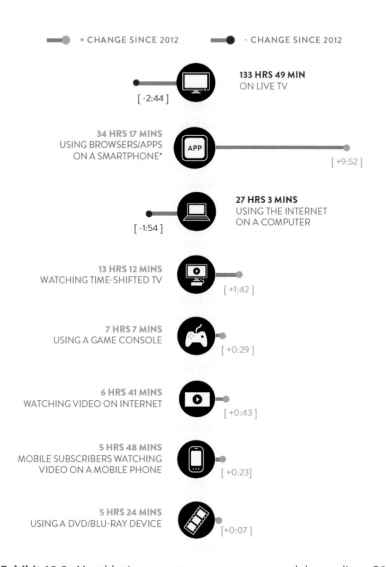

Exhibit 13.2 Monthly time spent per person per month by medium, Q3 2013 *(Source: The Digital Consumer February 2014, Nielsen).*

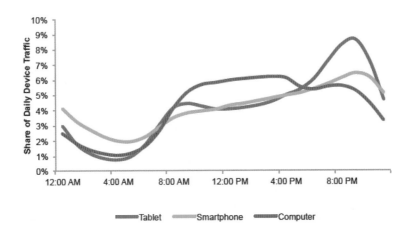

Exhibit 13.3 Share of browser-based page traffic by hour for computer, smartphone and tablet platforms *(Source: comScore Device Essentials, U.S., Monday, 21 January 2013).*

- According to the Nielsen survey, more than half the small but growing group of broadband-only homes fall in the 18–34 age group. 80% of these homes own game consoles (i.e. twice the national average) and 41% own tablets.
- Mobile is booming (as we all know). While the consumption of media increased slightly in 2013 over 2012, there is a substantial shift from traditional TV to mobile devices and time-shifted TV (Exhibit 13.2). Consumers are increasingly using devices that allow them to consume media when and where they want.
- According to YouTube mobile makes up almost 40% of their global watch time.
- YouTube reaches more young adults in the US aged 18-34 than any cable network.

- Free WiFi hotspots at university campuses, shopping centres, coffee shops and offices make it easier for consumers to tap the internet without subscribing to any internet service.

- In the media industry tablets have earned the moniker "vampire" media. They come out at night, cannibalizing primetime TV (See Exhibit 13.3).

- 2012 was a turning point too for digital music sales in the US. According to Nielsen SoundScan, in 2013, digital track sales fell 5.7% from 1.34 B to 1.26 B units.

- While digital music sales and pay-TV subscribers are down, audio and video streams increased 24% in the first half of 2013 to a whopping 50.9 billion. Streaming is an attractive option, but it comes with limitations — it misses out on local programming, live sport events, and premium channels.

- According to eMarketer more than 50% of internet users in the US will watch digital TV in 2014.

- The proportion of US consumers who use Netflix to watch TV programmes has increased from 16% in 2012 to 25% in 2013 (*Source*: Nielsen 2014).

- Netflix alone accounts for 30% of all internet traffic in the US during peak hours. 38% of US consumers say they used Netflix to stream video in 2013, up from 31% in 2012. They are streaming both within as well as outside of the home using a wide range of devices including — computer, smartphone, smart TV, regular TV (using gadgets like Apple TV, Roku TV and Google Chromecast), Tablet, internet-connected Blu-Ray, Wii, PS3 and Xbox.

- Despite the increase in consumption of media, viewership of primetime serials and major TV programmes continues to decline due to media fragmentation.

The trends we are witnessing are driven by the force of a generation. A generation that has been growing up in the digital world — it is where they work and where they play. In the late 1990s, they were the teenagers who "discovered" SMS. (Text messaging took off when they started to explore their hand-me-down cell phones). Later they spawned the iPod revolution and the social media revolution. Undoubtedly, these early adopters have an influence on the rest of us — "Look Ma …"

As these trends persist and more content moves online, traditional television and radio sets may no longer remain the most popular devices for watching and listening to programmes. Smart television sets will become one of many devices that stream audio and video.

Consumers are increasingly seeking the following from media providers:

- Mobility. "The future is mobile", a refrain we keep hearing all the time, certainly does apply to the media industry. Consumers want the ability to consume media wherever and whenever.
- Individualistic experience. Considering the demise in social TV viewing, media providers should offer more individualistic viewing friendly services. Currently, however, in most countries, cable operators charge extra for each additional TV.
- Attractive fees. With so much content on the net that is available for free, fewer subscribers will be willing to pay high premiums for media services.

Online Video Distribution Trends

Pay-TV carriers and content owners are responding to the consumer trends, as they prepare for the challenges posed by the new market environment. They are actively supporting/developing services for watching video on tablets and smartphones, and boosting internet speeds to support online distribution.

Content creators are essentially indifferent to carrier dynamics, so long as they get paid well. For now the cable/satellite/telco service providers offer by far the most lucrative monetization model. The disruption of this model by online platforms is an obvious concern; consumers are not accustomed to paying as high a premium for content on the net.

The market will remain in a state of flux, as new developments transform the industry. Opportunities of online video distribution have attracted a host of technology companies. Google, Netflix, Hulu, Vevo, Amazon, Microsoft, Apple and Yahoo present both an opportunity and a threat for traditional producers of TV content. Some of these companies are owned and operated by big networks, studios, and music corporations. Hulu for instance is owned by NBC, Fox, Disney–ABC, and Vevo is run by a joint venture comprising Universal Music Group, Google, Sony Music Entertainment and Abu Dhabi Media.

Vevo, in March 2013, launched Vevo TV, an advertising-supported internet television channel running 24 hours a day, featuring blocks of music videos and specials.

Meanwhile, in April 2014, Amazon added multiple scripted and animated shows to its subscription-based Prime service, and released the Fire TV box meant to stream the content directly on to televisions.

We are witnessing the confluence of a number of forces that, taken together, will further accelerate the growth in online media consumption. Consumers' viewing preferences and habits continue to steadily shift to online devices. Supply and distribution is better aligned with their tastes and preferences. And advancements in technology provide for superior consumer experiences.

Improvements in streaming technology and faster broadband links have dramatically reduced the time it takes for content to load. Developments in these fields also permit content providers and advertisers to engage with viewers in a number of different ways.

While many of the market developments in the past have been US-centric, the momentum is now moving to Europe and rest of the world. Netflix, for instance, which started its international operations in Canada in 2010, now offers its service to over 40 countries; and it sees international markets as its biggest growth opportunity.

Interactive Television

If consumers pay less for content on the net, media enterprises will need to turn to advertising to sustain incomes. One technology that could improve the effectiveness of advertising is Interactive Television (iTV).

iTV is television with a "return path". Information flows not only from the network to viewer, but also back from viewer to network. This is useful provided the system has the ability to customise viewers' content.

Some degree of interactivity, such as on-demand delivery and online shopping and banking, has existed for some time. But to be truly interactive, the viewer should be able to control the viewing experience. For instance if you are watching a tennis match, with iTV you could choose to watch at an angle where the camera focusses on your favourite player.

Interactivity has four main applications:

- Customized viewing experience: Viewers are able to control their viewing experience.
- T-commerce: Viewers will be able to use their remote to shop for products advertised on the screen without dialling a phone.
- Other frills: Viewers can pause live TV or record shows, click on advertisements (or other content) for more details.
- Consumer Analytics: Analysis of the clickstream can provide marketers with a profile of each viewer, revealing their needs and preferences. This should help better direct advertising (addressable advertising) and direct marketing efforts.

Addressable advertising could greatly improve advertising effectiveness by targeting products and advertising messages that are better attuned to individual households. The click stream would tell marketers which ads are being accessed, and allow them to alter ad messages in real time.

Interactivity is still experimental for now, yet companies are hoping that in-built interactive elements will serve to differentiate their content, enhance customers' viewing experiences, and permit advertisers to better direct their marketing efforts.

Internet Basics

The Internet is a gigantic decentralized global network of networks connecting hundreds of millions of computers, and the World Wide Web is a way of accessing the information over the Internet. Anyone connected to the net can use a web browser to view web pages that may contain text, audios, images, videos, and other multimedia and navigate between them via hyperlinks.

Each page has a unique web address called a URL (unique resource locator). A user may retrieve a web page by typing the URL into the web browser's address bar. But usually users simply navigate to pages via hyperlinks from search engine result pages or from some other web page.

A suite of protocols, the TCP/IP (Transmission Control Protocol/Internet Protocol), provide end-to-end connectivity on the internet. The methods, common languages, and set of rules outlined in these protocols are required to ensure that devices can connect and communicate on the net.

As far as public information goes, the internet is virtually all encompassing. By way of example, Wikipedia comprises about 33 million pages covering 4.5 million articles. If it existed in hard copy the average library would not be able to contain it, yet any page of information that we seek from its depths can easily be retrieved via a search engine, within a few seconds.

From the marketer's perspective, it is pertinent that the days that people rely on hard copy brochures and manuals for information are numbered. Nowadays the vast majority of customers simply google the information they seek. For businesses to survive they need to exist in cyberspace and ensure that their customers find them there.

Both for businesses as well as individuals, their sites (website, blog, social network etc.) are essentially their "properties" in cyberspace. Depending on their purpose, these sites, in the course of time, are becoming immensely valuable to their owners.

Engaging billions across the world, the internet is buzzing with activity. People go there to indulge their passions, learn something new, or simply have a relaxing or enjoyable experience. It is where they congregate to interact with friends. Marketers are striving to attract customers, and create the right kind of buzz on their cyber properties. Whether these properties constitute websites, blogs, social networks, advertisements, or other online media, marketers realize that in the digital era, cyberspace has become the new marketing frontier.

CHAPTER 14

Digital Marketing

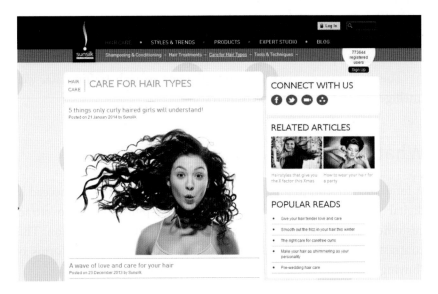

Exhibit 14.1 Hindustan Unilever's Sunsilk website offers tips on hair care.

Preview

As businesses embrace digital marketing, they need a strategy to attract customers to their websites with content that is useful, relevant and interesting. This requires a shift in mindset for marketers who previously focussed on pushing their products to customers.

This chapter comprises five major sections — building online assets, advertising on the net, digital advertising formats, search and web analytics.

Building online assets pertains to the common platforms for creating, maintaining and spreading content online, including websites, social networks, blogs, and internet forums. It discusses the importance of content, and the different forms of personalization.

The *advertising on the net* section includes a discussion on the challenges facing low involvement categories, and the challenge of reaching out to the masses.

The *advertising formats* covered include web banner, pop-up and pop-under, floater, video and search advertising. The range of mobile advertising formats is also covered.

The *search* section provides an overview of the search process and search engine optimization (SEO).

The final section, *web analytics* pertains to web traffic data, web intelligence, and controlled website tests.

What Works Online

A fundamental shift in mindsets must occur for marketers to succeed in digital marketing. On the web, they need a pull strategy to attract customers by serving useful, relevant and interesting information. This contrasts with conventional media which involves different forms of "buying" attention to push products to customers.

A pull strategy is even more important for products that consumers do not usually seek information about on the net. Take shampoo for instance — consumers do not usually go to the net to decide what shampoo to buy, yet they do discuss their hair issues there. According to NM Incite's white paper (December 2012) there were 2.3 million messages on hair care on social media in the US, for the first 6 months of 2012, and only 4% of these pertained to specific hair care brands. Top google searches in hair care, depending on country, usually cover topics such as hairstyles, hair fall, haircuts, hair colour, shampoo, long and short hair and hair salon.

When initially launched in June 2006, Hindustan Unilever's Sunsilkgangofgirls.com exemplified the pull strategy. Proclaimed as India's first "online all-girl community" the site provided social networking space and consumer generated content features such as

Exhibit 14.2 P&G's BeingGirl.com offers advice on puberty and periods.

blogs and communities (gangs). Content-wise it focussed on hair, beauty and fashion, and prominently featured hair care experts.

Promoted through a media blitz, the site attracted a high level of interest from its target group. By November 2006, the website had garnered about 250,000 registered users and 25,000 gangs. It had reached almost 200 million hits and was attracting an average of 12–13 million page views per month. Today the total number of registered users is close to 774,000.

The website evolved over time and is now more brand-centric (see Exhibit 14.1) than it used to be. Linked with Sunsilk's Facebook brand page and Twitter, the website now places less emphasis on social networking — you can no longer form a "gang" on the site. It does however continue to serve the information that target consumers are seeking, offering tips from hair experts on hair care, hair trends and fashion, in addition to information about the Sunsilk brand.

P&G's BeingGirl.com (Exhibit 14.2), which offers advice on puberty and periods for teenage girls, in a teen-friendly manner, is another apt

Exhibit 14.3 Sugarpova was launched with a budget of US$500,000, using primarily new media.

example of a helpful and informative site. According to Velvet Gogol Bennett, P&G's North America's feminine care external relations manager: "It's a safe place where they can go for information about changes they are experiencing but are too embarrassed to discuss."

Pampers.com, which offers baby and parenting advice, is yet another example of a site that attracts consumers by providing the information that they are seeking. The site is also a good example of the use of personalization in crafting a website. When a mother visits www.pampers.com, the content on the website is filtered and displayed according to her baby's age group.

As mentioned earlier, the internet is a great leveller. A new or unheard of brand, could gain awareness, and build relationships with consumers without having to spend the kind of money that is required in conventional advertising. Sugarpova is one such example.

At an initial investment of only US$500,000, Maria Sharapova made effective use of the new media to market Sugarpova, a new candy line. On 20 August 2012, armed with her star power, and 10.5 million Facebook fans and 400,000 followers on Twitter, she launched the premium candies without mainstream advertising.

It was candy veteran Jeff Rubin who conceived of the product concept and coined the name Sugarpova. The candies are available in a variety of flavours which come with labels such as "Flirty", "Smitten Sour", "Sassy", and "Splashy". They may be bought online on Sugarpova's website (Exhibit 14.3) or at select outlets in a number of countries across the globe.

About a year after the launch of Sugarpova candy, Maria Sharapova introduced a range of clothing and accessories under the same label. Later in 2014 she launched "Speedy", a yoghurt gummy that comes in the shape of the iconic Porsche 911.

Sugarpova got off to a good start with global sales of US$6 million in 2013. It is a remarkable illustration of the effective use of the new media, to enter consumer markets.

Building Online Assets

Digital media offers a high level of customization that paves the way for building relationships with stakeholders. Customers/prospects may have an account of their own that provides for a personalized experience. And sites can be crafted such that they are relevant for curious browsers as well as existing customers; novices as well as experts.

There are many platforms for creating, maintaining and spreading content online; common among these are websites, social networks, blogs, and internet forums.

Websites

A company's website is its business hub in cyberspace, the place where the company interacts with all stakeholders. From a commercial standpoint, for products and services that are suited to digital marketing, the website is the most valuable digital asset that a company possesses. Described frequently as a "conversion engine", it is the place where the company gets to move interested browsers down the prospecting funnel, converting leads to inquiries, inquiries to prospects, and prospects to customers.

Conversion is aided by the use of web analytics to personalize customers' experiences, and by various calls-to-action — e.g. encouraging visitors to subscribe to email newsletters, add your blog to their Real Simple Syndication (RSS) reader, fill out a form to request for a call from a sales representative, or purchase something.

As a hub the company website becomes the source of information on products and services, press releases, advertising, promotional information and so on. It also links visitors to all of the company's other online assets — blogs, social media networks etc.

Blogs

A blog (web log) is a web page or site that one or more authors maintain and update like a diary. From a marketing standpoint it offers the opportunity for companies to demonstrate thought leadership within their domain of expertise.

It is an ideal place for marketers to converse with customers about topics of mutual interest. To facilitate the dialogue, blogs should let readers leave comments and allow them to subscribe by RSS or email.

It is beneficial for companies to integrate their blog with their website. This enhances the content within the website and provides a seamless, cohesive experience for visitors.

Internet Forums

Internet forums are sites where people can converse with one another by posting messages. They are ideal places for communities to congregate, discuss issues and seek help from one another. Companies like Microsoft are blessed with forums where experts connect with one another to resolve technical issues and seek guidance. Customers around the world are able to support each other, instead of relying solely on the company to do so.

Social Media

Consumers are creating content and uploading it on a variety of online media platforms. These platforms are increasingly becoming the "places" where people get together and converse. All over the world they are communicating online on social networking sites like Facebook and Google+, microblogging services like Twitter, and content sharing services like YouTube and Instagram.

From the consumer marketers' perspective, since this is where their consumers are hanging out, it is where they should engage with them. Most networking sites provide the means for doing so. Facebook for instance allows users to create a fan page that may serve business objectives.

The wide range of facilities and features that sites like Facebook offer, make it easy for users to expand their network, and create and share content with friends. Social is highly conducive to viral marketing; it can fuel and propagate campaigns to generate considerable buzz and awareness for a brand.

Pop musicians and movie stars, unsurprisingly, top the list of the most popular Facebook pages. Among brands, Coca-Cola tops with 91 million fans (December 2014), followed by McDonald's (55 million), Red Bull (45 million), Converse (41 million), Samsung Mobile (40 million), PlayStation (39 million), Oreo (38 million), Nike Football (38 million), Starbucks (38 million), KFC (36 million),Walmart (35 million) and Pepsi (34 million).

Content is King

To state the obvious, content is what draws the target audience to a site, and keeps them coming back. It has always been of paramount importance for media in general; what differentiates the web tools, however, are the possibilities and capabilities they have to offer. The user experience on a site may be personalized to a much greater degree.

Traditional media tends to be linear, page by page, from start to end. In contrast, an online site is an interconnected network of pages, akin to the biological network of neurons. The pages may contain text interspersed with image, audio or video, and embedded with code and links. The hyperlinks allow the content to flow with the viewers' thoughts, providing meaningful paths to pages within the site, as well as to pages at other sites.

Securing inbound hyperlinks from influential external sites is a priority for any commercial website. These are the crucial pathways that bring traffic to the site. Moreover, since they are a reflection of the "authority" of a site, the quantity and the quality of inbound links is a key measure for page ranking by search engines like Google. Thus, the site's potential to secure links is a key barometer for success. And it all boils down to content — a site with useful, noteworthy content will draw attention and attract links.

A site can serve a wide audience with different requirements. It may serve a customer well, irrespective of whether she is a subject expert or a novice. She controls her on-site journey, and chooses the path she wants to take through the network of pages. She can easily customize her experience, reading into as much detail, or as little detail as she chooses.

She may also have the opportunity to collaborate on a site. As mentioned, internet forums can bring communities together to discuss topics of relevance, raise questions and issues, seek answers, and share interests. These sites become information systems that often serve their communities better than a user manual or guide, or even the company's support staff.

Sites can also personalize user experiences based on information that the site accumulates about the user (e.g. on-site behaviour, details provided by the system or the user). Personalization customizes the user's interaction by serving content that is of relevance to her. As the website content grows, this capability improves its usability, increases loyalty and encourages desired behaviour (i.e. conversion, sales).

Sites offer all of the aforementioned possibilities and benefits, yet while there are examples of really well-crafted business sites that resonate with their target audience, the majority of sites do not fully exploit the web's true potential. They tend largely to be "brochureware" or advertising-centric sites, replicating the company's printed brochures or TV advertising onto cyberspace, in virtually the same passive state as they existed in conventional media. Customers seeking information or guidance are often confronted with nothing more than sales pitches.

This suggests that there remains considerable scope for improvement as businesses transition from offline to online. As mindsets shift from push to pull, and as they make better use of web tools, businesses will be better placed to exploit the full potential that the web has to offer.

Personalization

When a mother visits www.pampers.com, the content on the website is filtered and displayed according to her baby's age group. Similarly if she has an account with Amazon, the company's website recommends her products that match her tastes and preferences.

This ability to personalize user experiences is a key advantage that online has to offer. It is also a much needed capability because websites are overloaded with content — Amazon, for instance, with over 50 million books listed on its site, has a very long tail.

Personalization customizes the user's interaction by bringing to the foreground content that is of greater relevance to her. The goal is to deliver the right content, to the right person, at the right time.

There are broadly two types of personalization — prescriptive personalization and adaptive personalization.

Prescriptive personalization is based on a set of predefined rules or business logic. The logic may be based on a number of factors including profile, on-site behaviour, landing page, where the user came from (e.g. search engine), context (e.g. search phrase, time of day, season), location, transaction details and so on. Users are segregated into profile-based groups or "personas", and content is tailored for each persona.

Prescriptive personalization is further divided into two forms — explicit and implicit. With explicit personalization the users' profiles are often based on details provided by the users. For example, at the Pampers site, parents use a slider scale to set their baby's age.

Implicit personalization does not require a user to create an account or provide any details. It tracks the user's behaviours, their clicking activity, to determine the user's preferences and accordingly filters the content. The Amazon site, for example, takes this approach — based on what the customer is browsing, the site displays products that other customers, who shopped for the same product, also shopped for.

Adaptive personalization does not require set up — the system itself creates the logic and rules that govern what content is to be displayed. Historical behaviour of website users is modelled to categorize users and their preferences, and this data is used to personalize content.

The ability for sites to self-manage customization makes adaptive personalization much easier to implement and maintain than prescriptive customization. It is therefore a compelling option for sites that are seeking the benefits of personalization, and should become widely used in the future, as the technology evolves.

Advertising on the Net

One of the realities of the new media is that it is difficult to make money selling content on the internet. The glut of free content has diminished its perceived value in cyberspace. The majority of entities in the business of disseminating content on the web need to therefore rely more on advertising income than subscription income. Online advertising is therefore growing as more and more content moves onto the internet.

The other reality is that the intensity and growth of the competition, coupled with poor response rates, translates to low and declining advertising rates. Yet the internet continues to thrive. And advertising volume is growing so rapidly that it more than compensates for the declining rates.

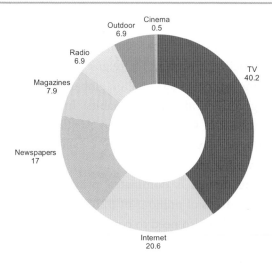

Exhibit 14.4 Share of global ad spend in 2013 by medium. Total spend for the year was estimated to be $503 billion (*Source: ZenithOptimedia*).

As always market forces are fundamental to driving growth. Armed with smartphones, tablets, PCs and smart TVs, people are spending more and more time throughout the day on the internet. Businesses too are thriving on the internet where they are discovering value propositions that never existed before. Many B2B firms and small and medium enterprises that scarcely advertised on conventional media, are increasingly doing so on the net where they are better able to target their ad spend. Global consumer marketing companies too are shifting ad spend to where their consumers are hanging out.

Furthermore, as CPM (cost per thousand impressions) rates go down, publishers are compelled to put more ads on their site to breakeven/maintain profits. Needless to say, the number of sites and the quantity of content on the web is soaring. And so we are experiencing both an increase in demand and an increase in supply. What this clearly portends is that netizens shall continue to be bombarded with an ever increasing slew of advertisements.

According to ZenithOptimedia, the internet's share of global advertising (20.6%) overtook newspaper in 2013 (Exhibit 14.4). As eyeballs continue to shift from conventional media to online media, advertising on the net grew by 16%, with mobile soaring at 77% driven by the rapid growth in usage of smartphones.

For the time being, however, TV reigns supreme, commanding a share of 40% of the estimated $532 billion global ad spend in 2014. This is not surprising considering viewing habits. In the US for instance, based on Exhibit 13.2 in Chapter 13, *New Media*, the average person spends 4 h 28 min per day glued to the TV — which by far exceeds the time spent on any other medium.

TV advertising though is dominated primarily by big consumer brands. For the hundreds of millions of B2B companies, and small and medium enterprises that also need to connect with their customers, TV is less viable. With finely targeted customers in specialized categories, they rely heavily on direct marketing, and in the past, their advertising would be confined mainly within trade magazines.

The internet is the perfect medium for these organizations; it is where their customers have become accustomed to engaging with them, and where prospective customers, who may not have heard of them, can find them. And it helps save costs by cutting down on the traditional approaches to direct marketing — sales calls, mail, tradeshows etc.

Challenge Facing Low Involvement Categories

There is absolutely no doubt that the web as a medium is of paramount importance to businesses. It is also evident that customers seeking high value, high involvement products and services, search for vendors on the internet. But what about mega brands in low involvement categories?

A Google study of "heat maps" (Google, April 2011) revealed that for travel, automotive, technology and a range of financial products and services, most consumers search online for information, sometimes weeks or months in advance of their purchase, and that the search has a strong influence on their purchasing decision. On the other hand for groceries, beauty and personal care, over-the-counter (OTC) health, and restaurants, the process of decision making occurs at the point and time of purchase.

When it comes to buying FMCG products, it is unlikely that the consumer will seek information or advice on the net. Most of the time for FMCG shopping, she habitually picks brands in her repertoire from the supermarket shelves. It is possible that for specialized personal care or exotic foods, she will sometimes consult the web, yet she will not have the inclination to do so for the vast majority of the items that are found in her shopping basket.

So how should a soda, soap or shampoo brand engage with consumers on the internet? We know that while consumers do not usually go to the net to decide what shampoo to buy, they do go there for information on hair care issues. Sites like Sunsilk.com, BeingGirl.com and Pampers.com that attract traffic bear content that relates to topics that consumers are interested in. While a Sunsilk brochure on the net will not attract much interest, a discussion on hair fall could generate interest in a variant of the brand.

Similarly for advertising on the net, if a campaign has ambitions of going viral it must tap into people's interests, passions, concerns and emotions. Dove talks about real beauty. Coca-Cola talks about happiness, togetherness and harmony. They both talk about the values people cherish, the concerns people are passionate about, and they tap into people's feelings and emotions to stimulate and arouse their attention. It is classical conditioning at work; the brand starts to represent those values and emotions that the advertising evokes.

Challenge of Reaching the Masses

Going Viral is a Tall Order

The Old Spice commercial ("Smell like a man, man") of 2010, the fastest growing online viral video campaign in its time, received 6.7 million views on Day 1 and 23 million by Day 3. On the net it has the benefit of remaining on the backlist and its views reached 50 million by 2014. The Blendtec viral video series "Will it Blend?" has crossed 300 million views since it debuted in 2006. Recent successes include Evian's "Baby & Me" (96 million) and Dove's "Real Beauty Sketches" (65 million).

Eventually there will be advertisements that cross the 100 million mark, within days instead of months or years.

Though impressive, 100 million viewers represent less than 0.14% of the world's population — far too small a proportion for global FMCG brands that need to reach out to the masses. Advertisements moreover, rarely go viral. The viral impact of the average online advertisement on the masses is therefore fairly insignificant.

Viral campaigns that people choose to view on their own *free will*, compete with all of the content that already exists on the web, as well as whatever continues to pour in! They can only do so by entertaining people in the manner they want to be entertained, or informing them about things that interest them. And it would only serve their purpose if in addition to the entertaining content and interesting information, they can effectively communicate the message they want to communicate about their brand.

It is a tall order. There can be no doubt that to reach out to mass audiences, it is much easier for advertisers to ride on the entertainment industry than to compete with it. Despite the ills of interrupt advertising, it presents a win-win, if not the only solution for mass marketers. Advertisers benefit from the reach, and the entertainment industry benefits from advertising revenue. From the consumers' perspective, while ads interrupt their viewing experience, they do fund the entertainment industry, which otherwise would need to rely more on subscription fees to pay for content.

Online Advertising for Mass Marketers

Broadly speaking, there are two approaches that marketers can take to communicate online to consumers — inbound marketing, which relies on a pull strategy to channel the buzz onto their sites; and outbound marketing, which relies on advertising. Ideally marketers would like to rely more on inbound marketing to generate traffic, but advertising may be more effective for mass marketers to reach larger audiences.

The audience is spoilt for choice on the web. As users explore and discover their unique personal tastes amidst the enormous glut of web

1. Google	6. Amazon	11. Google.co.in
2. Facebook	7. Wikipedia	12. Live
3. YouTube	8. Taobao	13. LinkedIn
4. Yahoo!	9. Twitter	14. Sina
5. Baidu	10. Qq	15. Tmall

Exhibit 14.5 The 15 most popular websites (*Source: Alexa, May 2014*).

pages, media consumption on the net is shattered into numerous miniscule fragments.

There is also considerable consolidation on the web. The 15 most popular websites listed in Exhibit 14.5 attract the largest number of eyeballs, and the majority of these sites support advertising. The big three — Google, Facebook and YouTube — have crossed a billion unique viewers per month. As of October 2014, Facebook has 1.35 billion active users, each with their home pages, and YouTube viewers have a choice of 25 million reference files.

Website publishers are able to segregate their users into audience segments or personas based on their online behaviours, demographics, socialgraphics, locations etc. The ad servers can direct different advertisements to different browsers. This allows advertisers to finely target their advertisements to audiences based on their traits, thus increasing the effectiveness of the ad. Audiences are also likely to be more receptive to advertising that is aligned with their interests.

The web also affords a high level of transparency and controls on the reach and exposure of advertisements. This allows for better budget controls through a variety of pricing models based on impressions and clicks.

The high level of flexibility and transparency makes advertising on the web conducive both for niche brands as well as mass marketers.

The web is also ideal for testing advertisements before airing on relatively expensive conventional media, thereby greatly reducing financial risks. The Old Spice commercial for instance, was aired on the Super Bowl, after its YouTube success.

As it grows to contribute to a larger component of a brand's communication mix, it is increasingly important that online marketing is well integrated with offline marketing. All marketing initiatives must be tightly interwoven to create a synergistic impact.

TV Remains Most Effective Medium for Mass Marketers

Consider the following statistics on some of the most watched TV broadcasts:

- On average, 80 to 90 million people from the United States are tuned into the Super Bowl, and over 100 million tune into Super Bowl Sunday.
- The clash between India and Pakistan, at the 2015 Cricket World Cup attracted over a billion TV viewers. At the earlier 2011 edition, their encounter at the semi-finals was watched by about 988 million people.
- Estimates of TV viewership of the 2008 Summer Olympics opening ceremony varied between one and four billion.
- Around 704 million tuned into China's 2014 Lunar New Year extravaganza on TV.
- On 20 July 1969, 530 million people watched the first humans ever to walk on the surface of the moon.

(Sources: Wikipedia, Adweek, China Central Television and The Hollywood Reporter)

While it is the blockbusters that attract huge audiences, primetime viewership also remains high, in spite of media fragmentation. According to Nielsen the top 10 primetime broadcast programmes in the US (April 2014) were watched by 17 million to 9 million viewers on the same day. The US ratings (i.e. the percentage of TV homes tuned into television) ranged from 11 for the top programme to 6 for the 10th most watched programme. Ratings in India, a heterogeneous country with many languages and cultures, vary from 10 to 2 for the top 10 programmes. In comparison, ratings in a smaller country like Hong Kong range from 30 to 20 for the top 10 programmes.

As these figures suggest, no other medium comes close to television when it comes to reaching a mass audience. By placing ads on multiple channels and programmes, advertisers are able to reach a far greater audience on TV. It is the only medium that can reach over 100 million viewers over a few hours.

Yet, as internet download speeds improve worldwide, as the penetration of smart TVs increases and as the influence of the present and future internet generations grows, online content will gradually erode offline media. Even now there is clear evidence that the level of cannibalization is substantial and growing — while 704 million viewers tuned into China's 2014 Lunar New Year extravaganza on TV, another 110 million tuned into the same programme online.

Digital Advertising Formats

Since the time they first appeared in 1994, advertisements on the net have been evolving. The earliest advertisements were in the form of banner ads that appeared at the top of web pages. Charges to run banner ads used to vary from US$30 to as high as US$100 per thousand impressions. Those early rates, which were benchmarked on magazine page ad fees, became unsustainable as advertisement space exploded on the net and as advertisers became aware of the low click-through rates for banner ads. Today's advertisement rates vary from below a dollar CPM (cost per thousand impressions) to over US$30 CPM depending on the site and the ad format. (According to rough estimates for 2013, market average CPM for video is around US$25, mobile is US$3, general display US$2, and premium display US$10).

Over the years, a variety of advertising formats have emerged yielding improvements in click-through rates and ROI. The range of display advertising include top banner, bottom banner, sidebar, side box, button, pop-up, pop-under, floating, expanding videos etc.

Web Banner

Web banners typically are ads displayed within a web page. They may use rich media to incorporate video, audio, and a host of interactive elements. One disadvantage of banner advertisements is they are easy to ignore, and average click-through rates are low (generally in the range of 0.05% to 0.15%).

Pop-up and Pop-under

Pop-up and pop-under ads are displayed in a new web browser window. They infuriate viewers because they clutter the desktop and take time to close. They do however generate significantly higher click-through rates than web banners, and hence command a premium.

Floater

These ads float for a few seconds superimposed over the content when the viewer enters a web page. They can be particularly annoying because they obscure the page's content and often block mouse input as well.

They cannot be ignored because they fully interrupt the viewer's experience much like conventional TV advertising. The ads may however provide the means to escape such as a close button.

Floater ads make use of rich media (animation and sound effects) and command a premium due to their high click-through rates.

Video

Video ads play like a TV commercial, usually in a pop-up or pop-under advertisement. The ads usually act as hyperlinks — viewers who click on them to seek further information are transported to a relevant external website.

The visual and narrative richness of video can enthral and inform audiences in a way that no other medium can. The medium was constrained in the past, due to low download speeds that made it tedious to watch video on the net. Since download speeds have improved considerably in recent years, in most countries, one expects that video advertising will outgrow other online formats. Its trajectory can be gauged by viewership trends over the past 12 months. According to data sourced from comScore online video advertising exploded in 2013 in the US, topping 35 billion views in December and achieving year-on-year growth of 100%. Video ads also achieved highest click-through rates among all digital ad formats. Viewers are 20 to 30 times more likely to click through online video ads than standard banners.

YouTube, which gets a billion unique viewers per month, is an ideal platform for video advertising. As of October 2014, the most popular video on the net (PSY's Gangnam Style) amassed over 2 billion views. Top videos on YouTube include songs by pop music artists like Justin Bieber, Jennifer Lopez, Miley Cyrus, Katy Perry, Rihanna etc. and a variety of entertainment videos. (As this list suggests, YouTube viewership is currently driven by the internet generations. It is where many budding artists get their first big break).

Display ads and in-video ads are the two common formats on YouTube. The display ads appear alongside YouTube videos, or as pop-ups within YouTube videos. The in-video overlay ads appear as pop-ups within videos that are targeted by selected queries. Destination URLs within in-video ads can also go to locations outside of YouTube.

In-stream advertising that plays before or during a video is an increasingly popular format on YouTube. The advertisement plays for a few mandatory seconds, after which viewers may choose to keep watching or skip the rest of the ad.

Pricing Models

There are a wide range of pricing models for online advertising, including the ones listed as follows:

- CPM (cost per thousand [mille] impressions) — An impression is display of ad to a user.
- CPC (cost-per-click), cost-per-completion — Applicable for video ads — advertiser pays only if viewer watched complete ad.
- CPA (cost per acquisition) — Advertiser pays on basis of acquisitions delivered by ad.

Targeting

A key advantage on the internet is the ability to manage and control advertising at the individual (device) level. Unlike TV where all those watching a programme get to see the same advertisements, on the net the ad server may direct different advertisement to different browsers. This customization allows advertisers to finely target their advertisements to increase the effectiveness of the ad.

Advertisers use the following approaches, among others, to target viewers:

- Behavioural targeting: By collecting data about a viewer's online behaviour, across several websites, advertisers are able to create a picture of the viewer's interests, and direct advertisements that relate to these interests.
- Demographic targeting.
- Geotargeting (geographic location using for instance, the Internet Protocol [IP] address or a phone's Global Positioning System [GPS] receiver).
- Persona-based targeting: Advertisers may group viewers according to traits that allude to their objectives. For instance landing pages, or traffic sources (i.e. referring site), keywords searched, or event based (e.g. filling a form, or buying something). This information may be used for delivering relevant advertisements.
- Contextual/semantic targeting is used when advertiser choose to deliver ads that relate to the content of the web page where the ads appear.

Effective targeting increases the relevance of advertising to viewers, thus improving the advertiser's return on investment.

Internet advertising is also highly transparent. Advertising platforms allow marketers to track and measure the performance of their ad campaigns by means of analytic tools that trace users as they click the ad and traverse the destination site. Advertisers are able to gauge the number of leads and increase in sales resulting from the ads.

Mobile

The gamut of mobile advertising encompasses the following formats/capabilities:

- Mobile Web: Short Message Service (SMS) tagline, mobile web banner (top of page), mobile web poster (bottom of page banner), rich media mobile ads.
- Multimedia Messaging Service (MMS), ads within mobile games and mobile videos.
- Interstitials which appear while requested content is loading, audios that can take the form of a jingle before a voice recording, or an audio ad played while interacting with an Interactive Voice Response (IVR) service.
- Ads that use the phone's utilities such as vibrations and camera.
- Campaigns that provide interactive experiences.
- Location sensing capabilities make it feasible for ads to offer consumers what they need, when they need it, and where they need it.

Due to the numerous advantages it has over other devices, mobile proffers tremendous potential. Mobile phones are the only devices that people usually carry wherever they go. As marketers make better use of the phone's location sensing capabilities, they could influence people at the point and time of purchase.

The penetration of mobile phones is also far greater than that for other digital media devices. Globally it is estimated that there are 6.8 billion mobile phone subscriptions, which translates to 97 subscriptions per 100 people (*Source:* International Telecommunication Union). Note, however, that penetration will be substantially less than 97% because many individuals have more than one subscription.

Search Advertising

Search or pay-per-click (PPC) ads are sponsored links that appear at the top, bottom or alongside the search engine result pages. Since the space allocated for the ads is limited, advertisers have to bid for keywords. Search advertising platforms such as Google AdWords offer advertisers the flexibility to craft ad text, set budgets, target customers based on demographics and location, and, as the name PPC suggest, pay on a per click basis.

Accountability is a key advantage as users can be traced as they traverse the web site. It is possible to track increase in leads and sales resulting from search advertising. These ads are also non-disruptive.

YouTube's AdWords for videos is structured along similar lines as Google's AdWords.

Search

Overview of the Search Process

According to Google, as of 2014, there are 60 trillion individual pages on the net. Search engines like Google, Yahoo and Bing help us retrieve relevant content from this gigantic information glut, in a timely manner. In order to do this they maintain a page index containing information that their algorithms need, to generate search results.

Search engines use automated programmes called spiders or bots (short for robot e.g. Googlebot) that crawl the web pages from link to link and retrieve data about the pages. The search engines store the information into a massive database called the index. The size of the Google index is over 100 million gigabytes.

As a user seeking information types into the engine's search box, algorithms interpret the information he is seeking and identify the relevant pages in the index. The search engine then ranks the results based on several factors, and presents the results in rank order to the user in the form of search engine result pages (SERPs).

Securing a high rank on these pages is of such enormous interest that a whole industry has emerged to help marketers optimize their websites.

Search Engine Optimization

Search engine optimization (SEO) is the process of boosting the ranking of a site on SERPs. It is of crucial importance because the ranking greatly affects site traffic. Most users do not look beyond the first SERP (each Google SERP contains 10 results), and the higher a site ranks on this list, the higher the probability the user will visit the site. According to Google 94% of users click on a first page result and 35% click on the top result.

A typical user query generates millions of web pages with helpful information. Google's algorithms rely on more than 200 unique signals or "clues" that make it possible to guess what the user might really be looking for, and accordingly rank the results. These signals include the website's content in the context of how well it relates to the search query, the freshness of content, region, and most importantly PageRank, an algorithm used for determining the *authority* of a web page based on the number of inbound links.

PageRank is based on the notion that the most important pages on the internet are the pages with the most links leading to them. (This approach is similar to the citation based criteria for assessing the importance of academic research papers.) However, PageRank is not a simple count of inbound links; recursive in nature, it weighs the importance (i.e. PageRank) of the page that contains the link. Links arriving from pages with higher PageRank have more weight than links from pages with lower PageRank.

The other signals that Google employs are used to assess the *relevance* of the page to the information or the services that the user is seeking. To score on relevance, marketers need to craft the content on each page such that it relates tightly with what their prospects are seeking, and serves the intended site objective. In particular they need an understanding of the range of words and phrases that target customers enter into the engine's search box, when they are seeking the information or services provided by the site. Those words and phrases, known as *keywords and keyword phrases* form the basis for SEO.

"Knowing your customers", the immutable success formula remains as relevant for e-commerce as it does for direct sales. On the net, marketers are empowered by web analytic tools that allow them to "see" what their prospect are doing, and track the words and phrases they use to get to specific pages on their sites and their competitors' sites. They may also use PPC advertising campaigns to test alternative keywords in their ability to draw traffic and convert prospects.

The selection of keywords and keyword phrases to target for optimization is a vital step in SEO. Marketers should narrow the possibilities down to a manageable list, choosing those keywords and keyword phrases that are not only relevant, but also more specific (i.e. less generic) to their site.

For example, a company that specializes in simulation methods for training marketing professionals in the consumer goods sector might consider the phrase "experiential learning programme in consumer marketing" (option 1), or the phrase "consumer marketing training" (option 2), or the phrase "marketing training" (option 3). The search volumes vary drastically for each of these phrases. Google search for instance yielded 2 million results for option 1, 174 million for option 2, and 912 million for option 3.

Clearly option 3 is too generic and poorly targeted; it will likely draw visitors from non-consumer goods sector. Moreover, it will be far too difficult to secure a high rank amidst the millions vying for a place on the first SERP. Option 1 is finely tuned and will drive well targeted volume to the site. In addition, the company might also consider option 2 ("consumer marketing training"), which is less generic than option 3, and may attract prospects who are open to experiential learning, though that may not be their prime consideration.

The company might also need to consider alternative phrases like "simulation based consumer marketing training" or use terms like "FMCG", "CPG" and "consumer durables" to cover a wider range from the vocabulary that prospects are likely to use. Note, however that it is not necessary to cover all synonyms because Google does that for you. Their algorithms recognize words with similar meanings.

Since search engine algorithms operate at the page level (SERPs is a list of landing pages, not sites), optimization efforts need to be directed on a page basis. This provides for greater flexibility — different landing pages on the site may target different prospects, with different set of key words.

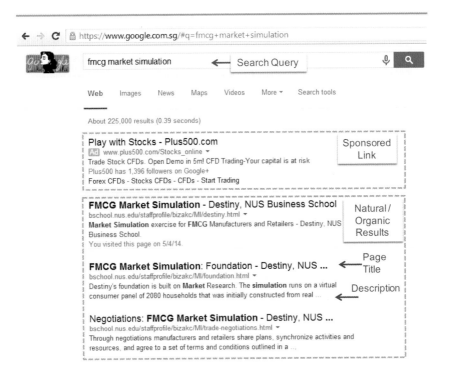

Exhibit 14.6   Screen shot of a SERP (search engine research page). Note the titles are also the hyperlinks to the listed web pages.

Once chosen, the keywords for each page need to be weaved into the content for the page, especially in the following areas which strongly influence page ranking:

- Page Title: Information intended for the browser is contained in the page's title tag. Titles are accorded great importance by the search engines for ranking, and should therefore contain the most important keywords. The order in which they appear within the title also influences the search results.

- Meta-description: The description of the web page (which is stored within the page's meta-description tags) appears below the title, on the SERP (refer to Exhibit 14.6). Should any of the words that users use in their query, appear in the title/description, they are highlighted. Thus by weaving keywords into the description, marketers may draw the users' attention and increase the likelihood that they visit the page. However, unlike the title, the description is not used by the search engines for ranking purposes.

- URL and domain name: The URL (i.e. the address of the web page) is another criteria used by Google for ranking pages. The same applies for the domain name, which appears in all URLs on the same website. This incidentally explains why keyword-rich domain names are being sold at premium prices. Keywords also make the URL text more meaningful; particularly when the URL acts as the anchor for inbound links to the web page.
- Headers (h1, h2, h3) that are keyword-rich improve the web page's ranking for those key words.
- Images: HTML (HyperText Markup Language), the language used for creating web pages, provides an attribute called "alt" that may be used to describe images. Search engines use these descriptors for ranking images, and some engines also use them for page ranking.

Web Analytics

Web analytics is the analysis of the behaviour of internet users. It serves the following key objectives:

- Monitor the health of a website — Track and measure web traffic to assess performance vis-à-vis benchmarks and metrics.
- Improve effectiveness of the website in terms of conversion rates and other performance parameters by means of controlled website tests.
- Improve effectiveness of elements of the marketing mix. For example testing/evaluating digital marketing campaigns.

Web Traffic Data

When a visitor accesses a web page, the site's web server receives relevant information about the visitor's request and visitor's computer.

This information which is saved and maintained in *webserver logs*, usually contains the following data:

- IP address of the client (visitor's) computer
- Time, date
- URI (unique resource indicator) of the requested resource
- URL (unique resource locator) of the webpage that the request emanated from
- Information about the client's browser, operating system etc.
- Information about the requested resource — file size etc.

The data divulges a host of useful parameters such as the users' geographical location (based on IP address), the time of arrival, the site where they arrived from and, in case they came via a search engine, the search query strings used to enter the site. It also reveals information on pages visited, and the duration of time spent on each page.

In addition to maintaining logs, web servers can also use *cookies* (small text files) to store information on client computers' local hard drives. There are a few different types of cookies that meet different requirements. A *transient cookie* is one that is created at the start of every session, and deleted at the end of the session. On the other hand a *persistent cookie* outlasts the user session. It is created when the user first enters the server's website, and is updated each time the user re-enters the site using the same computer.

Cookies are primarily intended to improve the user's on-site experience. For instance cookies can store information to allow users to re-enter sites without having to log in. The stored data usually includes unique user IDs and user preferences.

The use of persistent cookies provides for more accurate tracking of users, and determining how many client computers actually visited the site. The IP address cannot be relied to track this information because of ambiguity arising due to proxy servers, caching and so on.

Besides logs and cookies, an alternative method called *page tagging* allows outsourced services to perform web analytics. This process which requires the insertion of a few lines of code on every page of web site, has gained wide acceptance since SaaS (software as a service) vendors like Google Analytics and Statcounter started providing web traffic data analysis for free.

Website Intelligence

Web analytics tools use information from logs, cookies and/or page tagging processes to segment site visitors, and track their progress down the prospecting funnel, from leads to enquiries, enquiries to prospects, and prospects to customers. The software tools keep track of conversion rates at each stage of the prospecting funnel.

It is possible also to keep track of incoming traffic from advertisements placed on external sites. To isolate these visitors appropriate parameters are added at the end of the linking URL.

Here is a list of metrics that are useful for assessing the health of a website and benchmarking performance:

- Unique Visitors: The number of users who visit the site over the reporting period.
- New Visitor: The number of first-ever unique visitors (Assumes cookies have not been deleted).
- Repeat Visitor: The number of unique visitors who visit the site more than once during reporting period.
- Conversions: Number of visitors who complete a target action such as purchasing something, subscribing to newsletter etc.
- Conversion Rate: Proportion of visitors who perform a target action.
- Bounce Rate: Proportion of visitors who leave the site without visiting any page other than their landing page.
- Abandonment Rate: Proportion of visitors who start a target action, but do not complete it.
- Cost per Conversion (CPCon): Cost of an advertising campaign divided by the total number of conversions resulting from the campaign. (This requires that the inbound URL from the ad has been tagged so that analytic tools can distinguish the traffic resulting from the campaign).

Considering the vast amount of information as also the large number of metrics, one can easily get inundated while examining the data. It is important therefore to begin with objectives and key issues, and drill down to relevant information that addresses those issues.

Online is one of a number of ways that marketers engage with their customers. In order to improve their understanding of the overall relationship with customers and how each platform contributes to the development of the relationship, it is important for marketers to take a holistic view. They need to interpret website intelligence in the context of other sources of market information.

Controlled Website Tests

Analysis of web traffic reveals a great deal about the behaviour of users, i.e. what people do on websites. The data however does not explain why they do what they do. And this is often crucially important if marketers wish to act on the information.

The understanding of "why people to what they do" typically involves a two stage process — constructing hypothesis or scenarios, and testing those hypothesis. Marketers may need to conduct qualitative research to explore issues, and draw conclusions and hypothesis. For instance, if an advertisement or some other stimuli is not having the desired impact, a focus group discussion can unearth the objective, subjective and emotive reasons why this is so.

As regards testing hypothesis and alternatives, the website itself is the ideal platform. A technique known as multivariate testing allows marketers and web designers to test different combinations of elements (e.g. headlines, paragraph text, images, call-to-action buttons, testimonials etc.) on a web page and assess the impact of those changes on the site's performance.

Multivariate testing is conducted in a live, controlled environment. The web page is dynamically generated and rotated among incoming visitors so that each gets to see one of the different combinations of elements. The visitors are tracked and their behaviours recorded as they navigate the site, to determine which elements (i.e. independent variables) on a web page make the biggest impact on the site's performance, where site performance is measured in terms of a specific objective metric (i.e. dependent variable) such as conversion rate.

A/B testing (or split testing) is a relatively simpler way to test changes on a web page. In A/B testing (or A/B/C or A/B/C/D testing) different versions of the web page are tested to gauge and compare the performance of each version.

If a marketer or web designer wants to choose between one of two or more versions of a web page, in that case A/B testing is the appropriate methodology. On the other hand if she is seeking to optimize the elements of a web page, multivariate testing will reveal which elements she needs to focus her attention on.

The net affords great flexibility for evaluating digital marketing campaigns. It is possible to pre-test campaigns (A/B testing) before they are launched, and continue to evaluate them in real time after they are launched. It is easier to manage, control and execute test programmes on the net. It is also much less expensive. For these reasons, consumer marketing companies will increasingly evaluate campaigns on the net before airing them on TV.

Testing can be outsourced easily to analytics service providers by inserting code in the pages that are required to be tested.

SEO and controlled website testing are of great interest as they help to maximize the ROI of a website. By boosting the ranking of a site on SERPs, SEO helps internet marketers to bring more visitors to their site. By improving the design and content of web pages, multivariate and A/B tests help to increase the probability that visitors will take the desired action once they arrive at the website.

CHAPTER 15

Advertising Research

Exhibit 15.0 Telepics of the Coca-Cola Hilltop ad: "I'd like to buy the world a Coke and keep it company" *(Source: Coca-Cola website).*

Preview

"Advertising people who ignore research are as dangerous as generals who ignore decodes of enemy signals." — David Ogilvy.

In the 19th century John Wanamaker lamented: "Half the money I spend on advertising is wasted; the trouble is I don't know which half." Since his time, and especially during the latter half of the 20th century, many theories and models emerged that have enhanced our understanding of advertising and its impact. Yet uncertainty still clouds advertising to a great extent. Many of us believe we have the data and the methods to accurately assess the short term impact of advertising; what we are not so confident about is the assessment of its long term impact.

We know that advertising works in many different ways. Marketers' advertising objectives vary substantially depending on the nature of the product, its lifecycle, brand history, corporate priorities, competitive environment and a host of other factors. Their objectives must be keenly considered while evaluating advertising, as was highlighted by a consortium of 21 leading US advertising agencies.

This consortium which assembled in 1982, released a public document that laid out the Positioning Advertising Copy Testing (PACT) principles on what constitutes good copy testing. PACT stressed the need for multiple measurements — "because single measurements are generally inadequate to assess the performance of an advertisement". It emphasised that a good copy testing system should provide measurements which are relevant to the objectives of the advertising, and that there was need for clarity and agreement about how the results will be used in advance of each specific test.

The key themes that shed light on advertising were reviewed in Chapter 12, *How Advertising Works*. According to those themes, the success of advertising hinges on its ability to:

- generate salience;
- persuade consumers;
- differentiate from competitors;
- generate affinity for the brand;
- associate the brand with values, symbols and images;
- build relationships with consumers, and increase their involvement with the brand;
- generate feelings and emotions;
- and convey relevant messages — its proposition, its mantra.

This chapter dwells on the current practices in pre-testing (copy testing) and post-testing (tracking) advertising. It reviews the imperatives in advertising research, and how key facets, such as those listed above, are tested and measured. Emphasis is given to the practices of the major global firms such as Millward Brown and Ipsos ASI that specialize in advertising research. It also covers Millward Brown's awareness index model which provides a framework for measuring the effectiveness of advertising in generating awareness.

Market response models that use analytic techniques to assess the impact that advertising and other elements of the marketing mix have on sales, are covered later in Chapter 18, *Market Mix Modelling*.

Copy Testing (Pre-Testing)

Advertising pre-testing or copy testing is suited for taking go/no-go decisions, and can reveal insights on how to improve the effectiveness of the advertisement. With over 100,000 ads tested since its launch in 1989 till 2013, Millward Brown's Link™ is the most widely used copy testing solution in the industry.

By and large copy testing is a two-stage — quantitative and qualitative — interviewing process. The quantitative stage usually consists of 125 to 200 respondents who are shown a clutter reel comprising the test ad and some 8 to 10 other commercials, at a central test location. A second viewing where only the test ad is shown follows the first viewing.

Amongst the leading research suppliers, Ipsos ASI's Next*TV solution adopts a more rigorous approach that uses both in-home viewing of the ad and day-after-recall. Participants are asked to review a 30 min television programme broadcast on an unused cable channel in their homes. The actual intent, however, is to evaluate the commercials embedded within the programme. Responses are collected a day after exposure. Though relatively expensive compared to a central location test, in-home viewing methodology better simulates the natural viewing environment.

In general, respondents are interviewed three or four times during the quantitative stage — at recruitment (screening questions), before the first viewing, after the first viewing and after the second viewing. The questions test for advertising awareness and brand recognition, attention to brand, purchase intent, comprehension, recall of messages, and various diagnostic questions and measures. These metrics, and the methods deployed to measure them are described in the sections that follow in this chapter.

The qualitative stage consists of a subset of about 25 to 30 respondents with relatively strong opinions on key questions. These respondents participate in group discussion/in-depth interviews where projective techniques are employed to elicit insights from their thoughts and feelings.

Similar metrics and methods are used for testing of print advertising. To test a magazine ad, respondents are given fake magazines with the test ad imbedded, and asked to flip through and give their initial reactions. In the first round of questions, they are asked what ads they recall seeing. They are then given more time to look through the magazine and asked questions pertaining to recall, persuasiveness of the ad and message recall. Respondents are then directed to the test ad itself, and asked to read it. The final set of questions which follow, pertain to ad comprehension and diagnostics.

Copy testing is rich in diagnostics and can guide advertising creative development. As it does not replicate real life, unmotivated viewing and long term memory, it should not be used for making predictions on the performance of the test ads. It does however, provide a ballpark view of how a commercial will perform on-air, and is used for taking go/no-go decisions.

Testing Advertising Online

The internet is a ruthless medium; it exposes poor content by its insignificance. On the upside, truly engaging campaigns get spotted quickly on the web and can then be rolled onto the relatively expensive conventional media with greater confidence.

As such, the net is a low cost, efficient medium to pre-test ads. A video advertisement uploaded on the web could be tracked on success measures such as click through rate (for those with call to action), completion rate and viewer comments.

A/B testing could also be performed to evaluate two or more options, or test for different approaches to the execution.

The prime advantages of testing advertising online are that it is real time, employs accurate web analytics based success measures, and yields unsolicited feedback.

Online provides hard measures that advertisers will find hard to refute. It is however relatively weak on diagnostics, and would therefore combine well with copy tests, which are strong in this regard.

Advertising Tracking (Post-Testing)

Advertising tracking research monitors the effectiveness of on air advertising. Continuous tracking via interviews conducted throughout the year, is recommended for major brands in FMCG categories that are heavily advertised. Dipsticks however may be appropriate for smaller brands with limited research budgets.

In the past these studies were conducted mainly via telephone or face-to-face interviews. Nowadays online is the most widely used method for data collection.

Millward Brown's current in-market tracking service is called AdNow (formerly ATP — Advanced Tracking Program) and Ipsos ASI's service is called BrandGraph (known earlier as Ad*Graph). Ipsos also recently set up Ipsos ASI|digital, a global practice dedicated to online advertising research.

Gross Rating Points

The metric commonly used for weight of advertising is called Gross Rating Point or GRP in short. It measures quantum in terms of the size of the audience reached, and is computed as the product of the percentage of the audience reached by a campaign times the frequency they see it. This is the same as the sum of the % viewership of the programmes where the campaign is aired.

For example, if in a particular week a brand's advertisement is aired five times over different programmes, and the viewership across these programmes is 40%, 25%, 15%, 30% and 5%, then the GRP for that week is 115 (40 + 25 + 15 + 30 + 5).

Share of Voice is the brand's advertising weight (GRP) expressed as a percentage of relevant market (category or segment). Share of voice may also be expressed in terms of share of advertising expenditure.

Audience Measurement

GRP is typically measured by means of a device called the *people meter*. It is a little box hooked to the TV that reports which programme is being watched when the TV is switched on. The box is accompanied with a remote control with push buttons allotted to each member of the household, so that individuals may identify themselves when they are viewing the TV.

The key disadvantage of the people meter is that it involves the viewer's proactive involvement. Newer audience measurement methods are based on hypersonic facial recognition technologies. These solutions combine biometric authentication and neural network processing to passively detect and identify viewers.

Continuous Interviewing versus Dipsticks

Advertising tracking studies may be conducted continuously (a few interviews every day), or as a series of surveys, referred to as *dipsticks* (or *pulsed* interviews) that dip into the market over time (e.g. pre- and post-advertising).

Continuous interviewing offers a number of advantages over dipsticks. Like a video, it provides an uninterrupted record of measurements with no gaps or missing time periods in the data, capturing all trends and changes in the market. And unlike dipsticks, which tend to be biased to the media schedule of the company's own brands, continuous tracking is better suited for monitoring competitive activity. It is appropriate too for analysing multimedia campaigns.

Continuous tracking data also blends well with other continuous data streams such as GRPs or advertising expenditure, and sales, and can be used for developing market response models. Metrics derived

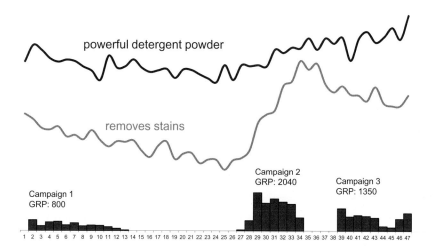

Exhibit 15.1 Image tracking for a detergent brand — 4 weekly moving average.

from models such as Millward Brown's awareness index, provide an assessment of the effectiveness of advertising.

To contain costs, continuous tracking is reported on a 4-weekly or 8-weekly rolling data basis. If for example the required sample size for reporting is 300, then for reporting on basis of 4-weekly moving average, 75 interviews need to be conducted each week.

Dipsticks are like images or snapshots in time. Their prime advantage is that they are less expensive than continuous tracking, and can be concentrated into a short time interval to provide more accurate pre- and post-measurements for a particular advertising campaign.

Tracking Questionnaire

A typical tracking study covers the following aspects of brands and their advertising:

1. Brand awareness
2. Purchase behaviour
3. Brand image
4. Advertising awareness
5. Advertising diagnostics

This order sequence in which topics are covered minimizes the incidence of *order effects* and biases. Unaided brand awareness comes first because succeeding questions make respondents aware of brands they might not have otherwise known. Similarly question pertaining to brand image should come before exposing respondents to any advertising content.

Brand and advertising awareness are measures that gauge the extent to which the advertisement registers in people's minds. Respondents' purchase behaviour is measured in terms of trial, consideration and current usage.

In typical tracking studies image attributes ratings are plotted vis-à-vis campaigns in the manner depicted in Exhibit 15.1. This highlights the impact of individual campaigns on respondents' perceptions. In this example notice how Campaign 2 has a marked impact on the image of the detergent brand, particularly on the attribute *removes stains*.

Details about how awareness is measured are covered later in the section *Branded Memorability*. The way brand image is tracked and analysed was covered in some detail in Chapter 1, *Brand and Brand Image*.

Advertising Research Imperatives

Advertising is tricky to evaluate because it works in many different ways and its impact is both immediate and long lasting. The nature of a product, its lifecycle, brand history, competitive environment and a host of other conditions, influence the objectives and outcomes of advertising; and it is important that due emphasis is given to stated objectives, while diagnosing the effectiveness of a campaign.

For the aforementioned reasons, advertising research agencies use a broad set of *evaluative and diagnostic components* to test advertising. The key evaluative components, applicable both for copy testing and advertising tracking, are as follows:

- Branded Memorability
- Persuasion
- Uniqueness
- Likeability
- Image and Symbolism
- Involvement, Relationship
- Emotion
- Communication

Ad diagnostics answer the following questions: Do consumers like the ad? Is it "talking to them" personally? Are they more likely to buy the brand? Does it reinforce commitment? Does the advertising/brand stand out? Is it different/unique? Is the message getting through?

Branded Memorability

People tend to only remember what is interesting and involving in a commercial. These creative elements that leave long-lasting memories, must serve the intended purpose of the advertisement. Which is why copy tests, like Millward Brown's Link™, emphasize the importance of "functional creativity" — creativity that relates tightly to both the intended message and the brand.

To assess branded memorability, we typically ask this question in a copy test: *There are some adverts that people remember but never know which brand they are for. Which of these phrases applies to this advertisement?*

- *You could not fail to remember the ad was for [brand].*
- *The ad is quite good at making you remember it is for [brand].*

- *The ad is not all that good at making you remember it is for [brand].*
- *It could have been an ad for any brand of [category].*
- *It could have been an ad for almost anything.*

The development of *brand and advertising salience*, as mentioned earlier, is a core objective of advertising. Salience is measured in terms of the percentage of consumers who claim they are aware. Top-of-mind awareness is the first brand (advertising) that comes to mind. Spontaneous or unaided awareness is brand (advertising) recall without prompting, and aided awareness is brand (advertising) recall with prompting.

Ipsos ASI's day-after responses approach enables the company to track the proportion of respondents who claim they have seen the ad, and those who are able to play back elements of the ad that are either general or exclusive to the execution.

Once a commercial has been aired, advertising awareness and brand linkage is tested via brand-led claimed awareness as well as de-branded recognition.

Brand-led claimed ad awareness is not execution specific; it measures a perception or belief that a brand has been advertised. Typically we ask this question to measure brand-led claimed awareness: *"Have you seen any television advertising for [brand] recently?"*

On the other hand recognition is execution specific; it measures exposure to and recall of a particular piece of advertising creative that's shown in the form of telepics. It is de-branded — so for example, if we were to use the telepics shown in Exhibit 15.0, the Coca-Cola branding on the bottles would have to be masked.

The question is phrased along the following lines: *"I'm going to read out a description of [show you] an ad for a brand of [category] that has been on television recently, and I'd like you to tell me if you have seen the ad or not."*

Those respondents who claim to be aware of the ad are then asked what brand it was for.

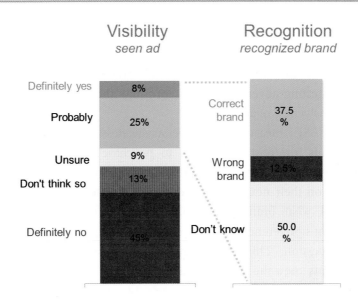

Exhibit 15.2 Branded Memorability — visibility and recognition (branded linkage).

Exhibit 15.2 presents the results from a specific research study. In this example branded memorability is weak. Only a relatively small proportion (one in three) of the respondents claimed they *definitely* or *probably* saw the ad. Furthermore one in two who claimed to have seen the ad, could not recall the brand, and one in four (12.5/50) who claimed they knew what brand was advertised, got it wrong! This advertisement was weak both in terms of visibility as well as brand recognition.

While in this example the results are quite straight forward, conclusions should normally be based on benchmarks provided by the research agency. For instance, Ipsos ASI computes a benchmark measure called the *Reach Index* based on visibility and recognition or brand linkage:

$$Reach\ Index = Visibility \times Recognition,$$
$$= 33\% \times 37.5\% = 12.5\% \text{ (for the example in Exhibit 15.2).}$$

A high reach index means more people noticed the ad and associate it with the brand.

Persuasion

A key advertising objective, particularly for a new product, is to persuade consumers to try the brand. Research solutions for pre-testing and post-testing advertisements accordingly incorporate measures for the persuasiveness of advertising.

Ipsos ASI's measure of the persuasiveness of an ad is based on respondents' pre/post disposition to purchase the advertised brand. Prior to watching, respondents are asked what brand they are likely to purchase on their next purchase occasion. Post exposure, respondents are asked what brand they would prefer to win. Asking for the respondent's preference in a different context helps to mask the purpose of the question. This lessens the possible bias that could arise if respondents knew the intent of the question.

An alternative approach is to use two groups — a test group exposed to the ad and a control group not exposed to the ad. This approach which eliminates bias, requires two well-matched sample groups, and is therefore more expensive.

The *persuasion score* is the shift between the purchase intent and purchase frequency after seeing the test ad and before being exposed to it, or the difference between the test and the control groups. Ipsos ASI computes a benchmark expected persuasion scores called *Predicted Average Result (PAR) Shift* based on market, brand strength, category loyalty and market fragmentation. A *persuasion index* is computed based on persuasion score divided by the PAR shift.

In copy testing, for advertisement effectiveness, Ipsos ASI computes the *copy effect index (CEI)* as a combination of reach and persuasion.

$$CEI = Reach\ Index \times Persuasion\ Index.$$

In a post-testing scenario, in addition to pre/post disposition to purchase, measures of sales response may also be used to gauge the impact of the advertisement in generating short term sales. This is not straightforward because the impact of advertising on sales is usually drowned by causal influences such as in-store promotions. Market response modelling, which is covered in Chapter 18, *Market Mix Modelling*, can help decompose the impact of each of the individual

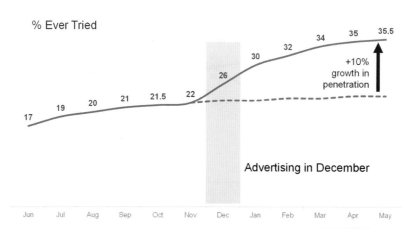

% Ever Tried

Exhibit 15.3 Consumer panel data reveals a large improvement in trial as this brand attracts new/lapsed buyers. This improvement in the brand's penetration is due to the advertising campaign during December, as well as other marketing efforts.

elements, and is particularly useful in assessing short term influences of advertising.

Disaggregate level consumer panel data is quite revealing, in that it can separate trial from repeat purchase. The chart in Exhibit 15.3 reveals a 10% point lift in trial of a brand due to the impact of an ad campaign in December, as well as other marketing activities. This is a good measure for the persuasiveness of the overall marketing effort in attracting new consumers. However, unless we decompose the impact of each of the marketing elements, we cannot deduce how much of this impact is due to advertising alone.

Uniqueness

To assess the novelty or uniqueness of an advertisement, respondents are asked to rate the ad on how much it differs from other advertisements. Uniqueness is of great importance particularly for new products that need to stand out to persuade consumers to try them.

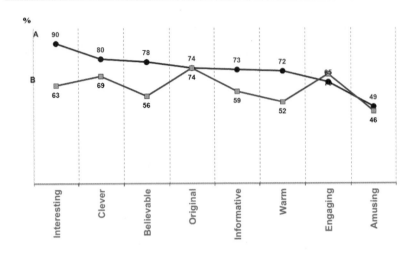

Exhibit 15.4 Selection of measures relating to affinity. Scores for the two campaigns are based on the top 2 box ratings by respondents.

Likeability

The likeability of an ad is usually measured in terms of rating on aspects such as enjoyable, entertaining, fun, appealing, interesting as well as overall like/dislike. Often a selection of questions is used, such as shown in Exhibit 15.4 where two advertising are compared against a set of measures.

Overall liking is tracked both in absolute as well as relative terms in the context of other brands in the category.

In-market tests also measure the level of advertising fatigue, in terms of the percent of respondents who claim they are getting "fed-up with seeing" the ad.

Image and Symbolism

Imagery and, to an extent, symbolism can be measured using agree-disagree rating scales as described in Chapter 1, *Brand and Brand Image*. Symbols however can be relatively hard to measure. For instance, how do we measure symbols that are non-verbal or nebulous or indescribable, such as logos and mnemonics?

Involvement

Consumers' relationships and their involvement with brands are complex in nature, and consequently difficult to measure. In an overall sense it is possible to gauge "relationship" via statement like "it is meant for people just like me" or "it makes me more comfortable about buying brand X". However, it is often not easy to articulate the nature of the relationship.

Emotion

Verbal responses often fail to reveal the true nature of emotions. Consumers find it hard to verbalize emotions, and they may not even be conscious of their existence. Moreover, some emotions are personal and perhaps embarrassing to express aloud. There are also subjectivities in languages and cultures. In some countries for instance, people are less willing to express negative opinions. For these reasons, the focus on emotion research is shifting to indirect interviewing methods and non-verbal approaches.

The approach adopted by Ipsos ASI makes use of Emoti*Scape™, a show card containing a map of 40 emotions (see Exhibit 15.5), each represented by an illustration of a facial expression (emoticons) and a verbal description of the feeling expressed. Respondents are asked to indicate where on this emotions landscape best represents their feelings for each of the following:

- What feelings do you have from this ad?
- What feelings is the advertiser trying to use and portray within the ad?
- What emotions do you associate with being a brand user?

Their responses are summarized to reflect the emotional reactions and responses to the advertisement and the brand.

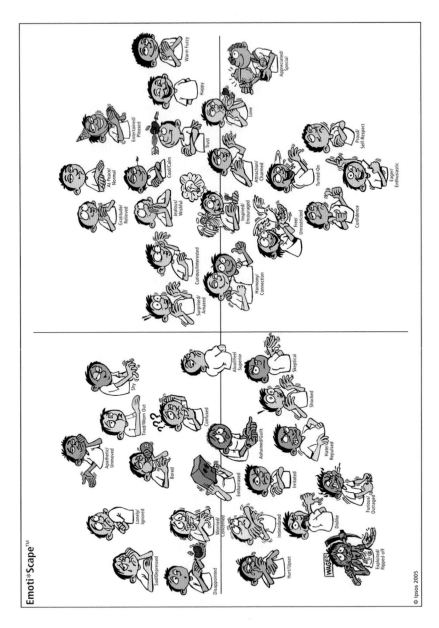

Exhibit 15.5 Ipsos ASI's Emoti*Scape™, an emotions landscape.

Exhibit 15.6 *Fourier One* is a medical-grade, dry and wireless EEG headset developed by Nielsen Neuro *(Photo courtesy of the Consumer Neuroscience division of Nielsen).*

There are also a number of physiological methods of testing advertisements that measure the respondents' involuntary reactions to stimuli. For instance, research on autism at the MIT Media Lab and the University of Cambridge has spawned non-verbal technologies to measure emotional response.

One of these is a wearable, wireless biosensor that measures emotional arousal via skin conductance (aka galvanic skin response). It is based on the fact that electrodermal activity grows higher during states such as excitement, attention or anxiety and lower during states such as boredom or relaxation.

Emotional states such as liking and attention may also be gauged from facial expressions. Neuromarketers have accordingly developed tools that read facial expressions using a webcam to give insights into consumers' response to advertising.

The development of portable, wireless electroencephalogram (EEG) (see Exhibit 15.6) scanners has enabled neuroscientists to gain insights into how the mind responds to stimuli. Sensors covering the entire area of the brain can comprehensively capture synaptic (brain) waves, and amplify and dispatch them to a remote computer. The resulting streams of data reveal participants' subconscious responses to advertisements, and capture their emotion, attention and memory retention during the course of the commercial.

EEGs are appropriate for capturing signals about attention, arousal, fatigue and surprise, which are emitted from the brain's surface. They are not as effective in picking up signals from deeper within the brain, that are key for decision making. EEGs therefore are better suited for testing feelings and emotions, and not appropriate for testing informational ads or commercials that require thinking.

The need for laboratory environment makes EEGs somewhat restrictive and removed from the natural settings in which advertisements are processed. Even so the use of EEGs is picking up as equipment costs decline.

EEGs are often used in conjunction with eye tracking devices, particularly for images and print ads. These devices trace eye movement to identify reading patterns and point out what portions of the ad gets most attention. The analysis is done with a camera that monitors the movement of the subject's eyes 60 times every second.

Communication

In diagnosing advertising we need to understand the extent to which it succeeds in imparting key messages. Do consumers recollect the messages that the advertising intended to communicate? What messages and impressions from the advertising do they recall?

Advertising message recall is measured by the following open-ended questions to which respondents give unaided, spontaneous answers:

Execution: You said you noticed advertising for [brand] on TV recently. Please write down everything you remember that was shown or said.

Message Comprehension: What messages can you remember from the recent TV advertising of [brand]? What was it saying? What impressions did it give you about [brand]?

To assess comprehension, respondents are also asked in an overall context whether the ad was confusing or easy to follow.

These questions determine if the intended messages are getting through to respondents. They also provide an indication of the consumer's memory distortion and learning effects over time.

It is often observed that some portions of an ad are recalled far more than their airtime might suggest. Indeed if the advertisement is well crafted, creative elements amplify the intended thoughts, feeling, images and messages so that their presence is magnified in people's minds.

Awareness Index Model

Market response models use statistical methods of analysis of historic market data, to estimate the impact of advertising and other elements of the marketing mix on sales. The topic is covered in some detail in the Chapter 18, *Market Mix Modelling*. This section is devoted specifically to Millward Brown's Awareness Index (AI), a widely used metric for gauging advertising "efficiency". It estimates the ability of an advertisement to generate awareness at a given level of media weight.

The origin of the Awareness Index dates back to 1986, when Gordon Brown introduced the notion in his paper, "Modelling Advertising Awareness." In 1987, Brown published another paper "The Link between Sales Effects and Advertising Content", and the Link pre-test was developed a year later.

The Awareness Index purports to measure the incremental awareness an advertising execution generates over and above a "baseline" awareness level, per 100 GRPs. The model measures the efficiency of advertising in generating awareness. It is based on the premise that advertising awareness depends on:

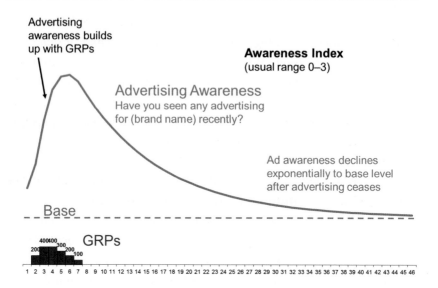

Exhibit 15.7   Awareness index and base.

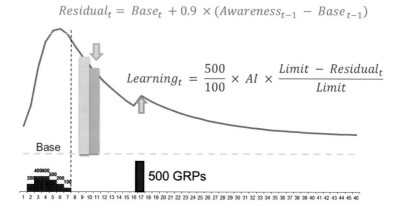

Exhibit 15.8   Residual awareness and learning.

- Quantum (GRP) or spend
- Current GRP, past GRP
- Quality (ad content)
- Advertising heritage, i.e. prior legacy of advertising

The measure used for advertising awareness is brand-led claimed advertising awareness: *"Have you seen any advertising for [brand] recently?"* The word "recently" curtails the time frame so that conclusions relate largely to current/recent campaigns.

Awareness Index is the measure of ad quality, representing the incremental level of claimed ad recall generated per 100 GRPs.

The model introduces the notion of "base level" advertising to reflect advertising heritage. *Base level* is the level to which recall will gradually decline when advertising stops. It represents the proportion of people who would claim to be aware of recent advertising, even if there is no advertising for some time.

Brands with historically high levels of memorable advertising tend to have higher base levels. Brands without memorable advertising or without much advertising history have low base levels.

The model states that awareness is a combination of *residual awareness* from previous advertising plus *learning*. As shown in Exhibits 15.7 and 15.8, awareness decays exponentially towards base level, and learning is the proportion of people who become aware of the brand's advertising due to its presence on air in the current week.

$$Awareness\ (A_t) = Residual\ Awareness\ (R_t) + Learning$$

$$R_t = Base_t + Retention \times (A_{t-1} - Base_{t-1})$$

$$Base_t = Base_{t-1} + constant$$

$$Learning = Awareness\ Index\ (AI) \times \frac{GRP}{100} \times \frac{Limit - R_t}{Limit}$$

$$Retention = 0.9, \quad Limit = 90$$

$$A_t = Base_t + 0.9(A_{t-1} - Base_{t-1}) + \\ AI \times \frac{GRP}{100} \times \left(\frac{90 - [Base_t + 0.9(A_{t-1} - Base_{t-1})]}{90} \right)$$

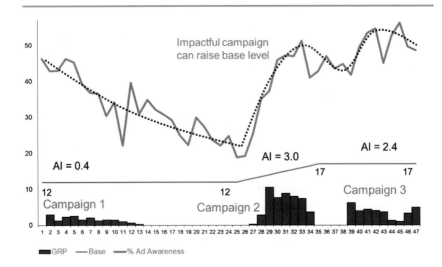

Exhibit 15.9 Awareness Index model of the advertising of a major brand.

The maximum possible claimed awareness level *(limit)* and the *retention rate* are hard-wired into the model:

- Retention rate is assumed to be 90%. In other words, awareness decays exponentially at the rate of 10% to the base level.
- Limit = 90. Assumes maximum achievable awareness level is 90%.

The base line is assumed to be linear, increasing (or decreasing) gradually at a constant rate every period. Because the retention rate (0.9) is fixed, the pace at which advertising declines is determined by the base level. Only powerful, memorable, heavy advertisement campaigns are capable of raising base levels.

A key issue with this model is that base level and awareness index are interdependent. It follows that a number of combinations of base level and awareness index may fit the model equally well. The baseline is usually set by the modeller based on experience as well as norms sourced from a database of historical studies.

The strength of the model lies in its ability to distinguish the performance of different advertising campaigns, as can be seen from Exhibit 15.9, which pertains to the advertisements of Surf Ultra, a concentrated detergent powder, soon after its launch in India. According to the model, Campaign 2 (the memorable "daag dhondte reh jaonge" commercial) registered a high awareness index of 3.0 and succeeded in raising the base level. In contrast the initial campaign for Surf Ultra was relatively weak. Diagnostics for that campaign revealed the inability of the campaign to differentiate the concentrate variant, Surf Ultra, from Surf, the mother brand.

PART V

Price and Promotion

PART

Price and Promotion

CHAPTER 16

Price

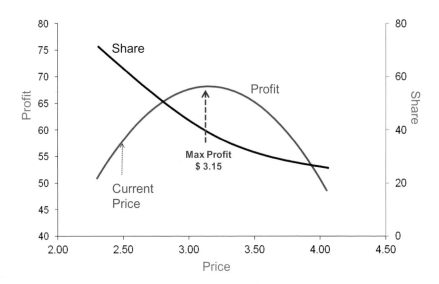

Exhibit 16.1 Demand and profit curves — taking a pricing decision.

At What Price Should We Sell Our Product?

The answer to this question invariably depends on your objectives. For instance, considering the typical scenario portrayed in Exhibit 16.1, what price adjustment would you recommend?

If the objective is to maximize profit, you might consider raising price all the way up to $3.15. However if you do this, your market share will plummet from about 60% to 40%, and your competitors' collective share will soar to 60%. If the market size does not change and if their variable costs increase proportionately, the competitors gain 50% growth in volume, value and profit. You, on the other hand, will gain about 19% in profit, and lose considerably in volume and value. So by maximizing your profit, you will be conceding competitive advantage to your competitors.

If the objective is to grow market share, you might consider reducing price. But if you do this, your profits will plunge, and you might trigger a price war.

Low-cost leaders might aggressively engage in price wars with the intent of squeezing competitors out of the market. Yet the outcome may not always be what they are hoping for.

For instance, when IBM, under competitive price pressures in 2005, sold off its PC business to Lenovo, the change in market dynamics did not favour Dell. Lenovo, which already possessed a low cost manufacturing base, got armed with the talent that came with the IBM business. Much of IBM's customer relationships, and a lot of its brand equity, got transferred to the new owners. According to Gartner, with a share of 16.9% in 2013, Lenovo became the leader in the global PC market.

Price-fixing is illegal in most countries, but the temptation may be alluring for oligopolies. That particularly holds for categories like cigarettes where governments also want prices to go up to dissuade smokers. The three conglomerates that control the cigarette market in a number of countries might be tempted to raise prices to the levels that the governments are targeting. By doing so they could get to "keep the money", rather than let it go to the government in the form of increases in excise duty.

Unless there are sustainable competitive advantages, high-price, high-margin tactics lower the barriers of entry for competitors. When cigarette prices were fixed upwards in a particular country, the market was soon flooded by imports from a Chinese manufacturer. The commotion that followed led ultimately to the sharpest increases in excise duties in that market.

As can be seen from some of the above examples, pricing decisions are fraught with hidden risks. The tendency quite often is to take a blinkered view to the problem, not foreseeing the impact on competitors and other industry players, and not anticipating the sequence of events that might follow a pricing decision.

The answer to the question posed above, hinges on several factors. You need to take into consideration company objective, price positioning, cannibalization, profit, revenue, market share, competitive scenario, competitive response, and where applicable, government's response. You also need to make a clear distinction between pricing strategy and pricing tactics.

Preview

The above discussion emphasizes the intricacies and risks involved with pricing decisions. As is often highlighted, price is the variable in the marketing mix that generates revenue. Getting it right therefore warrants careful attention to marketing and financial considerations.

The following section, which pertains to the basics of pricing research, reflects on the notion of price elasticity of demand and the factors affecting it. It highlights, too, the importance of realism in pricing research.

The chapter is devoted mainly to pricing research methods including Gabor–Granger, Van Westendorp's price sensitivity meter, brand price trade-off, conjoint analysis and discrete choice models. The applications and the strengths and weaknesses of these methods are reviewed.

The Yakult case study, at the end of Part V, facilitates the development of a deeper understanding of the application of pricing research, and the issues involved in taking pricing decisions.

Basics of Pricing Research

An understanding of how price affects demand forms the basis for taking pricing decisions. Typically this understanding is derived from various research techniques that reveal the sensitivity of demand to price, i.e., the price elasticity of demand.

One might wonder why not simply ask consumers how much they are willing to pay for a product. This does not help because what consumers claim they are willing to pay for a product differs from what they are actually prepared to pay during a purchase occasion. Survey questions usually elicit cursory answers. A direct question on how much they are willing to pay for a product often elicits bargaining behaviour with consumers stating prices lower than they would actually pay. It may also elicit a desire to please the researcher, or to not appear stingy, prompting consumers to state a higher price than they would actually pay.

Taking an indirect approach, asking consumers whether they would buy a product at a pre-selected price, yields answers that are potentially useful. By asking them to select a brand from *choice sets* in a manner that reflects the real world more closely, will yield responses that more closely reflect their true behaviour.

Importance of Realism in Pricing Research

Except for price, marketers are usually interested in a comparative assessment of the elements of the marketing mix. For example, what factors are more important in driving brand choice? Or which consumer segment should we target? Or what product formulation would target consumers like more? Or which advertisement campaign do consumers find more appealing?

All of the above research questions are relative in nature, comparing a set of possible alternatives. In contrast, pricing research must project the relationship between price and demand, in absolute terms. Whereas some bias may be acceptable in a comparative assessment, realism is of great importance in pricing research. The factors that influence a pricing decision must be replicated in the design of the research study.

Price Elasticity of Demand

Elasticity refers to the degree of responsiveness of one variable to another. Price elasticity of demand is a measure of the responsiveness of demand (sales quantity) to a change in price, and it is determined by the following equation:

$$\varepsilon = Price\ elasticity$$
$$Q = Sales\ Quantity$$
$$P = Price$$

$$\varepsilon = \frac{\%\ \text{Change in Sales}}{\%\ \text{Change in Price}} = \frac{dQ/Q}{dP/P} = \frac{P}{Q}\frac{dQ}{dP},$$

The notion of elasticity of demand, applies similarly for other elements of the marketing mix. Advertising elasticity for instance is the percentage change in sales volume due to a percentage change in advertising.

The definition of elasticity is units-free; a pure measure of responsiveness, its value can be compared across products, markets, and time. One can also compare a product's price elasticity with the elasticity of other variables. A product's price elasticity for instance, according to research findings, tends to be 15 to 20 times higher than its advertising elasticity.

Since sales quantity typically decreases with increase in price, price elasticity is usually a negative number. However, it is normally reported as an absolute value.

Price elasticity of demand may be interpreted as follow:

- $\varepsilon > 1$: Demand is elastic. If price is increased, revenue (price × sales volume) will decrease. The increase in price is offset by a proportionately larger reduction in sales volume.
- $\varepsilon < 1$: Inelastic. If price is increased, revenue will increase.
- $\varepsilon = 1$: Unit elastic. There is no change in revenue with change in price. The proportionate change in sales volume is same as the proportionate change in price.
- $\varepsilon = 0$: Perfectly inelastic demand. Sales volume is constant.
- $\varepsilon = \infty$: Perfectly elastic demand.

Factors Affecting Consumers' Sensitivity to Price

Consumers' knowledge of prices of products is usually sketchy particularly for low cost items. And their behaviour is often inconsistent with their claims. For instance, according to claims, they would be more price elastic towards an impending price increase than reflected in their behaviour at the time the price increase takes place.

Understandably consumers are much more sensitive to a discounted price promotion (i.e. a temporary price reduction) than a regular price reduction. The discount elasticity of demand (i.e. promotional price elasticity) is a lot greater than the price elasticity of demand — and marketers should be careful not to confuse one with the other.

The availability of similar, substitutable products increases consumers' sensitivity to price. On the other hand a well differentiated, unique product is less elastic to price changes.

Products that are deemed necessary tend to be less sensitive whereas luxury products may be more elastic. Also, low-cost products that take up a smaller proportion of the consumers' budget are less elastic compared to those that take up a greater share of the budget.

Consumers' price elasticity is also observed to diminish when shopping with a friend, or when being persuaded by a salesman perceived as an expert.

Easy access to information about price and product features also increases consumers' sensitivity to price. As consumers increasingly make web-based price comparisons at home and on the go, they are becoming more sensitive to prices.

It is believed that price points may also affect the price elasticity of demand. For instance a reduction in price from $10.00 to $9.99 is noted to have greater impact than a reduction from $9.99 to $9.98. This incidentally has led to the practice that is referred to as "odd pricing", where retailers set prices ending with ".9".

The cost of many ingredients and raw materials has fluctuated widely over the years, partly because of large increases in demand from big markets like China. Take for instance the global milk trade price index, which soared from 693 in June 2006 to 1,691 in October 2007. Manufacturers usually protect themselves from these types of fluctuations by entering into long term contractual agreements with suppliers. Yet when contracts are re-negotiated, they are often compelled to pass the sharp increase in price of their ingredients onto consumers.

In such situations, where manufacturers are compelled to pass a large increase in price to consumers, they often do so in part by reducing the pack size. For instance when milk prices soared in 2007, and powdered milk manufacturers were obliged to increase prices per kg by as much 30% to 40%, many of them imparted a proportion of the price adjustment by reducing pack sizes (e.g. from a 1 kg pack to 900 gm pack). This helps cushion the impact — studies have shown that consumers are less sensitive to a reduction in volume than they are to an increase in price.

Studies have also shown that consumers' sensitivity to an increase in price is different from their sensitivity to a reduction in price.

These examples illustrate a diversity of factors affecting consumers' sensitivity to price, that further complicate the task of setting price.

With view to the uncertainties clouding pricing decisions, marketers should rely on research studies that reveal how price affects the demand for their brands and their competitors' brands.

Pricing Research Methods

Pricing research is a relatively young and developing field of market research. Interest on the subject grew in the 1960s, initially within FMCG, and has since spread across industry sectors.

Exhibit 16.2 categorizes a number of well-known pricing research methods. Some of the earliest organized studies in pricing were conducted in the UK in the 1950s to examine influence of price of FMCG products on consumer behaviour. In the 1960s, economists Andre Gabor and Clive Granger conducted a small-scale survey on price consciousness and developed the "Buy Response" curve or the demand curve.

In 1976, a Dutch economist, Peter van Westendorp introduced the price sensitivity meter (PSM). The PSM is a technique for determining the acceptable price range for new products.

Conditions of Measurement

Variables measured	Uncontrolled	Experimentally controlled
Actual Purchases Behaviour	**Econometrics** • Store scan/audit data • Consumer/loyalty panel data	**STM** • Controlled store test • Laboratory purchase experiments
Claimed Preferences & Intentions Attitudes	• Buy-response surveys (Gabor–Granger) • Van Westendorp's Price Sensitivity Meter	• Brand/Price trade-off analysis • Conjoint analysis • Discrete choice models

Exhibit 16.2 Pricing research methods.

Indirect Approach

Gabor–Granger buy response curve and the PSM are examples of the indirect or psychological approaches to pricing research where respondents are presented with a product or service at different price points, and asked their likelihood to purchase at those prices. These methods are better suited for inferring price-related behaviour of new categories where direct comparison of alternatives at point-of-decision is not realistic.

Direct Approach

In contrast to indirect methods, the direct (or representational) approach presents a "purchase scenario" to respondents, complete with competitive products and their prices. It reflects a more realistic scenario for many consumer goods, where products are displayed alongside each other at retail outlets. Direct approach methods include brand price trade-off (BPTO), conjoint analysis and discrete choice modelling.

Conjoint analysis was developed by Paul Green at the Wharton School in the 1970s. It is a predictive technique that may be used to determine customers' preferences for the different products at different price points. Brand price trade-off, which is a simpler, easy to implement, predictive technique, was developed around the same time.

In the 1980s Richard Johnson (founder of Sawtooth Software) developed adaptive conjoint analysis, and Jordan Louviere (University of Iowa) developed choice-based approaches to conjoint analysis. Choice-based conjoint or discrete choice models gained popularity in the 1990s.

Econometrics

In addition to ad hoc survey based methods, market response modelling techniques are extensively used for accurately determining price elasticities in situations where historical data (e.g. scan data or consumer/loyalty panel data) is readily available. Chapter 18, *Market Mix Modelling* covers these methods in some detail.

Because econometrics relies on historical data it is not possible to use it to test new products, or to test for price points that significantly differ from historical levels.

Simulated Test Markets

Typically used for new product launch validation, simulated test markets (STMs), which are covered in Chapter 11, *Product Validation*, provide sales estimates of a new product *prior* to their launch. These methods are used by management to make the "go/no-go" decision at the end of the new product development process. They allow marketers to fine-tuning elements of the mix including price.

Gabor–Granger

Respondents are presented with the product/service, along with contextual information, and asked their likelihood, on a 5-point scale, to purchase at different price points.

The data can reveal price thresholds beyond which the demand for a product falls sharply. For instance the output depicted in Exhibit 16.3

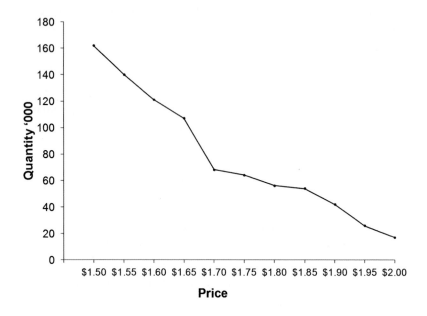

Exhibit 16.3 Buy response curve derives using Gabor–Granger method.

reveals a kink in demand at $1.65. When price is increased from $1.65 to $1.70, sales plunge by roughly 40%.

Kinks are not commonly observed in practice. They are known to arise due to factors relating to competitive response. For instance when government duties go up for products such as petroleum or cigarettes, if only a minority of suppliers take prices up, they will experience a sharper than expected fall in demand.

Similarly, if a company takes successive price drops, it will experience relatively smaller gains in volume if competitors follow suit.

Gabor–Granger is a simple, speedy technique that provides fairly rough estimates. It may be used as ballpark for products where direct comparison of competitor offerings is not realistic.

Besides failing to take competitive scenario into account, the Gabor–Granger method suffers from the bias due to consumers becoming sensitized to price. This is typical of methods where respondents are presented with multiple price options of an identical product offering. When they become sensitized to price, respondents' response to price changes gets exaggerated. This may be averted by using monadic tests where each respondent is asked for one price only, and prices are varied between different respondents in the overall sample. Monadic tests however require much larger samples, and consequently cost much more.

Van Westendorp Price Sensitivity Meter

Price sensitivity meter (PSM) is used for new products where no obvious benchmarks or competitor equivalents exist, for instance a new gadget, such as when the iPad was first introduced. And though it is not based on any theoretical foundation, the PSM provides a useful framework for assessing the price range for unique new products.

Respondents are shown the test item (a new product or service), and they are presented with contextual information and a price scale. The scale covers a wide range of price points from well below the likely minimum price point, to as much as three times the likely upper price.

Four questions are then posed to the respondents — at what price on this scale you would consider this product/service to be:

- A bargain? (inexpensive)
- Priced so cheaply that you would question its quality? (too cheap)
- Priced expensively? (expensive)
- Priced so expensively that you would not buy it? (Too expensive)

An example of a PSM output is shown in Exhibit 16.4, where the cumulative responses to these questions have been plotted. The intersection points in the graph constitute price thresholds — optimum price, indifference price, and upper and lower limits of acceptable prices:

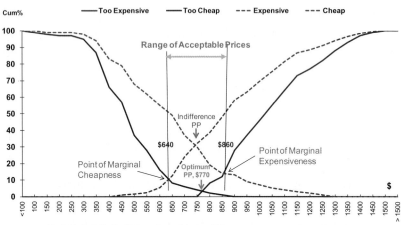

Exhibit 16.4 Price Sensitivity Meter — example output.

- The "*Optimum*" *Price Point* is the price at which the number of respondents who consider the product too cheap is equal to the number who consider it too expensive.
- The *Indifference Price Point* is the price where the number of respondents who regard the price as a bargain is equal to the respondents who regard the price as expensive. This generally represents the median price or the price of one of the leading brands.
- According to Van Westendorp, the range of acceptable prices lies between the *Point of Marginal Cheapness* and the *Point of Marginal Expensiveness*.

Like Gabor–Granger, the PSM is quick and easy to administer. Its strength lies in that, unlike other established pricing techniques, PSM provides a continuous assessment of price sensitivity across a very wide range of prices. The range of acceptable prices sets boundaries that are useful for crafting pricing strategies and tactics, and for price positioning.

Because there is no prompting or competitive set, responses are based on respondents' perceptions of competitive offerings and prices. This however assumes respondents know the market. Moreover, since

PSM lacks any assessment of sales, for making pricing decisions, it is often combined with one of the direct approaches to pricing research.

PSM may be used for determining the acceptable price range, at the stage where a product is conceptualized. It is particularly useful in new product development areas where there is no realistic (or feasible) alternative to provide direct comparisons, or markets where products may not face direct competition (e.g. new pharmaceutical products, new technology products etc.). It may also be used for product offerings such as insurance, where direct competition may exist, but straight choices are not realistic.

Brand Price Trade-off

Brand price trade-off (BPTO) employs a relatively simple direct approach to gain insights into consumers' sensitivity to price in a competitive purchase scenario.

Method

The study is usually conducted online or at a central location. The respondent is presented repeatedly with choice of brands relevant to her purchase decision, and their prices. The prices vary, starting at the lowest level of the test range, and moving upwards as the exercise progresses.

At each step the respondent is asked to choose from a set of brand/price options. After the respondent chooses an option, the price for the chosen brand is increased to the next price point while that for the other brands remains unchanged. Respondent is then asked to make her next choice, and the exercise continues till all options are exhausted.

Consider the example in Exhibit 16.5 for a range of cars with similar specifications, targeting the same consumer segment. The exhibit reflects the choices made by a particular respondent, from the start to the end of the exercise. This respondent is much less sensitive to price compared to the respondent in Exhibit 16.6 who switches brands 13 times over the price range.

1st Choice

Hyundai Avante	$54,000			
Nissan Sunny	$56,000			
Toyota Corolla	$69,000			
Honda City	$65,000			
Mitsubishi Lancer	$63,000			

4th Choice

Hyundai Avante		$55,000		
Nissan Sunny	$56,000			
Toyota Corolla			$71,000	
Honda City	$65,000			
Mitsubishi Lancer	$63,000			

2nd Choice

Hyundai Avante	$54,000			
Nissan Sunny	$56,000			
Toyota Corolla		$70,000		
Honda City	$65,000			
Mitsubishi Lancer	$63,000			

5th Choice

Hyundai Avante		$55,000		
Nissan Sunny	$56,000			
Toyota Corolla				$72,000
Honda City	$65,000			
Mitsubishi Lancer	$63,000			

3rd Choice

Hyundai Avante	$54,000			
Nissan Sunny	$56,000			
Toyota Corolla			$71,000	
Honda City	$65,000			
Mitsubishi Lancer	$63,000			

6th Choice

Hyundai Avante		$55,000		
Nissan Sunny	$56,000			
Toyota Corolla				$72,000
Honda City		$66,000		
Mitsubishi Lancer	$63,000			

Exhibit 16.5   A BPTO answer sequence (fictitious example).

Hyundai Avante	$54,000 **3**	$55,000 **6**	$56,000 **13**	$57,000
Nissan Sunny	$56,000 **1**	$57,000 **2**	$58,000 **4**	$59,000 **15**
Toyota Corolla	$69,000 **9**	$70,000 **12**	$71,000	$72,000
Honda City	$65,000 **7**	$66,000 **11**	$67,000 **14**	$68,000
Mitsubishi Lancer	$63,000 **5**	$64,000 **8**	$65,000 **10**	$66,000

1: Nissan, $56,000
2: Nissan, $57,000
3: Hyundai, $54,000
4: Nissan, $58,000
5: Mitsubishi, $63,000
6: Hyundai, $55,000
7: Honda, $65,000
8: Mitsubishi, $64,000
9: Toyota, $69,000
10: Mitsubishi, $65,000
11: Honda, $66,000
12: Toyota, $70,000
13: Hyundai, $56,000
14: Honda, $67,000
15: Nissan, $59,000

Exhibit 16.6   Example of hierarchy of choices for a price sensitive respondent.

Analysis

The analysis method commonly used, called *Essential Rank Analysis* is based on each respondent's hierarchy of choices. For illustration consider the following brand/price options:

Honda	$66,000
Toyota	$70,000
Hyundai	$54,000
Nissan	$58,000
Mitsubishi	$66,000

For the respondent whose choices are listed in Exhibit 16.6, *Honda $66,000* brand/price option ranks 11th, *Toyota $70,000* ranks 12th, *Hyundai $54,000* ranks 3rd, *Nissan $58,000* ranks 4th, and *Mitsubishi $66,000* is not ranked. This respondent, for the options listed above, will therefore choose *Hyundai $54,000,* as it lies uppermost in her hierarchy of choices.

In a similar manner, the highest ranking choice is taken for all respondents, and projected to provide an estimate of the brands' share at the mentioned price points, as well as for the other price points covered in the study. This yields the demand price relationships for the brands, which may be used to estimate price elasticity and cross price elasticity of demand at the price points of interest to the marketer.

BPTO can be modified to allow for gauging consumers' sensitivity to downward price movements. This is useful for markets where consumers' sensitivity to an increase in price may differ from their sensitivity to a reduction in price.

Limitations

When it comes to estimating volume, like other pricing research methods, BPTO makes a number of assumptions. It assumes consumers have perfect knowledge and awareness of products; and that other elements of the marketing mix, in particular distribution and promotions, are constant. Importantly, BPTO measures preference, not volume. For instance in FMCG where consumers purchase a repertoire of brands, estimates of volume are likely to be less accurate. A consumer, for instance, in overall terms, may prefer Sunsilk shampoo over Pantene or Head & Shoulders, but she could be using all three products.

BPTO is less widely used nowadays because the nature of the BPTO exercise heightens price awareness. As respondents become sensitized to price, their claimed response to price changes is considerably exaggerated. So, unless some adjustment is employed to normalize the data, one would not recommend the use of BPTO for taking decisions on price adjustments. As we will see later, discrete choice models, reflect the real world more closely, and yield responses that more accurately reflect consumers' true behaviour.

Conjoint Analysis

Utility, as you might recall, is central to the theory of conjoint analysis. It reflects how desirable or valuable an object is in the mind of the respondent, and is assessed from the value (part-worth) of its parts. Conjoint analysis examines respondents' choices or ratings/rankings of products, to estimate the part-worth of the various levels of each attribute of a product.

When used in the context of pricing research, conjoint analysis focusses mainly on two attributes — brand and price. The part-worth for all brand and price levels is computed, for each respondent, using the methodology covered in Chapter 11, *Product Validation*. In the example shown in Exhibit 16.7, based on her choices, this particular respondent values the Toyota Corolla brand more than the Nissan Sunny and the Nissan Sunny more than Honda City and so on.

To establish what the respondent would choose in the scenario depicted in Exhibit 16.8, the brand/price option utility is computed by adding the part-worth of brand and price for each of the five options. In this case, the choice would be Nissan Sunny $54,000, because its utility is higher than that for the other four options.

Brand	Part–Worth	Price	Part–Worth
Toyota Corolla	1.9	$54,000	0.8
Honda City	0.4	$58,000	0.3
Nissan Sunny	0.9	$62,000	0.1
Mitsubishi Lancer	-0.6	$66,000	-0.5
Hyundai Avante	-2.6	$70,000	-0.7

Exhibit 16.7 Part-worth for brand and price levels for a respondent.

Brand	Price	Utility	Part–Worth Brand	Part–Worth Price
Toyota Corolla	$70,000	1.2	1.9	-0.7
Honda City	$58,000	0.7	0.4	0.3
Nissan Sunny	$54,000	1.7	0.9	0.8
Mitsubishi Lancer	$66,000	-1.1	-0.6	-0.5
Hyundai Avante	$54,000	-1.8	-2.6	0.8

Exhibit 16.8 Product utility computed for the above brand/price options, for the respondent in Exhibit 16.7.

Choices for individual respondents across the study's price range are aggregated and weighted to yield the consumers' share of preferences over the price range. This yields the demand price relationships for the brands, which may be used to estimate price elasticity and cross price elasticity of demand at the price points of interest to the marketer.

Discrete Choice Modelling

Discrete choice models reflect the real world more closely than other claimed preferences based approaches for pricing research. In these models, respondents evaluate multiple sets of alternatives, and choose one alternative from each of the *choice sets*.

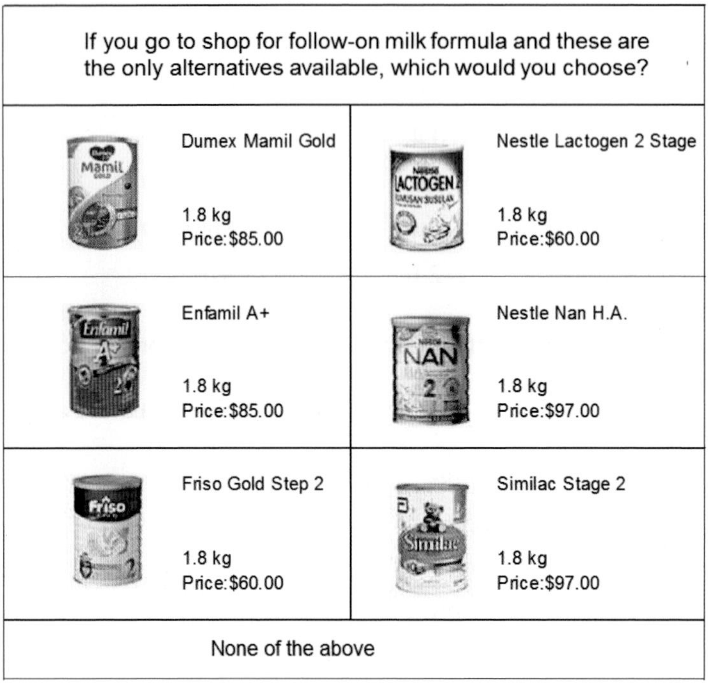

Exhibit 16.9 A choice set used in a research study on follow-on milk formula.

The choice sets must satisfy a few conditions. Firstly, the alternatives in each choice set must be collectively exhaustive, so that respondents necessarily choose an alternative from the set. The inclusion of a "catch-all" alternative such as "none of the above" is usually required to make a choice set collectively exhaustive.

Secondly, the alternatives must be mutually exclusive, i.e. choosing one alternative means not choosing any other alternatives. Respondents can choose only one alternative from the set.

Thirdly, the choice sets contain a finite number of alternatives, as opposed to some other modelling techniques where the dependent variable can theoretically take an infinite number of values.

For pricing research the choice sets are sets of brand/price options such as the one shown in Exhibit 16.9. Respondents are asked to select a brand from each of the sets used in the study.

Discrete choice models can be based on the notion of utility, where respondents are assumed to maximize utility. The models may take multiple forms including multinomial logit, conditional logit, multinomial probit, nested logit, generalized extreme value models, mixed logit, and exploded logit.

Case Example — Rationalizing Brand Range

The adulteration of milk by Sanlu and a few other Chinese manufacturers in 2008, which resulted in the death of 6 infants and the hospitalization of 54,000 other babies, left deep scars in the minds of Chinese mothers. In a market where premium infant formula was already a fast growing segment, its importance became even more pronounced after the scandal.

At that time a major manufacturer that produced both a low and a high cost variant of infant milk under the same brand name, considered the possibility of withdrawing the lower cost variant, in favour of shifting resources to grow the premium variant. To gauge the impact on consumer preferences that such an action might incur, this manufacturer undertook choice-based conjoint analysis to simulate the impact of the withdrawal of the lower cost variant.

For illustration purposes, the two variants of this infant formula are referred to as $X+$ and $X-$. $X-$, which was priced significantly lower than $X+$, targeted more price conscious consumers, had leaner margins and was experiencing declining sales. $X+$ on the other hand, was a premium product.

In general, if a brand is stretched in different directions, as was the case with X, its positioning tends to get fuzzy. This sometimes leads to confusion in consumers' minds, and may vitiate the brand's equity.

These reasons — i.e. consumer preferences, poorer margins, declining sales, fuzzy positioning — prompted the manufacturer to consider the withdrawal of $X-$. But if $X-$ was to be withdrawn, the overall share of brand X would drop substantially. So one option considered at that time was to adjust the price of $X+$ to retain some of the loss in sales due to the withdrawal of $X-$.

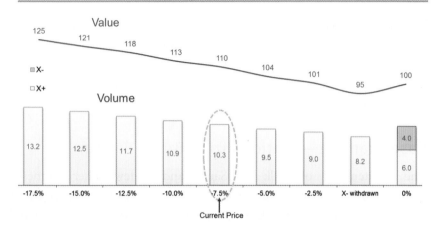

Exhibit 16.10 Trend in volume share and value as variant *X*− is withdrawn, and the price of *X*+ is reduced.

Based on the results, from the discrete choice model, depicted in Exhibit 16.10, the manufacturer was able to deduce that with a 7.5% reduction in price, the premium variant could retain the entire share that the brand was likely to lose if the lower priced variant was withdrawn.

To elaborate, variant *X*+ had 6% market share and *X*− had 4% at the time of the analysis. Based on the study results, if *X*− was withdrawn, brand *X*'s share would drop from 10% to 8.2% (i.e. an 18% fall), and sales value would decrease by 5%. However, if at the same time as the withdrawal of *X*−, the price of *X*+ is reduced by 7.5%, the brand would retain volume share. While this would yield a 10% gain in value, without data on cost, it is not clear to what extent profits will be eroded. There may be the need to consider adjustment in pack size, or minor changes to product formulation, to partially restore margins.

Note too that while considering any drop in price, the manufacturer should also consider how competitors might respond. The scenario changes considerably if the price of some competing brands is reduced in line with *X*+. These alternative scenarios can easily be simulated with respondent level disaggregated data obtained from the model.

CHAPTER 17

Promotion

Exhibit 17.1 Dove in-store display & promotion *(Courtesy TAD Network).*

Preview

The promoted sales volume for a majority of FMCG brands accounts for a very substantial proportion of their total sales. In New Zealand, for instance, which is one of the most heavily promoted markets in the world, according to Nielsen, nearly 60% of grocery purchases in 2012 were promoted products.

But how effective are these promotions? Considering that the proportion of on-promotion sales is so high, one would imagine that companies can barely afford not to understand their impact.

This chapter dwells on the different forms of trade and consumer promotions, the need to rationalize them, and the metrics and methods to evaluate them. It explains the basic approach to assessing promotions in terms of gain in volume, value and profit. It introduces the topic of market modelling for promotions evaluation, and outlines the basic design of models. These econometric based methods, however, are covered in greater depth in the next chapter, *Market Mix Modelling*.

In-Store Promotion and Media

Retail formats, particularly upper trade formats like hypermarkets and supermarkets, present unparalleled opportunities to influence shopper behaviour at point of purchase. Take for instance consumer promotions like discounts, banded packs, collectibles, sampling, loyalty programmes and special displays; or for instance in-store media such as television, shelf talkers, cart and floor vision, and interactive sampling via promoters.

These activities have important bearing on store choice and brand choice. From the retailer's standpoint they draw shoppers and increase their store loyalty. For manufacturers, they serve to attract new or lapsed consumers as well retain and reward existing consumers.

In-store activities have acquired far greater significance with the consolidation of retail, and the fragmentation of media. In many countries the incidence of shopping at a major chain is often far greater than primetime TV viewership. Consequently the need to engage with shoppers at point of purchase has grown in importance.

Displays, discounts and co-op advertising result in considerable gains in sales. In-store merchandising and communication, special displays such as that for Dove in Exhibit 17.1, facings and other types of promotions, generate visibility, shape brand image and store image, and trigger purchases.

Exhibit 17.2 Co-op advertisement of an in-store promotion.

Types of Promotions

Broadly speaking there are two major categories of promotions — consumer promotion and trade promotion. Consumer promotions offer consumers short term incentives drawing them into stores to purchase goods.

Trade promotions on the other hand, help manufacturers secure their trade partners' support in procuring, distributing, promoting and merchandising their products. Their purpose is to push products down the sales pipeline to the points of purchase.

Trade promotions also help to fuel consumer promotions as trade incentives are often intended to be passed onto shoppers.

Exhibit 17.3 Coca-Cola's collectible contour glasses at McDonalds.

Trade Promotion

Trade promotions take precedence over consumer promotions because the brand must first gain and hold distribution before consumers can buy it. They come in many different forms including trade discounts, free of charge (FOC) goods, contribution to cooperative advertising, promotions support, cash payments, payment for product displays and other selling aids, year-end rebates (monetary and non-monetary), sales on consignment basis, and acceptance of returned good.

Cooperative advertisement or feature advertisement is a joint advertisement by retailer and manufacturer, the cost of which is shared by both parties. It usually communicates promotional offers such as the exclusive promotion shown in Exhibit 17.2, of Pepsi at FairPrice supermarkets on May Day.

Exhibit 17.4   Coca-Cola F&N banded prosperity pack (F&N carbonated drinks were bottled by Coca-Cola till Sept 2011).

Exhibit 17.5   Example of a lucky draw promotion.

Consumer Promotion

Consumer promotions like the one in Exhibit 17.2 can be very effective in generating sales. During that particular May Day week, Pepsi sold more 24s can promo packs than the combined rest of year sales for that pack size, at Singapore's FairPrice supermarket chain.

There are many different types of consumer promotions including discounts, banded packs (in/on packs), refunds and rebates, displays, bonus packs, premiums, lucky draw (Exhibit 17.5), contests, collectibles (Exhibit 17.3), sampling, coupons and loyalty/continuity programmes.

Exhibit 17.4 provides an example of a banded pack promotion. The Coca-Cola F&N banded prosperity pack made a special appearance during Chinese New Year (CNY) 2009 (Orange, which symbolizes "gold", is considered auspicious during the CNY festive season).

Displays are special presentations of products to attract and entice shoppers at point of purchase. There are a wide variety of displays in existence today, some of which are quite creative, such as that for Dove in Exhibit 17.1.

The Need to Rationalize Promotions

The promoted sales volume for a majority of FMCG brands accounts for a very substantial proportion of their total sales. In New Zealand, for instance, which is one of the most heavily promoted markets in the world, according to Nielsen, nearly 60% of grocery purchases in 2012 were promoted products.

Exhibit 17.6 plots the weekly sales trend of a market leading brand. The chart reveals that the on-promotion volume of this brand accounts for 43% of the total sales, and the gains resulting from the promotions constitute 26% of sales.

But how effective are these promotions? Considering that the proportion of on-promotion sales is so high, one would imagine that companies can barely afford not to understand their impact.

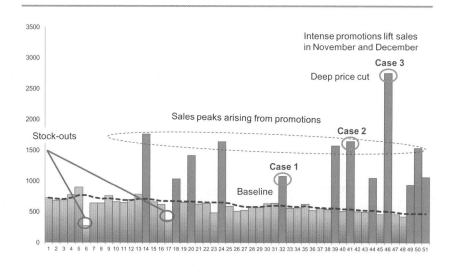

Exhibit 17.6 Sales of a major brand reflecting the impact of promotions.

Some promotions work better than others; some items respond better than others; some promotions generate big gains, whereas others cannibalize; some promotions are profitable, others incur loss.

There is realization too that excess levels of promotions can impair a brand's image and weaken its loyalty. Furthermore, the total cost of promotions is high and has been growing steadily over the years.

Their scale and significance leave us with no doubt of the need to rationalise promotions. Managers need to weed out less effective promotions and focus on those that yield superior results.

Promotion–Commotion–Demotion

Recurring promotions encourage consumers to lie in wait for attractive deals, and maintain high pantry stock. Highly attractive promotions entice consumers to stockpile for future consumption resulting in post promotion losses — i.e. dip in baseline or regular sales in the weeks immediately succeeding the promotions. Baseline sales are also affected by the intensity of promotional activities. For instance, reflected in Exhibit 17.6 is a declining trend in the baseline as the intensity of promotions increases over the course of the year.

Promotions also induce brand switching, compelling competing brands to strike back. As competitors get drawn into the battle ground of promotions, brands retaliate in quick succession creating *commotion* in the market place.

The growing incidence of promotions heightens their awareness in people's minds, and induces brand switching. The resulting erosion of brand loyalty leads to the *demotion* of brands.

Theoretically if no brand promotes it is a "win–win". In reality however new brands need to promote to induce trial, and established brands promote to continue to attract new or lapsed consumers as well as retain and reward existing consumers. If they do not promote, they land on the "lose" side of the fence in a "win–lose" situation. And so the vicious circle of promotion–commotion–demotion becomes the reality of a competitive marketplace.

Promotions Evaluation — Metrics

The impact of promotions on sales is usually short term and is assessed through analysis of baseline sales and sales gains, and metrics such as discount elasticity of demand, and discount cross elasticity of demand (cannibalization).

Baseline sales or *base volume* is the expected sales volume in the absence of short term causal influences such as promotions. It is a function of manufacturers' marketing actions such as regular price, advertising and distribution, and other factors including competitor activities. Also as mentioned earlier, the baseline is influenced by the historical levels of promotions. If a brand has a history of recurring promotional activity, consumers lie in wait for the deals, leading to the lowering of the baseline.

Sales gain/loss or *incremental volume* is the sales volume above the baseline. It is the gain or loss in volume on account of short term causal factors, including temporary price reductions (discounts), displays, features, distribution fluctuations (stockouts for instance), seasonal factors and competitor activities, during that time period.

	Case I	Case II	Case III
Regular Price $/kg	39.50	41.70	38.40
Variable Cost $/kg	30	30	30
Actual (promo) Price $/kg	37.60	36.28	31.60
Discount %	5%	13%	18%
Baseline Sales Volume kg	603	544	506
Baseline Sales Value $	23,819	22,685	19,430
Baseline Variable Cost $	18,090	16,320	15,180
Baseline Gross Margin $	5,729	6,365	4,250
Sales Volume kg	1,073	1,644	2,749
Gain: Volume kg	470	1,100	2,243
% Gain: Volume	78%	202%	443%
Sales Value $	40,345	59,643	86,868
Cost of Promotion $	2,000	5,000	4,500
Gain: Value $	14,526	31,958	62,938
% Gain: Value	61%	141%	324%
Variable Cost $	32,190	49,320	82,470
Gross Margin $	6,155	5,323	(102)
Gain: Margin $	426	(1,042)	(4,352)
% Gain: Margin	7%	-16%	-102%

Exhibit 17.7   Basic evaluation of promotion in terms of gain in volume, value and margin.

Basic Assessment of Sales Promotions

How much did my brand gain in volume, value and profit? This is first question on the sales manager's mind after she promotes her brand. The answer to the question provides a preliminary understanding of the impact of a promotion.

Sales gain/loss or *incremental volume* is the sales volume above the baseline. It is the gain or loss in volume on account of short term causal factors, including temporary price reductions (discounts), displays, features, distribution fluctuations (stockouts for instance), seasonal factors and competitor activities, during that time period.

Consider the three cases — 1, 2 and 3 — circled in Exhibit 17.6. Exhibit 17.7 provides additional details such as the regular price and baseline sales for this product at the three time periods. The gain in volume for each of these promotions is the difference between the sales volume and the base line sales volume. Similarly the gain in value is the difference between the sales value and the base line sales value, and the gain in margin is the difference between the margin and the base line margin.

Because of the price discounts, the gains in value are lower than the gains in volume, and the gains in margin are much lower. In Case 3, where the brand is heavily discounted, the gross margin is totally wiped out, and the brand incurs a loss.

Each of these three promotions has a different impact, and plays a different role. The promotion in week 46 (Case 3) was a tactical promotion run by a local retailer during the week that a major global hypermarket chain entered into this market with the opening of their flagship store. Price was slashed by 18%, volume soared 5.4 times, yet at that level of discount, profits were wiped out.

The Case 1 promotion on the other hand is profitable and may therefore be repeated more frequency. It yields a healthy 78% increase in volume with a 5% reduction in price.

Market Modelling

The basic assessment of sales promotions reveals the impact of the promotions on sales, revenue and profitability. It does not however answer a number of critical questions, included the ones listed below:

- What elements of the promotion are more effective in driving sales? What is the impact of the discount, the display, and the cooperative advertisement?

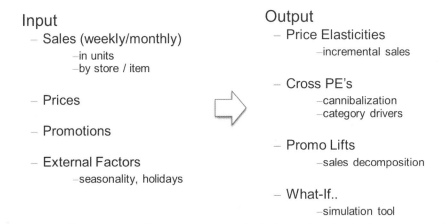

Input
- Sales (weekly/monthly)
  - in units
  - by store / item

- Prices

- Promotions

- External Factors
  - seasonality, holidays

Output
- Price Elasticities
  - incremental sales

- Cross PE's
  - cannibalization
  - category drivers

- Promo Lifts
  - sales decomposition

- What-If..
  - simulation tool

Exhibit 17.8 Overview of promotions response modelling.

- Does the promotion cannibalize manufacturer's own brands? Or does it "steal" share from competitor's brands?
- To what extent does the promotion help build category volume?
- How much more volume could be gained if the discounts are further increased?
- What is the optimum promo mix that maximizes sales volume without incurring any loss in profit?

Econometric promotions response modelling can provide answers to all of the above questions. The outline of the models, in terms of inputs and outputs, is shown in Exhibit 17.8. These models analyse data to establish the impact of each individual element of a promotion on sales. The sales response functions derived from these models yield estimates of discount elasticity of demand, discount cross elasticity of demand, and sales lifts due to displays, co-op advertising and other causal factors. It is possible to decompose sales into all of the elements contributing to the volume. Promotion response models can also forecast what impact a possible combination of initiatives will have on sales. These econometric modelling methods are covered in some detail in the next chapter *Market Mix Modelling*.

Chapter 18

Market Mix Modelling

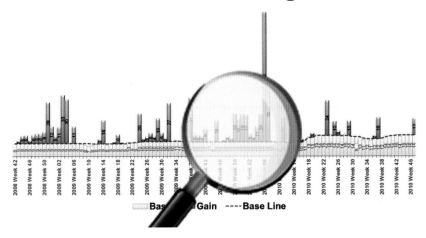

Bas... Gain ----Base Line

Exhibit 18.0 Market mix modelling assesses the impact of the elements of the mix, on sales and ROI.

Preview

"It is difficult to hide from the illumination of a market response model." —
Hanssens et al. (2003).

Marketers need to align their brand's marketing mix into a coordinated programme designed to drive revenue and profit. To achieve desired goals, they need an understanding of the level or combination of the mix variables that optimizes the brand's performance. This in turn, requires an appreciation of how sales respond to the expenditures on these variables. It would be useful if there was a method to assess the impact of the elements of the mix, on sales and ROI.

Though far from perfect, there is such a method — it is referred to as market mix modelling or market response modelling. These models use statistical methods of analysis of historic market data, to estimate the impact of various marketing activities on sales. They reveal the effectiveness of the marketing mix elements in terms of their contribution to sales and profits, and can be benchmarked against costs to compute ROI. This knowledge empowers marketers to craft plans that optimize the use of resources, and infuse marketing decisions with the logic and discipline of analytics.

This chapter provides an outline of the key design considerations for market mix models. It guides you on how to apply them, and how to interpret and analyse the output of these models.

While an effort is made to keep the content simple and easy to understand, it does assume an understanding of statistics and econometrics. Market modelling in general requires specialized skills; unless you are interested in developing models, you do not need to know how market models are created. What you need to know is how to interpret and apply them. So if you suspect you lack the required knowledge of statistics, do feel free to skim the sections on design considerations and methodologies, and focus more on the section on analysis and interpretation.

Market response modelling is a vast topic covering a wide spectrum of methods and techniques. The discussion that follows is confined to a few such methods that are widely used by practitioners. None of them is ideal — the ideal model ought to be able to capture the full dynamics of the marketing mix, and its impact on sales. No such model exists today, though there are many that can turn data into actionable insights.

Design Considerations

Market mix models are multifaceted, often including the interactions and interdependencies within marketing mix variables, lagged responses, competition, and simultaneous relations. This section highlights some of these factors that need to be taken into consideration while developing superior market models.

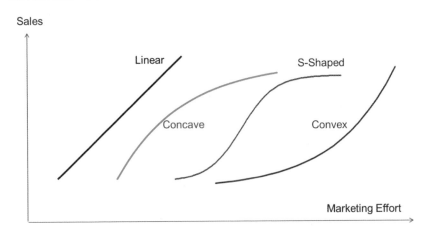

Exhibit 18.1 Shapes of different sales response functions.

Sales Response Function

Marketing mix models embody "sales response functions" to relate the effects of marketing activities on sales. The dependence of sales on the different element of the marketing mix is estimated from historical market data using econometric and time series analysis methods. The resulting sales response functions depict the effect of the different elements of the mix on sales.

The functional form specifies the relationship between the dependent variable (sales) and the independent variable (e.g. price, advertising, promotion etc.). It determines the shape of the sales response curve, and reflects the nature of the marketing activity.

Fundamentally there are four basic shapes — linear, concave, convex and S-shape — as shown in Exhibit 18.1.

Constant Returns to Scale (Linear) Models

The simplest functional form is the linear model which represents constant returns to scale:

$$S = \alpha + \beta X.$$

Where:

S is sales, the dependent variable, and

X is the independent variable representing the marketing effort for the marketing mix element.

α and β are model parameters. α is the intercept — the sales when there is no marketing effort. β is coefficient for X. A unit change in X results in a change of β units in sales.

The linear model is theoretically unsound because it suggests that sales increase indefinitely. However from a practical point of view, for a relatively small operating range, a linear model can provide a satisfactory approximation of the true relationship.

Diminishing Returns to Scale (Concave) Models

One of the most commonly used forms in market mix modelling is the concave shape, which is characterized by diminishing returns to scale as the marketing activity increases. This aligns well with the expectation that as the intensity of discounts, displays and advertising increases, the returns diminish.

The *semilog* (semi logarithmic) model is an example of diminishing returns to scale function:

$$S = \alpha + \beta \ln(X).$$

Another functional form that meets the diminishing return to scale requirement is the *power model*:

$$S = e^{\alpha} X^{\beta}, \quad X > 0 \text{ and } 0 < \beta < 1.$$

The power model is also known as the *constant elasticity model* due to its property that the power coefficient is the elasticity of demand of the marketing mix variable X:

$$\varepsilon = \frac{\delta S}{\delta X} \times \frac{X}{S} = \beta e^{\alpha} X^{\beta-1} \times \frac{X}{e^{\alpha} X^{\beta}} = \beta.$$

The most widely used marketing mix model is a variation of the power model, called the *multiplicative model*:

$$S = e^{\alpha} X_1^{\beta_1} X_2^{\beta_2} X_3^{\beta_3} \dots X_J^{\beta_J},$$

Where X_1 to X_J are variables representing the marketing effort for various marketing mix elements, and X_1 to $X_J > 0$.

This nonlinear structural model can be transformed into an estimation model that is *linear in parameters* by taking logarithms on both sides. The advantage of this transformation, which is shown below, is that the parameters of the original nonlinear model can be estimated using linear-regression techniques.

$$\ln(S) = \alpha + \beta_1 \ln X_1 + \beta_2 \ln X_2 + \beta_3 \ln X_3 \ldots + \beta_J \ln X_J.$$

The multiplicative form is widely used in marketing mix models such as Nielsen's Scan*Pro, to evaluate promotions.

Increasing Returns to Scale (Convex) Model

The *exponential* model $\left(S = e^\alpha e^{\beta X}\right)$ is an example of a convex shaped, increasing returns to scale model. This may apply for price, provided it is represented as 1/P:

$$S = S_0 e^{-\beta P}, \beta > 0.$$

The model assumes that the sales response to decreases in price may exhibit increasing returns to scale.

S-shaped Response Model

In the S-shaped response function, sales exhibit increasing returns to scale at low levels and diminishing returns at high levels of marketing effort. This is plausible for advertising which at low levels gets drowned by the noise, and hits an upper limit at very high levels. Besides advertising, the S-shape response function is also used for modelling the effect of shelf space on sales in store.

The S-shape captures the notions of *threshold* and *saturation*. Below the threshold, marketing effort has no impact on sales, and above saturation, there is no further increase in sales. Above/below these bounds, consumers become insensitive to the marketing stimuli.

If it truly reflects the response of advertising to sales, the S-Shape response function has implications on how advertising should be flighted — drip versus burst or pulse. An advertising *burst* is a heavy dose of advertising over a short interval. It would ensure that advertising levels cross threshold levels. In contrast drip or continuous advertising is much lighter weight of advertising spread over a much longer time frame. If thresholds exist, marketers should use less *drip* advertising and more burst or *pulse* advertising — an approach that falls between burst and drip, with advertising going on and off air over the weeks.

While conceptually appealing, there is not much empirical evidence to support the existence of an S-shape response to advertising effort. It is hard to prove or disprove considering that historical data tends to lie well within these theoretical upper and lower bounds, i.e. if they exist.

The *logistic* model depicted below takes a functional form that conforms to the S-shape.

$$\ln\left(\frac{S - S_0}{S^0 - S}\right) = \alpha + \beta \ln(X), \text{ with } 0 \le S_0 \le S^0,$$

Where, S_0 is the intercept and the threshold level, and S^0 is the saturation level.

The elasticity of demand, for a variable with an S-shaped response with sales, follows an inverted bell-shape, starting at 0 at threshold level to a maximum, and back to 0 at the saturation level.

A related but rare phenomenon is the notion of *supersaturation*. It refers to the excessive use of a marketing instrument, such as advertising, that theoretical may repulse consumers, creating a negative response to sales. It is rarely witnessed because marketers' budgets are usually constrained; they operate below saturation levels and well below supersaturation levels. The supersaturation effect can be represented by the quadratic model ($S = \alpha + \beta_1 X - \beta_2 X^2$).

Interaction Effects

The marketing mix works as a co-ordinated programme designed to achieve business imperatives. It is therefore not surprising that often the elements of the mix interact synergistically, to produce an effect greater than the sum of their individual effects.

For example the elements of consumer promotions, like discounts, displays and co-op advertising, often have a synergistic impact lifting sales more than the sum of their individual impact on sales. Or for example, investments in marketing instruments such as theme advertising strengthen a brand's equity, resulting in the lowering of consumers' sensitivity to changes in price.

These interaction effects affect the sensitivity of one or more elements of the marketing mix, to changes in another element of the mix. They are captured in response functions by including an additional term $(X_1 \times X_2)$ that is formed by the product of the two variables that interact.

The *multiplicative* model implies that the dependent variable is affected by an interaction of the variables of the marketing mix. Its functional form is written as:

$$S = e^\alpha \overset{variables}{\underset{j}{\prod}} X_k^{\beta_k} = e^\alpha X_1^{\beta_1} X_2^{\beta_2} X_3^{\beta_3} \dots X_J^{\beta_J}, \qquad X_k > 0$$

In its logarithmic form however the interaction effects are no longer explicit:

$$\ln(S) = \alpha + \beta_1 \ln X_1 + \beta_2 \ln X_2 + \beta_3 \ln X_3 \dots + \beta_J \ln X_J,$$

If there is the need to include interaction effects after taking logs, the *transcendental logarithmic (translog)* model is one approach for doing so:

$$\ln S = \alpha + \beta_1 \ln X_1 + \beta_2 \ln X_2 + \beta_3 \ln X_3 \dots$$
$$+ \beta_{12} \ln X_1 \ln X_2 + \beta_{13} \ln X_1 \ln X_3 + \beta_{23} \ln X_2 \ln X_3 \dots$$
$$+ \beta_{11} (\ln X_1)^2 + \beta_{22} (\ln X_2)^2 + \beta_{33} (\ln X_3)^2 \dots$$

A related notion, *interdependency*, exists when a company's decisions on one element of the marketing mix impact its decisions on some of the other elements of the mix. This may result from the outcome of concerted strategies, or the trade-offs that companies need to make with limited budgets. For example, pricing decisions impact margins, which in turn may have a bearing on the brand's budget on other instrument such as advertising. Interdependence may also exist within different forms of an instrument — conventional and online advertising for instance.

Competitive Effects and Market Share Models

Markets exist in a competitive environment. How consumers respond to a product is not only a function of what the product has to offer, but also a function of what competitors' products have to offer.

Take price for instance. When a product's price is increased by a substantial amount, say 20%, it is likely to lose a large proportion of its business to competitors that target the same consumers with similar products. On the other hand if all market players take prices up by 20%, as might occur when excise duties or raw material prices soar, the impact on product sales may be insignificant. For the majority of consumer sectors, product categories *as a whole* are relatively inelastic to price adjustments. If individual brands increase prices substantially, they lose share ... but if petroleum, milk, coffee, shampoo or cigarette prices increase by even as much as 20%, the demand for these product categories is unlikely to plunge.

In conclusion, rather than absolute, it is the relative price that has greatest significance on the demand for a product. This applies not only to price, but also the other elements of marketing mix.

The relative form of variables is often expressed in terms of an index or share — price index for relative price, share of market for sales, or share of voice for advertising (*Share of voice,* which is the share of GRP or advertising expenditure within the product category, is a measure that relates to the impact of advertising in a competitive setting).

Cross elasticity is the construct that quantifies competitive effects. The cross elasticity of demand determines the responsiveness in the sales of a product when a change in marketing effort takes place in a competing product. When a product drops price, increases advertising, improves product quality or expands distribution, it cannibalizes competing products. The shift in business from one product to the other, on account of a change in marketing effort, is captured by the cross elasticity of demand.

Market Share Models

One approach to capturing competitive effects is via market share models, known also as attraction models. These models are based on the notion that marketing effort generates "attraction" for the brand, and that the brand's market share is a function of its share of total marketing effort. This supposition is captured as follows:

$$Market\ Share,\ M_b = \frac{S_b}{\sum_j^{brands} S_j} = \frac{A_b}{\sum_j^{brands} A_j},$$

Where M_b and S_b are brand b's market share and sales, and A_b is the effort expended over the brand's marketing mix.

A commonly used form for A_b is the following multiplicative functional function:

$$A_b = e^{\alpha_b} \prod_{k=1}^{K} X_{kb}^{\beta_{kb}} \cdot e^{\delta_b},$$

Where $X_{ki} > 0$ are the K elements of the marketing mix.

The model as a whole is referred to as the Multiplicative Competitive Interaction (MCI) Model. The MCI model without taking cross-effects into consideration becomes:

$$M_b = \left(e^{\alpha_b} \prod_{k=1}^{K} X_{kb}^{\beta_{kb}} \right) e^{\delta_b} \bigg/ \sum_{j=1}^{B} \left[\left(e^{\alpha_j} \prod_{k=1}^{K} X_{kj}^{\beta_{kj}} \right) e^{\delta_j} \right].$$

This nonlinear model can be transform into a linear model by applying what is referred to as the log-centring transformation (Cooper & Nakanishi, 1988). After applying this transformation the model takes the below form:

$$\ln\left(\frac{M_b}{\overline{M}}\right) = \alpha_b^* + \sum_{k=1}^{K} \beta_k \ln\left(\frac{X_{kb}}{\overline{X}_k}\right) + \delta_b^*,$$

where $\alpha_b^* = \alpha_b - \bar{\alpha}$ and $\delta_b^* = \delta_b - \bar{\delta}$. Similarly $X_{kb}/\bar{X}_k$ can be expressed in log-centred format as X_{kb}^* ($\bar{M}$ and $\bar{X}_k$ are the average market share and the average marketing effort for mix element k).

This model may be expanded to include terms that capture the cross effect between variables, i.e. $\beta_{ki} \ln(X_{ki}/\bar{X}_k) \, for \, i \neq b$.

MCI model is essentially the normalized form of the multiplicative model. Similarly by specifying the attraction function (A_b) in terms of an exponential form $\left(A_b = e^{\alpha_b} e^{\beta_{1b}X_{1b}} e^{\beta_{2b}X_{2b}} e^{\beta_{3b}X_{3b}} \ldots \right)$, we derive what is referred to as the *Multinomial Logit (MNL)* model, which after applying the log centring transformation, takes the below form:

$$\ln\left(\frac{M_b}{\bar{M}}\right) = \alpha_b^* + \sum_{k=1}^{K} \beta_k (X_{kb} - \bar{X}_k) + \delta_b^*,$$

Market share models have several advantages. They capture competitive effects. They meet logical consistency requirements — brands' market shares lies between 0 and 1, and the sum of their estimated market shares equals 1. Their response curves are characterized by diminishing returns to scale at high levels of marketing activity. The MCI models are concave in shape, whereas the MNL models are S-shaped.

One limitation of these models however, is that they are static in nature. Marketing efforts are assumed to impact only the time periods when they occur. And the market environment is assumed to be static — the model parameters remain fixed over time.

Dynamic Effects

The impact of some marketing initiatives on sales is often felt not only at the time of the initiative, but also before or after the duration of the initiative. Consumers for instance may respond in anticipation to a price adjustment. Sales may dip after a promotion. Advertising campaigns take time to wear-in, and after they have been aired several times they begin to wear-out.

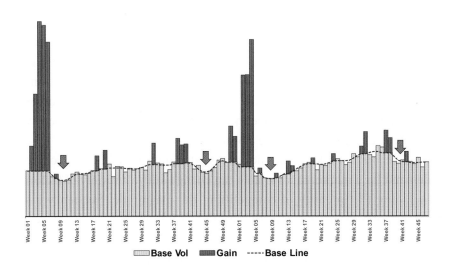

Base Vol   **Gain**   -----**Base Line**

Exhibit 18.2   Take home sales of a FMCG brand reflects dip in sales post festive season as consumers stockpile promoted items.

The *wear-in* effect is like an ad that grows on you. Its effectiveness in generating sales increases after consumers are repeatedly exposed to the advertisement, and messages start to register in their minds.

After a prolonged period however, ads starts to *wear-out*. The persuasive impact of advertising, which is important especially for new products, is short term. The repetition of the same message is unlikely to evoke a different response from consumers who are not persuaded to try it. Wear-out also occurs when fatigue sets in — consumers start to get "fed-up" of seeing the same commercial again and again.

Carryover effects may also occur due to various delay factors — consumers' inter-purchase intervals, delays due to retailer pipeline/lack of adequate stock in trade, delayed consumer response, or the time interval before word of mouth effects kick in. These carryover effects tend to be short in duration.

Promotions are known to impact sales before, during and after the duration of the promotion. In Exhibit 18.2 for example, the sales of take home packs of a major FMCG brand are seen to dip significantly after festive periods. These post-promotional losses occur when consumers stockpile goods, and are observed in markets after periods of intense festive promotions (e.g. mega sales during Christmas, Chinese New Year or Hari Raya). A brand may suffer post promotion losses not only when consumers stockpile the brand, but also when consumers stockpile a collection of competing brands. In other word, competitive or interaction effects also have a bearing.

Over time market dynamics also undergo change. The elasticity of demand for a market mix variable can change due to a variety of factors, including the intensity of competition, the magnitude, frequency and recency of prior marketing activities, and various exogenous factors.

All these effects that are spread over time are referred to as *dynamic effects*. For the sake of completeness, it is advisable to capture their impact into response models.

Stock Variables — Adstock

One approach to capturing carry over effects is the use of *stock variables*, *adstock* for instance. Adstock implicitly distributes the amount of an advertising exposure over several periods. Advertising that is effective at a given time is equal to residual adstock (what is "left over" from previous advertising), plus learning (adstock gained from current advertising). Specifically if $A_1, A_2, \ldots A_t$ represent the advertising effort (GRP) in periods *1* to *t*, then the adstock is computed as follows:

$$Adstock_t = \frac{1-r}{f(1-r)+r}(fA_t + rA_{t-1} + r^2A_{t-2} \ldots + r^{t-2}A_2 + r^{t-1}A_1),$$

$$A_t = \text{GRP}_t.$$

Where, r is the retention (or decay) rate, and f (fade) is the impact in the first period. These two parameters may either be pre-fixed by the modeller or determined by the data.

Half-life, the time duration by which the advertising effort has had half its total effect, is a commonly used benchmark for setting *f* and *r*.

Advertising Quality — Adfactor

The overwhelming evidence from research studies suggests that the quality of the creative material is critical in advertising. It is important therefore to include advertising quality as a measure when modelling advertising response.

The advertising quality is specific to the commercial, and it may be assessed in terms of consumers' perception of the advertisement on various measures. One approach used by research firm Millward Brown is based on their Awareness Index (AI). This index, which is explained in Chapter 15, *Advertising Research*, is essentially a measure of efficiency of a commercial in generating awareness. It represents the incremental level of claimed ad recall generated per 100 GRPs. An adstock type variable called Adfactor is constructed by using '*GRP × Awareness Index for the commercial*' as the measure for advertising:

$$Adfactor_t = \frac{1-r}{f(1-r)+r}(fA_t + rA_{t-1} + r^2 A_{t-2} \ldots + r^{t-2}A_2 + r^{t-1}A_1),$$

$$A_t = \text{AI} \times \text{GRP}_t.$$

Where, r is the retention rate, and f is the impact in the first period.

According to Hanssens *et al.* (2003), Millward Brown has illustrated through examples that use of adfactor results in models that reflect substantially higher contribution of short term advertising effects.

Leads and Lags

Dynamic promotion effects can also be explicitly modelled by incorporating variables that capture lead and lag effects, i.e.:

$$S_t = f(X_{t+k}), \ S_t = f(X_{t-k}).$$

Commonly used in marketing, the *Geometric Distributed Lag (GL) model* has a functional form that is structurally similar to that used for stock variables, i.e.:

$$S_t = \alpha + \beta(1-\lambda)\sum_{l=0}^{\infty} \lambda^l X_{t-l} + \delta_t, \qquad \text{where } \delta_t \text{ is disturbance term}$$

This relation, which is nonlinear, may be converted to a linear estimation model by applying the *Koyck* transformation:

$$S_t = \alpha + \beta(1-\lambda)X_t + \beta(1-\lambda)\sum_{l=1}^{\infty} \lambda^l X_{t-l} + \delta_t$$

$$-\lambda S_{t-1} = -\lambda\alpha - \beta(1-\lambda)\sum_{l=1}^{\infty} \lambda^l X_{t-l} - \lambda\delta_{t-1}$$

$$S_t - \lambda S_{t-1} = (1-\lambda)\alpha + \beta(1-\lambda)X_t + (\delta_t - \lambda\delta_{t-1})$$

$$S_t = \beta_0 + \beta_1 X_t + \lambda S_{t-1} + v_t$$

Where $v_t = \delta_t - \lambda\delta_{t-1}$, $\beta_0 = (1-\lambda)\alpha$ and $\beta_1 = \beta(1-\lambda)$.

In general for multiple marketing mix variables, the Koyck model becomes:

$$S_t = \beta_0 + \sum_{k=1}^{K} \beta_k X_{kt} + \lambda S_{t-1} + v_t.$$

This model however captures only monotonically decaying carryover effects that do not have a hump. Moreover, estimating the carryovers is tricky when there are multiple independent variables, each with its own carryover effect. Even so the model may provide a fairly good approximation of the underlying response function.

The *Autoregressive Distributed Lag Model (ADL)* which contains an autoregressive component for sales and a moving average distributed lag component for the mix variables is a general model that captures all types of carryover effects.

$$S_t = \beta_0 + \sum_{p=1}^{P} \lambda_p S_{t-p} + \sum_{k=1}^{K}\sum_{q=1}^{Q} \beta_{kq} X_{k,t-q} + v_t.$$

The rate at which the carryover effects peak and decay is controlled by λ, and the number of peaks and their heights is controlled by β.

Parameter Functions

The coefficients of the marketing mix variables in the response models we have discussed so far are assumed to be constant for the analysis period. It is a tenuous assumption considering that many of the dynamic effects imply that these parameters do vary. Parameter functions may be crafted to capture the impact of a variety of these effects, including:

- The magnitude, frequency and recency of prior marketing activities;
- Wear-in and wear-out of advertising;
- Quality of the creative material in advertising;
- Media effects (i.e. differences in ad response due to choice of TV programme, or section of newspaper).

For instance consider quality of advertising. We know that the effectiveness of advertising is dependent greatly on the creative material. One approach to capturing this effect is by means of a variable that captures both quantity and quality, the adfactor for instance. We could also capture the ad quality effect by means of a process function for the advertising coefficient, i.e. $\beta_{advt} = f(ad\ campaign)$.

Similarly the price-promotion elasticity (discount elasticity) of products can change due to the magnitude and frequency of previous discounts. If heavy promotions are repeated too frequently, their impact begins to fade. Frequent, attractive promotions also tend to induce an opportunistic behaviour — consumers lie in wait for the deals, resulting in the lowering of the base line. The parameters for price discount, promotion (e.g. display, co-op advertising) and baseline (i.e. store intercept) are therefore a function of historical levels of promotions.

One approach to capturing the dynamic nature of the market is by means of multistage models where the coefficients of the mix variables estimated at the first stage become the dependent variable in the next stage. In the second stage, where the coefficients of the mix variables are treated as the dependent variables, the independent variables are the characteristics that influence the coefficient.

Long Term Effect (Advertising)

It is generally accepted that the impact of advertising on sales is primarily long lasting. By attracting new users, many of who stay with the brand, the persuasive element of advertising has a prolonged impact on sales. Furthermore advertising effects gets carried over time as they imbue brands with symbols, values, feelings and meaning. Their short term impact on the other hand tends to be weak — advertising elasticity, based on various research findings, is usually 15 to 20 times lower than price elasticity.

According to Millward Brown, the long term effects of advertising outweigh short term effects in 80% of cases. And the scale of the impact is generally believed to be several times greater in the long term, than in the short term impact.

Though there are some approaches for doing so, capturing long term effects is not one of the strengths of market mix modelling. The dynamic effects discussed earlier capture mainly the short term lead and lag effects. Long term effects are more difficult to tie back specifically to advertising.

Assessing the short term impact of advertising is useful of course, for the short term. Moreover, experts claim that you do not get long term impact from advertising without achieving short term success. Yet short term gains do no guarantee the long term effectiveness of the ad.

Because most market models do not capture long term effects, it is not advisable to use market mix models to measure the ROI of advertising.

The research methods covered in Chapter 15, *Advertising Research* are best suited for assessing the long term potential of advertising. They dwell on the ability of advertising to build empathy with consumers, increase their disposition to purchase the brand, emphatically communicate the value proposition and positioning, and generate impact through salience and differentiation. Though these methods provide detailed understanding of the impact of advertising, they do not forecast the impact of advertising on sales, nor do they provide any estimate of the ROI of advertising.

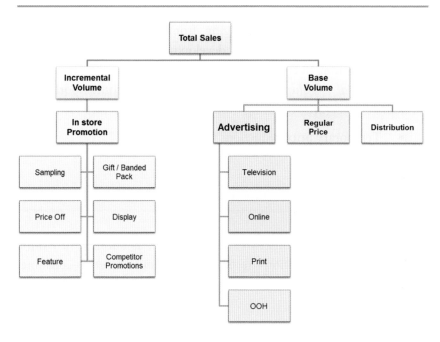

Exhibit 18.3 Market mix modelling — sales drivers.

Baseline and Incremental Volume

The fundamental approach to modelling the marketing mix involves estimating the *baseline sales*, i.e. the sales volume expected in the absence of in-store promotions.

$$Sales\ Volume \equiv Baseline\ Volume + Incremental\ Volume$$

Baseline Sales or Base Volume is a function of manufacturers' marketing actions such as:

- Regular price (base price)
- Advertising (advertising stock)
- Distribution
- Competitor activity

A variety of techniques ranging from smoothing functions to econometric methods are used for developing baselines such as the one depicted in Exhibit 18.2.

Incremental Volume specifically means contemporaneous, immediate gains (lifts) resulting from in-store causal factors such as:

- Temporary price reductions (discounts)
- Displays
- Features
- Distribution fluctuations (stockouts)
- Seasonal factors

Note however that this two stage approach, as outlined in Exhibit 18.3, assumes no interaction effects between manufacturer-to-consumer initiatives driving the baseline and retailer-to-consumer (in-store) influences.

Promotions Response Model

The following multiplicative model is commonly used to model sales responsiveness to promotions:

$$S_{ikt} = \left[\prod_{b=1}^{brands} \left\{ \left(\frac{P_{bkt}}{\bar{P}_{bkt}} \right)^{\beta_{ibc}} \gamma_{1bic}^{D_{1bkt}} \times \gamma_{2bic}^{D_{2bkt}} \times \gamma_{3bic}^{D_{3bkt}} \right\} \right]$$

$$\times \left[\prod_{w=1}^{weeks} v_{icw}^{W_w} \right] \left[\prod_{s=1}^{stores} \alpha_{is}^{O_s} \right] \times e^{\omega_{it}}.$$

Where:

S_{ikt} : Sales for brand *i* in store *k* in week *t*.

P_{bkt} : Actual Price of brand *j* in store *k* in week *t*.

$\bar{P}_{bkt}$: Regular (median) Price of brand *j* in store *k* in week *t*.

D_{1bkt} : Indicator for display. 1 if brand b in store k is displayed and *not* feature advertised in week t. Otherwise 0.

Note indicators (dummy variables) appear as exponents in a multiplicative model, otherwise sales will be zero when the indicator is off (value is zero).

D_{2bkt} : Indicator for feature 1 if brand b in store k is featured advertised and *not* displayed in week t. Otherwise 0.

D_{3bkt} : Indicator for display and feature. 1 if brand b in store k is featured advertised and displayed in week t. Otherwise 0.

W_{kw} : Indicator for week in store k (to capture seasonality). 1 if observation is in week w, otherwise 0.

O_{st} : Indicator for store. 1 if observation is from store k, otherwise 0

β_{ibc} : if $b = i$ price (promotion) elasticity, otherwise if $b \neq i$ cross price (promotion) elasticity, in chain c. (The model has the attractive property that the power coefficients can be directly interpreted as elasticity. It is also referred to as the constant elasticity model).

$\gamma_{1bic}, \gamma_{2bic}, \gamma_{3bic}$: if $b = i$ Display/Feature Advertisement/Display + Feature Advertisement multiplier, otherwise if $b \neq i$ cross multiplier, in chain c. (A multiplier value of m means that brand sales increase m times when the brand's promotion activity occurs).

v_{icw} : Week w seasonal factor for brand i, in chain c.

α_{is} : Store s' intercept for brand i. This is the store's baseline sales for brand i (i.e. regular sales for the brand when price equals the regular price and there are no promotion activities for any of the brands).

ω_{ikt} : Disturbance term for brand i in store k in week t.

As mentioned earlier this multiplicative structural model can be transformed into an estimation model that is linear in parameters by taking logarithms on both sides.

This approach to evaluating promotions is adopted in Nielsen's Scan*Pro model, which has been used to assess thousands of commercial application. Besides Scan*Pro, IRI PromotionScan is a model that is commonly used for modelling FMCG products. These models are designed to help marketers evaluate their promotions and refine their promotion plans.

Aggregation of Models

In the promotions response model, discount elasticities, and promotional and seasonal lifts are assumed to be the same for stores in the same chain, and different for stores in different chains. In other words, parameters β_{ibc}, γ_{1bic}, γ_{2bic}, γ_{3bic}, ν_{icw} are heterogeneous across chains and homogeneous within chains.

This store-level model with chain-specific parameters provides for greater accuracy, according to Foekens *et al.* (1994) who compared the forecast accuracy for store level, chain level and market level models.

While it is preferable to construct models with chain-specific parameters, due to data confidentiality clauses restricting the use of chain level data, the estimation of the parameters may be restricted to the aggregate channel or market level. This usually results in overestimation of the promotional effects.

From a business perspective, store level data is highly actionable for day to day tactical decisions — sales personnel and trade marketers need to know what promotions to run when and where. For manufacturer-to-retailer decisions and activities, key account, chain level data would seem most appropriate. On the other hand marketing decisions and initiatives (manufacturer-to-consumers) need to be based on regional or country level data.

Dynamic Model

One limitation of the promotions response model is that it is static in nature. Causal factors are assumed to impact only the time periods when they occur, and carryover effects are not taken into consideration. Moreover the market environment is assumed to be constant — model parameters remain fixed over the duration of the model.

Markets however do change. And as mentioned earlier, post-promotional losses occur when consumers stockpile goods, and are observed in markets after periods of intense festive promotions. Consumers' response to price discounts and other causal factors fades if promotions are repeated too frequently. Frequent promotions also tend to induce an opportunistic behaviour — consumers lie in wait for the deals, resulting in the lowering of the base line. The parameters for price discount, promotion (e.g. display, co-op advertising) and baseline (i.e. store intercept) are therefore a function of historical levels of promotions.

The two ways that the dynamics of the marketplace can be captured are described in a paper by van Heerde *et al.* (2002). Firstly, the parameters may be set to vary while the structure of the model remains unchanged. In particular, functions are crafted to capture changes in price parameters (β), the promotion multipliers (γ) and the store intercept (α) arising from the magnitude, frequency and recency of promotional activities.

Alternatively dynamic promotion effects can be captured by incorporating leads and lags for promotion variables, into the original model.

Model Validity: How Good is the Fit

The validity and reliability of market models must be assessed in terms of statistical accuracy as well as practicality. Is the model commonsensical? Does it meet the required accuracy standards?

Metrics/tests that help assess the goodness-of-fit and the reliability of the model include:

- Adjusted R^2 (coefficient of determination): measures the proportion of the variation in the dependent variable (Sales) accounted for by the explanatory variables (Marketing Mix variables). It adjusts for the degrees of freedom associated with the sums of the squares.

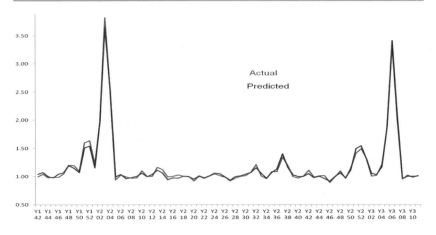

Exhibit 18.4 Goodness-of-fit.

- Estimated Standard Error: provides the average error for the model as a whole and can be used to calculate confidence intervals for forecasts and scenario simulations.

- Tests to assess the significance of the individual coefficients, i.e. the α and β values, which represent key parameters such as base and the elasticity of demand.

- Holdout tests to assess the reliability of the model. These tests use the estimated model coefficients to predict the sales for a further 8 to 12 weeks. The sales prediction is then compared with the actual sales data of those weeks to assess the quality of the model.

- Tests to check for bias. Bias occurs when any variables that influence sales are omitted or when spurious variables are included. If a variable is overlooked, its effect is incorrectly allocated to the remaining variables that comprise the model. This results in the distortion of the importance of these variables.

Because it is easier to comprehend, greater emphasis is given to the R^2 measures. It is important however that due consideration is given to all the above tests, or else the conclusions derived from the model could well be misleading.

Watchouts and Guidelines

Experienced market modellers will concur that it is easy to construct market models that are visually impressive, where the predicted and actual data match closely (e.g. Exhibit 18.4), the R^2 value is high, and yet the model is invalid or even nonsensical. As a user of market models, you therefore need to be a reasonably good judge of the quality of a market model.

Inclusion of All Sales Drivers

First and foremost, when it comes to developing market models, the knowledge of the market is as important as the knowledge of econometrics. The decision maker who uses the model and the econometrician, who builds it, need to work closely to create a practical solution based on market realities. It is very important that the market dynamics are clearly understood by the developer, that all of the variables that drive performance are included.

All too often in an era of commoditization of market modelling, data is shipped from the marketer to the market modeller, without the necessary information about the characteristics or nuances of the market. A modeller based overseas may have no knowledge of the Hungry Ghost festival, the exclusion of which may result in spuriously high discount elasticities for some FMCG brands in Singapore.

The exclusion from a model of any factor that significantly influences performance is likely to compromise the validity of the model. Unfortunately measures like R^2 will still look good despite the omission. This is because marketing initiatives often occur concurrently, so the impact of the missing variables is attributed to other variables that comprise the model. The point to note is that all factors that significantly influence the dependent variable (sales), including external exogenous factors, should be included, irrespective of whether or not they are key to the objective of the research.

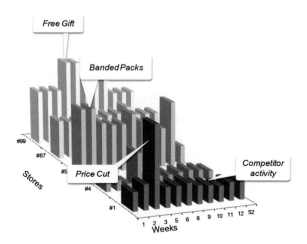

Exhibit 18.5 Store level modelling allows the modeller to isolate and measure the impact of price and promotion activities at store level.

Store Level Modelling

Greater levels of disaggregation provide for more robust and reliable market models. If 500 stores across 104 weeks (2 years) are modelled at store level, this yields 52,000 individual observations, i.e. this gives us very many degrees of freedom. Moreover, by modelling each store individually (Exhibit 18.5) the modeller is able to cut through noise, and isolate and measure the impact of price and promotional activities at store level.

When store level data is not available or accessible, modellers need to work with chain or channel level data, which introduces inaccuracies due to variations at the store level. Despite these imprecisions, chain/channel level data yields useful, fairly reliable models.

As regards the accuracy of the raw data from retailers, this is less of an issue now that relatively clean, weekly store level point-of-sale (POS) scan data is readily available in most markets.

Potential Difficulties in Estimating Parameters

Modelling works by correlating fluctuations in sales to those in the explanatory factors. If in the data there does not exist any variation in the movement of a factor, its potential effect is not calculable. (You

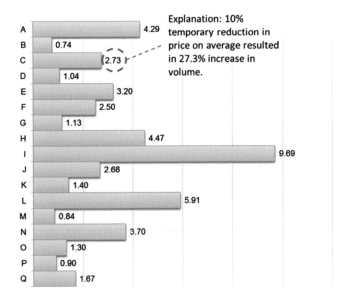

Exhibit 18.6 Discount elasticity — an illustration.

cannot compute the discount elasticity of demand, if the product was historically not offered on discount.)

Note also that when two or more factors always occur simultaneously and in similar proportions, it is not possible to untangle their individual influences.

Interpretation and Analysis

Discount Elasticity

Price elasticity (discount elasticity) is a measure of the responsiveness of sales quantity demanded to a (temporary) change in price, and it is determined by the following equation:

$$\varepsilon = \frac{\delta Q}{\delta P} \times \frac{P}{Q},$$

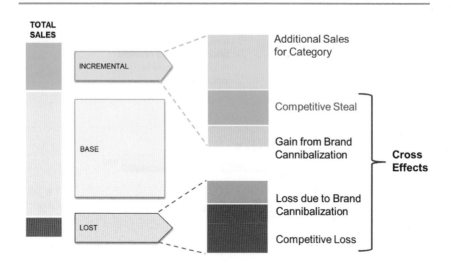

Exhibit 18.7   Cannibalization: Source of gains and loss.

If $\varepsilon > 1$, demand is elastic. Any dip in price due to a price-off promotion is offset by a disproportionately large increase in sales volume. On the other hand, if $\varepsilon < 1$, demand is inelastic, a dip in price will result in a decrease in revenue.

Discount elasticity is essentially the price elasticity due to a temporary price reduction. Since consumers are much more sensitive to a discounted price promotion than a regular price reduction, the discount elasticity is a lot greater than the price elasticity.

Exhibit 18.6 provides an illustration of discount elasticity. The SKUs in this chart, with discount elasticity of less than 1 (such as B, M and P) will experience a decline in revenue (sales value) when promoted. Items such as these with low elasticity tend to possess high brand equity and can command a price premium. Discounting these products will result in the loss of revenue and profit.

Price promotions should be considered in the context of discount elasticities as well as the SKU's profit margin. Low margin products need to be highly elastic to retain profitability when promoted.

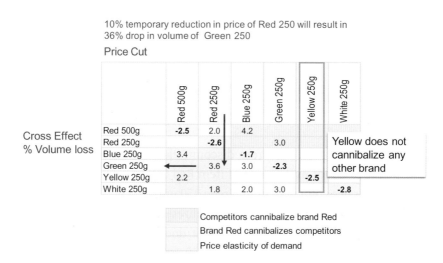

Exhibit 18.8 Discount elasticity and cross discount elasticity.

Cannibalization

In a competitive environment, the demand for a product is not only a function of what the product has to offer, but also a function of what competitors' products have to offer. The source of an item's gains and losses, as depicted in Exhibit 18.7, are largely the result of consumers shifting volume to and from other items, including those items belonging to the same brand.

When a product drops price, increases advertising, improves product quality or expands distribution, it cannibalizes competing products. *Cross elasticity of demand* is the measure for these competitive effects. It determines the responsiveness in the sales of one product when a change in marketing effort takes place in a competing product.

Cross Price Elasticity, Cross Discount Elasticity

When evaluating the impact of marketing efforts, it is important not only to consider the elasticity of demand, but also the cross elasticity of demand. Manufacturers do not want to drive initiatives if they merely cannibalize their own brands.

Cross price elasticity (cross discount elasticity) is a measure of the responsiveness of sales quantity of a product to a (temporary) change in price of another product:

$$\varepsilon_{A,B} = \frac{\% \ change \ in \ quantity \ of \ product \ A}{\% \ change \ in \ price \ of \ product \ B} = \frac{dQ_A/Q_A}{dP_B/P_B} = \frac{P_B}{Q_A} \frac{dQ_A}{dP_B}$$

Exhibit 18.8 depicts a cross discount elasticity analysis. It tells us that a 10% discount in the price of item Red 250 gm will result in a 36% drop in the sales volume of item Green 250 gm.

Note that Red 250 gm also cannibalizes Red 500 gm. On the other hand when Red 500 gm is promoted, it does not cannibalize Red 250 gm. Instead it steals share from Blue 250 gm and Yellow 250 gm. The manufacturer of Red should therefore consider promoting Red 500 gm more often than Red 250 gm.

From the retail chain's perspective, it is beneficial to frequently promote Yellow 250 gm. Since the brand does not cannibalize other items, category sales, within the chain, will increase when it is promoted.

Displays and Cooperative Advertisement

Exhibit 18.9 illustrates the impact that special displays can have on brand and category sales. In this example permanent displays were set up at a retail chain for a category that comprised primarily of two brands D and E.

The impact of displays, co-op advertising and seasonal effects is usually presented as sales *lift* (see Exhibit 18.10), the percentage increase in sales volume due to the incidence of the marketing effort.

The brands D and E, shown in Exhibit 18.9, experienced sales lift of 70% and 23% respectively. As is evident from the trends lines in the exhibit, the displays helped to reverse the decline in category sales at the retail chain.

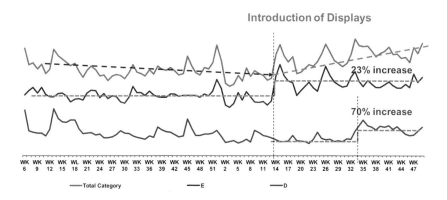

Introduction of Displays

23% increase

70% increase

——Total Category ——E ——D

Exhibit 18.9 Introduction of special displays boosts brands E and D's sales, and invigorates category sales at a retail chain.

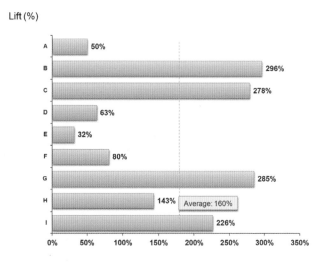

Lift (%)

A	50%
B	296%
C	278%
D	63%
E	32%
F	80%
G	285%
H	143% Average: 160%
I	226%

0% 50% 100% 150% 200% 250% 300% 350%

Exhibit 18.10 Sales lift represents the percentage increase in sales due to marketing initiatives such as display and co-op advertising.

Sales Decomposition and Due-To Analysis

Market Mix Models decompose sales into the baseline and each of the factors driving sales. For instance, Exhibit 18.11, which pertains to a promotions evaluation analysis, depicts the incremental gains arising

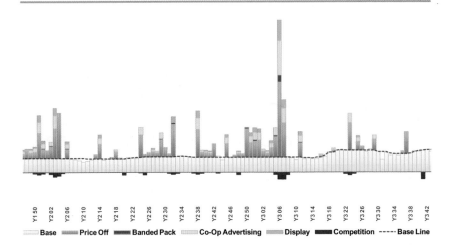

Base — Price Off — Banded Pack — Co-Op Advertising — Display — Competition ----- Base Line

Exhibit 18.11 Decomposition provides understanding of the contribution of each element in the promo mix.

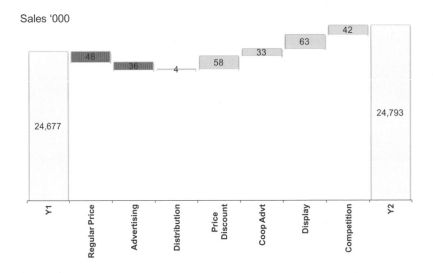

Exhibit 18.12 Due-to analysis for a brand.

from price discounts, banded packs, displays, cooperative advertising and competitive effects.

'Due-to' analysis, such as the one shown in Exhibit 18.12, reveals the impact of each element of the marketing mix on the year-on-year sales.

Items	Current					Simulated					
	Volume (L)	Share (%)	Value ($ '000)	Pack Price ($)	%Price Off	Pack Price ($)	Volume (L)	Gain (L)	Share (%)	Value ($ '000)	Gain ($ '000)
A	127	7.8	207	0.54	-5.0	0.51	144	17.7	8.8	225	17.2
B	21	1.3	49	1.17		1.17	20	-1.6	1.2	46	-3.7
C	66	4.1	126	3.76	-10.0	3.38	84	17.3	5.1	143	17.0
D	69	4.3	126	7.22		7.22	57	-12.4	3.5	103	-22.6
E	61	3.8	91	14.79	-15.0	12.57	91	30.1	5.5	115	24.6
F	206	12.7	249	1.82		1.82	206		12.5	249	
G	103	6.4	116	3.39		3.39	103		6.3	116	
H	13	0.8	13	4.54		4.54	13		0.8	13	
I	55	3.4	74	2.72		2.72	36	-18.5	2.2	49	-25.2
J	40	2.5	51	1.92		1.92	40		2.4	51	
K	24	1.5	30	1.86		1.86	24		1.5	30	
L	52	3.2	54	1.57		1.57	52		3.1	54	
M	31	1.9	33	1.57	-12.5	1.37	36	5.3	2.2	33	0.8
N	101	6.3	108	1.60		1.60	93	-8.3	5.6	99	-8.9
O	43	2.6	98	4.55		4.55	39	-3.5	2.4	90	-8.0
P	20	1.2	28	0.47		0.47	20		1.2	28	
Q	58	3.6	61	1.58		1.58	58		3.5	61	
R	28	1.7	28	1.50		1.50	28		1.7	28	
S	54	3.3	55	1.52		1.52	54		3.3	55	
T	383	23.7	396	1.55		1.55	383		23.3	396	
U	61	3.8	60	1.48		1.48	61		3.7	60	
Total	1613	100	2053				1639	26.2	100	2044	-8.8

Exhibit 18.13 What-if analysis for price discounting.

The chart reveals the incremental shifts in volume due to causal factors as well as the shifts in base volume due to factors such as regular price, advertising and distribution.

What-if Analysis

The output of a market model is a set of equations that spell out the relationship between sales and the variables of the market mix. With these equations one can predict what will happen if changes are made to the mix variables. Exhibit 18.13, for instance, provides an example of a "What-if" analysis tool to simulate the impact of price discounting. By changing the discounts in "%Price Off" column the user is able to see how those discounts will affect the sales volume and sales value, for the items in the category.

CASE V

Yakult

Exhibit C5.1 A 5s pack of Yakult cultured milk.

Yakult contains 30 billion live Lactobacillus casei Shirota, a probiotic strain of good bacteria strong enough to survive the journey through the stomach's gastric juices to reach the small intestine alive, where they help maintain an ideal balance of beneficial bacteria. Probiotics help control the number of harmful bacteria that naturally exist in the digestive system. They replenish and balance the level of beneficial bacteria which helps with the digestion of food and absorption of nutrients.

Products like Yakult are categorized as cultured milk. In Singapore, this market comprises of two brands, Yakult and Vitagen, available in only the standard (5s) pack size shown in Exhibit C5.1. Yakult's volume market share is 67%, and the brand's average retail price is $2.60 compared to $2.40 for Vitagen.

Note: The data provided in this fictitious case study is disguised.

Price Evaluation

Interested in reviewing price, Yakult commissioned a $9.99 pricing research study to understand how consumers respond to changes in price. From the research it was observed that as Yakult's price is increased from $2.60 to $3.10, its market share declines from 67% to 52%, and when its price is reduced to $2.30 the brand's share increases to 76%. *The total market volume for cultured milk, however, does not change over this price range.* Details of the research methodology and the findings of this research are provided in the following section.

$9.99 – Research to Determine the Price-share Relationship for Yakult

$9.99 is an approach to predicting the sensitivity of demand to price where respondents in separate matched panels are asked to indicate their purchase intent for each brand using a constant sum scale. The price of the test brand is varied across the panels while the price of other brands is maintained at their market level. Estimate of market share for test brand is obtained at different price levels based on the purchase intent of each respondent in each panel. The research design is summarized as follows:

- Category: Cultured milk.
- Study centre: Singapore.
- Target group: Household decision makers across all race/income groups.
- Brand portfolio: Yakult and Vitagen.
- Price range (see Exhibit C5.2):

    Yakult: $2.30, $2.60, $2.90, $3.10.
    Vitagen: $2.40.

- Panel matched on race, income group and brand usage.
- Details of sample size and sampling frame are provided in Exhibit C5.3.

	Panel #	Yakult	Vitagen
	1	2.30	2.40
Current price	2	2.60	2.40
	3	2.90	2.40
	4	3.10	2.40

Exhibit C5.2 Test price range ($).

Panel #	Yakult	Yakult & Vitagen	Vitagen	Total
1	200	100	100	400
2	200	100	100	400
3	200	100	100	400
4	200	100	100	400
Total	800	400	400	1600

Exhibit C5.3 Sampling frame.

Case Exercise

You are required to:

1. Compute the price elasticity of demand for Yakult at $2.30, $2.60, $2.90 and $3.10.
2. Assuming trade margin is 20% and cost per unit is S$1.17, estimate the price at which Yakult will maximize profit. (Note that as mentioned earlier, the total market remains fixed at the tested price range).
3. What are the key implications of taking price up/down? Make a recommendation on the selling price for Yakult.

Notes on Price Elasticity of Demand

Price Elasticity of Demand relates change in price to change in sales volume.

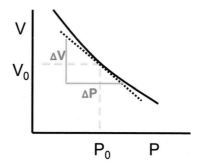

e = Price elasticity
V = Volume
P = Price

$$e = \frac{P \, dV}{V \, dP}$$

The price elasticity at P_0, V_0 is:

$$e_0 = \frac{P_0 \, \Delta V}{V_0 \, \Delta P}$$

Notes on Gross Profit

Yakult's Gross Profit = *Revenue* – *Variable Costs*
= *Sales Value* – *Trade Margin* – *Variable Costs*

The following table is provided for guidance on computing the gross profit for Yakult. It is one of many approaches for computing gross profit. You could also, for instance, work with the equation that relates gross profit to price, and use differentiation to locate the price point at which Yakult will achieve maximum gross profit.

	I	Current	III	IV
Retail Price	2.30	2.60	2.90	3.10
Share	76	67	58	52
Sales Volume (Index)	?	67	?	?
Sales Value (Index)	?	174.2	?	?
Trade Margin	20%	20%	20%	20%
Revenue (Index)	?	139.4	?	?
Variable cost/unit		1.17		
Variable costs (Index)	?	78.4	?	?
Gross Profit (Index)	?	61.0	?	?

PART VI

Retail

CHAPTER 19

Retail Tracking

THE NIELSEN CODE

IMPARTIALITY.	Be influenced by nothing but your client's interest. Tell him the truth.
THOROUGHNESS.	Accept business only at a price permitting thoroughness. Then do a thorough job, regardless of cost to us.
ACCURACY.	Watch every detail that affects the accuracy of your work.
INTEGRITY.	Keep the problems of clients and prospects confidential. Divulge information only with their consent.
ECONOMY.	Employ every economy consistent with thoroughness, accuracy and reliability.
PRICE.	Quote prices that will yield a fair profit. Never change your price unless warranted by a change in specification.
DELIVERY.	Give your client the earliest delivery consistent with quality - whatever the inconvience to us.
SERVICE.	Leave no stone unturned to help your client realize maximum profit from his investment.

A. C. Nielsen

President

Exhibit 19.0 The original Nielsen Code, 1931.

Preview

"If we have data, let's look at data. If all we have are opinions, let's go with mine." — Jim Barksdale.

Metrics like market share, sales and distribution, which are estimated by the retail tracking service, are fundamental to formulating marketing strategies and sales plans.

This chapter covers in some detail the six key processes — universe definition, retail census, sample design and recruitment, data collection, data processing, analysis and interpretation — that make-up a retail tracking service. It explains the metrics supported by the service, relates the benefits and applications of the service, and illustrates how the data is interpreted.

Most of the cases featured in this book make use of retail tracking data. The Little People case at the conclusion of Part VI, which is based entirely on retail audit data, facilitates a deeper understanding of the application of distribution and sales data.

Founding of the Nielsen Company, and the Nielsen Code

"The price of light is less than the cost of darkness." — Arthur C. Nielsen.

Adversity in the form of the Great Depression inspired the creation of what became the largest market research agency. The A. C. Nielsen Company which conducted performance surveys of industrial equipment nearly went bankrupt at the onset of the Depression. The company's founder Arthur Nielsen Sr., turning to a business proposition relatively immune to business cycles and war, created the Nielsen Food and Drug Index, a research service that recorded the retail flow of grocery and drug brands by ongoing audits of a sample of stores. A first of its kind, this retail tracking service provided manufacturers an estimate of their product sales and share of the market.

The science of tracking sales through retail outlets has since become the established methodology for the measurement of the sales of goods to consumers. Arthur Nielsen and his team went on to develop the science for measuring radio and television audiences for advertisers.

Among his many contributions to the field of market research, Nielsen left behind a code of conduct called *The Nielsen Code* (Exhibit 19.0). Enduring and timeless, the eight precepts in this code that dates back to 1931 form the guiding principles for a market research agency. According to David Calhoun, Nielsen's Executive Chairman, 2013, the code remains "a cornerstone of our brand, and it guides and inspires our employees around the world."

Applications of Retail Tracking

The retail tracking service yields metrics like market share (a term coined in 1935 by Arthur Nielsen), sales and measures for distribution. These measures, which are fundamental to formulating marketing strategies and sales plans, have numerous applications, including the following:

- Develop market strategies;
- Monitor brand health in terms of sales and distribution;
- Monitor competition;
- Understand market opportunities and threats;
- Develop sales plans;
- Evaluate performance in trade;
- Diagnose issues in distribution;
- Set goals and targets;
- Evaluate performance of individuals — business leaders, marketing and sales personnel.

The Data

Exhibits 19.1 and 19.2 provide a high-level view of the nature of retail tracking data. The charts depict a visual summary of the sales of a

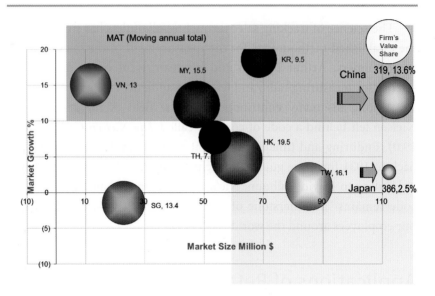

Exhibit 19.1 Attractiveness of product category across some Asian markets.

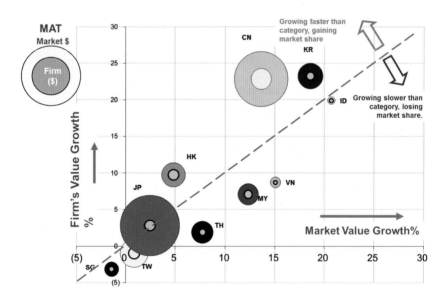

Exhibit 19.2 Firm's growth across the Asian markets.

product category and the sales of a firm's products in that category, across a number of Asian markets. They are configured to reveal the overall category and corporate performance, across the different markets in the region.

Whereas Japan (JP), in this example, is the biggest market in the region in terms of category sales, China (CN) is the most important market for this company. The inner circles in Exhibit 19.2, which represents the firm's sales, reveal that it is the firm's largest market; one where it is experiencing a 22.5% growth in value terms on a moving annual total (MAT) basis, which is well above the average category growth of 13.5%. Note too that this firm is also gaining share in South Korea (KR) and Hong Kong (HK) and losing share in Thailand (TH), Vietnam (VN), Malaysia (MY) and Singapore (SG). A macro view of this nature serves as a regional overview, highlighting the firm's performance across countries.

To act on the information, marketers need to drill down to markets, segments, and brands, identify opportunities and threats, and take strategic and tactical decisions. Brand and sales managers are therefore typically interested in the data at a brand and item level — variants, pack sizes — across segments, across chains, channels and markets, and across time periods — weeks, months, years. They need to know sales, market share and growth rates. They need to know distribution in terms of numeric, weighted, in-stock and out-of-stock. And they need this information for their brands and their competitors' brands.

Considering that a FMCG category typically comprises a few thousand stock keeping units (SKUs — i.e. items stocked), the data turns out to be quite a lot of information for marketers to access, and for their minds to process. Fortunately it is supported on user friendly software that permits speedy access to relevant information.

Performance Evaluation

Retail index is also increasingly used by firms for setting targets and for evaluating the performance of business units, business leaders, and marketing and sales associates. For example, during his tenure as CEO, Bart Becht benchmarked Reckitt Benckiser's (RB) performance on

Nielsen's estimate for category growth rate. RB's growth targets were set at +2% points ahead of Nielsen's growth estimate.

The research agency's estimates are viewed as accurate, objective, third party measures of the firm's performance, and key metrics like market share and growth are treated as the firm's KPIs.

One drawback of this use of data for performance evaluation is that it politicizes the retail index. Besides heightening pressures and expectations on data integrity, it can, occasionally, divert attention from the core objectives of the research.

Retail Index, Consumer Panels and Customized Research

The retail index yields a host of very useful metrics for formulating market strategies and sales plans. Basic measures like market share, sales and distribution serve also as key brand health indicators. For deeper *diagnosis* of brand health, however, it is advisable to use the retail index in conjunction with quantitative and qualitative customized research as well as consumer analytics data from sources such as consumer panels and loyalty panels.

Consumer analytics reveal behavioural information that provides for an improved understanding of the factors affecting a brand's health.

To diagnose issues, marketers also need to understand consumers' minds — Why are they buying what they are buying? This can be crucially important when it comes to acting on the information, and it falls within the scope of customized consumer research, both qualitative and quantitative

All the three forms of research — retail tracking, customized research and consumer analytics have their strengths and limitation. They do, however, combine well to provide marketers with a holistic and powerfully diagnostic understanding of business issues in general.

It is needless to add that it is neither necessary, nor, in the case of small brands, desirable to purchase all forms of research, on an ongoing basis. Marketers should procure research based on their needs, weighing the costs and the benefits of doing so.

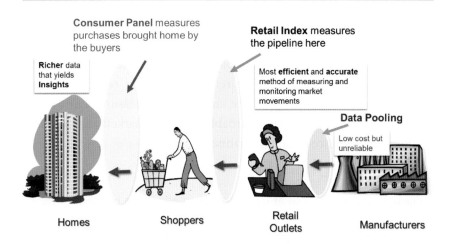

Exhibit 19.3   Variety of ways to measure sales of goods.

Where to Measure Sales?

As goods flow from manufacturers to retailers and from retailers to consumers, there are multiple points in their path where it becomes feasible to measure sales.

The sales pipeline commences with *primary sale*, the sale from manufacturer to distributor. Sale from the distributor to the retailer is called *secondary sale*. Manufacturers also sell directly to the bigger retail chains. At the end of the pipeline, the sale from the retail outlet to consumer is called *retail sale, consumer purchases* or *consumer offtake*.

Sales may be estimated by measuring the flow of goods at a number of points in the pipeline as depicted in Exhibit 19.3. The common methods for tracking and measuring sales include the retail index, consumer panel and data pooling. These methods, which are described in the following paragraphs, vary in terms of the "richness" and accuracy of the information they provide. The data collection processes also differ; some are more efficient and cost less, whereas others yield potentially more diagnostic information.

Retail Index (Retail Tracking)

Retail sales or the sale of goods from retailers to shoppers may be tracked through syndicated retail panels, and projected to reflect total sales for the market. Commonly referred to as the retail index, this approach offers the most accurate and efficient measurement of sales and distribution, at relatively affordable costs, for markets characterized by flow of goods through retail channels.

Consumer Panel

Sales may also be tracked at the point when goods are brought home by consumers. Estimates of consumers' purchases are obtained from a representative sample of homes called a consumer panel.

Syndicated household consumer panels are neither as efficient nor as accurate as the retail indices, for tracking sales. They also miss out on goods that are consumed out of home.

Consumer panels, however, are highly valued because disaggregate data (i.e. household level) is richer, and better suited for diagnosing issues. Intended for this purpose, they are usually not the preferred choice for tracking sales, in markets where retail indices exist.

Consumer panels are covered in detail in Chapter 7, *Consumer Panels.*

Data Pooling

Data pooling refers to the exchange, among manufacturers, of their sales data. This is usually undertaken by an intermediary agency that collects, compiles and re-distributes the processed data to the participating manufacturers. It is feasible when a few manufacturers control a large proportion of the market. And its prime advantage is low cost.

The pipeline that lies between primary sales and consumer offtake can be long and porous. Furthermore, primary sales tend also to be quite volatile due to trade promotions and other sales efforts that may result in the build-up of stock in the pipeline. As such it is not as good a reflection of consumer demand as the retail index.

Importantly, data pooling relies on data that is sourced from competitors. Instances where the arrangement falls apart due to incorrect or missing data, are not uncommon.

Retail Measurement Services

Retail measurement services (RMS) exist in a wide range of industry sectors including FMCG, consumer durables, pharmaceutical, vision care, pet foods (pet shops), Chinese tonics (Chinese Medical Halls), writing instruments, computers and peripherals, mobile phones/telecom products, and hardware and sanitary ware.

Within FMCG, Nielsen is the largest global service provider. IRI has a strong presence in North America, Aztec (acquired by IRI in 2013) is leading in the Pacific, and Intage is the sole service provider in Japan (Nielsen discontinued its Japan retail index in 2009). GfK is dominant in consumer durables, and IMS in pharmaceuticals.

The following steps outline the key processes in the development of a retail index:

- Universe definition
- Census
- Sample design and recruitment
- Data collection
- Data processing
- Analysis and interpretation

Steps 1 to 3, the universe definition, census (i.e. universe estimation), and sample design and set up, pertain to the design and development of the service. They form the foundation for the measurement service.

Steps 4 to 6 constitute the ongoing measurement process that is repeated every reporting period.

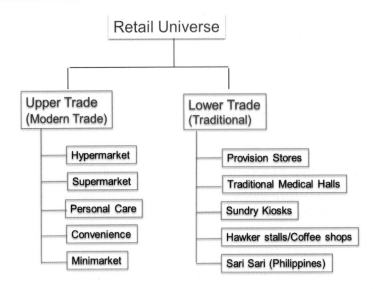

Exhibit 19.4 FMCG Retail Universe (an example).

Exhibit 19.5 Nielsen's retail universe (2008) excludes rural areas and the sparsely populated Western region of China.

Define Universe

Among the different classes of goods, the FMCG retail environment is the most complex and widest spread. At the broadest level, as shown in Exhibit 19.4, it may be split into the upper and the lower trade. The upper trade, which refers to the organized sector or modern trade, includes store formats such as supermarkets like Walmart, Tesco and Carrefour; convenience stores like 7-Eleven, Circle K and Lawson; and personal care and health outlets like Boots, Walgreens and Watsons. The lower trade comprises a collection of traditional, independent stores such as provision stores and sundry kiosks. Based on Nielsen's estimate for 2012, the upper trade represents only 1.6% in terms of number of stores in Asia, yet it constitutes 53% of total FMCG sales in value terms.

Typically the channels that sell FMCG products comprise many outlets that for a variety of reasons are not covered by the retail index. For instance it may not be feasible for the service provider to access outlets at schools, offices, tourist locations, hotels, bars, construction sites, army camps, and transient hawkers and so on. Some chain of stores may refuse to participate in the service. For large countries like China (see Exhibit 19.5), it may be too expensive to cover the entire geography, and the service may exclude less densely populated provinces and villages.

The retail universe is therefore a subset of the real world, and should be clearly defined by the service provider. This definition typically provides an outline of the channels and geographical areas that are covered as well as those that are excluded.

The shortfall in the retail index sales estimate for a product is the called the *coverage gap* (refer to Exhibit 19.6). It is usually represented as a ratio — i.e. the measured purchase volume as a proportion of the firm's total shipments within the market.

The shortfall is due to two factors:

- The difference in the product's sales area and the agency's universe, and

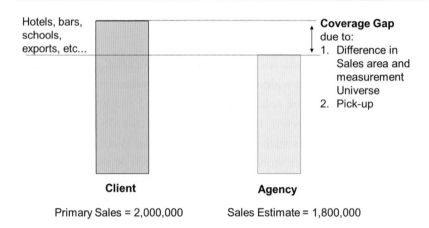

Exhibit 19.6 Coverage gap is the shortfall in the retail index sales estimate for a product.

- The difference between agency's sales estimate and the brand's shipments to the agency's universe. The ratio, *agency's sales estimate/shipments to universe*, is referred to as pick-up.

Retail Census

Once it is defined, an establishment survey called a retail census is conducted to measure the size and characteristics of the universe. These estimates, which are updated on a regular basis, are used to:

- Identify different outlet types and quantify number of outlets in a universe by type.
- Provide key statistics for setting up a representative retail panel.

Details collected in a retail census typically include: outlet name, address, telephone number, outlet type, use of scanning equipment, presence of air-conditioning, refrigeration facilities, number of hours open per day, monthly turnover, floor space, and presence of major product categories.

For the organized trade, most of these details are readily available from secondary sources including retailer websites.

For the traditional trade, field personnel armed with area maps and questionnaires, go street by street collecting the relevant information. Most of the information is gathered by observation, and the remainder may be obtained from store owners/employees.

Information on monthly turnover for the stores of participating retailers is obtained from their data. As for non-participating retailers, some store owners may refuse to divulge data of this nature. For these stores, the missing data is projected by statisticians based on store characteristics such as store type, location, floor size, number of major categories, facilities etc.

It is usually neither practical nor cost-effective to undertake a complete census covering the entire country. Instead the retail census takes the form of an establishment survey, i.e. a survey to estimate the scale and characteristics of the retail universe. To ensure that the data has low statistical error the establishment survey is undertaken over a very large sample covering the defined universe.

For sampling purposes, the defined universe is split into a number of mapped areas called primary sampling units (PSU). The PSUs are categorized by some measure of size usually provided by government, e.g. cities, towns, villages or polling districts. For the establishment survey, statisticians select a representative sample of PSUs. Every outlet within the sample is surveyed, and the results are projected to the universe.

A common approach called the *rolling census* is used for relatively small, important geographical areas such as cities. The PSUs are divided across a set of *"replicas"* in such a manner that all replicas have very similar characteristics — spread across geographical areas, store types, location types. Once these replicas are defined, the survey periodically (e.g. once every six months) rolls from one replica to another, so that over time all replicas are covered.

In Singapore, for example, the retail audit PSUs were originally based on the polling districts demarcated for the 1994 general elections.

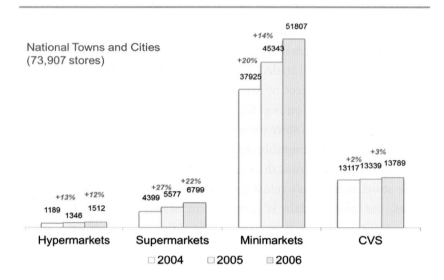

National Towns and Cities
(73,907 stores)

Exhibit 19.7 China's modern trade during the boom years — 2004 to 2006.

These 640 PSUs were split into four replicas — roughly identical in terms of spread across housing estates, regions, retail channels and so on. The establishment survey is conducted over a six month period, rolling from one replica to another. Within a period of two years all four replicas are covered, and the cycle continues.

Because each replica is so similar to the others, projecting it to the universe provides for a reasonably good estimate. However, since certain biases do creep in, a more accurate approach is to adopt projection techniques that account for these biases.

The core purpose of the retail census is to establish a basis for the sample design, and the foundation for the retail tracking service. It does however serve a number of secondary objectives. For instance, store census information is used by sales management for developing sales plans. And the aggregate data provides an understanding of retail trends in countries and regions across the globe. Exhibit 19.7 for instance illustrates the rapid growth of modern trade in China, during the boom years of 2004–2006.

Sample Design and Recruitment

The sample design is crucial to the accuracy and cost of the service. A well designed sample ensures that the desired data quality is achieved in an efficient and effective manner.

The key aspects that constitute a sample design are the sampling methodology, the accuracy standard and the ideal sample size.

Stratified Sampling is the norm for retail tracking. Stratification is a process of dividing a universe into groups (called strata or cell) for the purpose of selecting the sample, and projecting each one separately. Since the retail universe is composed of distinct *market breakdowns* (MBDs, e.g. supermarkets, convenience stores, provision stores etc.), it is amenable for stratification. Compared to random sampling, stratified sampling allows for the same level of precision with substantially smaller samples.

The determination of sample size is a commercial decision that weighs the costs with the benefits. Small unreliable samples are not meaningful, and large, overly accurate samples, may not be affordable. An *ideal sample* is one that precisely meets specifications — it is neither over specified, nor underspecified. The specification of ideal sample size is dependent on the following factors:

- Population variability — the larger the variance the larger the sample size.
- Sample design — for retail tracking, compared to other methods, stratified sampling allows for substantially smaller sample sizes.
- Specified level of accuracy — the greater the required precision, the larger the sample size. The standards for sampling error are set by the service provider.

It is pertinent to note that sample size is *not dependent on Universe size*. Countries like China and India require big samples because store variability is large, and product distribution is low.

The accuracy standards reflect the acceptable tolerance level of error, at a specified level of confidence. Nielsen's global standard for sampling error, set at 90% level of confidence and applicable to categories that are available in 80% of the universe, is as follows:

National Market	±3% of sales level
Major Market Breakdowns/Channels	±6% of sales level
Minor Market Breakdowns	±6–10% of sales level

According to this standard, the sample should be configured such that for a national market the probability that estimated sales value will lie within ±3% of actual value is 90%.

Once the sample is designed, the process of recruitment commences. To eliminate bias and eradicate systematic errors, the sample is recruited via a controlled, randomised selection process.

Further details of accuracy standards, sampling methods, and the statistics of sampling are provided in Appendix A.

Data Collection

Scan Data

Scan sales data, captured at the point-of-sale (POS) terminals, is usually broken down by weeks. The weekly cycle should preferably coincide with the chain's promotional week.

Scan data provides volume and value sales, and price information. It does not provide us with stock or purchase data. Distribution is based on sales (sales distribution), i.e., no sales for a time period means no sales distribution.

Manual Audits

Data collection for manual audits is conducted on a monthly cycle by field personnel called retail auditors. They collect the following information from each store in the retail sample:

- Stock count in the outlet (on the store shelves as well as storeroom).

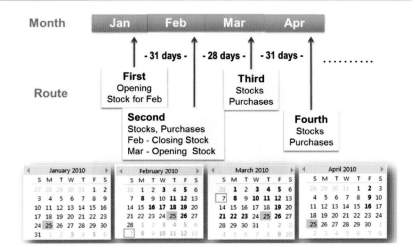

Exhibit 19.8 Monthly audit cycle.

- Retail selling price from the price tags.
- Purchases made by the outlet since last visit. This data is obtained from invoices maintained by the retail stores in the sample.

The auditors have monthly work cycle plans, and they usually audit the same stores on the same day of the month. In the example in Exhibit 19.8, a new store is added to the retail panel in January. The auditor conducts the first audit for the store on 25 January at which time information on purchases is not available. The store is re-visited on the 25th of each month. The stock count on 25 January becomes the opening stock for the period 25 January to 25 February. Stock count on 25 February is the closing stock for the same period, and the opening stock for the period 25 February to 25 March.

Data Processing

Manual Audit — Sales Derivation

In the case of manual audits, sales is derived from stocks and purchases. As portrayed in Exhibit 19.9, retailer purchases move stock into the store, increasing the in-store stock; and consumer purchases move stock

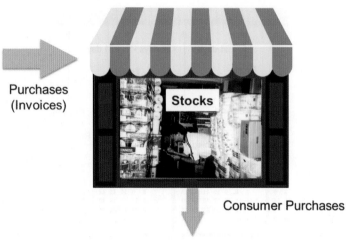

Purchases
(Invoices)

Stocks

Consumer Purchases

Consumers

Exhibit 19.9 Derivation of sales: Consumer offtake is retailer purchases plus the difference between opening and closing stock.

out, depleting the in-store stock. Consumer purchases are therefore equal to retailer purchases plus the difference between opening and closing stock (see example in Exhibit 19.10).

Consumer Purchases
$$= Retailer\ Purchases + Opening\ Stock$$
$$- Closing\ Stock - Credit\ Returns\ and\ Transfers$$

Data Projection

Ratio Estimation

The methodology commonly used for projecting data is called *ratio estimation*. The ratio projection factor is usually based on the all commodity value or ACV. ACV is the sales value of the product categories (i.e. those that are tracked by the research firm) sold by store. The ACV of sample stores reflects the relative size of these stores compared to the universe.

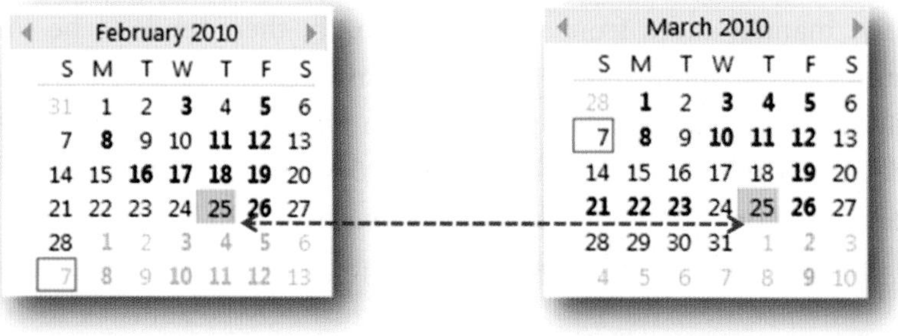

25th Feb Audit
Stocks = 500
(opening stock for March)
(closing stock for Feb)

25th Mar Audit
Stocks = 700
(closing stock for March)
Purchases = 1200

Sales (25th Feb to 25th Mar) = Opening Stock − Closing Stock + Purchases

= 500 − 700 + 1200 = 1000

Exhibit 19.10 Example — Computing Sales for March (25th Feb to 25th Mar).

If the universe for a market breakdown is 1,000 outlets, and the sample size is 100 (i.e. 10%), the numeric projection factor would be 10 times. If the ACV of the sample stores is estimated to be 12.5% of the ACV of the universe (i.e. these are somewhat larger stores on average), in that case the ratio projection factor is 8 times. By factoring the size of the stores in the sample, ratio estimation provides for greater accuracy.

Ratio estimation also reduces erroneous fluctuations in sales estimates arising due to any churn of stores within the sample. This is important because some amount of churn is expected on account of attrition of the sample stores. If a relatively small store in the sample is replaced by a relatively large store; in that case the numeric projection method would tend to inflate sales. Since ratio estimation factors the store ACV into the projection, it is able to contain any swings in the data arising due to changes within the sample.

Lapsed Audit Days — Adjustment Factor

For the manual audit, from month to month, there tends to be some variation in the audit time interval. For instance the retailer purchases data collected on 25 March for the store in Exhibit 19.10 pertains to the 28-day interval between 25 February and 25 March. For consistency this time interval or lapsed days is adjusted to reflect a 30.5-day interval, so that each of the 12 monthly periods are equal in size. The 1000 units of sales estimated in Exhibit 19.10 would accordingly be adjusted to 1089 ($= 1000 \times 30.5/28$) units.

Audit — Reporting Period

You may have noted that the data in our example pertains neither to February nor March; it pertains to the period 25 February to 25 March. In the retail index report, it falls under March. This is a peculiarity of manual audits — the actual time period varies from one store to another depending on the audit cycle for that store. Considering that stores are audited throughout the month of March, for stores that audit at the start of the month, the estimates for March reflect more of February sales than March. In interpreting manual audit data, one must bear in mind that the retail audit report for any month pertains partly to sales during that month and partly to sales over the previous month.

Data Imputation Techniques, Matrix Projection

Typically for scan channels, the MBD estimates are based on those chains that collaborate with the agency. Estimates for the stores of non-collaborating chains are made based on a combination of stores within the sample that have similar characteristics. If a non-collaborator's stores are distinctly different from the stores in the retail panel, in that case the non-collaborating chain should preferably be excluded from the universe definition.

The service relies on many external factors that lie outside the agency's control, and time and again situations arise that need to be resolved. To manage foreseeable situations, the agencies maintain a prescribed range of standardized techniques that are used to improve the quality of the data.

For instance, occasionally data sourced from a collaborating retailer may contain unusable or missing data for some stores. When this occurs, data for the missing stores is imputed based on prior period data for the same stores and projected to reflect the trend (increase/decrease) in other similar stores, for each and every item.

Consider for instance the following sales data for a brand in stores X and Y:

	Jan	*Feb*
Store X	1200	missing data
Store Y	1000	1050

If store Y is similar to store X, one may estimate Feb sales of the brand in store X, by projecting the increase in sales in Y (1050/1000 = 1.05) to that of the sales of the brand in Jan:

$$\text{Estimated Feb Sales in Store } X = 1200 \times 1.05 = 1260$$

This imputation technique which is commonly used for estimating missing sales data is called *matrix projection*.

Analysis and Interpretation

Retail tracking data is essentially 3-dimensional — product, market and time (refer to Exhibit 19.11), and each dimension has a hierarchical structure. For instance the product dimension can be broken down to category, segment, sub-segment, manufacturer, brand, variant and item.

The following are some metrics or facts supported by the retail index:

- Sales Volume.
- Sales Value.
- Year-to-date (YTD) Sales Volume and Value: The sum of sales volume/value from the beginning of year to the latest period.

	Product
	Segment
	Manufacturer
	Brand
	SKU (item level)

The data is essentially
3-Dimensional
   Product
   Market
   Time
... Data Types

Market
National
Regional
Trade Sectors
Account Specific

Time
Annual (MAT)
Monthly
Weekly(Scan services)

Exhibit 19.11   Retail tracking data is three dimensional.

- Moving Annual Total (MAT) Sales Volume and Value: The sum of the total sales volume/value for the 12 months ending with latest period.
- Average Price: Sales Value ÷ Sales Volume.
- Retailer Purchases Volume and Value.
- Forward Stock: Stock in the store's selling area which can easily be accessed by customers. Includes stock placed on shelf, on special display, on the shop floor space, inside chillers, freezers, cabinets and so on.
- Total Stock: Stock in the store's selling area plus stock in the store room (aka backroom or stock room).
- Stock Cover (Stock Cover Days): Number of days that stock would last, assuming sales continue at the same rate. Example: If stock is 300 units and sales is 600 units per month, then stock cover days = 300/600 = half a month.
- Out of Stock: Percentage of stores in the universe that sold the product in the audit period but having no stock at the time stock was counted.

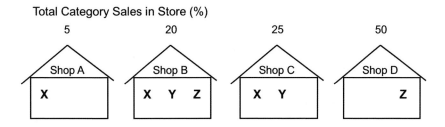

Exhibit 19.12 What is the numeric and weighted distribution of brands *X, Y* and *Z*? (Universe is shops *A, B, C* and *D*).

- Numeric Distribution: Percentage of stores handling product. A store is considered a product handler during an audit period, if it stocked that product at any time during that period.
- Weighted Distribution: Percentage of stores handling product weighted by *product category* store sales (equal to share of category sales by handlers).

Numeric and Weighted Distribution

Consider the example in Exhibit 19.12. Brand X is handled by shops A, B and C; its numeric distribution therefore is three out of four or 75%. Its weighted distribution is the total weight of shops A, B and C in terms of category sales, which is equal to 50% (5 + 20 + 25). Note also that the brand's weighted distribution (50%) is the same as the trade share of shops A, B and C, which handle brand X.

Unless otherwise specified, distribution is weighted in terms of category *value* sales. Defined as a percentage of where money is spent on the product category, it reflects the quality of distribution.

Considering that brand X's weighted distribution (50%) is lower than its numeric distribution (75%), one may conclude that the quality of the brand's distribution is relatively weak. In comparison brand Z with 50% numeric and 70% weighted distribution is handled by stores that contribute more to category sales.

Occasionally categories are weighted in terms of ACV (i.e. sales value of all categories sold by store). This is advisable in case of small,

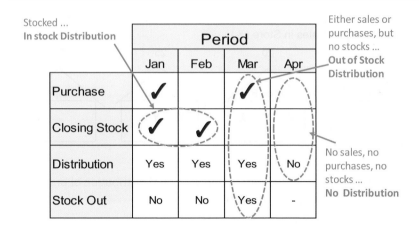

Exhibit 19.13 Stockout and loss of distribution.

new/growing categories with few brands. For such categories, ACV weighted distribution provides a better reflection of the quality of distribution.

In-Stock and Out-of-Stock Distribution

Consider Exhibit 19.13, which depicts a brand's incidence of purchase and stocks over four time periods. The brand has in-stock distribution in January and February, and it has out-of-stock (OOS) distribution in March. The brand lost distribution in April because there are no sales, no purchases and no stocks — it did not exist in the store at any time during the month.

Now suppose there was some closing stock in March, and as before, no purchases in April and no stocks by end of April. In this case, the status in March changes from OOS distribution to in-stock distribution. Is the store still considered a non-distributor in April? (No, because the stocks at the end of March are opening stocks for April. These stocks would have sold during the month.)

Benefits — Market Understanding

With view to analysis and interpretation, retail tracking data is fundamental to formulating marketing strategies and sales plans. In particular the data yields insights in the following areas:

- Market Structure: The information on size and growth of category, segments and brands provides an understanding of the opportunities and threats. Consumer trends such as, for instance, in convenience and health, are spotted first by the retail index.

- Channel Performance: The size, growth and development of channels and chains, feeds into channel strategies.

- Brand Health: Brand growth, share, distribution, price are some of the key metrics that help assess the health of a brand.

- Competition: The index reveals the activities of competitors, as also their strengths and weaknesses.

- Sales Evaluation: With metrics like distribution, stocks, stock cover, OOS and so on, the retail index is ideal for sales evaluation and distribution diagnostics.

Analysis and interpretation of this data, in the context of sales and distribution, is the topic of Chapter 21, *Sales and Distribution*.

CHAPTER 20

Retail Analytics

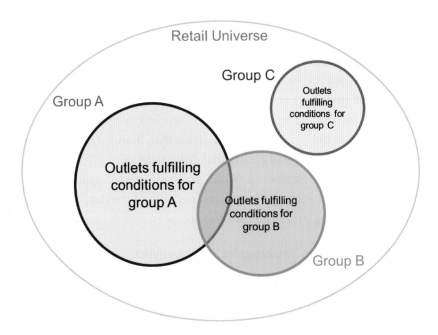

Exhibit 20.1 Forming outlet groups.

Preview

The term "retail analytics" is commonly in use in recent years, often in ways that tend to overlap with related areas such as "consumer analytics" and "retail tracking". Since each of these topics is covered separately in this text, let me clarify by outlining the scope of this chapter and how it differs from the other two.

In the current context, *Retail analytics is defined as the analysis of continuous outlet level data to address business issues in retail.*

Retail Tracking Databases for Retail Analytics

Retail tracking, which sources data from point-of-sale (POS) scan terminals and retail audits, generate continuous transaction databases that feed into retail analytics. Whereas the chapter on retail tracking focussed at the aggregate level (i.e. market breakdown — chain, channel, country, region), in this chapter, we analyse disaggregate or outlet level data.

Fundamental to retail analytics is the filtering of retail outlets to form outlet groups. For instance a retailer or a supplier might be interested in examining outlets that stocked a particular brand compared with outlets that did not stock that brand. Or outlets that offered a promotion versus outlets that did not do so.

This chapter describes a wide array of outlet group analysis addressing aspects such as brand handlers', brand overlap, assortment, shelf space, pricing, promotion and rate of sales.

Customer Transaction Databases for Retail Analytics

Customer transaction databases (e.g. sales transaction data, consumer panel data, loyalty panel data) also feed into retail analytics. These databases have the customer dimension in addition to outlet dimension, thus adding an additional layer of diagnostic capabilities. This data can be used to compute chain or outlet penetration, spend per customer, chain loyalty, cannibalization among outlets and so on, using similar concepts, tools and techniques that are applicable for the analysis of consumer panels.

The analysis outlined in this chapter include customer profile, loyalty and propensity, assortment analysis, overlap, outlet group, outlet repertoire, gain–loss, trial and repeat visit, penetration and repeat rate, and sales forecasting. A case example pertaining to the opening of a new petrol station illustrates a number of these analyses.

Outlet Group Analysis Using Tracking Data

Retail analytics using tracking data (retail audit/scan data) essentially involves filtering the data to form one or more outlet groups (refer to Exhibit 20.1). The groups may be defined based on the physical characteristics of the outlets (e.g. location, size, type of outlet, type of facilities etc.) or on the sale and distribution of products.

Outlet grouping serves the purpose of drilling into relevant data. If a particular retail issue is to be evaluated, the groups are configured so that they provide a deeper understand of that issue. For example:

- Handlers' analysis: Outlets are filtered according to whether they stock a product, or any combination of products.
- Assortment analysis: E.g. outlets that stock 1 or 2 models of Sony TVs, outlets that stock 3 to 6 models, and outlets that stock more than 6 models.
- Brand overlap: E.g. outlets that only distribute Coca-Cola, outlets that only distribute Pepsi and outlets that distribute both Coca-Cola and Pepsi.
- Shelf space analysis: E.g. in the breakfast cereals category, outlets with less than 10% forward stock and outlets with more than 10% forward stock of health cereals.
- Pricing: Group stores according to the average price at which some product was sold. Or group according to comparative pricing, e.g. stores where Pantene shampoo is cheaper than Sunsilk, and stores where it is more expensive.
- Promotion: E.g. petrol stations that promoted RON 92 fuel and those that did not promote.
- Rate of sale: Group stores into heavy, medium and light on the basis of their rate of sales for a category.

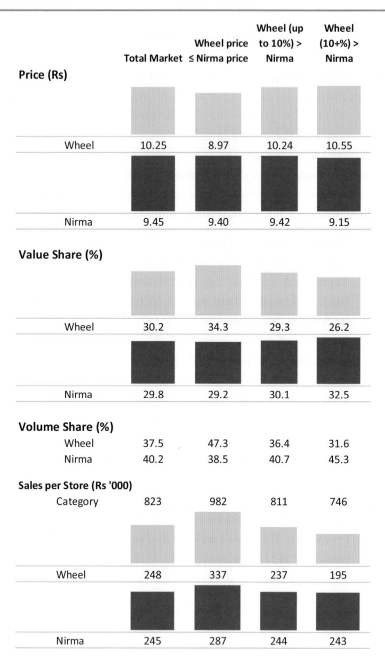

Price (Rs)	Total Market	Wheel price ≤ Nirma price	Wheel (up to 10%) > Nirma	Wheel (10+%) > Nirma
Wheel	10.25	8.97	10.24	10.55
Nirma	9.45	9.40	9.42	9.15
Value Share (%)				
Wheel	30.2	34.3	29.3	26.2
Nirma	29.8	29.2	30.1	32.5
Volume Share (%)				
Wheel	37.5	47.3	36.4	31.6
Nirma	40.2	38.5	40.7	45.3
Sales per Store (Rs '000)				
Category	823	982	811	746
Wheel	248	337	237	195
Nirma	245	287	244	243

Exhibit 20.2 Price analysis for Wheel and Nirma (fictitious data).

Case Example — Wheel and Nirma Pricing Analysis

Wheel and Nirma are direct competitors in the low price segment of the Indian detergent bar market. The analysis shown in Exhibit 20.2 demonstrates the very significant impact relative price has on the market share of the two brands.

Both brands have a 30% value share in the total market. However in stores where Wheel's price is cheaper or same as Nirma, the brand's value share increases to 34%. In volume terms the increase is even more pronounced — Wheel's share varies from 31.6% in outlets where it is priced more than 10% higher than Nirma, to 37.5% where it is priced up to 10% more, and 47.3% in outlets where it is priced the same or cheaper than Nirma.

Analysis Using Transaction Data

The tools and techniques used for consumer panel analysis are also applicable for retail analytics. The focus however shifts from brands to outlets.

The range of analysis includes:

- Customer profile analysis
- Loyalty and propensity
- Assortment analysis
- Overlap analysis
- Outlet group analysis
- Outlet repertoire analysis
- Gain–loss analysis
- Trial and repeat visit analysis for new outlets
- Penetration and repeat rate
- Sales forecasting (relevant for new outlets)

The case example, "Evaluation of opening of new petrol station", which comes later in this chapter, illustrates the application of some of these analyses.

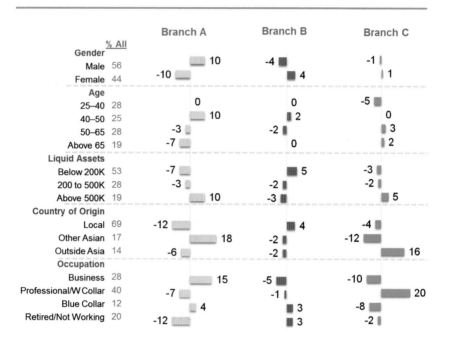

Exhibit 20.3 Profile (skew) analysis of "affluent" customers at different branch offices of a bank.

Note that data confined to the retailer's own transactions, as is the case with loyalty panels, curtails the scope of the analysis. The analysis is then restricted in context to the retailer's customers and their transactions at the retailer's outlets.

For example, penetration would be redefined as proportion of loyalty card holders. The analysis of gain–loss between stores will not be able to capture switching between competing chains. Forecasts would be confined within the boundaries of the retail chain. And metrics such as loyalty and propensity cannot be computed. Both these measures require an assessment of customers' transaction across the entire market.

In the FMCG sector, where they are prevalent, consumer panels provide a holistic view of the market and work well for most of the above analysis. They are however expensive to set up and maintain, and sample sizes would tend to be relatively small compared to sales transaction data or loyalty panel data.

Customer Profile Analysis

Profile analysis reveals an outlet's customer profile in terms of customer segment or demographic groups. It can be conducted for a store, or any cluster of stores.

The analysis basically reveals the demographic makeup of the customers at an outlet. For example, the skew analysis shown in Exhibit 20.3 depicts the profile of private banking customers at three branch offices. In addition, profile analysis provides an understanding of the importance of each group in terms of transaction volume and value.

Loyalty and Propensity

Customers visit a repertoire of outlets, and they spread their transactions across these outlets. Retailers therefore get only a proportion of their customers' spend. Behavioural loyalty tells us what that proportion is. It is defined as the retailer's share of category sales among its customers, and it may be measured in terms of volume or value.

Take for example the consumer panel data on the FMCG fabric wash category depicted in Exhibit 20.4. The total market size is $1 billion. Shoppers that shop at a particular retail chain spend a total of $300 million across all of the outlets where they shop. Of this amount they spend $120 million within the retail chain. Their behavioural loyalty to the chain is therefore 40% (= 120/300).

Related to loyalty is the notion of *buyer conversion*. It is the proportion, among its customers, of category buyers who buy the category at the retailer's outlets.

The retailer can theoretically grow category sales by improving chain loyalty. In this example, sales could increase to a maximum value of $300 million, if loyalty rose to 100%. The retailer could also grow category sales by attracting more shoppers to shop at its stores

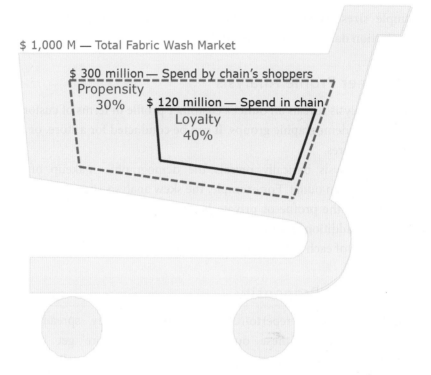

$ 1,000 M — Total Fabric Wash Market

$ 300 million — Spend by chain's shoppers

Propensity
30% $ 120 million — Spend in chain

Loyalty
40%

Exhibit 20.4 Loyalty and propensity.

(increasing store traffic), or by increasing the amount they spend on the category.

This leads to the concept of retailer propensity which is the proportion of total category sales coming from the retail chain's shoppers. In the earlier example the retailer's propensity for fabric wash is 30% (= 300/1000).

It follows from the stated definitions that a chain's share of trade in a category is the propensity of its shoppers to shop for that category multiplied by the behavioural loyalty of the shoppers.

$$Market\ share = Propensity \times Loyalty$$

Due to variations in the consumption habits of their shoppers, retailers can have relatively high propensity for some categories, and

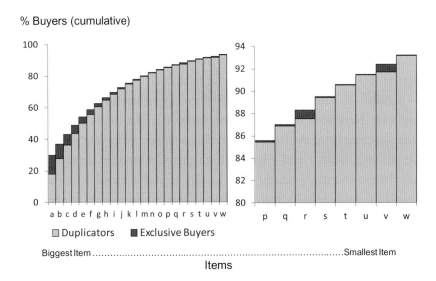

% Buyers (cumulative)

Exhibit 20.5 Assortment optimization.

low for others. For instance, if the chain's shopper's demographic profile is skewed towards families with babies, then its propensity for categories like infant milk and diapers is likely to be high.

Note: As mentioned earlier loyalty and propensity cannot be computed with data that is confined to the retailer's own transactions, as is the case with loyalty panel data. Both these measures require an assessment of customers' transaction across the entire market.

Assortment Analysis

Retailers are grappling constantly with a vast number of brands and items, as also the continual requests to list an ever increasing parade of new products. Their space is finite — as new items get listed, some items on the shelf need to be de-listed.

One approach to optimizing assortment is on the basis of sales volume, sales value and profitability. This is covered in detail in Chapter 21, *Sales and Distribution*. It is important also for the retailer to examine the proportion of shoppers who buy (% buyers), and particularly those who *exclusively* buy listed items. A low selling item might have relatively high base of shoppers who exclusively buy it. If the item is de-listed, some of the shoppers may switch to other stores, in which case the retailer stands to lose their total spend in store.

Exhibit 20.5 depicts an analysis of exclusive buyers and cumulative duplicate buyers of items for some category. The items are listed in order starting from the item with the biggest base of buyers. Observe, at the tail end, items *r* and *v* have a high proportion of exclusive buyers. Since these shoppers exhibit high loyalty to items *r* and *v*, the retailer should probably refrain from de-listing them; or do so only after careful consideration.

Case Example — Evaluation of Opening of New Petrol Station

This example pertaining to the opening of a new petrol station is based on analysis of loyalty panel data. It computes the trial, repeat usage rate and usage index to provide an estimate of the outlet's share or contribution within chain. It also examines the source of volume of the new station, and the overlap in usage of the motorists frequenting the new station with the chain's other stations.

Outlet Trial

For a new outlet to flourish, it must develop a base of regular customers — i.e. motorists who try it and continue using it. The outlet's success hinges therefore on trial and repeat usage.

Trial or cumulative penetration at a time *t* is the percentage of customers who transacted at the outlet from the time it was opened till time *t*.

As can be seen from Exhibit 20.6, the proportion of loyalty card holders who pumped petrol at the new station rose steadily to 21% by the 47th week after its opening. The penetration of the other petrol stations in the chain has also been increasing over time, and total penetration (all stations) is 96% in week 47.

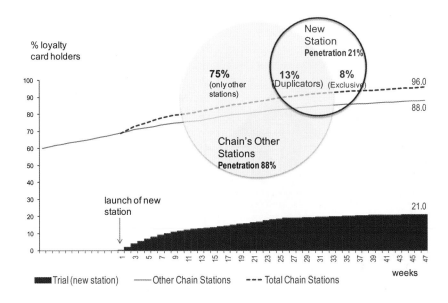

Exhibit 20.6 Trial and overlap analysis for new station.

The stable repeat usage rate (RUR) estimate was 28%, and the usage index was 1.02. These measures akin to RBR (repeat buying rate) and buying index are covered in detail under the Parfitt–Collins model in Chapter 11, *Product Validation*. Based on this model, the estimated contribution of the new petrol station to the chain's total volume is 6.0% (= 21% × 28% × 1.02).

It would interest the chain's management to know how many of the motorists who frequent the new station exclusively pump at that station, and how many of them are "duplicators" who are also pumping at the chain's other stations. This information may be gleaned from the overlap analysis which is also presented in Exhibit 20.6.

Overlap Analysis

The overlap analysis splits the chain's base of loyalty card holders into three groups depending on where they fill petrol — *only new station users, new and other stations users* (i.e. duplicators) and *only users of other stations*.

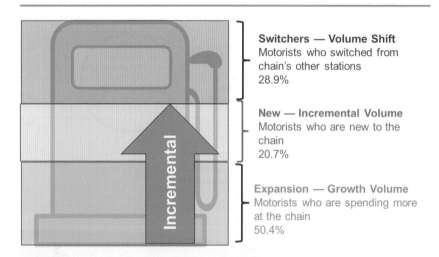

Exhibit 20.7 Source of growth analysis for new station (analysis over the 13 week period — weeks 35 to 47 versus the 13 weeks prior to opening).

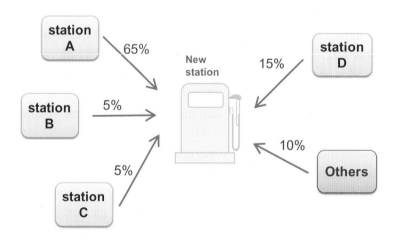

Exhibit 20.8 Analysis of cannibalization.

The analysis reveals that 8% of the loyalty card holders pump the chain's fuels exclusively at the new station. These motorists may also be going to competing chains, but they have not been going to the chain's other stations. They therefore represent the incremental gain in motorists resulting from the addition of the new station. It is also possible to analyse these motorists further in terms of measures such as their consumption levels, and how that compares with the chain's other motorists.

The presence of "duplicators" suggests cannibalization. This is inevitable whenever a new station is added to an existing chain. Gain–loss analysis can reveal the extent to which the new station increases the amount of petrol the duplicators consume at the chain, and the extent it cannibalizes other stations belonging to the same chain.

Gain–loss

Refer to Chapter 7, *Consumer Panel* for details on the gain–loss methodology. The analysis depicted in Exhibit 20.7 reveals the sources of volume for the new petrol station. About 21% of the volume is from motorists who started purchasing fuels from the chain only after the new station opened. This is purely incremental volume for the chain.

Also incremental is the 50.4% of the volume of fuels sold at the new station, which represents an increase in fuel consumption at the chain by motorists who were pumping at the chain's other petrol stations. The remaining 29% is due to cannibalization. This is the proportion of business that the new station acquired from other stations belonging to the chain.

The high incremental volume (50.4% + 20.7%) suggests that the new outlet gained considerable volume from competition. However, since the analysis is based on the chain's loyalty data, it is not possible to identify which competing petrol stations contributed to the new outlet's growth.

The data does however reveal which of the chain's petrol stations were cannibalized by the new station, and how much volume the new station acquired from these outlets. This analysis is presented in Exhibit 20.8. It tells us that the majority of the cannibalized (switching) volume (65%) came from station A. Stations D, B and C were also substantially affected.

CHAPTER 21

Sales and Distribution

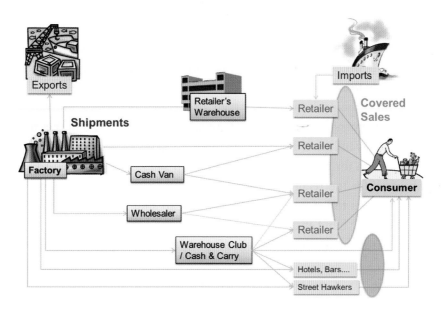

Exhibit 21.0 Distribution network, retail universe and covered sales.

Preview

This chapter addresses sales and distribution priorities in five key areas — building distribution network, targeting the right channels and chains, optimizing assortment, securing retailer support and managing stocks in trade.

A wide array of metrics are reviewed to address these priorities, including measures for stock and distribution, metrics for depth of sales such as share in handlers, rate of sales, cash rate of sale and rate of gross profits. The chapter also covers a host of techniques and metrics for evaluation of assortment including average number of items stocked, stock turns, portfolio analysis and fragmentation analysis.

Interdependence of Demand and Supply

A mousetrap, irrespective of how good it is, will not sell if consumers cannot find it. And irrespective of how widely it is distributed, consumers would not buy it if they do not want it. It takes both demand and supply to achieve sales.

Supply, the push factor, is largely driven by sales efforts, including the management of distribution channels and trade marketing. Yet it is also strongly influenced by the demand for the product.

Demand for a brand generates a pull in sales. It yields a return on inventory for the retailer. As a brand's *turns × earns* improve, more retailers want to list it, and they are willing to allot it more shelf space. On the other hand if demand is declining, the brand's stock turnover deteriorates, retailers reduce its shelf space, trim its range and ultimately de-list it.

While it is predominantly created through marketing efforts, demand is also influenced by availability and retailer support, and the impact of in-stores activities is growing. The consolidation in retail coupled with fragmentation of media, makes the store an attractive place to market products. Manufacturers are increasingly using in-store displays and in-store media to engage with their consumers.

In-store activities including displays, price-offs, sampling and in-store launches, raise brand awareness, shape perceptions and generate the desire among consumers to purchase the brand.

The use of *in-store media* on shelves (shelf talkers or shelf stoppers), floors, carts, chillers, as well as walls and ceiling is quite extensive. In-store presence of digital has been growing. Beyond signage and touch screen kiosks, we are now witnessing hectic growth in the use of *mobile devices* as a means to engage with shoppers.

Components of Sales — Width and Depth

Sales may be broken down to two components — width and depth — the number of stores distributing, and the sales per store.

$$Sales = Number\ of\ stores\ distributing \times Sales\ per\ store$$

These components are interdependent — as the number of stores distributing a product expands, the stores start to cannibalize one another, adversely affecting the sales per store.

A wide range of metrics are used by managers to assess the sales and distribution of their brands, and to formulate sales strategies and plans. The metrics pertaining to the sales per store are covered in detail under the section "Measures of Assortment".

Measures for distribution were initially introduced in Chapter 19, *Retail Tracking*. These measures are covered in more detail in the following paragraphs.

Measures for Distribution (Width)

Distribution, the metric commonly used for product availability, has a number of variations: purchase, sales and handler distribution; in-stock and out-of-stock (OOS) distribution; forward stock and total stock. It may be measured in numeric and weighted terms, and it may be weighted in terms of volume or value. Some of these terms are explained below:

- Handler: A store is considered a product handler during an audit period if it stocked that product at any time during that period. (If there is any opening or closing stock, purchase or sale, then the store is a handler.)
- Numeric Distribution: Percentage of stores handling product.
- Weighted Distribution: Percentage of stores handling product weighted by product category store sales. If the weight is in value terms, which usually is the norm, then weighted

distribution is the same as the value share of category sales by handlers.

- Numeric/Weighted Sales Distribution: For the upper trade, information on stocks is not captured in their scan data. For scan stores, therefore, the numeric and weighted distribution is computed in terms of numeric *sales* distribution and weighted *sales* distribution.
- Numeric Sales Distribution: Percentage of stores selling product.
- Numeric Purchase Distribution: Percentage of stores purchasing product.
- Weighted Sales Distribution: Percentage of stores selling product weighted by product category store sales. (Equal to share of category sales by sellers.)
- Weighted Purchase Distribution: Percentage of stores purchasing product weighted by product category store purchases.
- Numeric distribution tells us the proportion of stores distributing a product. Weighted distribution, on the other hand, reveals the product's presence as percentage of where money is spent on that category. It is a better reflection of the quality of distribution.
- Usually the weighted distribution of a product is greater than its numeric distribution. This is because bigger stores typically carry more brands; they tend to be the stores that brands would enter into first.
- All commodity value (ACV) weighted distribution: Occasionally categories are weighted in terms of ACV (i.e. sales value of all categories sold by store). This is advisable in case of small new/growing categories with few brands. For such categories, ACV weighted distribution provides a better reflection of the quality of distribution.

Sales and Distribution Priorities

Knowing that it is neither viable nor feasible to get all retailers to carry all your products, it is important that you get the right retailers to carry the right products. To optimize your distribution and assortment, you need to address the following priorities:

- Build distribution network.
- Target channels and chains: Which are the right channels/chains for your products?
- Optimize assortment: How many items in each channel? Which items in which channel?
- Secure retailer support: How to get listed at a retail chain?
- Manage stocks in trade.

The remainder of this chapter details how the above imperatives may be addressed through the application of market research methods.

Distribution Network — Basics

A distribution network is a set of interdependent organizations engaged in making goods and services available to customers. It includes primary channel partners such as wholesalers, distributors, retailers, agents and brokers who form the pipeline or link between manufacturer and customers. It also involves ancillary channel members who provide generic facilities such as transportation (logistics), financing, storage, promotion and other such services. These primary and ancillary intermediaries make the flow of goods to target customers efficient and cost-effective.

Distribution channels vary from one class of goods to another, and channel strategies too can differ from manufacturer to manufacturer.

The FMCG distribution network in particular is complex and widespread, and usually takes the form of a conventional channel, such as that depicted in Exhibit 21.0. The retail universe, as mentioned in the chapter *Retail Tracking*, comprises both the upper (modern) and the lower (traditional) trade. The trade formats are diverse varying from

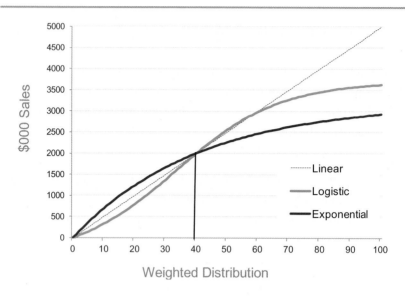

Exhibit 21.1 Relationship between sales and distribution.

very basic to advanced retailing concepts like virtual shopping. Key FMCG trade formats are described in the next chapter, *Category Management*.

The pipeline characteristics vary depending on the nature of the product and the size of the market. Markets covering large geographies such as China and India have extensive and elaborate distribution networks.

Products like bread that have a short shelf life require distribution networks that can cater for daily deliveries to retail outlets. Other products like pasteurized milk and fresh foods require cool chain distribution, whereas ice creams and frozen foods require cold chain distribution.

A soft drink like Coca-Cola is distributed not only in a very large number of stores, it is also available at food and beverage outlets, and at many other indoor and outdoor locations through vending machines. On the other hand premium quality, niche and exclusive products like gourmet foods or luxury personal care brands are only distributed in select outlets.

Building, and sustaining, a channel network for products that are widely distributed is time consuming and expensive. There are benefits as well as costs. As manufacturers expand their distribution, at some stage an optimum level is reached; the gains of distributing to additional outlets do not justify the cost of servicing them. To know whether it is *cost-effective*, manufacturers need an understanding of how much sales and profits they stand to gain from further expansion in distribution, and how much this will cost them.

Consider Exhibit 21.1, which depicts the relationship between sales and distribution of a brand which has sales of $2,000,000 and weighted distribution of 40%. As the sales manager crafts plans to build distribution, he needs some understanding on how much the brand stands to gain in sales, if its distribution is increased to 50% or 60% or 80%?

If the relationship between sales and distribution is linear, doubling distribution from 40% to 80% will result in doubling of sales to $4,000,000. Sales will increase to $3,000,000 if distribution is expanded to 60% and $2,500,000 if it is grows to 50%.

The linear model, however, is theoretically unsound because it suggests no cannibalization of sales between stores, no store switching behaviour, and a homogenous trade channel.

It is more realistic to assume either a logistic or an exponentially declining relationship between sales and distribution. Most products that are launched with substantial marketing efforts and investments would tend to exhibit an exponentially declining relationship, where incremental sales from expansion in distribution decline with increase in distribution. As the velocity of sales decreases with expansion of distribution into smaller stores, it becomes increasingly less viable for these smaller retailers to stock the brand, and for the manufacturer to distribute it.

Like the exponentially declining functional form, the logistic relationship captures the notion of saturation. This is the point at which cannibalization will offset the impact of any further gains in distribution. The logistic relationship also assumes that at low levels, the impact that distribution has on sales will be limited. This may hold true for products that have limited advertising, and rely on their in-store presence and in-store initiatives to gain share of mind.

Right Channels, Right Chains

Your products need to be where your consumers usually go to buy them. Targeting the right retailers with the right products requires good understanding of channel and chain characteristics, and retail trends. The key considerations are sales density, shopper profile and store positioning.

Sales Density

Different classes of goods (e.g. FMCG, durables, clothing, petroleum, fast food etc.) sell in different types of outlets. Even within the same class of goods, channels can vary in importance for different categories, segments or brands. In FMCG for instance, cheeses, cakes, cigarettes, colas and cleansers sell in different types of stores.

In general the sales force should target those channels and chains with high sales density for their product segments and variants. Usually this is self-evident at the category level. However sales personnel need to keep track of trends and changes in shopping behaviour so that they know what segments, variants, and pack sizes to prioritize at which stores. A brand's market share is severely affected if the distribution of variants, pack types and pack sizes is not aligned with shoppers' preferences.

For instance the sales of a major sanitary napkin brand were constrained because it was not available at Watsons, at that time a fast growing personal care chain in parts of Asia. Once the importance of the chain was revealed, the manufacturer was prepared to accept the relatively high listing fees that the chain commanded. In addition to sales, the brand's consumer profile also improved — young women tended to shop more at Watsons.

In another instance, a brand of batteries experienced low market share because shoppers prefer to purchase large pack sizes in supermarkets, and this brand was not available in large pack sizes.

In yet another instance, a breakfast cereals brand experienced sluggish sales because it was not available in small packs. In the Asian market that the brand had entered, people who are not accustomed to consuming breakfast cereals preferred to try small packs before they started buying the bigger packs.

Shopper Profile and Store Positioning

Brands target consumers, and retail banners target shoppers. Both from the viewpoint of the manufacturer and the retailer, it is important that brands are more visible in banners where the shopper profile is aligned with the brands' target consumer profile. This forms an important basis for prioritizing distribution as well as in-store activities and in-store communication.

Manufacturers need to be mindful of the retailer's role and positioning, because the mere presence of a brand in a chain colours consumers' perception of the brand.

Take for instance high end department stores and mainstream personal care chains. While these are the two most important channels for facial care products, they differ in almost every aspect of their retailing mix, and target contrasting shopper segments.

Even within a channel such as department stores or supermarkets, positioning may differ greatly. There are department stores that primarily sell premium designer labels, while others focus on masstige and mid-range, and still others that specialize in low price popular products.

Mindful of the way the channels and chains are positioned, manufacturers target different brands for different outlets. For instance, L'Oreal's Plenitude and Garnier ranges of facial care products are usually not seen in the same outlets. Plenitude is distributed in upmarket department stores, whereas Garnier sells in mainstream personal care chains.

Right Assortment

Conventional wisdom suggests that consumers prefer greater variety. This is relevant especially within the realms of a physical brick and mortar world where shelf space is finite and limited.

Yet sometimes consumers are overwhelmed by the profusion of choices that confront them. They may appreciate a wide selection of movies, songs, books, breads and soups, and juices. But do they need to choose from 20 different brands of pineapple juice?

In a natural experiment using data from nearly 800,000 employees, Sheena Iyengar concluded that participation rates for a retirement savings plan fall as the number of fund options increase (Iyengar *et al.*, 2004). The team's results confirmed that participation in the retirement savings plans is higher in plans offering a handful of funds, as compared to plans offering ten or more options.

In another study on the benefits and detriments of variety, Vries-van Ketel (2005) concluded that "an optimal level of assortment size seems to exist for simple grocery products ... more variety is more appealing to consumers, but that variety also has its limits." Based on her empirical findings, consumers find it harder to cope with variety in assortments of complex products. For these products, optimal assortment level is lower than that for simpler products.

For instance the task of purchasing a digital camera is complex because it entails the understanding and trade-off of a large number of attributes, some of which an average buyer might not fully comprehend. In this case great variety becomes a burden for consumers confronted with the difficult task of selecting a complex product.

There also exists in people's mind, the fear for later regret, i.e. what if I choose the wrong product? The potential for regret is greater for products that are complex and long lasting, and it increases with increase in choice.

Expertise of the buyer too has a bearing on her preference for variety. Experts are able to better cope with the complexity of choice. They presumably are more inclined to learning more about the product, and prefer large assortments so that they may choose exactly what they want.

Vries-van Ketel's study also stresses the importance of merchandising. Her research suggests that products should be placed on the shelves in an organized manner, so that consumers find it easier to choose what they want. This reduces the "cost" of variety to consumers.

As regards costs, from the manufacturer's perspective, adding brands and variants reduces the economy of scale per item, heightening manufacturing, marketing, sales, logistics and inventory costs.

From the retailer's perspective too, greater variety translates to higher costs. The increase in assortment and consequently the reduction in turns per item, adversely affects inventory, delivery, merchandising, administration and purchasing costs.

It is important to stress that while some research studies have shown too much choice is not good, in majority of sectors and product categories, retailers are well below the optimum levels of assortment. Rather than too much choice, physical constraints such as finite shelf space are the prime limitations. Thus, the majority of research studies have concluded that increasing assortment will increase store traffic as well as spend levels.

In view of this, the challenges confronting retailers in most consumer goods industries are as follows:

- Shelf space is limited — retailers are unable to accommodate the wide selection of brands and products offered by suppliers.
- Consumers want more variety. (Though there are upper limits, current levels of assortment, for most categories, are far below these levels.)
- Consumers expect products to remain in-stock. Retailers need to ensure that products are stocked on shelves in adequate quantities, so that they are unlikely to run out-of-stock.

The limited shelf space that is available in a store must be optimized so that consumer may benefit from a wide range of choices, with minimum incidence of stockouts.

Managing Assortment

Nowadays items on sale in retail stores are usually distinguished by a bar code that is scanned at the checkout. Every book for instance has a unique International Standard Book Number (ISBN). In FMCG an item's bar code is referred to by various abbreviations — stock keeping unit (SKU) number, Universal Product Code (UPC) in the US, European Article Number (EAN), Global Trade Item Number (GTIN), Japanese Article Number (JAN) etc.

The average supermarket has roughly 10,000 to 20,000 SKUs in stock. That sounds like a large number of items, but it is small compared to what the suppliers have to offer.

To gain some understanding of the scale, some time back I asked for a count of the number of active items on Nielsen's item master in Singapore. I was told that there were 2,137 shampoos, 4,714 facial products, 3,441 biscuits, 2,376 chocolates and 2,110 soft drinks. Besides wondering what all you can do to your face these days, there is the question of how retailers cope with this glut.

Brick and mortar stores can stock only a small fraction of the items that manufacturers have to offer. They need to manage this carefully because assortment is a key driver of store choice. It impacts consumers' perception of their chain, their store loyalty and the amount they spend in store. The limited shelf space that is available in a store must be optimized so that consumers may benefit from a wide range of choices, with minimum incidence of stockouts.

From the manufacturer's perspective, the brand's range and its distribution is aligned to its marketing strategy. In trade channels however it is faced with a battle for shelf space. Ultimately how much of the brand's range is stocked by a retailer is a function of several size factors:

- Size of the store.
- Size of the category. Importance of the category. Destination categories, for instance, would get higher priority on space.

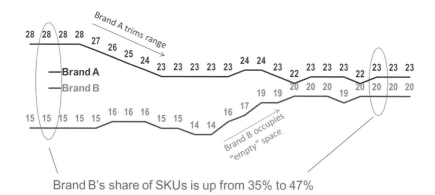

Brand B's share of SKUs is up from 35% to 47%

Exhibit 21.2 Average number of items (SKUs) of cat food in supermarket over a period of two years (monthly data).

- Size of the brand. Importance of the brand. Brands that are better aligned with the identity of the retailer get higher priority.
- Size of item.

Bigger stores accommodate more categories and offer more space for each category. For instance supermarkets stock over 30 SKUs of Campbell's soup, whereas provision stores on average stock less than 5. Campbell's management team needs to take a decision on which items it will sell through which store in each of the channels, and ensure that these items remain in stock.

Battle for Shelf Space

During a presentation to a cat food manufacturer, I observed the interesting trend depicted in Exhibit 21.2. The number of SKUs for the client's brand *A* was trimmed from 28 to 22, as part of a cost cutting initiative. The retailer responded by sourcing more items from the competitor, and brand *B*'s range expanded from 15 to 20 variants.

This led to very substantial sales gains for brand *B*. A year by year comparison revealed a 30% growth for brand *B*, whereas brand *A*'s volume dipped by about 2%. Brand *B*'s market share went up from 42% to 49%.

Cat food is one among a number of categories where a brand's share of space has a strong bearing on market share. Brand *A*'s margins may have improved a little over the two year time frame, yet, by trimming its range, it yielded some competitive advantage to brand *B*.

The battle for shelf space stems from the relationship between share of space, share of mind and share of sales. By expanding its range on the shelf, a brand is able to offer consumers greater choice. It usually gets more facings to accommodate the additional items. This gives it greater visibility, i.e. more mind space. At the same time the incremental shelf space must be relinquished by some other brand. As a result of all these factors the brand usually gains market share.

Needless to say that though the temptation may be there to grab space, each item in a brand's range must earn its place on the shelf. If it fails to do so, it will erode the retailer's and the manufacturer's margins, and reflect poorly on the brand and the manufacturer. Ultimately, if it fails to perform, it will get de-listed.

Measures of Assortment

To better manage assortment there are a number of questions that retailers and manufacturers need answers to:

- How many items or lines are stocked by a retailer? More specifically there is the need to assess:
  o Average number of brands of a category in a store.
  o Average number of items of a category in a store.
  o Average number of items of a brand in a store.
  o Brand's share of total category items.
  o Efficiency rate — How efficient is a brand in securing depth of distribution of variants, where it is listed?
- Which items should the retailer stock? As mentioned earlier this is a function of size in terms of volume, value and profit. The relevant metrics are as follows:
  o Sales per point of weighted distribution

    o   Share in handlers

    o   Average sales per store

    o   Rate of sale (adjusted average sales per store)

    o   Cash rate of sale

    o   Rate of gross profits

    o   Portfolio analysis

- What is the extent of concentration/fragmentation across different categories? Fragmentation analysis.

- How many of brand buyers are exclusive buyers? Exclusive buyers and cumulative duplicate buyers' analysis (refer to Chapter 20, *Retail Analytics* for details of this analysis).

Number of Items Stocked

Consider the following example. Flat screen TVs are available in 90% of stores (numeric distribution) carrying consumer durables. There are only three brands in the market:

- Panasonic is in 60% of stores;
- Philips is in 40%;
- Sharp is in 80%.

For simplicity, suppose there are exactly 100 stores. In which case 60 would carry Panasonic, 40 Philips and 80 Sharp. This adds to the brands' distribution count of 180 (60 + 40 + 80) over 90 stores. Since only 90 stores carry flat screen TVs, the average store is therefore carrying 2 brands (180/90).

As can be seen from this example, the *average number of brands (in category) stocked in stores* is the sum of the numeric distribution of the brands divided by the category numeric distribution:

$$\frac{Sum\ of\ Brands\ Distribution}{Product\ Category\ Distribution},$$

Sum of Brands Distribution: 60 + 40 + 80 = 180
Product Category Distribution: 90

Average number of brands = 180/90 = 2

Similarly the average number of items stocked in stores:

$$\frac{Sum\ of\ Items\ Distribution}{Product\ Category\ Distribution}$$

And the average number of a brand's items stocked in the stores carrying the brand:

$$\frac{Sum\ of\ the\ Brand's\ Items\ Distribution}{Brand\ Distribution}$$

Example: A brand has 80% numeric distribution, and its three items have distribution of 80%, 50%, 70%. The average number of a brand's items stocked in stores carrying the brand is computed as follows:

Brand distribution = 80% (*width of distribution*)

Item distribution (3 of) = 80%, 50%, 70%

Sum of the brand's items distribution = 80 + 50 + 70 = 200

Average number of items stocked = 200/80 = 2.5 (*depth of distribution*)

Example: Flat screen TVs are available in 90% of stores (numeric distribution) carrying consumer durables. There are only two brands in this market — Panasonic and Sharp. Based on the distribution of these brands and their individual models, as given in Exhibit 21.3, we can compute the following:

- Average number of flat screen TVs stocked per store;
- Average number of Sharp TVs stocked where Sharp is listed;
- Average number of Panasonic TVs stocked where Panasonic is listed;
- Efficiency rate for the two brands.

Average number of items stocked per store = (300 + 320)/90 = 6.9

Average number of Panasonic TVs stocked where brand is listed:

300/60 = 5,

Panasonic's efficiency rate: 5/6= 80.3%,

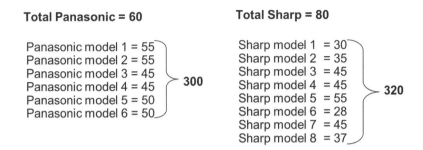

Exhibit 21.3 Numeric distribution of Panasonic and Sharp flat screen TVs.

Panasonic's share of items: 300/620 = 48.4%,
Average number of Sharp TVs stocked where brand is listed:
                              320/80 = 4,
Sharp's efficiency rate: 4/8 = 50%,
Sharp's share of items: 320/620 = 51.6%.

One conclusion from this fictitious example, is that Sharp has greater *width* of distribution whereas Panasonic has greater *depth*. It appears that Sharp has greater success in getting listed, whereas Panasonic is better at securing depth where listed.

Sales per Point of Weighted Distribution

In the previous example, considering that the average retailer stocks only 7 TVs, retailers and suppliers need to prioritize which models should be listed. The *Sales per Point of Weighted Distribution (SPPD)* is one of a number of metrics that helps you to do that. It is simply a ratio of sales (units or volume or value) divided by weighted distribution.

Sales per Point of Weighted Distribution (SPPD):

$$\frac{Volume\ Sales}{Wtd\ Distribution} \quad or \quad \frac{Value\ Sales}{Wtd\ Distribution}$$

For example if a brand's sales is 10,000 kg and its weighted distribution is 80%, then:

$$SPPD = 10,000/80 = 125\ kg.$$

Share in Handlers

As its name suggests, share in handlers means the share of sales (in *value* terms) within the stores carrying the product. Here is an example that illustrates how this conceptually meaningful metric is computed:

	$ Million
Television sales	$100
Panasonic sales	$20
Panasonic's market share is	20%
Television sales in stores selling Panasonic	$80
Panasonic's handler's share of television sales	80%

(By definition, this is Panasonic's weighted distribution)

Panasonic's share in handlers (% value)
= Panasonic's share in shops selling Panasonic
= $20/$80   25%

$$= \frac{Panasonic's\ Value\ Share}{Panasonic's\ Weighted\ Distribution}$$

In general, a brand's share in handlers is equal to:

$$\frac{Market\ Share\ (in\ value)}{Weighted\ Distribution\ (based\ on\ Product\ Category\ Value)}.$$

Average Sales per Store

The average sales per store is equal to:

$$\frac{Sales\ Volume}{Number\ of\ stores\ distributing\ the\ product}$$

$$Number\ of\ stores\ distributing\ the\ product =$$
$$Numeric\ Distribution \times Number\ of\ Stores\ in\ Universe$$

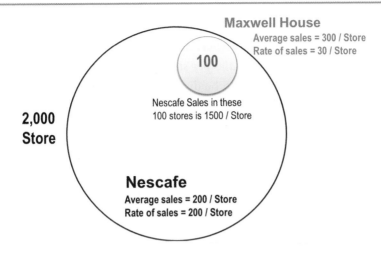

Exhibit 21.4   Rate of sales per store for Nescafe and Maxwell House (fictitious example).

For example, if sales volume = 10,000 kg, numeric distribution = 50% and the number of outlets in market breakdown = 800, then:

$$Average\ Sales\ =\ 10,000/(0.5\ \times\ 800),$$
$$=\ 10,000/400\ =\ 25\ kg\ per\ store$$

This measure, though simple and easy to comprehend, can be misleading as it does not account for the quality of distribution. For instance, consider the following data for Nescafe and Maxwell House.

Nescafe:
   Sold in 2000 *outlets*,
   Average sales per store is 200 *kg per month.*
Maxwell House:
   Sold in 100 *outlets*,
   Average sales per store is 300 *kg per month.*

The *average sales per store* suggests that Maxwell House is selling at a faster pace than Nescafe. But intuitively, this does not sound right. If Maxwell House can sell at a faster rate than Nescafe, why is its distribution confined to only 100 outlets, compared to 2,000 for Nescafe?

On drilling into the data, we find that Nescafe is selling 1,500 kg per month in those 100 stores where Maxwell House is distributed (see Exhibit 21.4). The *average sales per store* fails to account for the size of stores. Smaller brands tend to be distributed only in the big stores that carry a wide assortment, and account for a much larger share of trade than the average store. As a brand's distribution expands its *average sales per store* tends to drop, because of the effect of store size.

Rate of Sales (Adjusted Average Sales per Store)

The rate of sales adjusts the average sales per store to reflect what the sales would be if the stores handling the product were average in size.

$$Rate\ of\ Sales\ =\ Avg\ sales\ per\ store\ \times\ \frac{Numeric\ Distribution}{Weighted\ Distribution},$$

Or

$$Rate\ of\ Sales\ =\ \frac{Sales\ Volume}{Equivalent\ \#\ of\ stores\ distributing\ product}.$$

Reverting to our Maxwell House (MH) example:

$Sales\ Volume\ =\ 30,000\ kg/month$
$Numerical\ Distribution\ =\ 5\%$
$Weighted\ Distribution\ =\ 50\%$
$Number\ of\ Supermarkets\ =\ 2,000$
$\#\ of\ Stores\ \times\ Numeric\ Distribution\ =\ 100$
$=\ \#\ of\ stores\ distributing\ MH$
$\#\ of\ Stores\ \times\ Weighted\ Distribution\ =\ 1,000$
$=\ Equivalent\ \#\ of\ stores\ distributing\ MH.$

$Rate\ of\ Sales\ =\ Sales\ Volume/(\#\ of\ Stores\ \times\ Wtd\ Dist)$
$=\ 30,000/(2000\ \times\ 0.50)\ =\ 30\ kg/store.$

This means that *Maxwell House sells 30 kg per month per averaged sized store selling coffee in supermarkets.*

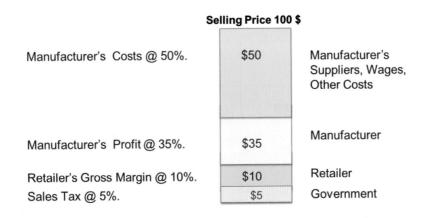

Exhibit 21.5   Distribution of profit from the sale of goods.

Cash Rate of Sale, Rate of Gross Profit

The cash rate of sales (i.e. the rate of sales in value terms) and the rate of gross profit are computed as follows:

$$Cash\ Rate\ of\ Sales\ =\ Selling\ Price\ \times\ Rate\ of\ Sales.$$
$$Rate\ of\ Gross\ Profit\ =\ Margin\ \times\ Cash\ Rate\ of\ Sales.$$

Unit, volume, value and profit are the different measures used to express the movement of goods. Production, purchasing and logistics work with units. The factory manager needs to know how many jars of coffee need to be produced.

Volume is the measure for the size of the market. For FMCG products kilogramme or litre usually is appropriate. Some products however are available in different forms. Coffee for instance is available in the form of powder and 3-in-1 sachets. The appropriate measure would be to translate the volume of these forms into an equivalent representing number of cups of coffee.

From a financial standpoint, sales value and profit are of prime importance. Money is required to pay for raw materials and supplies, salaries, taxes, dividends and so on.

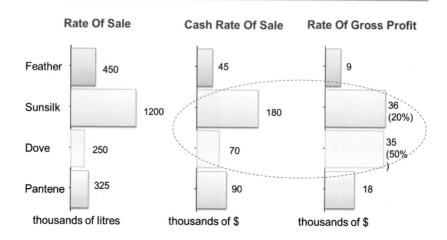

Exhibit 21.6 Comparison of rate of sales of four shampoo brands.

Exhibit 21.5 depicts how the $100 selling price for a product gets distributed across the various stakeholders — manufacturer, retailer, suppliers and government. In this example the manufacturer makes a margin of 35%, and the retailer's gross margin is 10%.

The notion of *turns* × *earns* sums up the retailing business model. It captures the two main components of retailing — to maximize the margins (earns) and the times they can earn that margin, i.e. the velocity of inventory turn. Turns are calculated by dividing the sales (cost of material sold) by the inventory (average inventory value). Earns is the gross margin. Categories tend to vary from high earn and low turn to low earn and high turn. The margin for products with high turns, detergents or cooking oils for instance, will tend to be lower than those with low turns, such as facial care and books. Retailer margins, for the majority of FMCG goods tend to lie between 5% and 30%.

Exhibit 21.6 provides a fictitious example for the rate of sales comparisons of four shampoo brands. Among the four brands, Sunsilk is the top brand consumed by shoppers and it contributes more than the other brands to the retailer's gross profit. Dove on the other hand, is a profit generator; its rate of gross profit is comparable to that for Sunsilk, despite much lower rate of sales.

	Weighted Distribution	Numeric Distribution
Outrageous Orange	78	62
Cheeky Cherryade	87	70
Ice Cream Soda	82	67
Original Sarsi	80	65
Fruitade	72	58
Groovy Grape	64	47
Zesty Zappel	62	40

Exhibit 21.7 Weighted and numeric distribution of the flavours of Rainbow, a soft drink brand. The brand's overall distribution is 85%.

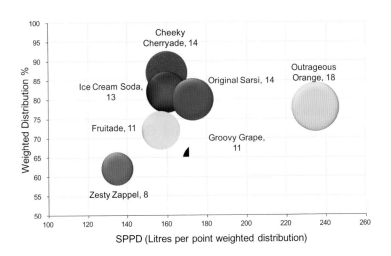

Exhibit 21.8 Weighted distribution and sales per point of distribution for Rainbow's portfolio of flavours. Label = sales value in $'000.

Portfolio Analysis

Exhibits 21.7 and 21.8 depict the portfolio of Rainbow, a soft drinks brand in a lower trade channel. Given that the brand's overall numeric distribution is 85%, based on the numeric distribution of its variants, the depth of distribution is 4.8 — the average store handling rainbow carries 4.8 of the 7 variants of Rainbow.

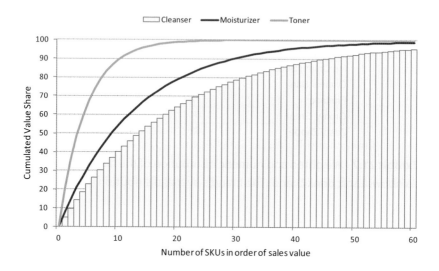

Exhibit 21.9 Fragmentation analysis for cleansers, moisturizers and toners.

The portfolio analysis in the exhibit suggests the need to expand the distribution of Outrageous Orange and Groovy Grape. Distribution should be prioritized on the basis of SPPD — other factors remaining constant, if a shop keeper wants to stock only one flavour, it should preferably be Orange, and if it is three, in that case — Orange, Grape and Sarsi.

Fragmentation Analysis

Fragmentation analysis (Exhibit 21.9) depicts the build-up of cumulative share with each additional SKU, starting from the largest to the smallest. It reveals the level of fragmentation/concentration within the category, and may be conducted at SKU or brand level.

In the exhibited example the toner category, where the top three SKUs account for close to 50% of market share, is highly concentrated. In contrast, it takes 14 SKUs in the fragmented facial cleansers category to touch 50% share.

Securing Retailer Support

To gain retailers' support, suppliers must demonstrate why their product deserves a place in their stores. Does it perform better than competing brands in term of return on inventory (earns × turns)?

For example consider a brand that is seeking distribution at a major supermarket chain. The brand is currently distributed in a few small supermarket chains; its value share in the supermarket channel is 2.5%, and its weighted distribution in the channel is 20%.

What facts should the trade marketer put forward that might help her secure the category manager's support to list the brand? Why should the retailer be interested in stocking the brand?

Based on the data, the brand has a 12.5% (=2.5/20%) share in handlers, i.e., its value share in those stores that are carrying the brand is 12.5%. That is quite a respectable share — depending on the level of fragmentation within the category, it possibly ranks among the top one or two in the category, where distributed.

Because it is conceptually meaningful, share in handlers is an apt measure to demonstrate the brand's potential, where the strength of the brand lies in its value share. Similarly measures such as SPPD, rate of sales or rate of gross profits, which also allow for a comparison with competing brands, are also appropriate for justifying the distribution of a product. Rate of gross profits would work best for brands that command higher margins for the retailer.

Other than measures that reflect the size of the brand, the synergy between the brand's image and the chain's role and positioning, is an important criteria. An upmarket retailer, for instance, would not consider listing a low end brand, irrespective of how big it might be where it sells.

Considering the perpetual parade of new products, it is usually challenging to secure retailer support for new, unheard of products or less established brands. In such instances, in addition to bearing the listing fees, manufacturers also use a variety of discounts to incentivize retailers to stock new products.

Importantly, a partnership built on trust greatly facilitates the alliance between trade partners. If relationships are not well developed, or if their resources are constrained, manufacturers may need to rely on distributors to market their products to retailers.

Managing Stock in Trade

The following metrics that are commonly used for measuring stocks in trade are useful in managing the stocks in the lower trade:

- Forward stock: Stock in the store's selling area which can easily be accessed by customers. Includes stock placed on shelf, on special display, on the shop floor space, inside chillers, freezers, cabinets and so on.
- Total stock: Stock in the store's selling area plus stock in the backroom (stock room).
- Stock cover (stock cover days): Number of days that stock would last, assuming sales continue at the same rate.
- Out of stock: Percentage of stores handling the product in the audit period but having no stock at the time stock was counted.

These metrics are supported in the retail audit data for the lower trade (non-scan) channels. For scan channels, though retailers keep track of some of the metrics, the information may not be readily available. In sectors such as apparel, footwear and luxury goods, where some retailers are adopting radio frequency identification (RFID) tags for storing electronic product codes (EPC), the process of collating and maintaining this type of information will become much easier.

The danger signals that manufacturers and retailers need to take note of are declining forward stock and growth in the incidence of stockouts. Both metrics are indicators of supply issues or loss of distribution.

Stock cover needs to be substantially greater than the manufacturer's sales cycle or retailer's procurement cycle. Whenever

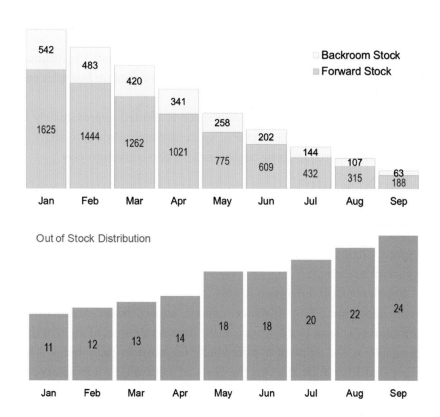

Exhibit 21.10 Declining forward & backroom stock and growth in the incidence of stockouts are indicators of supply issues or loss of distribution

stock cover days fall below the average sales cycle, incidence of stockouts will soar.

Trends in forward stock and out of stock distribution reveal distribution and stock management issues in trade. Exhibit 21.10, for instance, depicts a brand that is experiencing supply shortages resulting in reduction in inventory and high stockouts. From January to September, stocks in the channel have depleted from 2,176 units to barely 251 units. During the same period stockouts have soared from 11% to 24%.

Allocation of Shelf Space (Forward Stock)

It is of prime interest to retailers that the allocation of shelf space is well planned and well implemented. Poor allocation will lead to stockouts for some items and excessive stocks for others, resulting in lost sales and high inventory holding costs.

To optimize forward stock, shelf space is allotted approximately in proportion to demand (i.e. share of space is roughly equal to share of sales), though merchandising considerations also come into play.

Stock to Sales Ratio

In order to maintain wider range of products and accommodate small brands, the big brands tend to get somewhat less than their sales share of space. Chains also allocate more space to brands that are strategically important to them.

Retailers usually maintain norms for merchandising that impact on space allocation. For instance, many supermarkets maintain a minimum of at least two facings (i.e. the number of units of an item that are visible at the front of a store shelf) for most of their items. This benefits small brands that on the basis of sales might not deserve as much as two facings.

Stock to sales relationship therefore follows the pattern depicted in Exhibit 21.11, where the share of space is lower than the share of market for the bigger brands. On the other hand, the share of space for small brands exceeds their share of market as they get no less than the minimum number of facings stipulated by the retailer.

Stock to sales ratio, which is simply stock share divided by sales share is the measure usually adopted for comparison across products. In Exhibit 21.12, for instance, Item 1 is getting far less than its fair share of space, whereas Item 3 is getting substantially more space.

Stock Turns

Shelf space is the most valuable physical asset that retailers own. How well they utilize it ultimately determines the profitability of retail chains.

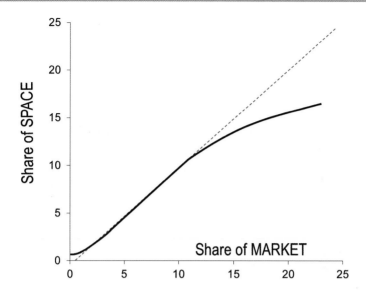

Exhibit 21.11 Relationship between share of market and share of space.

	Forward Stock %	Sales %	Ratio
Item 1	5.0	7.5	**67**
Item 2	5.0	5.0	100
Item 3	5.0	3.5	**143**

Exhibit 21.12 Stock to sales ratio.

Their business model therefore revolves around the notion of stock turns and return on inventory.

"Stock turns" is the number of times per year that the shelf inventory is turned over in relation to the sales revenue of a given product.

$$Stock\ turns\ =\ \frac{Annual\ Sales\ Volume}{Average\ Volume\ of\ Stock\ on\ Shelf}$$

If for example, the full year sale of an item in one store is 1,200 units and its average stock is 24 units, then its stock turns is equal to 50. This means that on a yearly basis the stock in the selling area is being replenished 50 times, or about once a week.

Cost of Stockouts

Consider the following information pertaining to a brand with 80% numeric distribution, and 100,000 unit sales:

Numeric distribution	80%
Universe of stores	500
Number of stores handling	400
Period sales	100,000
Average sales per store	250

If this brand experiences OOS of 10%, given the above information, what is the estimated loss in business — in terms of sales — due to the stockout?

OOS distribution	10%
Number of stores OOS	50
Average sales lost per store	250
Total lost sales	12,500

This assumes:

1. Probability of OOS at any store, at any point in time (during the period under investigation) is 10%. (Sounds reasonable.)
2. OOS = lost sales. (This is a questionable assumption. There are many options open to the shopper when she encounters a stockout. In instances where the brand loyalty is high a stockout may not result in the loss of brand sales.)

How a consumer responds when she is unable to find the item she wants depends on a number of factors including the following:

- Pack or variant loyalty
- Brand loyalty
- Product loyalty
- Store loyalty
- Urgency to use

Her response is determined by the influences that are of greater importance at the time of purchase. The possible outcomes include:

- She buys an alternative size/variant of the same brand;
- She buys a different brand — supplier loses;
- She buys from a different store — retailer loses;
- She delays purchase — both supplier and retailer could lose if this leads to a drop in consumption or a change of brand/store;
- She buys a different category — supplier loses.

According to what shoppers claim, the response to an OOS can vary substantially across categories. Based on the data in Exhibits 21.13 and 21.14, the cost of OOS to retailers is high for categories like infant milk which exhibit very high brand loyalty, and low for categories like carbonated drinks and chocolate, where the shopper is prepared to switch brands. Mothers are unwilling to try a new brand of infant formula, and would look for their chosen brand in other stores. On the other hand for carbonated drinks, shoppers are prepared to switch to some other brand when they experience a stockout.

True Cost of Poor Distribution

Manufacturers do not want to give their loyal consumers any reason to try competitors' products, let alone compel them to do so. For once these consumers experience something new, their loyalty might permanently shift to the competing product. In which case, in addition to the loss of current sales, the stockout results in the loss of future sales from that time onwards.

For the retailer, the top 10% of shoppers account for 30% to 50% of a store's sales. These core shoppers are most affected by stockouts. If some of them switch allegiance to other stores, the cost will be their total spend from that time onwards.

Whereas earlier we concluded that the estimated 12,500-unit loss in current period sales was an overestimate, from a long term perspective, taking the impact on brand loyalty and store loyalty into consideration, one concludes that the true cost of OOS, for both manufacturer and retailer is likely to be far greater. This goes to emphasize the importance of sustaining distribution and maintaining adequate stocks in trade.

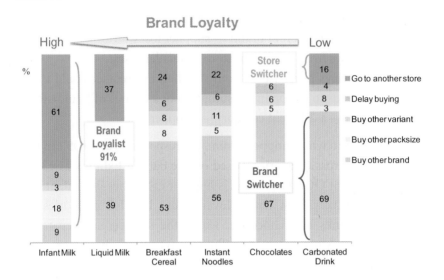

Exhibit 21.13   Claimed response to out-of-stock situations for different categories of FMCG goods *(Source: based on a Nielsen survey in Singapore).*

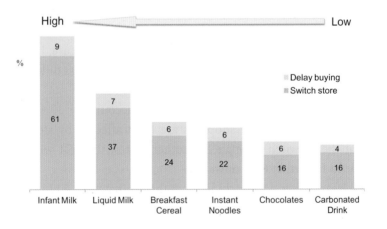

Exhibit 21.14   Based on exhibit 21.14, the cost of OOS to retailers is higher for categories like infant milk and liquid milk, and lower for categories like carbonated drinks and chocolate.

CHAPTER 22

Category Management

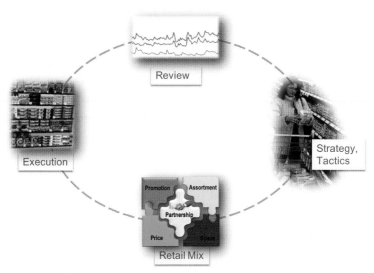

Exhibit 22.1 Category management process.

Preview

"There is only one boss. The customer. And he can fire everybody in the company from the chairman on down, simply by spending his money somewhere else." — Sam Walton.

The customer according to Sam Walton is the boss. To attract and retain her, retailers must align their retailing mix to cater to her needs and preferences. To achieve this they need to develop strategies and processes to manage their business in a customer-centric manner. These strategies and process fall under the realm of category management.

The topics covered in this chapter include an overview of category management, its processes, trade marketing, the partnership between retailers and manufacturers, category roles, category strategies, retail mix and space management.

The Inulas case study at the end of Part VI, is crafted to impart a deeper understanding of the category management process, and the application of space management.

Category Management Overview

Categories are the building blocks of a retailer's business, in much the same way as brands are the building blocks of a manufacturer's business. To manage their business, retailers need to manage their categories in a cohesive manner so that they are better placed to attract and retain customers. This is the premise of category management.

Strategy

At the onset, what is required is a sense of direction — a strategy. The retailer's *business strategy* is a long term course of action that the retailer is committed to. It sets a direction that distinguishes its chains from its competitors.

Like any enterprise, the retailer has a collection of strategies — category strategies, sourcing strategy, technology strategy. Its business strategy is the overarching strategy that harmonizes all these constituent strategies.

A sound business strategy is based on a deep understanding of shoppers, and full appreciation of the retailer's purpose and core competencies. It encompasses crafting the *retail chain's identity and value proposition;* partitioning shoppers into segments, and identifying which *target segments* to pursue with what categories; and distinctly *positioning the retail banner* in the minds of target shoppers.

Category strategies are established to fulfil the chain's value proposition, and clearly *differentiate* their banners from competition. Crafting them involves a number of tasks — *defining departments and categories*, assigning *category roles* and establishing goals, benchmarks and objectives.

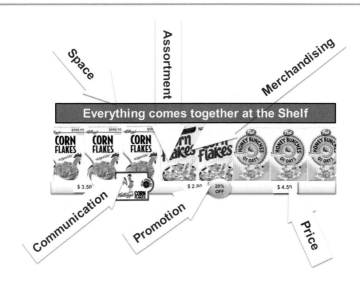

Exhibit 22.2 Retailers execute strategies and tactics on their shelves.

Strategies are not revamped every year. On the contrary, good strategies tend to be stable, yielding competitive advantage over the long term. However, as markets evolve, retailers need to continually tune and refine their strategies.

As a continuous ongoing process, category management is concerned with refining category strategies and tactics, aligning the retail mix, executing plans and reviewing performance. The cyclical sequence of tasks depicted in Exhibit 22.1 constitutes the process as a whole.

Retail Mix

Category strategies and tactics are translated into a coordinated programme that aligns the retail mix with the retailer's imperatives. The retail mix is the set of tasks that are required to manage categories in the store. It includes:

- *Merchandising*: Product *assortment* and *space* allocation should blend with the category's role, and meet the needs and preferences of target shoppers.

- *Pricing:* Products need to be priced in accordance with the banner's positioning, and the category's roles and strategies, taking financials into considerations. Low prices are a great attraction for shoppers, but they also impact heavily on profit margins.
- *Promoting:* Products are promoted to attract and retain target shoppers. The promotions should blend with category tactics/strategies.
- *Store Maintenance:* Stores are well maintained so that they provide appropriate service levels and quality standards to cultivate the desired *shopping environment*. Retail chains need to optimize their investment in these areas.
- *Location:* Stores are located within proximity of target shopper. The decision to open/close outlets reflects the critical trade-off between building the chain's presence and offering shopper convenience, and the cost of doing business. It requires alignment with the retailer's business strategy and financial goals.

Execution

The shelf is the retailing arena; it is where retailers execute their strategies and tactics. Elements of the retailing mix comprising space, assortment, merchandising, communication, price and promotions are aligned at the shelf into a coordinated programme designed to achieve desired outcomes.

Review

The category review evaluates the retailer's performance to assess the impact of category strategies and tactics, and the effectiveness of the retailing mix. It identifies opportunities and threats, and reveals the retailer's strengths and weaknesses in relation to its competitors. The objective is to *identify business issues and set imperatives (with objectives and targets) that address these issues.* Success hinges on how well the category managers can channel their limited resources to those initiatives that offer the best return on investment.

Category management should not be treated as a mega project to re-engineer or re-invent. Instead it should be regarded as an ongoing process of business improvement. Category managers review the progress of their categories on a regular basis identifying opportunities and threats as they arise. Tactics and strategies are tweaked to meet the requirements of a changing retail environment. The retail mix is refined so that the retailer is better aligned to address business issues and tap market opportunities. And the retail shelf remains in a perpetual state of flux as the retailer implements plans and executes strategies.

Partnership between Retailers and Manufacturers

"Every great business is built on friendship." — JC Penny.

Consumers buy brands, not categories. In the context of consumers, therefore, category management is essentially the management of a collection of brands in stores. It works best as a collaborative process involving the retailer and the manufacturers who market the brands. Their engagement creates synergies that constitute *marketplace equity*.

Marketplace equity (Exhibit 22.3) represents the incremental value a consumer derives from acquiring her repertoire of brands at a particular store. It is the outcome of brand and store equity and the extent to which they reinforce one other, and it serves the mutual interests of both the retailer and the manufacturers.

The foundation of category management, therefore, stems from retailers' and manufacturers' need to collaborate to pursue their mutual interests. It is the *retailer/supplier process of managing categories to achieve superior business results by enhancing marketplace equity.*

Retailers usually do not possess in-depth knowledge of categories and brands, and rely on manufacturers for guidance on products and consumers. In developed markets, it has become an industry practice for major retailers to appoint *category captains* for some of their

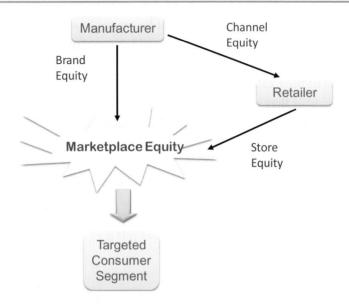

Exhibit 22.3 Manufacturers and retailers jointly contribute to marketplace equity *(Adapted from Anderson et al.,* Business Market Management*).*

important categories, and count on these manufacturers' expertise for advice on their category plans and strategies, and their retailing mix. While the category captaincy usually goes to one of the larger manufacturers, others participate as category advisors, collectively tweaking strategies in an effort to cohesively manage categories, so that retailers are better placed to attract and retain customers.

Manufacturers eagerly embrace category management as it affords the opportunity to collaborate with retailers to strengthen their categories and enhance the health of their brands. They recognize too that increasingly brand choices are made in stores. What is stocked, where, at what price and with what incentives has great influence on the consumers' buying behaviour and ultimately their choice of brand. They realize that the need to engage in category management is greater than ever before.

Category captaincy is also seen as a source of competitive advantage; the manufacturers appointed to assume these roles benefit from their proximity with retail partners.

Exhibit 22.4 Category manager's role encompasses marketing and merchandising in addition for purchasing.

Structure follows strategy. As the practise of category management permeated retail organizations, "buyers" transformed into "category managers". Their roles expanded to encompass operational and financial accountability for their categories. Besides purchasing, their responsibilities now encompass merchandising (assortment, and space allocation) and marketing (pricing, promotions, in-store marketing). This ensured a better co-ordinated approach to category management with category responsibility and authority placed under one team.

Meanwhile suppliers embraced the practice of trade marketing, a form of business-to-business marketing intended to strengthen trade relationships and improve business performance.

One of the outcomes of this transformation, though limited to more progressive retailers, was change in *purchasing orientation* or the philosophy that guides purchasing-related decisions. Whereas traditionally buyers focussed on obtaining the lowest prices and maximizing power over manufacturers, progressive category managers now seek growth in sales and profitability through a more collaborative approach.

Exhibit 22.5 The Partnership — it remains in the best interests of both manufacturers and retailers that categories are well managed.

Trade Marketing

"If you control your factory, you control your quality; if you control your distribution, you control your image."—Bernard Arnault, Louis Vuitton MH.

To fully appreciate the manufacturer's role and priorities in category management requires a basic understanding of trade marketing.

Manufacturers rely heavily on their trade partners — a brand must first gain and hold distribution before consumers can buy it. To secure their trade partners support in procuring, distributing, promoting and merchandising, manufacturers need to market their products to them. This form of business-to-business marketing where manufacturers seek to grow their business with their retailers, wholesalers and distributors by building value added relationships is of growing importance especially for products where brand choice decisions are increasingly made at point-of-purchase. Trade marketers are devoting considerable time and resource to partner retailers in developing their brands and categories in their stores. This is an ongoing process with long term commitment that yields business gains for both parties.

Trade marketing requires considerable business acumen as manufacturers and retailers strive to achieve the delicate balance between their shared goals and their distinct individual goals. On one hand these partners work together to enhance marketplace equity, and improve the overall performance and profitability of the category. On the other hand they are engaged in competition for the profit that can be generated from the sale of goods. They rely on different, sometimes conflicting, profit models. Manufacturers seek economies of scale and a return on investment, whereas retailers are interested in economies of scope and return on inventory.

That they share complementary resources and capabilities strengthens their bond and increases the likelihood that both achieve their respective goals. There is the need to ensure that the engagement does not hover solely on negotiating discounts and trading terms, and that attention is devoted to the development of brand loyalty, store loyalty and marketplace equity. To sustain and strengthen the relationship, it is important the partners continuously align and strengthen their mutual self-interests.

The process of category management has become a crucial component of the trade marketing process. It serves to bring manufacturers closer to their business partners in a constructive process that encourages sharing of plans and strategies, synchronizing activities and resources, as they jointly work towards building marketplace equity.

Origins of Category Management

Developments Leading to Category Management
The first Walmart opened on 2nd July 1962. It was a time when retail was fragmented comprising of a large number of small stores with no leverage over dominant manufacturers. The manufacturers largely controlled the elements of the marketing mix — price, distribution,

product, advertising and promotion. Today, except for a few developing countries, this scenario no longer exists.

Retailer/manufacturer relationships have changed greatly over the decades. Through consolidation major retailers amassed enormous influence within the marketplace (Walmart, for instance, generated 15% of P&G's worldwide revenue in 2012). They acquired greater control on pricing, distribution, promotions … and with the emergence and growth of house brands, their influence on product development also grew. Increasingly brand choices are being made at point-of-purchase in their stores, and they influence those decisions through their retailing mix.

This shift in the balance of power from manufacturers to retailers inevitably led to some adjustments. Manufacturers became vulnerable to the big retailers who used their leverage to wring low prices and concessions. There was the need to move away from an increasingly distributive relationship to a more constructive, integrative relationship.

While manufacturers were struggling to maintain their scope of influence, retailers were grappling with an increasingly complex marketplace. Over the years, mass markets splintered into numerous consumer fragments, each with their own tastes, needs and values. The number of products had exploded to meet the plethora of consumer needs. Retailers found it challenging to comprehend the needs of their ever growing base of shoppers and to cope with the continually expanding glut of products. They needed a scientific, fact-driven approach to optimize their retail mix.

The time was ripe for category management.

Advent of Category Management

The term "category management" was coined by Brian F. Harris, a former professor at the University of Southern California and the founder of The Partnering Group (TPG).

In the early 1990s, TPG developed a comprehensive eight-step category management process that became accepted as the industry standard. The eight cyclical steps are as follows:

- Define the category;
- Define the role of the category within the retailer;
- Assess current performance;
- Set objectives and targets;
- Devise strategies;
- Devise tactics;
- Implement plan;
- Review.

According to a number of industry reports, organizations that successfully adopted the disciplines of category management experienced significant gains in sales and profits. A study by Accenture (2000) for instance, claimed that retailers that adopted category management experienced up to 10% uplift in sales, 3% increase in profit margin and up to 15% reduction in inventory.

Experienced practitioners however, also pointed out that compliance has been an issue. A majority of the recommended actions specified in approved category business plans did not get implemented (TPG and Armature and Interactive Edge, 2001). So while there have been many successful implementations, the perceived promise of category management has yet to be fulfilled.

Practitioners of category management also feel that the process is complex and time-consuming; that it not only demands specialized data expertise and analytical skills, but also a high degree of coordination and cooperation between departments, and across organizations.

In part the problem probably lies with the interpretation of the TPG process. If the category management team starts with a blank sheet, the eight steps amount to a massive re-engineering exercise. Yet, today it is hard to envisage a major retailer who does not already have a number of the process steps chalked out, and an ongoing review process in place.

Instead of re-inventing category definitions, roles and so on, the category management teams need to focus on identifying business issues, and addressing them by tweaking strategies, tactics and the retail mix. Rather than a big project, category management should be run as an ongoing process of improvement. Many of the companies that practise category management know this, and have streamlined the process to contain costs and achieve results in a timely manner.

The bigger issue is the quantum and complexity of the data. The mountains of store level scan data, loyalty panel data, and shopper research data reside in silos, accessed via legacy systems. Understandably people get overwhelmed by the numbers, and too much time is diverted to the mechanical task of populating templates. What is required are integrated business intelligence systems that facilitate the analysis and reporting of information.

Trade Formats — FMCG

The FMCG retail environment is continually evolving. At the broadest level, it may be split into the upper or modern trade, and the lower trade, which comprises a collection of traditional, independent stores such as mom and pop stores, provision stores and sundry kiosks.

Diversity is particularly pronounced in Asia, which has developed rapidly in the past 20 years. The continent is a melting pot of formats, from the traditional Sari Sari stores in the Philippines and Chinese medical halls in North and Southeast Asian markets, to hypermarkets, sophisticated vending machines, and virtual shopping platforms.

The following are descriptions of the key channels/sub-channels prevailing in the upper trade, across the globe:

- Supermarket: Is a self-service store offering a wide variety of food and household products. Store layout is organized into aisles with fixtures of shelves used to display merchandise. The average supermarket has roughly 15,000 to 25,000 SKUs in stock spread over 1,000 to 4,000 sq. metres.
- Hypermarket/supercentre: Is a large retail facility combining a supermarket and a department store. In theory, hypermarkets allow customers to satisfy their routine shopping needs in one trip. They offer a wide range of products, including food and household products as well as general merchandise. On average

a hypermarket covers a floor space of 10,000 to 20,000 sq. metres, and stocks roughly 50,000 to 100,000 SKUs.

- Minimarket/superette: Is a small supermarket. Usually these stores have one or two check-out counters.

- Hard discounter: Is characterized by very low prices, small assortment size (500 to 1,500 SKUs) comprising primarily private labels, in relatively small stores (300 to 1,000 sq. metres). Hard discounters like Aldi and Lidl have spread over Europe. Aldi entered the Australian market in 2001.

- Soft discounter: Primarily sells limited range of food and household products at low prices. These stores stock roughly 1,500 to 3,000 SKUs, and their floor space varies from 300 to 3,000 sq. metres.

- Health and personal care store: Retails health and personal care products. Examples include Boots (UK), Watsons (Asia) and Walgreens (US).

- Convenience store: Is a shop with extended opening hours, stocking a limited range of food and household goods. It stocks about 500 to 1,500 SKUs and is usually less than 300 sq. metres in size. Examples include 7-Eleven, Circle K and Lawson.

- Warehouse store/warehouse club: is a retail facility, such as Costco and Sam's Club in the US, which offers food, household products and some general merchandise in bulk, at discounted prices. It offers a no-frills experience. The warehouse shelving is heavily stocked with merchandise intended to move at a fast pace. On average it stocks about 4,000 SKUs. Unlike a warehouse club, a warehouse store does not require membership or membership fees.

In addition to these retail channels, there are also a number of on premise channels such as coffee shops, drink stalls, hawker centres, bars/night clubs and dining.

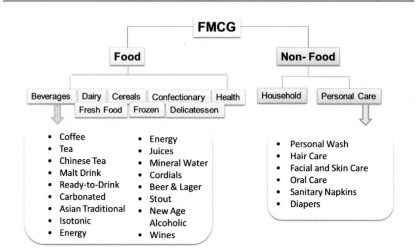

Exhibit 22.6 Some FMCG departments and categories.

Categories

Categories are groups of products that meet similar needs. Departments are groups of categories that meet related needs. The store is a collection of departments. Exhibit 22.6 provides examples of some FMCG departments and categories.

Consumer needs can be defined broadly such as "hair care", or more precisely such as "cleaning hair". A broader need is met by a super category (e.g. hair care category), which essentially is a group of related categories (e.g. shampoo, conditioner, hair colour). Categories comprise of sub-categories or segments (e.g. anti-dandruff shampoos).

Marketers need to be careful that they do not define categories too narrowly. For example, a definition such as "yeast based spreads", where a single brand commands 90% share of category, is unlikely to capture the market dynamics. The category should be defined such that it reflects the needs of the consumers, not merely the form of the product.

For retailers, their categories are central to their identity, and should be framed based on the needs and behaviours of their target shoppers. By and large, for established retailers, this task has already been performed. However, as markets evolve and new products get launched, the category definitions may need to be tweaked and updated.

Category Roles

Category strategies and plans must be crafted in the context of the retailer's overall portfolio, and in accordance with the retailer's business strategy. The category's role establishes the category's place within that portfolio and forms the basis for the allocation of resources.

The following factors relating to their importance serve as a basis for assigning roles for categories:

- Strategic Importance: Is there high synergy between the category and the chain? Is the category well aligned with the chain's purpose and identity? Is it important to target shoppers?

  Two measures that help assess the strategic fit with shoppers are chain loyalty and propensity. (Refer to Chapter 20, *Retail Analytics* for details). Another relevant metric is the Fair Share Index:

$$Fair\ Share\ Index\ = \frac{Value\ Share\ of\ Chain\ in\ Category}{Value\ Share\ of\ Chain\ in\ All\ categories}$$

- Category attractiveness: Size and growth rate in terms of volume, value, profitability.

The four roles — destination, routine, convenience and occasional/seasonal — suggested by The Partnering Group are described in Exhibit 22.7.

Destination categories would rank high on strategic fit as well as category attractiveness. They are central to the chain's identity and of strategic importance to their business.

For example, wine is a destination category at Cold Storage, an upmarket supermarket chain in Singapore. It is also the biggest

Destination: To be the primary category provider and help define the retailer as the store of choice by delivering consistent, superior target customer value.

Routine: To be one of the preferred category providers and help develop the retailer as the store of choice by delivering frequent, competitive target consumer value.

Occasional/Seasonal: To be a major category provider, help reinforce the retailer as the store of choice by delivering frequent, competitive target consumer value.

Convenience: To be a category provider and help reinforce the retailer as the full service store of choice by delivering good target consumer value.

Exhibit 22.7 Category roles (*Source: TPG*).

packaged foods category at the chain; this despite the fact that wine is a relatively small category in the country as a whole.

On the other hand, at Watsons, a personal care chain in Asia that targets young women, facial care is the destination category.

Routine categories rank medium to high on strategic fit and category importance. Their presence and offering also has an important bearing on store selection. They reinforce the banner's identity and image, but not to the same extent as destination categories. Tea and pet foods for example are routine categories at Cold Storage.

Supermarket chains usually stocks a limited range of magazines and newspapers, but usually no books. Some chains however made an exception for the exceedingly popular Harry Potter series, at the time the books were released. This served to excite their younger shoppers, and provided convenience to them and their parents.

Convenience categories such as books and stationery at supermarkets rank low on strategic fit and category importance. Their presence provides for a one-stop shopping convenience for the chain's shoppers.

Category Strategies	Category Purchase Dynamics
Traffic Building	High share, frequently purchased, high % of sales
Transaction Building	Higher ring-up, impulse purchase
Profit Contribution	Higher gross margin, higher turns
Cash Generating	Higher turns, frequently purchased
Excitement Creating	Impulse, lifestyle oriented, seasonal
Image Creating	Frequently purchased, highly promoted, impulse, unique items, seasonal
Turf Defending	Used by retailers to draw traditional customer base

Exhibit 22.8 Category strategies (*Source: TPG*).

Seasonal or occasional categories include New Year's greeting cards, Christmas and Chinese New Year goodies, and categories like sun block or insecticides in Europe.

Category Strategies

Category strategies are geared towards generating more money for the retailer. This can be achieving by one of the following means — increase traffic (i.e. shopper base) by attracting and retaining shoppers, increase basket of purchases (transaction volume and value), and improve the margins made in each transaction. The strategies listed in Exhibit 22.8 are different combinations of these three fundamental ways that the retailer can make more money.

These strategies may be adopted for the category as a whole, or for a segment or a brand. They may apply across an entire retail chain or across store clusters. They collectively form the retailer's overall blueprint to grow its business by attracting and retaining shoppers.

The objective of the traffic builder is to draw shopper into the stores. The Knife brand cooking oil at Carrefour (Singapore) serves as a good example of the use of a "loss leader" to build traffic. Carrefour wanting to make a bold statement (presumably: "We are not just a French hypermarket"), priced this local brand at a level lower than the price at which they purchased it.

(Incidentally Lam Soon, the manufacturer of Knife cooking oil, seemingly under pressure from retailers competing with Carrefour, took the hypermarket to court for "price fixing". The court case was won by Carrefour.)

There are two distinctly different types of transaction builders. There are products that are somewhat peripheral to the category that shoppers buy on impulse. This increases the shopper's purchase basket. For example, speciality flavours in soft drinks or pet supplies in pet care.

Transaction builders may also be products that people buy during their heavy shopping trips. For instance, rice. When a shopper, in a rice-eating country like India, Thailand or China, buys rice, it is observed that she spends significantly more than the average shopper. In view of this, the retailer is particularly keen to attract her when she intends to buy rice, because her transaction on those trips will be relatively large.

Profit generators are high margin products (e.g. premium wines and some facial care products).

A product that generates cash would be one where the sales value (price × volume) is high.

Excitement creating products tend to be trendy and innovative products. Some of these may also be occasional products — for instance the Harry Potter series, or chocolates in gift packs on Valentine's Day.

One of the objectives of image enhancing products is to attract new shoppers. Like turf defenders they also help to retain shoppers.

Review

The objective of the review is to craft action plans that address issues and take the business to the next level. This, broadly speaking, is a three steps process: identifying issues, investigating them and chalking out the plans.

Cash to Product

Product to Cash

Exhibit 22.9 Retailer's business revolves around turning inventory.

Identifying Issues

An issue may be an opportunity or a threat. To identify key issues the category management teams need to focus on the key health indicators. They are usually empowered with a suite of dashboards that provide at-a-glance view of the performance of the chain and its stores. Collectively, these dashboards comprise a store health kit that is made up of a wide range of measures, including the following:

- *Shopper*: Penetration, retention (measures in terms of repeat usage rate or repeat decay rate), spend per shopper, banner loyalty.
- *Store:* Sales, share, shopper penetration in-store, spend per shopper, store loyalty.
- *Transactions*: Sales volume and value, market share.
- *Profitability*: Gross profit, gross margin.
- *Inventory*: Turns × Earns or Gross Margin Return on Inventory Investment (GMROII).

These measures relate to the factors that make the retailer's business tick — attracting and retaining shoppers, increasing their transactions, and improving the margins made in each transaction.

The notion of turns × earns is central to the retailer's business model. This refers to the need to maximize the gross margin (earn) and the number of times they can earn that margin (velocity of inventory turn) (Exhibit 22.9). Annual turns are calculated by dividing the sales (cost of material sold) by the inventory (average inventory value).

Turns × Earns is equal to the GMROII:

$$GMROII = \frac{Gross\ Margin}{Inventory}$$

$$= \frac{Gross\ Margin}{Sales} \times \frac{Sales}{Inventory} = Earns \times Turns.$$

To identify issues, one needs to search for significant shifts in performance trends. Health measures that lie below target or benchmark are a concern. Typically when an issue arises, it is reflected across multiple measures.

Investigating Issues

Whereas dashboards help identify issues, to investigate them the team needs to drill deeper into the data. This process of exploration must remain focussed on the key issues. One of the perils of our data-rich age is the ease of drowning in the digital black hole. Over-analysis can lead to the point where the issue can no longer be recognized (the "analysis paralysis" syndrome).

A focussed investigation means diagnosing the issue and pinpointing the problem or opportunity areas. For example, suppose the retailer has lost share in the category due to decline in penetration. To investigate this issue one should determine which stores are affected, which segments and brands are affected, what is the profile of the shoppers that the chain is losing, where are they going to, how do their purchases in competitors' stores compare with purchases in the chain's stores, and which elements of the retailing mix (price, promo, assortment, distribution and stock) might have contributed to the loss.

The issues once diagnosed, must lead to recommendations and action plans that entail refining the retailing mix. To arrive at good action plans the team needs to keep asking tough rhetorical questions: What needs to be done to resolve the issues? How do we take the business to the next level? They are crucial because without action plans all we have is a theoretical exercise, i.e. an overhead.

Retail Mix

The dynamics of assortment, merchandising, space, price and promotion differ considerably depending on the role of the category. For instance, a destination category is likely to have an exhaustive assortment, attractive prices and many red hot deals. On the other hand a convenience category is likely to have a limited assortment of products that afford good margins.

The retail mix needs to be fully aligned with category roles and strategies, and should support the retailer's action plans.

Price

The adage "rich people love low prices, the poor need them" holds true universally. Price is undoubtedly among the most important drivers of store choice. It influences shoppers' perceptions of the store and impacts their shopping behaviour. As the variable that generates revenue and profit, it warrants careful consideration.

In theory retailers can use analytic techniques to determine the price elasticity and the cross price elasticity of demand of their products, and set prices optimally. With manufacturers' support some retailers do this for the major items in important categories.

In practice, however, there are also many complexities. Considering that the average supermarket is stocking roughly 20,000 SKUs, and that items are constantly being listed and de-listed, it is impractical to scientifically set prices for every item. Moreover the price of a product (e.g. a traffic builder) in one category affects the sales of products in other categories.

So in reality, most retailers set prices based on manufacturers' guidelines and pre-determined mark-ups. The mark-up is likely to vary across categories based on category dynamics (turns × earns), as well category/brand roles and strategies.

There are two approaches retailers have historically taken on pricing: high-low promotional and everyday low price (EDLP). The high-low promotional pricing involves setting regular prices at healthy margins but running frequent promotions to temporarily reduce prices for some products to much lower levels. With EDLP the retailer charges low prices for items all the time, making low but positive margins on them.

Pricing these days tends to be a hybrid of the two strategies. Stores may have some key products on EDLP, and the rest following high–low promotional approach. Additionally there may be privileges and discounts for loyalty card holders.

Promotion and In-Store Media

Retail formats like department stores, hypermarkets and supermarkets present unparalleled opportunity to influence shoppers at point-of-purchase through consumer promotions, in-store media and in-store events (e.g. product launches).

The promotional activities include price-offs, banded packs, collectibles, in-store sampling, special displays, cooperative advertising and loyalty programmes. They are often supported by the use of in-store media on shelves (shelf talkers or shelf stoppers), floors, carts, chillers, as well as walls and ceiling.

Mobile devices are being used at point-of-purchase to research products, compare prices and seek promotions.

These varied in-store activities have acquired far greater significance with the consolidation of retail and the fragmentation of media. In many countries the incidence of shopping at a major chain is often far greater than the incidence of primetime TV viewership. Hence the need to engage with shoppers inside the store has grown in importance.

Promotions and in-store media have important bearing on store choice and brand choice. From the retailer's viewpoint they are an important means to attract and retain shoppers. For manufacturers they serve to raise awareness, mould brand perceptions and draw new or lapsed consumers as well retain and reward existing consumers.

On-promotion sales account for a big proportion of total sales in FMCG. It is therefore, of high importance to evaluate and optimize them. Promotions evaluation is covered in Chapter 17, *Promotion,* and details of promotions response modelling are covered in Chapter 18, *Market Mix Modelling.*

Space Management

Within the finite boundaries of their stores, retailers seek to increase sales, offer wider variety, reduce inventories and associated carrying costs, and reduce incidences of stockouts. Space management's goal is to achieve the best trade-off between these conflicting objectives. It is a complex, yet crucially important task. Space, after all, is the most valuable physical asset that retailers possess. How they utilize it greatly impacts their success.

Space management addresses the management of three functional areas — assortment, merchandising and inventory. From a category perspective, we need answers to the following questions:

- Where to locate category in store?
- Adjacent to what other categories?
- How much space is to be given to the category?
- Which items to stock?
- How much space is to be given to each brand, each SKU?
- Where will the products be placed on the shelf?

Chapter 21, *Sales and Distribution* addressed the question: Which items to stock? As mentioned in that chapter, what the retailer chooses to stock is a function of several size factors — size of the store, size and importance of the category, size and importance of the brand and size of item. The chapter covers a wide range of metrics that can help marketers decide how many items to stock and which items to stock.

Specialized software packages such as SpaceMan, JDA Intactix and SAS' Retail Space Management help category management teams plan

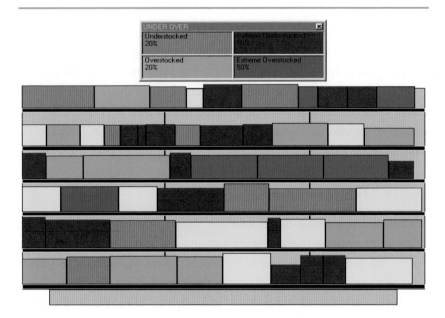

Exhibit 22.10   A planogram using colour codes to highlight items on the basis of their inventory levels.

the shelf layout in a manner that optimizes the amount of space given to each item, and the placement of the items on the shelf.

These packages use visual diagrams called planograms that depict the items in their correct proportions on the shelves. The planograms basically depict the number of facing (i.e. the number of units of a product that are visible at the front of a store shelf) of an item on shelf.

Planograms use colour codes to portray different characteristics about the items, such as brand name, segment, or for instance stock level. For example the planogram in Exhibit 22.10 uses colour codes to portray items that are extremely understocked, understocked, overstocked and extremely overstocked.

Based on various indicators, planogrammers adjust facings so that stock levels are in line with sales rate, and move products around and block them in a manner that is aligned with how people shop the category. Consumer decision trees which essentially identify and prioritize the decisions a shopper makes while shopping, provide a good basis for merchandising.

To optimize forward stock, shelf space is typically allotted in proportion to demand (i.e. share of space is approximately equal to share of sales). However merchandising considerations also come into play. In order to maintain wider range of products and accommodate small brands, the big brands tend to get less than their sales share of space. Retailers also make adjustments based on segment and brand strategies.

Product placement also has an important bearing on the performance of a product. When shoppers face a gondola (i.e. the freestanding fixture of shelves used to display merchandise), their peripheral vision covers about 12 feet, and they tend to look firstly at products placed at eye level, then to their left and right, and lastly from top to bottom. In view of this, major brands, or brands that the retailer wishes to prioritize, are kept at eye level.

As mentioned earlier, space management's goal is to achieve the best trade-off between many conflicting objectives. If well executed, the proposed planogram would be better aligned with shopper needs, lift sales, reduce inventory holding costs and working capital, and minimize the incidence of stockouts. On the whole it would make shopping at the chain's stores a much improved experience.

Execution

With regard to execution, it makes a crucial difference as to whether the category management exercise has top management's full support. It is important too that the category management team engages with all stakeholders early in the process, and has them on board. In terms of compliance, it makes considerable difference if store management and store personnel are well aware of the process, and understand its objectives. Promotions, cooperative advertising, product placement and logistic must be well synchronized for plans to succeed.

Benefits of Category Management

From a manufacturer's perspective, category management stimulates the growth of their category and their brands. The process allows them to collaborate with retailers to strongly influence consumers at the store. Moreover, as category captain or category advisors, participating manufacturers benefit from value added relationship with retailers.

Customers benefit from the improved shopping experience. They find the right mix of products, merchandised in a logical and attractive manner.

Category management helps retailers cope with the complexity of their operations and maximise their return on inventory investment. Improvements in product range and merchandising enhance shopper satisfaction and store loyalty, and reduce stockouts. These factors help to lift sales.

At the same time, retailers benefit from cost saving ensuing from the culling of poor performing items, optimization of inventory, and reduction of costs associated with inventory holding and working capital. These reductions in costs and the improvements in sales, combine to substantially improve profits for retailers.

Little People

You are an analyst at a market research company and are preparing a presentation to a new client, Little People.

Little People recently purchased retail tracking data for the first time. The company used to be the sole supplier of impulse ice cream in Little Country until a little over a year back when a new manufacturer, Little Mice entered the market.

Top management in the company is interested to know the impact Little Mice is having on the impulse ice cream market, and has asked you to address the following areas in your presentation:

1. Performance of Little Mice and factors contributing to its success/failure.
2. What impact is Little Mice having on Little People's sales? What are the reasons why Little Mice is affecting/not affecting Little People?
3. Briefly recommend a course of action for Little People. (List out the key actions the company should take.)

Impulse Ice Cream

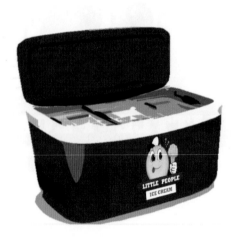

Exhibit C6.1 An ice cream cabinet.

Impulse or novelty ice creams are single-serve ice creams in cones, bars, sticks and cups; bought from vendors typically for on premise or outdoor consumption. The distribution of ice cream is relatively expensive as it requires a temperature-controlled supply chain. The cold chain as this network is called provides an uninterrupted series of storage and transportation facilities from the ice cream factory to the ice cream shop. At the shop, impulse ice cream is stored in ice cream cabinets such as the one shown in Exhibit C6.1. These ice cream cabinets are usually owned by the supplier, not the retailer.

Impulse ice creams sell best in small to medium size FMCG outlets such as convenience stores, minimarkets and provision shops. The data in this case study pertains to the relevant store universe covering all outlets that carry ice cream as well as those that have the potential to carry ice cream, even though they may not be doing so. Typically these stores have the space to accommodate two to three cabinets.

Retail Measurement Data on Ice Cream Sales and Distribution

The relevant retail tracking data for impulse ice cream sales in Little Country is provided in Exhibit C6.2. The metrics shown in the exhibit are defined as follows:

- Number of Stores or the retail universe is the count of all stores of relevance to the distribution of impulse ice cream.
- Stores Distributing: Count of stores that handle the product.
- Numeric Distribution: Proportion of stores in the retail universe that handle the product.
- Weighted Distribution: Value contribution (%) to impulse ice cream sales of those stores that handle the product.
- Sales/Store: Sales rate or the quantity sold in an average store.
- Product Class Distribution: Numeric distribution of the product class (i.e. impulse ice cream).

Y1

	Y1 Jan	Feb	Mar	Apr	May	Jun	Jul	Aug	Sep	Oct	Nov	Y1 Dec
Number of Stores	1,000	1,004	1,010	1,005	1,020	1,020	1,019	1,022	1,025	1,028	1,032	1,040
Little People												
Sales ('000 kg)	1,693	1,747	1,975	2,203	2,644	3,086	3,353	3,020	2,552	2,083	1,910	1,737
Sales ('000 $)	2,658	2,725	3,061	3,371	3,992	4,598	4,996	4,470	3,854	3,208	2,961	2,727
Stores distributing	600	602	596	613	632	643	642	644	646	637	640	634
Numeric Distribution	60	60	59	61	62	63	63	63	63	62	62	61
Sales/Store ('000 kg)	2.8	2.9	3.3	3.6	4.2	4.8	5.2	4.7	4.0	3.3	3.0	2.7
Average Price ($)	1.57	1.56	1.55	1.53	1.51	1.49	1.49	1.48	1.51	1.54	1.55	1.57
Product Class Distribution	60	60	59	61	62	63	63	63	63	62	62	61

Y2

	Y2 Jan	Feb	Mar	Apr	May	Jun	Jul	Aug	Sep	Oct	Nov	Y2 Dec
Number of Stores	1,045	1,058	1,061	1,063	1,060	1,068	1,065	1,068	1,071	1,070	1,067	1,069
Little People												
Sales ('000 kg)	1,791	1,845	2,089	2,333	2,813	3,293	3,588	3,261	2,750	2,238	2,037	1,836
Sales ('000 $)	2,812	2,878	3,217	3,546	4,191	4,808	5,203	4,696	4,043	3,335	3,096	2,827
Stores distributing	637	635	647	648	657	673	671	673	675	674	651	652
Numeric Distribution	61	60	61	61	62	63	63	63	63	63	61	61
Weighted Distribution	100.0	100.0	86.5	83.5	80.3	77.9	77.2	73.3	71.2	66.9	66.0	64.2
Sales/Store ('000 kg)	2.8	2.9	3.2	3.6	4.3	4.9	5.3	4.8	4.1	3.3	3.1	2.8
Average Price ($)	1.57	1.56	1.54	1.52	1.49	1.46	1.45	1.44	1.47	1.49	1.52	1.54
Little Mice												
Sales ('000 kg)			410	570	844	1,118	1,316	1,515	1,496	1,478	1,436	1,395
Sales ('000 $)			504	701	1,030	1,364	1,606	1,863	1,855	1,862	1,838	1,814
Stores distributing			95	117	159	224	266	310	343	375	395	417
Numeric Distribution			9	11	15	21	25	29	32	35	37	39
Weighted Distribution			13.5	16.5	19.7	22.1	25.8	33.7	38.8	45.1	46.0	49.0
Sales/Store ('000 kg)			4.3	4.9	5.3	5.0	4.9	4.9	4.4	3.9	3.6	3.3
Average Price ($)			1.23	1.23	1.22	1.22	1.22	1.23	1.24	1.26	1.28	1.30
Product Class Distribution	61	60	70	72	77	84	86	87	87	88	88	89

Exhibit C6.2 Retail tracking data for Little People and Little Mice.

CASE VII

Inulas
Management of the Breakfast Cereal Category

Inulas, a major supermarket chain in Joka, is well known for the width and depth of its range in food, grocery and personal care products. The chain was acquired recently by a regional retailer with the intent to grow revenue and profits by offering a superior range of products particularly in fresh foods. Accordingly, the new management launched a media campaign repositioning Inulas as "the Fresh Food People".

Soon after the takeover, you have been appointed Category Manager for breakfast cereal, a relatively small but high growth category. One of your current priorities is to chalk out the category's role in the context of Inulas' overall portfolio and business strategy. You are aware that the category has not been performing well at your chain, compared to competing supermarkets, and you are under pressure to revamp the category to improve business performance.

A key issue is the poor performance of the adult and health segments. According to internal sales data, their growth is weak compared to other supermarkets. The General Manager of Operations and a number of store managers are advising you to trim the range of these segments, and reallocate their space to the big brands in child cereals, which are frequently experiencing stockouts. To gain even more space they are suggesting that you remove all the small 30g packs.

To learn more about the category, you held meetings with the trade marketing teams of the three major manufacturers — Bianca, Anya and Nigella. The teams from Bianca and Nigella concur with the suggestion to trim the range and facings of the adult and health segments. The team from Anya, however, claims that sales of adult cereals are soaring

Note: The details presented in this case study have been disguised, and the data has been altered.

at other supermarkets, and that you need to review the category and examine your retailing mix, to better comprehend the reasons why the category as a whole, and adult cereals in particular is underperforming.

You are aware that Anya is the major supplier of adult cereals, and consequently, any reduction in space and range will adversely impact their company's performance. Compared to Bianca and Nigella, Anya is also a relatively late entrant into Joka and the rest of Asia. An American company, its focus has primarily been in the mature breakfast cereal markets of the western hemisphere. Since entering Joka about five years back, its market presence has grown rapidly in breakfast cereal, and its brands now contribute to a little over 25% of category sales (kg) at Inulas. Even so, you suspect that their range in terms of pack sizes and varieties is not as well aligned as it should be for the growing, undeveloped Joka market.

Faced with conflicting views, you propose to the general manager that you will complete a full review of the breakfast cereal category. With the assistance of the major manufacturers, you intend to analyse the reasons for the substandard category performance, in light of the existing trends in the market, and provide concrete recommendations on how Inulas can drive sales and profits for the total category.

Given his busy schedule, the general manager has allotted you a half hour session to present your review. After further discussion you agree to the following agenda for the session:

- Overview of the cereals market (Is Inulas getting its share of the growth?).
- In context of the consumer trends make recommendations on how to refine the retailing mix to lift sales and profits. You agree to be explicit on range, space, promotion and price, so that the store managers can easily act on your recommendations.
- Broad outline, in terms of segments, of layout for the breakfast cereal category in Inulas stores. For each of the segments, you will need to consider blocking, positioning and allocation of space.

Market Overview

Joka is a small, vibrant and affluent Asian city-nation with a population of 4 million people. Food and groceries in the country are sold in modern outlets like supermarkets and convenience stores, as well as a large base of traditional provision shops. The total market value for these products grew last year by 4.5%, driven mainly by supermarkets which grew by 7.8%. All other grocery outlets grew by 3%, on average.

Breakfast cereal (or just cereal) is a food made from processed grains that is usually eaten during breakfast. It is eaten hot or cold, usually mixed with milk and sometimes yogurt or fruit.

Though it is not aligned to the traditional breakfast eating habits of Asians in general, the category has experienced high growth in the region, spurred by the need for convenience. Sales last year touched $35 million in Joka, with supermarkets contributing 80% ($28 million). The category grew by 12% in value (and 10% in terms of weight) in the Supermarket channel, but only by 4% in Inulas. The chain's value share within supermarkets was 20%.

Segments

The category comprises of five segments — child, adult, staple, health and variety. What follows is a description of each of these diverse segments:

- **Child** breakfast cereals are targeted at toddlers and teenagers. They tend to be high in sugar content to appeal to children's palate and to provide an energy boost. The major brands are usually marketed as "fun" and enjoyable to eat cereals. Bianca and Nigella have been very active in this segment with products such as Bianca Frozzy and Nigella Kola Kopa.
- **Adult**: This relatively new segment is driven primarily by Anya. Products in this segment target adults looking for high quality cereal with fruits such as blueberries and

bananas, and nuts such as almonds and walnuts. These cereals command a premium retail price and afford high margins for the retailer.

- **Staples** are the traditional breakfast cereal products that target the mature, conservative and health conscious consumer. These "sensible" cereals are low in sugar and fat content. The big brands are Bianca cornflakes and Nigella cornflakes. They do not contain "unnecessary" additives like fruits and nuts. Consumers may add sugar, honey, fruit or nuts when they consume these cereals

- **Health**: These products target consumers interested in healthy cereals. They are low fat, low sugar products with healthy ingredients such as oats, wheat and bran.

- **Variety**: These products come in bundles of 6 to 10 single serve packs that combine different type of product packs. A variety multipack may contain staple, child, adult and/or health cereal packs in a single offering.

Segment breakdown in sales volume (kg), across the supermarket channel and Inulas, is as follows:

Segment	Supermarket	Inulas
	(% kg)	(% kg)
Child	37.3	43.3
Adult	28.5	22.3
Health	15.8	12.4
Staples	14.4	17.4
Variety	4.0	4.7

The Child and Staples segments grew by 6% and 2.5% respectively, in weight terms, in supermarkets, over the previous year. The Adult and Health segments grew at a faster pace, at 18.5% and 15.8% respectively, over the same time, whereas the growth of variety packs has been stagnant (0%).

Manufacturers

The list of breakfast cereal manufacturers and the breakdown of their sales volume (kg), across supermarkets and Inulas, is as follows:

Manufacturer	Supermarket (% kg)	Inulas (% kg)
Bianca	43.8	46.0
Anya	32.6	25.5
Nigella	9.8	12.4
Diana	6.2	6.3
Lucerne	5.4	5.3
Cyro	1.4	1.5
Inula	0.8	3.2

The relatively low contribution by Anya at Inulas reflects the chain's weakness in adult cereals. In discussions with the manufacturer's trade marketing team, you were informed that the following items are currently not listed at Inulas:

- Anya Adult Fibre Vita Crunch 300 G, Segment: Adult, Market Rank 11, Cost $3.90, suggested retail price $5.40
- Anya Crispy Crunch Wheat 453 G, Segment: Adult, Market Rank 17, Cost $3.10, suggested retail price $4.30
- Anya Multi Try Pack 8's, Segment : Variety, Market Rank 39, Cost $3.00, suggested retail price $3.80

Consumer

The proportion of households consuming breakfast cereal in Joka last year was only 40%. Consumer research commissioned by Anya suggests it could reach 50% by the end of this year. Other consumer studies revealed that households new to breakfast cereal will on most occasions purchase the small 30g packs before graduating up to the bigger packs. Of those who do try a small pack, 75% go on to buy at least one large pack. And households who regularly consume cereal products typically have four packs of cereal open at any time.

In addition, panel data revealed that a high number of consumer of adult cereals have traded up from the staples segment.

Overview of Breakfast Cereal in Inulas

Revenue and Margin

The sales and margin summary for the breakfast cereal category in Inulas, across the various segments is as follows:

Segment	Sales $ %	Margin %
Breakfast Cereal	100.0	24.4%
Child	43.3	21.4
Adult	21.9	27.9
Health	10.6	25.2
Staples	16.2	23.9
Variety	8.0	20.8

A full list of all items listed at Inulas, with details of movement, and store and market rank are provided in Exhibit C7.1.

Pricing

Price competition is intense in Joka, and Inulas prices its dry grocery products in line with its major competitors. This applies also to the cereal category, where products have been competitively priced, and the regular shelf prices for SKUs are set at the same level as that for the other major supermarket chains.

Promotion

In previous years, it was primarily the Child and Staple segments that were supported via promotions, and that too of the bigger size packs (300g+).

Name	Size	Manufacturer	Segment	Movement '000 units	Rank (Inulas)	Rank (S'Mkt)
Bianca Frozzy 30g	30	Bianca	Child	124.4	1	38
Bianca Berry Hoops 30g	30	Bianca	Child	106.3	2	44
Bianca Cornflakes 30g	30	Bianca	Staples	94.9	3	15
Bianca Choc Hops 30g	30	Bianca	Child	93.4	4	35
Nigella Moka Cereal 150g	150	Nigella	Child	73.5	5	7
Bianca Cornflakes 150g	150	Bianca	Staples	67.4	6	36
Nigella Kola Kopa 30g	30	Nigella	Child	67.0	7	1
Bianca Corn Frost 300g	300	Bianca	Child	64.1	8	31
Bianca Frozzy 450g	450	Bianca	Child	55.5	9	23
Bianca Choc Hops 300g	300	Bianca	Child	52.3	10	47
Nigella Moka 30g	30	Nigella	Child	51.0	11	3
Nigella Multi-Pack Cereal 150g	150	Nigella	Variety	38.6	12	43
Bianca Corn Hop 300g	300	Bianca	Child	36.3	13	45
Bianca Rice Crunchies 150g	150	Bianca	Staples	35.2	14	24
Anya Warf Krip 300g	300	Anya	Adult	35.0	15	8
Nigella Cornflakes Single 30g	30	Nigella	Staples	34.4	16	5
Nigella Honey Moons 150g	150	Nigella	Child	34.0	17	6
Bianca Choc Hops 450g	450	Bianca	Child	33.7	18	32
Anya Berry Day 300g	300	Anya	Adult	32.8	19	10
Anya Grainy 450g	450	Anya	Health	30.0	20	12
Nigella Kola Kopa 150g	150	Nigella	Child	29.4	21	2
Bianca Rice Crunchies 30g	30	Bianca	Staples	29.2	22	46
Bianca Variety Pack 300g	300	Bianca	Variety	27.5	23	51
Bianca Big G 30g	30	Bianca	Health	27.3	24	4
Diana Poh's Honey 300g	300	Diana	Adult	26.3	25	27
Bianca Honey Ps 300g	300	Bianca	Child	25.9	26	30
Nigella Honey Glis 30g	30	Nigella	Child	25.2	27	9
Anya Honey Bees 450g	450	Anya	Adult	25.1	28	19
Anya Ban Nut 450g	450	Anya	Health	25.0	29	29
Anya Honey Gees 450g	450	Anya	Adult	24.3	30	18
Lucerne Bixy 450g	450	Lucerne	Staples	24.2	31	48
Anya Branies 450g	450	Anya	Health	23.4	32	34
Diana Oat Qs 450g	450	Diana	Adult	23.2	33	42
Nigella Glis 150g	150	Nigella	Child	22.5	34	28
Anya Grape Flake 450g	450	Anya	Adult	22.1	35	21
Bianca Rice Loons 300g	300	Bianca	Staples	21.1	36	59
Bianca Coca 300g	300	Bianca	Child	20.6	37	99
Nigella Kola Kopa 30g	30	Nigella	Child	19.7	38	14
Inula 450g	450	Inula	Staples	19.5	39	145
Lucerne Bixy 300g	300	Lucerne	Staples	19.1	40	37
Bianca Big G 300g	300	Bianca	Health	18.8	41	20
Cyro Cheery 300g	300	Cyro	Adult	16.9	42	16
Nigella Cornflakes 150g	150	Nigella	Staples	16.5	43	26
Bianca Berry Hoops 300g	300	Bianca	Child	15.6	44	41
Bianca Fun Pack 150g	150	Bianca	Variety	15.2	45	50
Inula 150g	150	Inula	Staples	14.5	46	186
Diana Catnip 300g	300	Diana	Child	11.4	47	49
Nigella Cornflakes 300g	300	Nigella	Staples	8.0	48	25
Nigella Multi Cheery 300g	300	Nigella	Child	7.4	49	55
Lucerne Corn Flakes 300g	300	Lucerne	Staples	5.4	50	53
Bianca Choc Nut 300g	300	Bianca	Child	5.0	51	52
Bianca G Krisp 450g	450	Bianca	Adult	2.3	52	22
Anya Frisby 450g	450	Anya	Health	1.7	53	33
Nigella Gordon 300g	300	Nigella	Adult	1.3	54	61
Bianca Grapies Crunch 450g	450	Bianca	Health	0.9	55	57

Exhibit C7.1   Item list ranked by movement (unit sales).

Appendices

APPENDIX A

Sampling

More pixels

Less pixels

Exhibit A.0 Sample size is a commercial decision that weighs the costs of a larger sample against the benefits of greater accuracy.

Preview

"In God we trust. All others must bring data." — W. Edwards Deming.

A sample is a subset of the universe that is used for making conclusions or inferences about the universe. It reduces the time, effort and cost in estimating parameters of interest to marketers such as brand awareness, penetration, brand equity, market share, sales or distribution.

This appendix reviews the different sampling methods, and the mathematics of computing sample sizes for retail tracking and quantitative research studies. It covers the sampling standards commonly used by research firms. It also explains sampling and non-sample errors, and their impact on data accuracy.

Sampling Methods

Sampling methods can be broadly classified into two types — *probability* and *non-probability sampling.*

Probability Sampling

In probability sampling the probability of an element being included in the sample is known, though the probability of inclusion may not be equal.

Simple Random Sampling

Simple random sampling is an example of probability sampling where the chance of inclusion is equal for all elements in the target population. The achievement of a random sample requires not only a random sampling process, but also a 100% response rate. Since in practice, the latter is usually not achievable there is always some bias, however big or small it may be, in "random sampling".

Systematic Sampling

One drawback of simple random sampling is that it may lead to poor representation if large areas of the universe are excluded from the sample. This disadvantage is overcome through systematic sampling which relies on sorting the target population into an *ordered sampling frame,* and selecting elements at regular intervals through this ordered frame. The sampling interval or skip (k) is equal to the population size divided by the sample size (k = population size/sample size). At the start an element at random is selected from within the first to the kth element in the list, and then every kth element in the frame is selected. This approach ensures that the sample is evenly spread over entire target population.

Stratified Sampling

Stratified sampling is another probability sampling method where, unlike random and systematic sampling, the chance of inclusion of the elements is not equal. It is particularly useful when the target population is composed of distinct clusters or segments. For these populations, stratification provides the same level of precision with substantially smaller sample size.

Stratification is a process of dividing a universe into groups (called strata or cells) for the purpose of selecting a sample from each group and projecting each one separately. For example, in market measurement where stratification is the norm, retail channels such as provision stores, supermarkets, minimarkets and convenience stores form different strata. Each stratum is internally homogenous, and externally heterogeneous. Or in layman terms, a supermarket is similar to another supermarket and different from convenience stores.

Homogeneity in retail measurement is based on store characteristics such as store type, retail chain, geographical location and shop size.

The following example illustrates how the process of stratification can yield strata with greatly reduced variance:

> *Population of numbers:* {1,2,1,3,3,12,12,13,13,10},
> *Mean = 7,*
> *Variance = 28.9.*
>
> *Stratum I:* {1,2,1,3,3}.
> *Mean = 2,*
> *Variance = 1.0.*
>
> *Stratum II:* {12,12,13,13,10},
> *Mean = 12,*
> *Variance = 1.5.*

The population of the 10 numbers shown above comprises two distinct clusters. The total population has a variance of 28.9. If, however, we break the population into the 2 strata, the variance in each stratum is greatly reduced.

Consider a target population comprising two clusters, e.g. provision stores and supermarkets. The provision stores and supermarkets strata have much reduce variance compared to the variance of the total combined population of outlets. Since sample size, as we will see later, is proportional to variance, the sample requirement for the population is substantially reduced through stratification.

Non-Probability Sampling

Non-probability sampling involves subjective judgment in sample selection. Sampling errors cannot be computed because the probability of selection of any element in the population is unknown. Examples of non-probability sampling include:

- *Quota Sampling* is where the population is split into predefined groups and sample sizes are based on a pre-specified proportion. Quota sampling is more cost-effective than random sampling if the random response rates are less than 50%. Quota sampling is also used when no sampling frame is available. So for instance with online surveys, since there is no sample frame for the online population, quotas provide for a balanced sample profile. A well-crafted quota can reduce bias by achieving a well spread sample. The bias decreases with quotas that are set more finely; this however needs to be balanced with the resultant increase in data collection costs.
- In *Convenience Sampling,* an element is selected at the convenience of the researcher. For example interviewing people at a shopping mall (quant research).
- *Purposive (Judgment) Sampling* is where selection is based on certain criteria. For example a sample of brand users. Or a sample of experts in a particular field.
- *Snowball Sampling* is where respondents are asked to identify (or recruit) one or more of their acquaintances who they believe to be in-scope of the survey.

Sample Weighting

Weighting is required to adjust for imbalances in sample profile relative to the target population. Distorted samples create bias with over-represented groups having greater influence, and under-represented groups having reduced influence on the study metrics. Weight factors are applied on each of the sample components to correctly adjust their level of influence.

Sample Size

The determination of sample size is a commercial decision that weighs the costs of a larger sample against the benefits of greater accuracy. There is not much value in the information sourced from a sample unless it can be generalised to the target population. The ability to do so with some confidence depends on factors associated with sample design as well as non-sampling inaccuracies.

Small unreliable samples that do not permit generalization are not meaningful or useful. Large, overly accurate samples may be needlessly expensive. An ideal sample is one that precisely meets specifications — it is neither over specified nor underspecified. The specification of ideal sample size is dependent on the following factors:

- Population variability. The larger the variance the larger the sample required to achieve the desired level of accuracy.
- Sample design. For services like retail audits, a stratified sample design can yield a substantial reduction in sample size.
- Specified level of accuracy. The standards for sampling error are set by the service provider. The greater the required precision, the larger the sample size.

Other factors specific to the nature of the research also affect sample size. For instance, for retail audits, larger sample of retail stores are required if products are thinly distributed. Similarly for usage and attitude studies, if product usage is low, a larger sample of consumers will be required to achieve the desired level of accuracy.

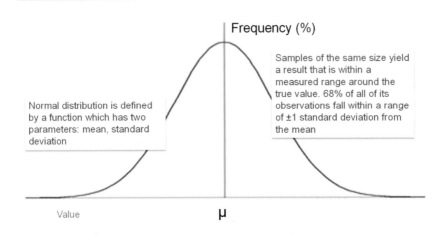

Frequency (%)

Normal distribution is defined by a function which has two parameters: mean, standard deviation

Samples of the same size yield a result that is within a measured range around the true value. 68% of all of its observations fall within a range of ±1 standard deviation from the mean

Value

μ

Exhibit A.1 Frequency distribution of estimates $\bar{x}_1, \bar{x}_2, \bar{x}_3, \bar{x}_4 \ldots$ of a variable X obtained from samples, taken from the universe, follows the bell-shaped normal distribution curve.

It is pertinent to note that sample size is *not dependent on universe size*. This may sound counterintuitive — if universe size is not a factor, why then do we need large retail audit samples in countries like China and India? The reason is because variability in these universes is much greater, and product distribution is low. Besides that for large markets we also have many more market breakdowns, such as regions, provinces, and cities. The sample size for each market breakdown must individually meets the specified accuracy standards, which adds to the total requirement.

Central Limit Theorem

The Central Limit Theorem (CLT) forms the theoretical foundation for determining sample size. The theorem states that the sampling distribution of the mean $\bar{x}$ (or the percentage value $\bar{p}$) of a variable X, derived from a simple random sample will be *normally distributed* as the sample size increases, even if the population distribution is not normally distributed.

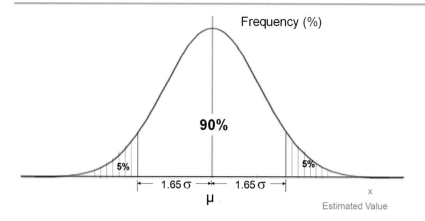

Exhibit A.2 Confidence interval = 90%: probability that estimated value lies between ±1.65σ is 90%.

For example:

> *Universe size = N*
> *Sample size = n*
> *Mean value = μ*
> *Sample mean values:*
>> *Sample 1: $\bar{x}_1$*
>> *Sample 2: $\bar{x}_2$*
>> *Sample 3: $\bar{x}_3$*
>> *Sample 4: $\bar{x}_4$ etc.*

According to the CLT, the frequency distribution of the average values $\bar{x}_1, \bar{x}_2, \bar{x}_3, \bar{x}_4 \ldots$ of a variable X, obtained from samples taken from the universe, follows the bell-shaped normal distribution curve shown in Exhibit A.1.

The *normal distribution* is said to represent an elementary "truth about the general nature of reality". It is a family of distributions, each defined by two parameters — mean (μ) and standard deviation (σ).

While each sample yields a different mean for the variable being measured, based on the theorem, it can be expected that all samples of the same size and design will yield a result that is within a measured range around the true value.

The CLT further states that if repeated random samples of size n are drawn from a large population along some variable X, having a mean μ and variance S^2, then the sampling distribution of sample mean will be a normal distribution having mean μ and variance $\sigma^2 = S^2/n$. The standard deviation σ is also referred to as the standard error of the mean.

A characteristic property of the normal distribution is that 68% of its observations are expected to fall within a range of ±1 standard deviation from the mean, and 90% of its observations are expected to fall within a range of ± 1.65 standard deviations from the mean. This is reflected in Exhibit A.2, by the non-shaded area lying between $\mu - 1.65\sigma$ and $\mu + 1.65\sigma$.

Sampling Standards in Retail Measurement

Retail measurement services providers maintain global standards for sampling error (aka relative standard error or RSE), reflecting the acceptable tolerance level of error, at specified level of confidence, for their retail audits. For instance, Nielsen's global standard for sampling error, set at 90% level of confidence and applicable to categories that are available in 80% of the universe, is as follows:

National Market	*±3% of sales level*
Major Market Breakdowns/Channels	*±6% of sales level*
Minor Market Breakdowns	*±6-10% of sales level*

According to this standard, the sample should be configured such that for a national market, the probability that estimated sales value will lie within ±3% of actual value is 90%.

Note also that accuracy standards are dependent on the availability of the category being measured. If it is available only in a small proportion of stores, the effective sample for the category is much lower, and that adversely impacts the sampling error for sales estimate. Hence the stipulation above, that the global standard applies to categories that are present in at least 80% of the universe of stores.

Sample Size — Random Sampling

If the level of confidence is 90%, the confidence interval, $\mu \pm 1.65 \varpi$, in Exhibit A.2, is equal to

$\mu \pm (RSE \times \mu)$,
or $1.65\,\varpi = RSE \times \mu$.

In general:

$Z\,\varpi = RSE \times \mu = e$
$\sigma = e/Z$

Where:

e: acceptable tolerance level of error in value = RSE × µ
Z: standardized value associated with the level of confidence. If level of confidence is:
90% then Z=1.65
95% then Z=1.96
99% then Z=2.58

According to the central limit theorem, the variance of the sampling distribution (σ^2) is dependent on the sample size (n), and the universe variance (S^2):

$$\sigma^2 = \frac{S^2}{n}$$

Substituting for σ^2:

$$\frac{e^2}{Z^2} = \frac{S^2}{n}$$

$$n = \frac{Z^2\,S^2}{e^2}$$

Example 1

If the standard deviation of the sale of a category in provision shops is *80*, and the average sales per store, *µ*, is about *200*, then the required sample size, so that the sales estimates fall within ±6% *(RSE)* of its true value with a confidence level of 90% is equal to:

$$n_{prov} = \frac{Z^2 S^2}{e^2} = \frac{(1.65)^2 (80)^2}{(0.06 \times 200)^2} = 121$$

Take note that in order to half a sampling error we need to quadruple the sampling size. If the sampling error was reduced to 3% (0.03), the required sample size will be 484.

Sample Size — Stratified Sampling

For stratified samples, which are the norm for retail measurement services, the formula for sample size is as follows:

$$n'_i = \frac{Z^2 S_i^2}{e^2} \times \frac{N_i S_i^2}{\sum_{j=1 \, to \, k} N_j S_j^2}$$

Where:
 n'_i: Sample size for strata$_i$ (k in all)
 N_i: Strata$_i$ population
 S_i^2: Strata$_i$ population variance
 Z: Standardized z value associated with the level of confidence
 e: Acceptable tolerance level of error

Example 2

The national universe for a retail audit comprises provision stores, minimarkets and supermarkets. Details for the provision stores are provided in Example 1 above. In the case of minimarkets, the standard deviation of the sale of the category is *100,* and the average sales per store is about *400.* The required minimarket sample size so that the sales estimates fall within ±6% *(RSE)* of its true value with a confidence level of 90% is therefore equal to:

$$n_{mini} = \frac{Z^2 S^2}{e^2} = \frac{(1.65)^2 (100)^2}{(0.06 \times 400)^2} = 47$$

The national universe comprises 200 supermarkets, 500 minimarkets and 2,000 provision stores, and the standard deviation of the sales in supermarkets is 400. If the acceptable tolerance level at the national market breakdown is ±3%, the required sample size for minimarkets is then equal to:

$$n'_i = \frac{Z^2 S_i^2}{e^2} \times \frac{N_i S_i^2}{\sum_{j=1 \, to \, k} N_j S_j^2}$$

$$n'_{mini} = \frac{(1.65)^2 (100)^2}{(0.03 \times 400)^2} \times \frac{500 \times 100^2}{500 \times 100^2 + 2000 \times 80^2 + 200 \times 400^2}$$

$$n'_{mini} = 19$$

To meet both criteria for RSE at the minimarket breakdown and national level, we need a minimum sample size of 47 minimarkets.

Similarly, for provision stores, $n'_{prov} = 124$, and the required sample size is the maximum of n_{prov} and n'_{prov}, which is equal to 124.

Population Proportions

Quantitative research studies are concerned frequently with estimation of measures in terms of population proportions. For instance — What proportion of the population are aware of brand X? What proportion of consumers claim they will buy brand X? What proportion of consumers prefers formulation X over formulation Y?

Based on the Central Limit Theorem, as the universe increases, the required sample size (n) for estimating percentage value $\bar{p}$ is:

$$n = \frac{Z^2 p(1-p)}{e^2}$$

Where:

p: is the probability for given response and varies from 0 to 1. It reflects the variability in the data. Note when p = 1, (i.e. variance = 0) no sample is required.

Z: is the standardized value associated with the level of confidence.

e: is the desired precision or the margin of error in percentage points.

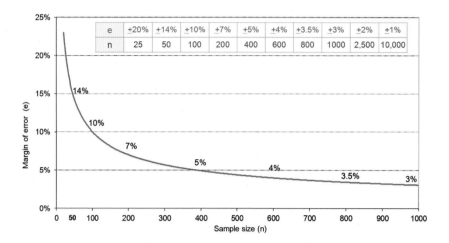

Exhibit A.3 Estimated sample size required for different margins of error at confidence level of 95%.

The probability for which we require the largest sample size is $p = 0.5$. For this "most conservative" value for p, and for a confidence interval of 95% ($Z = 1.96$), we can simplify the above equation:

$z = 1.96 \approx 2$ *for confidence level of 95%*

$p = 0.5$

$$n = \frac{Z^2 p(1-p)}{e^2} = \frac{2^2 0.5(1-0.5)}{e^2} = \frac{1}{e^2}$$

$$n = \frac{1}{e^2}$$

Based on the above formula, Exhibit A.3 shows how sample size n varies with the margin of error e. For example if $e = +5\%$, then for the confidence interval of 95%, we require a sample of n = 400. Or 384 to be precise if Z $(= 1.96)$ is not rounded off.

Finite Population Correction Factor

In the interest of saving costs, in cases where the universe size is not large, the sample size may be adjusted downwards. For medium size

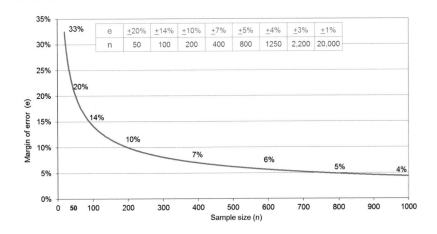

e	±20%	±14%	±10%	±7%	±5%	±4%	±3%	±1%
n	50	100	200	400	800	1250	2,200	20,000

Exhibit A.4   Required sample size at confidence level of 95%, across different margins of error, for differences in proportions.

populations, the sample requirement is adjusted downwards using this formula:

$$n_{adj} = \frac{n}{1 + n/N}$$

For example if N = 2000, e = 5% then

$$n_{adj} = \frac{384}{1 + 384/2000} = 322$$

Additionally if it is known that the proportions are skewed (i.e. p is not close to 0.5) the sample may be further reduced.

For small universe populations, 100 for instance, it is advisable to take census instead of sample.

Tracking Studies

For tracking studies where *independent* samples are taken at regular intervals, the change of a metric between intervals is of prime interest. Because both estimates are subject to sample error, change estimates have margins of error that are 41% (times √2) larger than the corresponding estimates from the individual surveys. The required sample size at confidence level of 95%, across different margins of error, for differences in proportions, is shown in Exhibit A.4.

To contain costs, continuous tracking studies use 8 weekly or 4 weekly rolling averages to track metrics. This helps to reduce sample sizes to 25 to 100 per wave (usually per week). The drawback is that since rolling averages flattens the data, it is harder to detect changes.

Alternatively *dipstick* studies may by conducted at less frequent intervals with larger samples that reveal changes more distinctly. Since they provide a snapshot in time, dipsticks are better suited for tracking the "before" and "after" impact of a marketing initiative. They are not usually recommended for studies where the objective is to track ongoing changes occurring in the market. For instance, in advertising tracking where several brands have campaigns scattered over multiple media through the course of the year, continuous tracking is better suited for establishing baselines, and capturing the ongoing nature of marketing activities and their impact in the market place.

Sample and Non-Sample Errors

Data errors can be broadly categorized as — *sample and non-sample errors*. Sample errors are the inaccuracies arising from taking only a sample of the target population. These errors, as we have seen, may be reduced by increasing the sample size or improving the sample design, and accuracy standards can be set in term of acceptable error levels at some confidence interval.

Apart from sample errors, research is subject to a variety of other errors commonly referred to as non-sampling errors. They arise in all forms of studies (including census) both from systematic and random causes. These errors tend to be difficult, if not impossible, to measure.

Non-sampling random errors are the unpredictable errors occurring during data collection and data processing. For instance, incorrect recording of data by an interviewer, or incorrect response by a respondent, or incorrect computation of some metric during

| Biased | Unbiased, random errors. | Unbiased and accurate |

Exhibit A.5 Inaccuracies due to systematic (bias) and random errors.

processing. They lead to an increased variability in the results, though they tend to cancel out if the sample is large.

Non-sampling systematic errors tend to accumulate over the entire sample, making the results unrepresentative of the population. For example poor wording of a question may inadvertently influence responses, or for example, coverage issues where some targets with different properties cannot be reached. These types of errors are of greater concern since unlike random errors, they often lead to a bias in the final results. Moreover unlike sampling inaccuracies, bias resulting from systematic errors cannot be reduced by increasing the sample size.

Non-sampling error can be reduced by maintaining reliable survey frames, well designed and properly tested questionnaires, good training of the data collection team (interviewers, auditors), monitoring and call-backs, and high standards in measurement and processing systems..

EXAMPLE A.5

Gain–loss Algorithms: Assumptions/Limitations

Preview

The objective of gain–loss is to measure competitive shifts in consumer buying in terms of the amount of business each product gains from other products. Also known as brand switching or brand shifting analysis, it analyses *transactional data* to answer questions relating to switching behaviours: What is my brand's source of growth or decline? Which brands are being cannibalized?

Though much-loved by consumer analysts and widely used especially within the FMCG (consumer packaged goods) industry, the assumptions and limitations of the gain–loss analysis are often not fully appreciated.

A description of the gain–loss analysis covering its application is provided in Chapter 7, *Consumer Panels*. This appendix dwells on the algorithms. It outlines the standard gain–loss algorithm, and highlights its limitations. It also proposes two alternative algorithms — nested and hierarchical gain–loss.

The nested gain–loss algorithm is run in a two-step sequence; first within sub-groups or product segments that are homogeneous, and then across the segments. It provides much improved approximation of switching behaviour in markets where products are differentiated, and the propensity for consumers to switch within category sub-groups, is greater than that across sub-groups.

In hierarchical gain–loss, products are segregated into homogeneous groups at the household level, based on historical purchasing patterns within the households. The gain–loss is run sequentially within the product groups for each household, and then across the groups.

Hierarchical gain–loss is theoretically appealing and rigorous. Yet it also adds another layer of complexity, and computationally, it is more resource intense.

Standard Gain–loss Algorithm

The standard gain–loss algorithm is essentially a two stage process:

Stage 1:

- For each household, for each brand, the gains/losses are computed as follows:

    Gain (Loss) = Purchases in Period II − Purchases in Period I

- The losses incurred by brands that lost volume are proportionately allocated to those brands that gained volume.

    The example in Exhibit B.1 illustrates the above process for three households. Note that for household III where the gains are greater than the losses, a dummy entity called "increased buying" is introduced to absorb the difference. "Increased buying" represents the increase/decrease in category purchases.

Stage 2:

- The estimates of gains and losses for the total market are the sum of the gains and losses across households. This output is shown in Exhibit B.3.

Limitations

Consider a possible scenario for Household II. The usual brands consumed by the household are Lipton tea and Bru coffee. Some members of this household drink only tea and others drink only coffee. The tea drinkers consume about 550 cups over period P1. If the period duration is six months, their consumption amounts to about 3 cups a day. The coffee drinkers consume roughly 300 cups over the same time.

The household bought a Brooke Bond tea pack of 400 tea bags, at a promotion during period P1. In P2, Bru was stocked out in stores, and the household switched to Nescafe, purchasing the equivalent to 200 cups of the brand, during this period.

In this scenario, the household switched part of their consumption from Lipton to Red Label in P1, and from Bru to Nescafe in P2. It is one of any number of possible scenarios, where the outcome differs vastly from the standard gain–loss result in Exhibit B.1.

By proportionately allocating losses to gains, the standard gain–loss algorithm assumes that the likelihood of a shift in volume between a set of brands is equal across brands. For our example, it assumes that the likelihood of switch from Nescafe coffee to Bru coffee, and from Nescafe coffee to Red Label tea is the same.

In the case of tea and coffee, it is pretty clear that this is not a sound assumption. Our understanding of hot beverage drinking habits suggests that consumers are more likely to switch within coffees or within teas, than from a coffee brand to tea brand or vice versa.

Whereas the distinction between teas and coffees is self-evident, even within narrowly defined categories, the intensity of switching will tend to vary across brands. Different products within the same category satisfy different need states. Within an individual's repertoire, in a differentiated marketplace, depending on the needs they satisfy, some brands compete more intensely than others. Proportionate allocation is valid only for categories where there are no segments; where brands are undifferentiated.

Note also that because it works on purchases, not consumption, and because it is unable to account for pantry stock, the gain–loss algorithm exaggerates the gains and the losses. If, for instance, the pantry stock for Brand A increases in a household, and that for Brand B decreases during the same period, in the same household, the gain–loss algorithm will incorrectly show that Brand A has gained volume from Brand B.

Indeed, only a fraction of the gain and loss that is classified under "new buyers", "lapsed buyers", "expansion" and "contraction" is due to a change in consumption, the remainder is due to change in pantry stock.

These overestimates often balance out in such a way that the estimate of "net gain" is not significantly affected. But there may also be occasions where the incidence of promotions, stockout or other causal factors affect consumers' inclination to stock a brand, leading to a scenario where purchase differs substantially from consumption.

In view of the limitations cited above, the following points should be taken into consideration when interpreting gain–loss results:

- The proportionate allocation of gains and losses underestimates interaction between brands that compete strongly and overestimates the interaction between brands that do not compete strongly.

- Variance in consumption of fast moving goods is much lower than the variance in purchase. People drink roughly the same amount of coffee every day, or every week; but they usually do not purchase coffee every week or every month. Some FMCG products are bought weekly, others once a month, or once in three months or even once in six months (toothbrushes for instance, according to the data for many markets).

- Because it works on purchases, not consumption, the extent of switching reflected in gain–loss outputs is usually an exaggeration — and the exaggeration is more pronounced if the length of the period chosen for the analysis is not substantially larger than the inter-purchase interval for the product category.

- In general the average pack sizes are bigger in large format outlets like supermarkets and hypermarkets. As these outlets grow in importance, they extend the inter-purchase interval of products for the market as a whole.

- Markets where per capita incomes are relatively low, the consumption of small packs is more pronounced. Single use sachets for instance sell better than larger pack sizes in some developing countries. In these markets where the inter-purchase interval is small, purchases more closely match consumption, and pantry stocks are limited.

From the standpoint of interpretation, gain–loss serves as a good comparative assessment. It accurately reveals the *direction* of the flow of the business as brands gain and lose to other brands. It tells us that a brand is gaining more share from some competitors than others. And it reveals the propensity of a brand to gain from or lose to other brands.

The limitations mentioned above, do however highlight some of the distortions that impact the analysis. Gain–loss does not provide an exact *absolute* measure of switching between brands, and it is prudent to remain aware of the exaggerations, and the biases highlighted earlier.

Refinements like the nested gain–loss help to considerably improve the estimates, and in particular reduce the extent of over/ underestimation of the gains and losses. Yet distortions continue to exist, and one must therefore interpret the results of any gain–loss, bearing their existence in mind.

Nested Gain–loss

In nested gain–loss the category is segregated into predefined sub-groups (typically product segments). The gain–loss is run in the phased sequence outlined below:

- In the first phase, gain–loss at the household level is run separately within each of the sub-groups. The losses incurred by brands that lost volume are proportionately allocated to those brands that gained volume *within the same sub-group*.
- In the second phase, the residual gains and losses that remain after the first phase are offset across the groups.
- Household level data is aggregated across homes to arrive at market estimate.

Instead of predefined product segments, the segregation of products into sub-groups may also be based on their interaction indices. Brands are segregated such that those with high interaction are grouped together. This approach is appropriate where predefined product segments do not accurately partition products in accordance with the way they are used or consumed.

Reverting to the hot beverage example, Exhibit B.2 illustrates the process for the three households, and Exhibit B.4 displays the aggregate result.

Running gain–loss in a nested manner prioritizes the interactions within predefined product sub-groups over interactions across the sub-groups. For the hot beverage category comprising sub-groups tea and coffee, it is known that consumers are more likely to switch from one tea to another tea, than from a tea to a coffee. In its initial run the algorithm allocates the amount of business each brand has gained from each other brand within teas, and separately within coffees. The residual values from this initial run are mapped across the sub-categories — i.e. from teas to coffees and vice versa.

Comparing Exhibit B.3 with Exhibit B.4, and Exhibit B.1 with Exhibit B.2, reveals substantial differences in the results derived from the two methods. With nested gain–loss, as one would expect, the interaction within teas and within coffees has increased substantially and the interactions across brands of tea and brands of coffee has come down (see Exhibit B.5). These indices are a measure of the extent of switching between brands. A high interaction index of 300 of Red Label with Lipton means that the propensity for Red Label to interact with Lipton is 3 times greater than that for an average brand.

Case Example — Detergent Bars, Powders and Concentrates

When concentrate detergent powders were first launched into the Indian detergent market in 1990, manufacturers were keen to understand the impact concentrate *powders* would have on detergent *bars*. Though distinctly different in form, due to the potency of concentrates, it was felt that the need for bars would diminish once consumers switched to concentrate powders.

Soon after Ariel Microsystem, the first concentrated detergent powder was launched into test market in a southern Indian town called Vizag, Hindustan Lever set up a consumer panel to study the impact it would have on wash habits. The nested gain–loss methodology outlined above was specifically developed at that time to analyse the interaction between concentrate detergent powders and detergent bars. The gain–loss results based on this approach (see Exhibit B.6) were far more satisfactory than the results obtained from the standard gain–loss algorithm.

Hierarchical Gain–loss

While it is a vast improvement over the standard algorithm, a drawback with nested gain–loss is that it applies the same product segregation based switching rules across households. Inherently, as far as switching behaviour goes, it assumes that the market is homogeneous. Yet even if their repertoire of brands is similar, the switching behaviours of households within their repertoire may differ substantially.

For categories where need-states differ substantially across the consumer base, a hierarchical approach that takes the heterogeneous nature of the market into consideration should provide an improved estimate of switching behaviour.

Accordingly products in hierarchical gain–loss are segregated into groups at the household level. For each individual household, based on historical purchase patterns of the households, interaction indices are computed and product groups formed. Gain–loss is then run sequentially — within groups, across groups.

Hierarchical gain–loss is theoretically appealing and rigorous. It does however add another layer of complexity, and its computation is resource-intensive.

Conclusion

It is important for marketers to appreciate that the gain–loss algorithms work with purchase transaction data, not consumption data, and that the algorithms assume certain predefined rules on switching behaviour.

On the whole results from the different algorithms provide a good sense of direction. You can, for instance, rely on the results to identify which brands compete more strongly, or the source of growth or decline of a brand. However because the assumptions are an approximation of reality, the results may not provide an accurate estimate of the switching volume between brands.

The standard gain–loss algorithm in particular underestimates interaction between brands that compete strongly and overestimates the interaction between brands that do not compete strongly. Nested and hierarchical methods, by prioritizing the interactions within predefined product sub-groups over interactions across the sub-groups, provide much improved estimates.

All three approaches suffer from the disadvantages of using purchase transaction data that fluctuates over time periods due to factors other than consumption. This volatility of transactional data considerably exaggerates the estimates for "gain", "loss", "new buyers", "lapsed buyers", "expansion" and "contraction". These overestimates often balance out in such a way that the estimate of "net gain" is not significantly affected. Sometimes however the incidence of promotions, stockout or other causal factors may affect consumers' inclination to stock a brand, leading to a scenario where purchase differs substantially from consumption.

While refinements to gain–loss do considerably improve the estimates, distortions continue to exist, and one must therefore interpret the results of any gain–loss, bearing their existence in mind.

Household I - purchases

	P1	P2
Nescafe	250	
Red L		500
Lipton	250	

Gain

Loss	N	R L	L	Total
Nescafe		250		250
Red L				
Lipton		250		250
Total		500		500

Household II - purchases

	P1	P2	L	G
Nescafe		200		200
Bru	300	200	100	
Red L	400		400	
Lipton	200	500		300
Total	900	900	500	500

Gain

Loss	N	B	RL	L	Total
Nescafe					
Bru	40			60	100
Red L	160			240	400
Lipton					
Total	200			300	500

Loss to Bru (100) and Red Label (400)
proportionately allocated to Nescafe and Lipton

Household III - purchases

	P 1	P 2	L	G
Nescafe	300		300	
Bru	200	300		100
Red L		400		400
Total	500	700		200
Increase	200		200	
Adj Total	700	700	500	500

Gain

Loss	N	B	RL	Inc	Tot
Nescafe		60	240		300
Bru					
Red L					
Increase		40	160		200
Total		100	400		500

Loss to Nescafe (300) and increase in household purchases
(200) allocated proportionately to Red Label Bru.

Exhibit B.1 Standard gain–loss: Losses proportionately allocated to gains
(P1 and P2 are time periods of equal duration).

Household I - purchases

	P1	P2
Nescafe	250	
Red L		500
Lipton	250	

Gain

		N	R L	L	Total
Loss	Nescafe		250		250
	Red L				
	Lipton		250		250
	Total		500		500

Household II - purchases

	P 1	P 2	L	G
Nescafe		200		200
Bru	300	200	100	
Red L	400		400	
Lipton	200	500		300
Total	900	900	500	500

Gain

		N	B	RL	L	Total
Loss	Nescafe					
	Bru	100				100
	Red L	100			300	400
	Lipton					
	Total	200			300	500

Loss to Bru (100) allocated to Nescafe. Loss to Red Label (400) is allocated first to Lipton and then to Nescafe

Household III - purchases

	P1	P2	L	G
Nescafe	300		300	
Bru	200	300		100
Red L		400		400
Total	500	700		200
Increase	200		200	
Adj Total	700	700	500	500

Gain

		N	B	RL	Inc	Tot
Loss	Nescafe		200	200		300
	Bru					
	Red L					
	Increase			200		200
	Total		100	400		500

Loss to Nescafe (300) is allocated first to Bru. The remainder goes to Red Label. Increase in household purchases (200) allocated to Red Label.

Exhibit B.2 Nested gain–loss: Losses allocated based on predefined nested hierarchy.

Gain

	Nescafe	Bru	Red L	Lipton	Decrease	Total
Nescafe		60	490			550
Bru	40			60		100
Red L	160			240		400
Lipton			250			250
Increase		40	160			200
Total	200	100	900	300		1500

Exhibit B.3 Standard gain–loss: Aggregation of gains and losses.

Gain

	Nescafe	Bru	Red L	Lipton	Decrease	Total
Nescafe		100	450			550
Bru	100					100
Red L	100			300		400
Lipton			250			250
Increase			200			200
Total	200	100	900	300		1500

Exhibit B.4 Nested gain–loss: Aggregation of gains and losses.

Standard Gainloss

	Nescafe	Bru	Red L	Lipton
Nescafe		167	124	
Bru	47			46
Red L	173			216
Lipton		200	186	

Sequential Gainloss

	Nescafe	Bru	Red L	Lipton
Nescafe		267	108	
Bru	93			
Red L	147			300
Lipton			250	

Exhibit B.5 Interaction indices.

Gains From	(Nov..Jun) % Gain	% Vol Share (Nov 90)	% Vol Share (Jun 91)	Growth Jun/Nov
Ariel		3.2	6.2	78.3%
Triple Power Rin	18	4.0	4.4	1.1%
Surf	44	20.1	14.9	-31.4%
Other Powders	38	72.6	74.5	-4.8%
Total Powders	100	100	100	
Powders	90	52		
Bars	10	48		

Exhibit B.6 Nested gain–loss analysis for Ariel — Vizag.

References

Aaker, David A. (1991). *Managing Brand Equity*. New York, NY: The Free Press.

Allen, Derek R. (2004). *Customer Satisfaction Research Management: A Comprehensive Guide to Integrating Customer Loyalty and Satisfaction Metrics in the Management of Complex Organizations*. Milwaukee, WI: ASQ Quality Press.

Accenture. (2000). *ECR 2000 Day-to-Day Category Management*.

Anderson, Chris. (2008). *The Long Tail: Why the Future of Business is Selling Less of More*. New York, NY: Hyperion Books.

Anderson, Chris. (2009). The Long Tail Blog, http://longtail.typepad.com/the_long_tail. Accessed 22 December 2014.

Anderson, James C.; Jain, Dipak; and Chintagunta, Pradeep. (1992). Customer Value Assessment in Business Markets: A State-of-Practice Study. *Journal of Business-to-Business Marketing*, 1(1), 3–29.

Anderson, James C.; Narus, James A.; and Narayandas, Das. (2009). Business Market Management, Understanding, Creating and Delivering Value. New Jersey: Pearson International Edition.

Bakken, David, and Frazier, Curtis L. (2006). Conjoint Analysis: Understanding Consumer Decision Making. In Rajiv Grover and Marco Vriens (Eds.), *Handbook of Marketing Research: Uses, Misuses, and Future Advances* (pp. 288–311). Thousand Oaks, CA: Sage Publications.

Bass, Frank M. (1967). A New Product Growth Model for Consumer Durables, Working Paper, Purdue University Krannert School of Industrial Administration Institute Paper No. 175.

Baum, J. and Dennis, K. E. R. (1961). The Estimation of the Expected Brand Share of a New Product. Paper presented at the 15th Esomar/Wapor Congress, Baden-Baden. Amsterdam: Esomar.

Bretton Clark, Product literature.

Brown, Gordon. (1991). How Advertising Affects the Sale of Packaged Good Brands. Millward Brown.

Bonamici, Kate, and Useem, Jerry. (2005, June 27). 20 That Made History. *FORTUNE Magazine*.

The Coca-Cola Company's Conversations Staff. (2012, November 14). The Real Story of New Coke. http://www.coca-colacompany.com/history/the-real-story-of-new-coke.

Cooper, Lee G. and Nakanishi, Masako. (1988). *Market-Share Analysis: Evaluating Competitive Marketing Effectiveness*. Boston, MA: Kluwer Academic Publishers.

Cooper, Robert G. (2001). *Winning at New Products: Accelerating the Process from Idea to Launch*, 3rd Edition. Cambridge, MA: Perseus Publishing.

Edwards, Jim. (2013, November 24). TV Is Dying, And Here Are The Stats That Prove It. *Business Insider*. http://www.businessinsider.com/cord-cutters-and-the-death-of-tv-2013-11#ixzz30MhPv0Fu.

Foekens, Eijte W.; Leeflang, Peter. S. H.; and Wittink, Dick R. (1994). A Comparison and an Exploration of the Forecasting Accuracy of a Loglinear Model at Different Levels of Aggregation. *International Journal of Forecasting*, 10(2), 245–261.

Gale, Bradley T. (1994). *Managing Customer Value: Creating Quality and Service That Customers Can See*. New York, NY: The Free Press.

Garau, Barbara and Rougier, Louis. (2012, June 28). Dispelling the Myths of the Fuzzy Front End, Ipsos Innoquest. Retrieved 22 December 2014 from http://www.ipsos.com/marketing/sites/www.ipsos.com.marketing/files/pdf/InnoQuest_Fuzzy_Front_End_POV.pdf.

Gerry Katz. (2011, November 29). Rethinking the Product Development Funnel, NPDP, Applied Marketing Science Inc. Retrieved 22 December 2014 from http://www.innovationexcellence.com/blog/2011/11/29/rethinking-the-product-development-funnel.

Godin, Seth. (1999). *Permission Marketing: Turning Strangers into Friends and Friends into Customers*. New York, NY: Simon & Schuster.

Google. (2011, April). The Zero Moment of Truth Heat Maps by Industry. Retrieved 22 December 2014 from https://www.thinkwithgoogle.com/research-studies/zmot-heatmaps-by-industry.html.

Gordon, Wendy and Langmaid, Roy. (1988). *Qualitative Market Research: A Practitioner's and Buyer's Guide*. Brookfield, VT: Gower.

Gordon, Wendy. (1995, March). Time to Face Marketing's Moment of Truth. *Research Plus*.

Hair Jr., Joseph F.; Black, William C.; Babin, Barry J.; and Anderson, Rolph E. (2009). *Multivariate Data Analysis*. 7th Edition. New Jersey: Prentice Hall.

Halligan, Brian and Shah, Dharmesh. (2010). *Inbound Marketing: Get Found Using Google, Social Media, and Blogs*. Hoboken, NJ: John Wiley & Sons, Inc.

Hanssens, Dominique M.; Parsons, Leonard J.; and Schultz, Randall L. (2003). *Market Response Models: Econometric and Time Series Analysis*, 2nd Edition. New York, NY: Springer.

Hauser, John R. (2008). Note on Product Development. Cambridge, MA: MIT Sloan Courseware.

Hauser, John R. and Clausing, Don. (May–June 1988). The House of Quality. *Harvard Business Review*.

Iyengar, Sheena S.; Huberman, Gur; and Jiang, Wei. (2004). How Much Choice is Too Much? Contributions to 401(k) Retirement Plans. In Olivia S. Mitchell and Stephen P. Utkus (Eds.), *Pension Design and Structure: New Lessons from Behavioral Finance* (pp. 83–95). Oxford, UK: Oxford University Press.

Jaruzelski, Barry and Dehoff, Kevin. (2011, March). How the Top Innovators Keep Winning. *Visions*, 35(1), 12.

Karolefski, John; Heller, Al; with ACNielsen. (2006). *Consumer-Centric Category Management: How to Increase Profits by Managing Categories Based on Consumer Needs*. Hoboken, NJ: John Wiley & Sons, Inc.

Keller, Kevin Lane. (1998). *Strategic Brand Management: Building, Measuring and Managing Brand Equity*. New Jersey: Prentice-Hall.

Kotler, Philip; Armstrong, Gary; Ang, Swee Hoon; Leong, Siew Meng; Tan, Chin Tiong; and Yau, Oliver. (2009). *Principles of Marketing: A Global Perspective*. New Jersey: Pearson. 2009.

Laney, Doug. (2001, February). 3D Data Management: Controlling Data Volume, Velocity, and Variety. Meta Group.

Lee, Edmund. (2014, March 20). TV Subscriptions Fall for First Time as Viewers Cut the Cord. *Bloomberg*. Retrieved from http://www.bloomberg.com/news/2014-03-19/u-s-pay-tv-subscriptions-fall-for-first-time-as-streaming-gains.html.

Li, Charlene and Bernoff, Josh. (2008). *Groundswell: Winning in a World Transformed by Social Technologies*. Boston, MA: Harvard Business Press.

Lilien, Gary L; Rangaswamy, Arvind; and De Bruyn, Arnaud. (2013). *Principles of Marketing Engineering*, 2nd Edition. State College, PA: DecisionPro.

Mahajan, V.; Mason, C. H.; and Srinivasan, V. (1986). An Evaluation of Estimation Procedures for New Product Diffusion Models. In V. Mahajan and

Y. Wind (Eds.), *Innovation Diffusion Models of New Product Acceptance* (pp. 203–232). Cambridge, MA: Ballinger.

Manyika, James; Chui, Michael; Brown, Brad; Bughin, Jacques; Dobbs, Richard; Roxburgh, Charles; Hung Byers, Angela. (2011, May). Big Data: The Next Frontier for Innovation, Competition, and Productivity. McKinsey Global Institute. Retrieved 22 December 2014 from http://www.mckinsey.com/insights/business_technology/big_data_the_next_frontier_for_innovation.

McGrath, Michael E. (1996). *Setting the PACE® in Product Development*. Boston, MA: Butterworth-Heinemann.

Moss, Michael. (2013, February 20). The Extraordinary Science of Addictive Junk Food. *The New York Times*. Retrieved 22 December 2014 from http://www.nytimes.com/2013/02/24/magazine/the-extraordinary-science-of-junk-food.html?pagewanted=all&_r=0.

Nielsen. (2001, April). Nielsen Pathfinder Analysis Library. Version 2.

Nielsen. Product literature and materials on various topics.

Nielsen. (2004, February). The Digital Consumer.

NM Incite. (2012, December). Delivering on the Promise, Five Ways to Drive Brand Effectiveness with Social Media, White Paper. Retrieved 22 December 2014 from http://www.slideshare.net/NMIncite/nm-incite-white-paper-delivering-on-the-promise.

Oliver, Thomas. (1986). *The Real Coke, The Real Story*. New York, NY: Penguin Books.

Netzer, Oded and Srinivasan, V. (2009). Adaptive Self-Explication of Multi-Attribute Preferences. *Journal of Marketing Research*, 48(1), 140–156.

Parfitt, J. H. and Collins, B. J. K. (1968). The Use of Consumer Panels for Brand-Share Prediction. *Journal of Marketing Research*, 5, 131–146.

Prahalad, C. K. and Ramaswamy, Venkat. (2004). Co-Creation Experiences: The Next Practice in Value Creation. *Journal of Interactive Marketing*, 18(3), 5–14.

Prahalad C. K. and Ramaswamy, Venkat. (2000). Co-opting Customer Competence. *Harvard Business Review*.

Rigby, Elizabeth. (2006, November 11). Eyes in the Till. *Financial Times*, UK.

Ryan, Damian and Jones, Calvin. (2012). *Understanding Digital Marketing: Marketing Strategies for Engaging the Digital Generation*, 2nd Edition. London, UK: Kogan Page.

Scott, David Meerman. (2011). *The New Rules of Marketing and PR: How to Use Social Media, Online Video, Mobile Applications, Blogs, News Releases, and Viral Marketing to Reach Buyers Directly*, 3rd Edition. Hoboken, NJ: John Wiley & Sons, Inc.

Tellis, Gerard J. (2006). Modeling the Marketing Mix. In Rajiv Grover and Marco Vriens (Eds.), *Handbook of Marketing Research: Uses, Misuses, and Future Advances* (pp. 506–522). Thousand Oaks, CA: Sage Publications.

Toubia, Olivier. (2006). Idea Generation, Creativity, and Incentives. *Marketing Science*, 25(5), 411–425.

TPG, Armature and Interactive Edge — Continuous Category Management Strategic Partners. (2001). Understanding Continuous Category Management.

Urban, Glen and Hauser, John R. (1980). *Design and Marketing of New Products*. Englewood Cliffs, NJ: Prentice-Hall, Inc.

Utterback, James M. (1994). Radical Innovation and Corporate Regeneration. *Research Technology Management*, 37(4), 10–18.

van Heerde, Harald J.; Leeflang, Peter S. H.; Wittink, Dick R. (2002). How Promotions Work: Scan*Pro-Based Evolutionary Model Building. *Schmalenbach Business Review*, 54, 198–220.

Vitale, Robert; Giglierano, Joseph; Pfoertsch, Waldemar. (2011). Business-to-Business Marketing: Analysis and Practice. New Jersey: Pearson.

Vries-van Ketel, Eline de. (2005). *How Assortment Variety Affects Assortment Attractiveness*. Rotterdam: Erasmus University, Erasmus Research Institute of Management (ERIM).

Wedel, Michel; Kamakura, Wagner A. (2000). *Market Segmentation: Conceptual and Methodological Foundations*, 2nd Edition. Norwell, MA: Kluwer Academic Press.

Weiser, Mark. (1998). Nomadic Issues in Ubiquitous Computing. Xerox PARC. Retrieved 22 December 2014 from http://www.ubiq.com/hypertext/weiser/NomadicInteractive.

Wheelwright, Steven C. and Clark, Kim B. (1992). *Revolutionizing Product Development: Quantum Leaps in Speed, Efficiency and Quality*. New York, NY: The Free Press.

Wise, T. A. (1966, September). I.B.M.'s $ 5,000,000,000 Gamble. *FORTUNE Magazine*, p. 118.

Zikopoulos, Paul; Eaton, Chris; deRoos, Dirk; Deutsch, Tomas; and Lapis, George. (2012). *Understanding Big Data: Analytics for Enterprise Class Hadoop and Streaming Data.* McGraw Hill.

Subject Index

Company and Product Index

People and Place Index